CHOSEN NATION

CHOSEN NATION

MENNONITES AND
GERMANY
IN A GLOBAL ERA

BENJAMIN W.
GOOSSEN

PRINCETON UNIVERSITY PRESS
Princeton and Oxford

Published by Princeton University Press
41 William Street, Princeton, New Jersey 08540

In the United Kingdom: Princeton University Press
6 Oxford Street, Woodstock, Oxfordshire OX20 1TR

press.princeton.edu

Cover photograph: Residents of the Molotschna Mennonite colony in southeastern Ukraine, including a cavalry squadron under the *Waffen*-SS, celebrate a visit from Heinrich Himmler, 1942. Courtesy of The Mennonite Heritage Centre, Winnipeg, Alber Photograph Collection 351-9

First paperback printing, 2019
Paperback ISBN 978-0-691-19274-1
Cloth ISBN 978-0-691-17428-0

Library of Congress Control Number 2017930424

British Library Cataloging-in-Publication Data is available

This book has been composed in Sabon Next LT Pro and Penumbra Half Serif

Printed on acid-free paper ∞

Printed in the United States of America

FOR MY FAMILY

CONTENTS

ACKNOWLEDGMENTS

I spent the first years of my life in a small Mennonite town in central Kansas. Pacifist Mennonites had settled the Great Plains during the 1870s, when thousands left Europe to escape newly established conscription laws. While most of these immigrants came from colonies in southern Russia, several hundred also left the German region of West Prussia. Among these were the ancestors of my paternal grandfather, Henry Goossen. I knew my grandfather as a thoughtful and congenial man, a retired minister who always arrived at church a half hour early and who habitually proclaimed himself a "proud Prussian." My fascination for what I considered the profound irony of my grandfather's dual identity—as a Mennonite and a German American—prompted me to undertake this study. The greatest ideals of Mennonitism, according to my understanding, were personal humility and the notion that one's highest allegiance should be paid to God. Germanness, by contrast, signaled pride and loyalty to an earthly nation. In the abstract, I found the two concepts irreconcilable. And yet, in the figure of my grandfather, I could not read one without the other.

My search took me to archives and historic sites across the Atlantic world. From the birth town of Menno Simons to the oldest standing Mennonite church, I visited places I had heard about since childhood. Traveling to rural parsonages, farmsteads, and cemeteries, as well as to Reformation-era sites of baptism, persecution, and hidden worship, I followed paths well-trodden by Mennonite pilgrims since the late nineteenth century. In congregations throughout Europe and the Americas, I encountered incredible hospitality and friendship, as well as many more *stolze Preußen*. My travels helped me both to understand contemporary Mennonites and to reconstruct the spatial world of earlier generations. Yet they also taught me I was asking only half the question I needed to pose. While I had set out to discover the influence of German nationalism upon Mennonites, I became increasingly skeptical that "Mennonitism" itself constituted a coherent historical category. At least as I had absorbed it as a child, the story of the Mennonites was a nationalist narrative in its own right.

As is so often true of Mennonite projects, this book has been a community effort. I would like to thank those who made it possible through their encouragement and support. Fellowships from the German Academic Exchange Service, the Fulbright Commission, Swarthmore College, and Harvard

University enabled research at home and abroad. The scope and shape of my project emerged from significant exchanges with Mark Jantzen and John Thiesen. I am grateful to Abraham Friesen for allowing me to use personal research materials; both Peter Letkemann and James Urry have shared their expertise on Imperial Russia and its successor states, as well as many unpublished documents. Conversations with Fernando Enns have informed my thinking about Mennonite peace theology. Robert Kreider has been a tireless conversation partner; his wisdom and enthusiasm for Anabaptism have been models for me.

I have received hospitality and assistance from many scholars and Mennonites. In Weierhof, Gary Waltner far exceeded his role as head of the Mennonite Research Center by sharing with me his home, culinary skills, and boundless knowledge of all things Mennonite. I thank Gary for the hours we spent discussing history and theology while sorting currants, savoring *Mohnkuchen*, and traveling to churches around Germany. Thanks also to my fellow researchers in Weierhof, including Hans-Joachim Wienß, Joachim Schowalter, Horst Gerlach, and Ortwin Driedger, for sharing their findings. Sonja Bartel, Manuela Bolick, Gundolf Niebuhr, Frank Peachey, Astrid von Schlachta, Conrad Stoesz, and Tillie Yoder helped me navigate archival collections on both sides of the Atlantic. I fondly remember an afternoon at the Bienenberg with Hanspeter Jecker, as a well as a tour he conducted in Bern as part of the Mennonite European Regional Conference. In Strasbourg, the staff of Mennonite World Conference shared information on transnational Anabaptist organizations from the sixteenth century to the present, and in Detmold, Krefeld, and Münster, the German Mennonite Historical Society sponsored fascinating sessions.

For their perspectives, I am indebted to Alfred Neufeld in Asunción; Benjamin and Wolfgang Krauß in Bammental; Jacob Thiessen in Basel; Ingrid and Horst Küger in Berlin; Irina und Heinrich Unrau in Bielefeld; Francisca and Uwe Friesen in Ebenfeld; Alex Teichreb in Emmendingen; Christel and Wolfgang Schultz in Falkensee; Lydia, Viktor, Naemi, and Luise Fast as well as Erich Dyck in Frankenthal; Isabell Mans, Corinna Schmidt, Bernhard Thiessen, Maren Schamp-Wiebe, Thomas, Sam, Tabea, and Janneke Schamp in Hamburg; Gabrielle Harder in Krefeld; Hannah Rosenfeld, Marius van Hoogstraten, Anne Hege, and Rebekka Sauer in Neukölln; Justina Neufeld and Floyd Bartel in North Newton; Eva, Johannes, and Matthias Dyck in Oerlinghausen; Brenna Steury Graber, Brad Graber, and Valentin dos Santos in Paris; and Cor Trompetter in Wolvega. All of these individuals as well as their families made me welcome in their homes and shared resources on Mennonite history. With appreciation for their hospitality, generosity, and sheer love of life, I thank Evi and Dieter Volpert, in whose home much of this book was written.

I have been blessed with learning environments that foster both academic scholarship and personal growth. At Swarthmore College, Universität Freiburg, Freie Universität Berlin, and Harvard University, students, professors, and alumni have been amazing resources on a daily basis. Elke Plaxton, Sunka Simon, and Hansjakob Werlen instilled in me a love of German literature and language; Timothy Burke, Allison Dorsey, and Robert Weinberg deepened my thinking on the craft of historiography; and George Lakey, Ellen Ross, Joyce Tompkins, and Mark Wallace encouraged my interest in Anabaptism. Randall Exon taught me more about art, including the art of German history, than he knows. Arnd Bauerkämper and Sebastian Conrad facilitated research in Germany. During presentations at Harvard University, Swarthmore College, the University of Winnipeg, Universidade de São Paulo, the German Studies Association, Mennonite World Conference, and numerous churches, audiences offered valuable suggestions. Special thanks to Miriam Rich, who encouraged me to engage issues of gender, and to Benjamin Van Zee, whose conversation and excellent restaurant choices enlivened winter in Berlin.

This study began as a thesis for the Swarthmore College Honors Program, and I am indebted to Helmut Walser Smith for agreeing to be my examiner. For her willingness to jump into this project partway through, I thank Alison Frank Johnson, whose vision and careful readings helped me see Mennonitism for the vibrant, pluralistic religion it is. Tara Zahra has offered masterful commentary on every chapter; these pages aspire to the elegance of her own writing. I am grateful for suggestions from Celia Applegate, Leora Auslander, Sven Beckert, David Blackbourn, James Casteel, John Eicher, Marlene Epp, Helmut Foth, Michael Geyer, Hans-Jürgen Goertz, Peter Gordon, Faith Hillis, Andrea Komlosy, Diether Götz Lichdi, Royden Loewen, Charles Maier, Terry Martin, Kelly O'Neill, Moishe Postone, John Roth, Walter Sawatsky, Steve Schroeder, Nathan Stoltzfus, Ajantha Subramanian, Paul Toews, Heidi Tworek, and Hans Werner. At Princeton University Press, Quinn Fusting and Brigitta van Rheinberg have made publication a rewarding process. Three anonymous reviewers provided stimulating, incisive feedback. As the main advisor to this project, Pieter Judson has been an outstanding teacher, mentor, and friend. His guidance has pushed me to think deeply about nationality and indifference to nation while allowing me to pursue my own course. I thank Pieter for discussing the connections between scholarship and activism, for asking about my faith, and for commiserating over the indecipherability of old German script. Pieter has greatly improved the nuance of my argumentation, and I have been inspired by his passion for history.

My parents, Rachel Waltner Goossen and Duane Goossen, and my sister, Elsa, have supported my interest in Mennonitism during countless discussions, travels, and Sunday services. Family trips to Anabaptist sites around Europe and the United States first exposed me to the joys of discovering history through inherited stories and the material culture of the past. I remember with particular affection our visits to the Amsterdam Mennonite Church, our search for the Felix Manz house in Zurich, an impromptu dash to the Pfrimmerhof, and that wonderful August afternoon in the cemetery at Heubuden. My grandmother, Lenore Waltner, has shared many of her own experiences. Corresponding with her during my travels deepened my understanding of the connections between faith, family, and history. Throughout the completion of this book, it has been the opportunity to explore these themes and to discuss them with others that has meant the most.

NOTE ON TRANSLATION

Except where otherwise noted, all translations are my own. While qualifications in brackets are mine, italicized words are emphasized in the original documents. I have used the English word "Mennonite" (*Mennoniten*) to describe all people whom self-identified members in German lands considered "coreligionists" (*Glaubensgenossen*), including those who did not formally adopt the name of the sixteenth-century reformer Menno Simons. "Anabaptist" (*Taufgesinnten, Täufer, Wiedertäufer*) serves as a catch-all for Mennonites, Amish, and Hutterites, although sometimes it refers specifically to the Reformation-era radicals who practiced adult baptism before Menno's conversion. "Confession" (*Konfession, Gemeinschaft*)—similar to "denomination" in the North American context—refers to religious groups such as Mennonites, Catholics, or Jews. Confessions not under state administration were "free churches" (*Freikirchen*). In most instances, I have translated *lutherisch, evangelisch, reformiert*, and *protestantisch* as "Protestant." While "evangelical" means gospel-oriented, some Mennonites invoked this term to affiliate with Protestant respectability. On Sundays, Mennonite "congregations" (*Gemeinden*) assembled in "meeting houses" (*Bethäuser*) or "churches" (*Kirchen*). Congregations that practiced lay ministry often had a three-tiered system with one "elder" (*Älteste*), several "preachers" (*Lehrer, Prediger*), and several "deacons" (*Diakonen*). Others paid professionally trained "pastors" (*Pastoren*). I have equated the doctrine of "nonresistance" (*Wehrlosigkeit*), meaning weaponless living, with "pacifism"—although at least until the mid-twentieth century, Mennonites differentiated religious *Wehrlosigkeit* from secular *Pazifismus*.

In Eastern Europe, Mennonites sometimes used Polish and German place names interchangeably. I have chosen to render only German names. Ukrainian place names are given according to standard present-day English-language equivalents, although I have retained German names for Mennonite settlements. When possible, I have used contemporary geographic nomenclature; the city of Marienburg, for example, was alternately in the Polish-Lithuanian Commonwealth, West Prussia, the Province of Prussia, once again West Prussia, East Prussia, Danzig-West Prussia, and Poland, depending on the decade. In order to denaturalize national categories, I have not identified individuals with national appellations. Rather than referring to "German Mennonites" or "Dutch Mennonites," I prefer "German-speaking Mennonites" or "Mennonites in the Netherlands." While such workarounds are not perfect (individuals often spoke multiple languages and moved between states), I hope they will highlight the inadequacy of nationalist language, while also acknowledging the profound ways that state borders and nationalist discourses shaped Mennonites' self-perceptions. I have translated *Volk* as either "people," "folk," "nation," "ethnicity," or "race," according to context. Much of this book is concerned with understanding how Mennonites deployed this word in changing circumstances.

CHOSEN NATION

INTRODUCTION

> And the Lord spoke to Abram: Go out from your fatherland and from your friends and out from your father's house to a land that I will show you.
>
> And I will make you into a great nation and will bless you and make for you a great name, and you will be a blessing.
>
> —GENESIS 12:1–2[1]

Soon after dawn on June 15, 1876, several dozen families gathered on the train platform outside the West Prussian village of Simonsdorf. A morning storm had settled over the town and the surrounding fields, and as the passengers arrived, rain drummed against their carefully packed trunks. The travelers were Mennonites, pacifist Christians who for generations had farmed the rich grain lands between the Vistula and Nogat rivers and who were departing their homes to seek freedom from military service. They had booked rail tickets to Bremen and from there, transatlantic passage to the United States. Once on the new continent, they hoped to settle the western prairies where ground was flat and fertile and where their sons would not be forced to bear arms for the state. In the rain outside the station office, the emigrants embraced those who had come to see them off. Peter and Agatha Dyck, departing with five of their nine children, took leave of those who would not be boarding the train. "In this way parents parted from their children," Peter recalled, "brothers and sisters, friends and acquaintances." Many of those remaining behind hoped to follow soon, perhaps in the next year. Some had not yet sold their land. Others wished to complete another harvest before making the costly journey across the Atlantic. But there were also many "who due to an unfortunate lapse in judgment, had been convinced to tolerate military service," and who now "took leave of their relatives forever."[2]

Peter and Agatha Dyck were among about two thousand Mennonites who departed Germany in the 1870s. For these pacifists, emigration signaled a rejection not only of military service, but also of German nationalism. During the territorial wars that had recently led to the founding of the German nation-state, the last privileges freeing Mennonites from military participation had been revoked. As German patriotism became tied to armed service, pacifists like the Dycks considered it unconscionable to praise the "the glory of fatherland and of the nation."[3] Since the emergence of Mennonitism in Central Europe more than three hundred years earlier, ministers had championed nonviolence as an inalienable tenet of Christianity. This belief colored nearly every aspect of daily life, providing a blanket rationale for inhabiting rural areas; for abjuring higher education and political participation; and for banning intermarriage with other confessions. By keeping among themselves, members believed external authorities would leave them unmolested. Parents admonished children to avoid "showing affinity for the military class," forbidding martial clothing and the growing of mustaches.[4] Any man wayward enough to become a soldier faced excommunication. Thus, in the aftermath of the Franco-Prussian War, militarist nationalism seemed an existential threat. Citing scripture and the Reformation-era theologian Menno Simons, pacifists condemned German exceptionalism: "Are not the French and other alleged enemies also our brothers? Are they not made in God's image and saved through the precious blood of Christ?"[5]

The vast majority of Germany's Mennonites, however, were willing to renounce pacifism. Allowing national pride to outweigh the doctrine of weaponless "nonresistance," 90 percent remained in the country. Belying their image as a tradition-bound minority, they demonstrated an adaptive faith—one whose most deeply held tenets were open to negotiation. Already by the mid-nineteenth century, some had begun to claim membership in a larger nation: "Love of the fatherland is a feeling as holy for us as it is for any other German."[6] To them, nationality seemed ontologically prior to religion. One chose to be Mennonite, but one was born German. Given their practice of Anabaptism—which allowed baptism only upon personal profession of faith—this was a significant distinction. Yet, in relation to traditional belief, it represented a theological sea change. While earlier generations had styled themselves as "pilgrims" or "wayfarers" who lived in but did not belong to the merely human kingdoms of earth, nationality now appeared a divinely ordered characteristic. "Our congregations are no longer the same as they were in Menno's time," one pastor explained. Since the sixteenth century, they had relinquished strict isolationism, realizing that "the Kingdom of God is supposed to be built not *outside of the world*, but *in the world*."[7] Military service provided a means of acknowledging and even praising the nation's God-given nature. Nationalists ridiculed pacifists for whom German soil was "at best a place of rest on their migration through the desert," charging that they "lacked any proper estimation of the value of noble goods like nationality and fatherland."[8]

The emergence of a German national consciousness among some Mennonites troubles the distinction usually drawn between religion and nationalism. Scholars have long portrayed nationalism as marginalizing older religious modes of belonging.[9] Zionism—a nationalism that emerged out of an older religious tradition, but whose character became largely secular—

seemed the exception that proved the rule.[10] Yet in the twenty-first century, these phenomena appear less to have diverged than to have grown together. With conflicts across the planet fueled by extremist violence and faith-based fundamentalism, innovative explanations are imperative.[11] Peter and Agatha Dyck may have considered the choice to board the train in Simons-dorf a clear dichotomy between faith and patriotism. But such categories are not intrinsically oppositional. While the Dycks saw those who aban-doned pacifism as entering a kind of voluntary excommunication, most who took this turn continued to call themselves Mennonite. Despite pre-dictions that "the congregations themselves must also perish," Prussia's communities survived the demise of pacifism, retaining a vibrant presence in Imperial Germany.[12] The adoption of nationalist attitudes, in fact, pro-vided them with an impressive new range of tools. Rather than assimilat-ing into a subsuming German whole, they harnessed nationalism for their own purposes—a decision with consequences not only for their own con-gregations, but for the entire confession.

Already by the turn of the twentieth century, spokespersons in Germany had, ironically, employed the language of nationalism to reconnect with pacifist coreligionists abroad. Depicting Mennonitism as the most Ger-manic form of Christianity, they posited the existence of a global German Mennonite diaspora. "The German country is the fatherland of the Men-nonites," one author asserted. "Wherever the German Mennonites travel among their coreligionists, they find, so to speak, a piece of the German homeland."[13] Such claims, unsurprisingly, were more fiction than fact. The confession's largest and most influential branches had developed during the Reformation, not in countries that would later form the German Empire, but in Switzerland and the Netherlands. Many early Anabaptists emphasized their religion's voluntary nature, allowing an uneven stream of converts—often with Polish or French surnames—to bolster their ranks, not to men-tion a growing number of individuals of color on mission stations across Asia, Africa, and the Americas. Outside German lands, few congregations celebrated German patriotism. "The reason our forebearers left Prussia in their day was primarily religious, namely restrictions on their nonresis-tance," noted one Russian-born leader. "German national ideals are foreign to us, just as are our [German-speaking] Lutheran and Catholic neighbors." But if commentators in Imperial Russia, North America, and elsewhere dis-missed German-centric accounts, many were attracted to nationalism itself. In the same years that Zionists began asserting a separatist Jewish national-ity, some Mennonites presented their own confession as a national body. Conjecturing that global wanderings and endogamous marriage had cre-ated a unique people, they believed that the "national characteristics of our Mennonitism are Mennonite and not German."[14] Here was a nationalism compatible even with pacifism.

As suggested by the malleability of both religious doctrine and national precepts, static understandings of collective identity are untenable. If Mennonite theologians could both justify and oppose pacifism, if Mennonite nationalists could both embrace and reject Germanness, it makes little sense to speak of either category as coherent, limited, or unchanging. This book rejects traditional definitions of both religion and nationality, whether as immutable identity markers or as ideological forces, capable of generating uniform communities. Rather, it sees "collectivism"—the representation of social groups—as a contestatory process. Socially constructed and historically situated, religious and national cosmologies are negotiated at each moment. By examining their evolving relationships, I hope to demonstrate how diverse modes of belonging informed one another. As scholars of collectivism have shown, the boundaries of national and religious groups are seldom clearly defined.[15] Members often hold multiple affiliations, while rarely expressing as much enthusiasm for particular collectivities as spokespersons would have us believe. Terms such as "German" and "Mennonite" are themselves imprecise symbols, incapable of providing comprehensive referents for the heterogeneous constituencies they claim to represent. The following pages provide a new framework for narrating collectivism—one in which global dispersion, ideological construction, and lived practice are given central importance. My aim is neither to reify collectivist myths nor to normalize their patterns of claims-making, but instead to tell a history of religion without religions, of nationalism without nations.[16]

Mennonites around the world have for centuries contested their collective identity. Whether in the foothills of the Black Forest or in the deserts of Mexico, anxieties about belonging made their way into sermons, prayers, dinnertime conversations, letters, poems, and disputations with God. In the age of nation-states, nationalists from Austria to Argentina maintained that all peoples harbored inalienable national characteristics, delineating global space with national units. Like members of other collectivities, Mennonites assessed such claims. On Sunday mornings, as wooden benches creaked and fingers flipped through well-worn Bibles, worshipers tested nationalist proposals against theological sensibilities. Some new ideas were welcomed, others reluctantly tolerated. Knowing when to identify as German—and when not to—frequently determined the difference between life and death. Affiliation could produce a corpse in a Kansas military prison or secure rail transport to a Siberian gulag. Even in German-controlled territory, it sometimes posed as much a burden as an asset. Surviving an SS murder squad along the Dnieper River might only preface the donning of a black shirt. A life saved, a soul lost. Ubiquitous and deadly, the question of nationality was always uncertain. From kitchen tables to the Politburo, rural pulpits to the UN, debates about Mennonites' collective identity influenced how people thought and fought about democracy, minority rights, and self-determination. Slipping an unexpected wedge between religious and national narratives, Mennonitism exposed collectivism as decentered, multivalent, and fragmentary.

RELIGIOUS NATIONALISM

In 1850, Leonhard Weydmann, a Mennonite preacher in the Prussian city of Krefeld, published a biography of Martin Luther. Presenting the sixteenth-century reformer as a "German and a patriot," Weydmann followed a trend across Europe to link nationalism and Christianity. Protestant theologians, especially, characterized the Reformation as the first great epoch of the German nation. These authors depicted the Middle Ages as a black era during which the continent surrendered to Catholic rule. In this darkness, Luther had ignited a mighty light. "There are some individuals who show the various national tribes their particular character," Weydmann explained. By casting off the yoke of papism, Luther had taught the Germans how to be German, enabling them to become "a pure nation, one that is unvanquished, never repressed, and free of foreign influences."[17] Such accounts held appeal for Mennonites like Weydmann. While earlier generations had suffered under Protestant order (Luther himself recommended that Anabaptists "should not be tolerated, but punished as blasphemers"), progressives now claimed membership in a larger reform movement.[18] Presupposing the existence of a nation to which he could belong, Weydmann cast nationality as pure, elemental, and ageless: "Just as we [Germans] do not speak a mixed language, but rather an ancient language, so have we also protected our original essential character and way of life."[19]

Unlike Weydmann and his Protestant contemporaries, few present-day historians consider nations to be eternal entities.[20] Revisionists, rather, have portrayed them as "invented traditions."[21] Projected retroactively into the past only after elites developed categories like Scottish, German, or Turkish, the first nations are said to have been products of modernization and industrialization. As argued by anthropologist Ernest Gellner, "it is nationalism which engenders nations, not the other way around."[22] Modernists like Gellner hold that prior to the Napoleonic Wars, "Germans" were not really German at all. They were rather subjects of a stratified, estate-based system, in which organizing principles like religion, political rank, and economic status held more weight than language use or cultural experience. Political scientist Benedict Anderson famously employed the term "imagined communities" to suggest that nationality is less a bodily property than a state of mind.[23] Attempting to explain why individuals affiliate with enormous collectivities, most of whose members they will never meet, Anderson attributed national sentiment to the circulation of print materials, military mobilization, and other forms of identity creation.

Yet to speak of nations at all—meaning groups with common traits, language use, and histories—is misleading. Such phrasing suggests that national communities, imagined or otherwise, constitute bounded entities, whose affiliates can be reasonably distinguished from one another. It is perhaps more useful to think of nationalism as a kaleidoscope of recombining patterns.[24] Members always also belong to other interlocking collectivities—professional, familial, municipal, and linguistic, to name only a few. Recent scholarship on Imperial Germany has demonstrated the plurality of individuals' allegiances. People in Bavaria, Prussia, or Wurttemberg could maintain local loyalties while also considering themselves German.[25] Religion has provided another avenue for deconstructing nationalism. Christian piety helped some practitioners criticize nationalist precepts, while Jews disillusioned with other European collectivities found an alternative in Zionism. Measured against religions' spatial breadth, nationalism often appeared stifling. "We want to be children of our [German] nation and to promote and protect its well-being," one Mennonite pastor wrote in 1911, "but our love of the fatherland should never become so shortsighted and petty that we fail to bind ourselves to our [spiritual] brethren in all lands."[26] Whether Jewish, Mennonite, or otherwise, pan-confessional movements typically crossed national borders, highlighting the relative youth of nationalism. The German nation-state, after all, was far younger than its major religious communities.

But it is not enough to replace one static category with another. Just as nations are amorphous to the point of incoherence, faith formations are themselves highly contested. Undifferentiated invocations of religion—whether Islam, Buddhism, or Presbyterianism—obscure more than they reveal. Just as a self-identified German might speak more than one language, hold dual citizenship, or profess a different understanding of Germanness than another of her alleged co-nationals, Christians in various communities might not practice compatible theologies or even recognize each other as followers of the same God. What common essence unites the 2.1 million Anabaptists of today's world? While some drive buggies and eschew electricity, others wear suits and run investment firms. Popular stereotypes of white, bearded or bonneted farmers not only elide the diversity of conservative members in the Americas; they simultaneously mask the reality that since the 1990s, most Mennonites live in the Global South and are people of color.[27] Writing in the context of ethnic studies, sociologist Rogers Brubaker has proposed sidestepping the vagaries of "identity" altogether. For Brubaker, ethnicity—like religion, nationalism, and other forms of collectivism—is primarily cognitive. Constructed not cumulatively among a population, but rather individually, it is called into being with each personal act of recognition. Although people may identify more closely with one ethnicity than another, constellations of allegiance constantly shift.

Moments of crisis (such as wars) or of celebration (such as holidays) can heighten the appeal of particular collectivities, while defeat or embarrassment can lower their potency. By refocusing attention from the communal to the individual, it is possible to imagine "ethnicity without groups."[28] Applied to the study of national and religious history, Brubaker's methodology allows heterogeneity to be taken seriously, without treating any iteration as normative. Like other collectivities, Mennonitism should not be understood as a single group—nor even as an amalgamation of many smaller groups. It is more revealing to ask what the idea of Mennonitism has meant for various observers, as well as how and why interpretations developed over time.

Current beliefs and practices cannot be meaningfully measured against those of the religion's earliest practitioners. Reformation-era Anabaptists, like their present-day namesakes, lived in different states, spoke different dialects, and held almost irreconcilable theologies. Emerging in the 1520s and 1530s across the Holy Roman Empire—primarily in areas that today are Austria, Belgium, the Czech Republic, France, Germany, Italy, the Netherlands, and Switzerland—they were a motley bunch, characterized by pious women, rebellious peasants, scholastic ex-priests, and apocalyptic polygamists. Particularly famous were the violent Anabaptists of Münster, who after seizing the city in 1534, forcibly rebaptized hundreds of townspeople and laid plans to conquer the world in the style of Old Testament kings. While the Münsterites made strange bedfellows with pacifists like Menno Simons, they have been considered common members of a "Radical Reformation," instigated to secure greater ecclesiastical reforms than those advocated by Protestant theologians such as Martin Luther, Ulrich Zwingli, and John Calvin.[29] According to later chroniclers, a majority of Anabaptists, seeking to distance themselves from Münster, renounced participation in worldly governments as well as proselytism through the sword—while also reaffirming the tenets of adult baptism, scriptural authority, and personal discipleship. Their writings nevertheless reveal divergent viewpoints on each of these issues. Rather than distilling a single vision from the chaos of the Reformation, it is more accurate to see Anabaptism as plural and polycentric.[30] Even the name "Mennonite" is little more than a misnomer. Renouncing Catholicism in 1536, the Frisian priest was a relative latecomer. Although Menno—as subsequent generations affectionately called him—quickly became a prolific writer and organizer, he was not the only major Anabaptist leader, and his influence in north Central Europe was far greater than in the south. Beginning in the 1540s, it was neither Menno nor his followers but state authorities who coined the term *Mennists*, and later, Mennonites.[31]

If the first Anabaptists were disunited in even basic principles, hostile governments did not hesitate to group them together. Pronouncing the faith heretical, Protestant and Catholic rulers dispatched bounty hunters to capture practitioners. From Bern to Amsterdam, they waged a campaign to eliminate every single Anabaptist. Those not converted or expelled were targeted for slaughter. Thousands faced drowning, beheading, or burning. After a humiliating interrogation, a lone believer might be murdered in a crowded square. Others were killed in groups—nine, ten, or several dozen at a time. Their bodies could be quartered and hung, severed heads mounted on city gates.[32] At an early stage, persecution forced Anabaptists underground or out of hostile regions. Carrying their faith and a burgeoning martyrology, survivors found refuge in tolerant states like East Friesland, the Palatinate, and the Polish-Lithuanian Commonwealth. Even in these areas, rulers curtailed Mennonites' civil and political rights. Restrictive marriage and inheritance laws prevented communities from growing through conversion—although social marginalization did not occur entirely against their will. Fusing Christian asceticism with political necessity, many were content to live as a separate people. Espousing simplicity in speech and dress, they became known as the "quiet in the land." One instructional handbook warned "against bearing rule according to the manner of the world ..., as well as against all vengeance ..., the swearing of oaths, and all worldly conformity."[33]

Statements of faith, however, were multiple and contested. Mennonitism's decentered nature—reinforced by the doctrines of lay priesthood and congregational independence—rendered communities vulnerable to rupture. There is some truth in the witticism that Anabaptist history can be told through a long list of schisms. In fact, it is often difficult to know who counted as Mennonite at all. Secessionists sometimes continued to use this name, as in the case of the Amish, who arose during the 1690s in Switzerland, France, and the south German states. At other times they did not, as in 1858 when two Baden congregations joined the pietistic Michelians.[34] The issue is further complicated by the ambivalence that members often held for the appellation. "I am against this label," one Munich resident wrote, "because it gives the appearance that Menno is the founder of our confession, which is not the case."[35] For a religion that touted God's authority above all else, was it not perverse to take the name of a mortal? Some found an alternative to sectarianism in overseas evangelism. Influenced by a broader movement across nineteenth-century Christianity, reformists began exporting their faith—while continuing to discourage mixed marriages in European contexts. If missionized populations in Indonesia, North America, and elsewhere were sometimes acknowledged to be Mennonite, it was only of a lower-tier variety. As implied by the growing dichotomy between white and non-white members, the religion's primary vector was understood to be heredity, not belief. At least nominally, most "old Mennonite families" continued to portray their faith as voluntary; a child facing admonishment for un-Anabaptist behavior might quip that since she had not been baptized, she was not yet a member. But in reality, such jokes implied exactly the opposite—that simply being born into a Mennonite household "generally already leads to baptism and membership in our congregations."[36]

It is no accident that at the same moment that some Mennonites began depicting themselves as a closed population, characterized by common surnames and collective memories stretching back to the Reformation, their communities appeared threatened by the rise of European nationalisms. During the eighteenth century, Enlightenment writers had begun connecting national duties and civil rights. Mennonites' doctrine of nonresistance seemed to pose the greatest barrier. "Love your enemies, bless them that curse you, do good to them that hate you, and pray for them which despitefully use you," Menno Simons had taught; "our weapons are not swords and spears, but patience, silence, and hope, and the Word of God."[37] Rarely did such ideas conflict with nascent nationalism more strongly than in the expansionist kingdom of Prussia. For rulers like the Hohenzollerns, conscription provided a means of constructing new citizenship norms. While earlier militaries had comprised standing forces at nobilities' behest, mass armies now arose out of the general population and mobilized in the name of the nation. State powers sought to induce conformity through common service, while sometimes excluding undesirable minorities, such as Jews, by restricting eligibility.[38] After the Partitions of Poland brought thousands of German-speaking Mennonites under Prussian control, King Friedrich Wilhelm II extended military exemption, but only in exchange for civil liberties. Although members retained pacifism, they relinquished property rights and paid steep taxes.[39]

As a perceived exception to the rule, Mennonitism helped stabilize nationalism as a European norm—in turn becoming understood as a quasi-national entity in its own right. Privileged status provoked resentment from other confessions. Moses Mendelssohn grumbled about European Jews' comparatively worse position, while during Napoleon's invasion, Protestants in the Vistula Delta refused to fight unless Mennonite neighbors also joined the militia.[40] Congregants appeared to face an inexorable choice: yield to nationalism or depart the fatherland. Immigration agents in both North America and the Russian Empire capitalized on the situation, enticing farmers with promises of religious freedom and vast untilled plains. Beginning in 1788, thousands from Poland and Prussia answered Catherine the Great's call for foreign settlers, establishing a pattern of colonization in southern Russia that would continue into the twentieth century. A Charter of Privileges granted full spiritual liberty, including exemption from conscription and oaths.[41] Although concessions in North America were less generous—in 1874, the US Congress rejected a "Mennonite bill" that would have allowed closed, Russian-style colonies—land was nevertheless cheap and military service could be avoided.[42] Of all members in German lands, some 18,000 (roughly 45 percent) emigrated abroad during the eighteenth and nineteenth centuries. Around half went to North America, half to the Russian Empire.[43]

The rise of a nationalist order strong enough to drive thousands of Mennonites to foreign shores heralded for many observers a new epoch of European modernity. Associating national consolidation with cultural progression, enlightened thinkers cast pacifism as antithetical to modern civilization. "The Mennonites, who forbid the ownership of weapons, live in peaceful backwardness," one critic wrote; "they do not honor the fatherland, because the notion of fatherland is unknown to them."[44] Indeed, the confession's most reactionary members affirmed such ideas, consciously positioning themselves as agrarian anti-modernists. While leaders had always questioned the morality of certain clothing, musical, and architectural styles, these discussions now acquired a chronological component. In 1847, one Königsberg elder commented unfavorably on Amish Mennonites in the south German states. "Contemporary ways of life are distasteful to them," he wrote, noting how they grew long beards and fastened garments with hooks instead of buttons. At home, they read little more than the Bible; household appliances were "quite antiquated."[45] Even their worship appeared outmoded, at least compared to more northerly coreligionists, who (emulating neighboring Protestants) had begun to build stylish churches, install organs, and hire salaried pastors—some of whom dressed in cassocks and delivered scholarly meditations from raised pulpits. The Amish, by contrast, sang simple songs, read sermons while seated behind a table, held meals in their service space, and knelt during prayer. As national renewal became indicative of modernity, it is no surprise that some Anabaptists considered it yet another temptation to be avoided.

While scholars have long linked the emergence of nation-states with sweeping economic transformations—from industrialization to modern capitalism—such associations are overstated. Most obviously, they fail to explain the appeal of nationalism in minimally industrialized societies. Some conservative Mennonites in Europe and the Americas appropriated nationalist strategies despite rejecting many technologies associated with modernism. Nor can these theories account for the anti-modernist strain in much of nationalist thought.[46] At a more fundamental level, nationalism and anti-nationalism, like any binary, were codependent. Religious separatism provided an opposite to which nationalists could point. And if conservative Mennonites contributed to nationalism's production, if only through dissension, its tie with modernism must surely fall away—not because horse-and-buggy Mennonites were unmodern, but because drawing them within the modernist circle renders its boundaries meaningless. This is not to deny a complex bond between nationalist and modernist systems of thought. But as historian Frederick Cooper has argued, it is less useful to reify modernity as an objective condition than to analyze a "historically rooted process of making claims and counterclaims in the name of modernization."[47] Far from a harbinger of modernity, nationalism played a more modest role.

It simply offered a new vocabulary with which individuals could articulate, as they always had, their place within shifting collectivities. A history confined to the Reformation—or any other period—could tell much the same story. Nor would it need to center on a religious community. Just as Mennonites of every era have negotiated competing groupings, all humans are enmeshed in social networks. Whether collectivities take the name religion, nation, ethnicity, race, or family is less a matter of kind than of context. While scholars have long sought to isolate these strands, their interwoven nature explains why such studies rarely yield satisfying results. Analyzing any one category risks effacing both the memory of its invention and the ways it evolved in relation to others. It would be more valuable to examine such groupings in situ, focusing less on ideal types than the ragged edges where collectivities trail off, turn into something else.[48] In 1911, for example, hymnists repurposed the tune of an old battle song. "Swing, brothers, swing Germania's banner," read the original.[49] The rewritten version: "A holy inheritance remains always for us Mennonites."[50] Blended in harmony, political culture and spiritual tradition lost their distinctiveness. This was collectivism in its rawest form: a multivalent sound, changing pitch and timbre as it traveled from vocal chords to tongue to ear. If certain collectivities crystalized at a particular instant, they were likely to crumble moments later. Malleability, rather than hegemony, explains nationalism's proliferation.

GLOBAL FANTASIES

A pastor in the Netherlands named Samuel Cramer piqued coreligionists' interest in 1902 with a manifesto entitled "International Mennonitism." Inspired by a unification movement among European Protestants, Cramer called upon Anabaptists across the globe to form a transnational bond of fellowship. From the earliest days of the Reformation until the mid-eighteenth century, he argued, they had comprised a decentralized but unified confession, bound by personal relationships and familial ties. Unlike state churches with their fixed territorial boundaries, early Mennonites had considered borders "entirely immaterial."[51] Much of Cramer's proof rested on global dispersion. At the time, approximately 50 percent of all members resided in North America, with as many as 140,000 in the United States alone. A smaller number had traveled to South America and Austria-Hungary, while 60,000 lived as settler colonists in Imperial Russia. Non-white converts, totaling at most a few thousand, went unmentioned. Yet while these migrations allowed Cramer to picture solidarity at a global level, it was diversity that made his injunction necessary in the first place. Whether pressured by local nationalists or enticed to assimilate, members in distant lands adopted foreign cultures. With each passing year, the Russian language made inroads among the colonies of Siberia and the Black Sea region; communities in the United States and Canada were preaching and publishing in English; and more members in France and Switzerland spoke French than ever before. Thus, for Cramer's readers, it was a truly aspirational fantasy that one day, it would "no longer be necessary to distinguish between Dutch, German, American, and Russian Mennonites," that all would set aside national differences and "recognize each other as brethren of the same tribe."[52]

Historians of transnationalism have studied cross-border movements—whether of people, commercial goods, humanitarian aid, or ideas—to overcome narrow methodologies.[53] Emphasizing the conceptual and territorial instability of countries like Germany, they have demonstrated boundaries' inadequacy as rubrics of analysis.[54] Yet if figures like Cramer worked transnationally, their thinking also reflected statist frameworks. Understanding this dialectic requires attention to individual "activists."[55] Theorists of collectivism, by deemphasizing groups, have instead elevated human agency. In their telling, the political was always personal. Particular national or religious accounts developed through the propagandizing of activists, who competed with each other for populations' allegiances. "We have made Italy," one nationalist reportedly jested in 1861, after helping form a new Italian state; "now we have to make Italians."[56] Similarly in German lands, politicians committed to the idea of a unified nation institutionalized their opinions in census forms, citizenship papers, and legal codes; educators restructured school curriculums; and cultural trendsetters attempted to recast civil society, literature, art, and almost everything else in a nationalist mold.

Such tactics were not lost on Mennonite observers. Confessional advocates learned that by appropriating nationalist discourses, they could promote forms of nationalism favorable to their own agendas. After the revocation of military exemption, for example, progressive leaders in Germany sought to nationalize their coreligionists. Downplaying older accounts of Dutch and Swiss origins, they proposed the creation of a German Mennonite collectivity. Asserting that "our congregations must be *reorganized*," they initiated an empire-wide renewal movement that would emerge in full force by the 1880s.[57] Mennonite activists—who were unusually urban, affluent, and well educated—conformed to demographic patterns of nationalist activism across Europe. Emblematic was the cultured and charismatic Hinrich van der Smissen, co-pastor of the large congregation in Hamburg-

Altona. Despite his Dutch last name, van der Smissen's brand of Menno-nitism was almost rabidly pro-German, and his florid essays on the confes-sion's essentially German nature drew frequent ire from coworkers in the Netherlands. Throughout his long tenure, van der Smissen played the roles of organizer, cheerleader, and historian of the German Mennonite project. During the same years in which he helped establish a Union of Mennonite Congregations in the German Empire, he was also president of an educa-tional institute designed to serve all congregations in Germany, as well as editor of a newspaper for German-speaking Mennonites worldwide.[58] Using the German Mennonite idea they had recently forged, leaders like van der Smissen sought to sway state authorities, a wider public, and their own congregations on a host of political and theological issues.

Unlike Samuel Cramer's vision of religious internationalism, pro-German activists offered a more restricted model. Coding Anabaptism within the language of German nationalism, they portrayed members as archetypal Germans. "Do not almost all Mennonites," one proponent asked, "wher-ever they may live—in Russia, in Switzerland, in Alsace-Lorraine, Galicia and Pomerania, in the United States and in Canada, in Mexico and Para-guay, yes even in asiatic Siberia and Turkestan—speak the same *German* mother tongue? Are not the Mennonites, wherever they go, also the pio-neers of German language, customs, and culture?"[59] Depictions of Menno-nitism as the German confession par excellence reflected a fascination emerging across the country's public sphere for "diasporic" colonists. Espe-cially after 1884, with Germany's procurement of territories in Africa and the Pacific, citizens followed their alleged co-nationals' march across the globe.[60] Settlers in Togo, North Dakota, Palestine, Brazil, or China were said to perform "German work," a trope—deployed in racist contrast to native populations—associating them with efficiency and productivity.[61] In 1904, the sociologist Max Weber famously linked the "Protestant ethic" of ascetic Christianity with a "spirit of capitalism." Mingled with ethnic chauvinism, Weber's analysis implied that the diligence of German speakers abroad and especially of German-speaking Mennonites—"whose otherworldliness is as proverbial as their wealth"—allowed them to tame foreign lands (and for-eign peoples) while fortifying them to retain German values and customs.[62]

Mennonites outside Germany, for their part, rarely considered them-selves German colonists. After all, those most opposed to nationalism had been likeliest to emigrate. With few exceptions, the attribute German na-tionalists most admired about external communities—their ability to pro-mote German culture abroad—meant little or nothing to settlers themselves. Most had departed for religious freedom or to pursue economic opportu-nity. If a majority continued to speak German—persisting in some cases across more than ten generations—this reflected less a political loyalty to Germany than a desire to distinguish their congregations from surrounding

German nationalist Mennonites emphasized the order, diligence, and industry of their coreligionists abroad, portraying settlements in other countries—such as this farm in south Russia's Molotschna colony—as bastions of diasporic Germandom.

non-Mennonite populations. In the same way that conservative Amish and Mennonites in North America refused to wear printed clothing, grow mustaches, or use electricity, many avoided English as a worldly language. Old German dialects, such as the "Pennsylvania Dutch" spoken from Virginia to Ontario, or the "Low German" of Imperial Russia's colonies, were cultivated for separatist reasons and not as part of an imperialist lingua franca. When faraway Mennonites did meet counterparts from German lands, culture differentiated as often as it united. At "every turn," one minister from Holstein wrote of an 1868 tour across the United States, "it was evident [we] had come into a new world; the familiar home customs were unknown here, perhaps even gave offense. And then the Pennsylvanian language—how strange it sounded to the newcomer!"[63] Similarly in the Russian Empire, spokespersons often presented themselves as a "little Mennonite nation," typically contrasted with "other nations," including nearby Catholic and Protestant German speakers.[64] "The difference between us and our German neighbors was so great," reasoned one leader, "that a period of over 100 years brought virtually no amalgamation through marriage." Considering Germany's expansionism both theologically and politically bankrupt, many rejected "the notion of being an 'outpost of Germanism in the east.'"[65]

German nationalist Mennonites—in the awkward position of having to convince coreligionists abroad that they were in fact German—faced remarkably similar challenges at home. That activists like Hinrich van der Smissen expended such energies toward unifying their own congregations suggests a deep-seated ambivalence or even hostility on the part of most members in Germany. Historians Pieter Judson and Tara Zahra use the term "indifference" to describe people unmoved by nationalist appeals. Portrayed as the inverse of activism, indifference has likewise been theorized through the language of agency. According to Judson and Zahra, it "refers to the attempt to maintain a degree of choice in one's life, in historical situations where such choices are being drastically limited, either by official fiat or local activist pressure."[66] Engaged in an ideological tug-of-war, indifferent persons attempt to maintain independence from larger collectivities, while activists seek to draw them in. When German nationalist Mennonites formed their national Union in 1886, only seventeen of the empire's seventy-one congregations joined. Unionists designed creative methods of attracting participation. Generating fears about shrinking birth and marriage rates, they tied membership to mutual aid programs and spun romantic tales of Reformation-era unity. But despite their efforts, many kept a distance.

Activists' accounts were certainly self-serving. Indeed, they were often better barometers of what coreligionists did *not* believe. But it would be incorrect to suggest that conservative Mennonites, either in Germany or abroad, were truly indifferent toward questions of affiliation. The concept of indifference was first developed by nineteenth-century nationalists, who employed it as a pejorative, intended to shame populations into performing nationalist acts. It thus presupposed a dualistic interpretation in which persons were either inside or outside of nationalism. As the history of Mennonitism demonstrates, however, there was no normative path from which skeptics could deviate. Religious, national, and other collectivities intermingled to such a degree that individuals' choice was not whether to associate with some larger grouping, but which one to adopt. It may be useful to think of each person as an activist in his or her own right, all advocating different narratives to suit private agendas. Even those wary of progressive change could agitate for stasis or for the strengthening of a given tradition.[67] By reasserting conventional practices against the perceived dangers of nationalism and modernity, conservative Mennonites made and remade their communities. Just as traits like piety and modesty required cultivation, collective practices and cultural artifacts—such as barn-raisings or broad-brimmed hats—developed in response to shifting conditions. Only in the era of electricity have oil lamps become a choice; only with the invention of automobiles did buggies become conservative. Less a retrenchment than the initiation of a crusade, opposition to change was itself new.[68]

Collectivism, of course, was never an ideological free-for-all. Embedded in larger fields of contestation, individuals were constrained by the situations in which they found themselves.[69] After the First World War, for instance, anti-German sentiment prompted Mennonites across Eurasia and North America to disassociate from Germanness. Inoculating against external prejudices, many embraced a Zionist-like form of religious nationalism. "Just as every star has its place in the heavens," one writer argued, "we have our place in the constellation of nations."[70] Combining Jewish nationalist terminology with Wilsonian self-determination, leaders won support from the League of Nations and multiple governments to establish a semiautonomous "Mennonite State" in rural Paraguay. During the Third Reich, a growing cadre pinned its hopes on the new German state. Echoing Hitler's call to "turn our gaze toward the lands in the East," pro-Nazi Mennonites asserted membership in a four-hundred-year-old "racial church"—an Aryan version of the Jewish "antirace"—entitled to a share of the *Führer's* spoils.[71] But global violence swung the pendulum once again. In the aftermath of the Second World War, more than 15,000 refugees shed their Aryan identity papers to secure transport across the Atlantic, most gaining UN assistance and entry into Canada or Paraguay's "Mennonite State" as non-Germans. One final turn: Beginning in the 1970s, the mass repatriation of nearly all Mennonites from the Soviet Union to West Germany reflected a widespread belief in members' German roots. The trick for historians, then, is not to discover who belonged to which group when, but rather to understand how larger events rendered certain affiliations desirable, whether German, Mennonite, or otherwise.[72] While these cases reveal the fluidity of group loyalty, they also highlight the limitations of elective affinity in the era of nationalism.

———————————

Mennonite history underlines the fragmentary nature of religious and national collectivities. That so many actors disagreed so fervently about the confession's true character suggests that depictions of coherence constituted a malleable resource. Members as well as outsiders could draw on such discourses, molding them to fit divergent needs—often redefining what it meant to be Mennonite in the first place. While German-centric accounts cast congregants abroad as diasporic nationals, observers both within and beyond German borders offered alternative readings. Colonists in Russia, Canada, or Paraguay were neither intrinsically German, diasporic, nor even Mennonite. Only in relation to broader hermeneutic systems did these terms acquire meaning. Forms of belonging rested on no permanent foundation. Nevertheless, collectivist language held immense power. If strategically deployed and liberally received, it could structure self-conceptions and world outlooks, circumscribing entire communities' range of political and intellectual motion. Individuals' decisions to affiliate with particular nations (or with no nation) rarely reflected free expressions of will. More often, local circumstances, personal histories, and collective expectations embedded subjects within rich but limited matrixes. As particular words or material objects—head coverings, flags, blond hair—developed significance, members engaged a process of mutual religious and national production. The resulting constellations aligned differently for each observer, as well as across time, evolving with the passage of years, decades, and centuries.

In 1876, when Peter and Agatha Dyck embarked from Bremen on the ocean liner *Rhein*, their voyage marked not just one family's journey from Germany to the United States, but also a critical moment in a string of confession-wide transformations. Subsequent events would reshape again and again the ways that Mennonites across the world perceived their nationality and their religion. In the summer breeze on the deck of the *Rhein*, the Dycks considered their departure a rejection of militarism and the threat it posed to pacifist theology, not an affirmation of German nationalism. The travelers could not have anticipated the myriad stories that future generations would tell about their emigration, the contradictory objectives it would be called upon to justify.

Once Germany's shoreline dipped below the horizon, the emigrants gathered in the *Rhein*'s dining compartment to send thanks to God. For his sermon text, Peter Dyck chose Genesis 12:1–4.[73] Like thousands of migrating Mennonites before and afterward, he and his listeners recalled the story of Abram, in which God calls the patriarch to enter the land of Canaan. Like Abram, the worshipers had answered their Lord, abandoning home and entering an unknown territory. They were apprehensive about what lay ahead, and yet filled with hope. Just as Abram's journey had presaged the creation of a new people, the emigrating Mennonites believed that God would reward their faith. Their congregations would flourish, and they would become a blessing and a great nation. Exactly how this process would unfold remained to be seen.

CHAPTER 1

BECOMING GERMAN

THE GEOGRAPHY OF COLLECTIVISM

> In my youth it was a generally accepted fact that we
> Mennonites were not native Germans, but rather of purely
> Dutch origin, and that through the charity of the princes
> and God's merciful guidance, we found an entirely new
> homeland on German soil.
>
> —HINRICH VAN DER SMISSEN,
> "ORIGINS OF THE GERMAN MENNONITES," 1917[1]

A visionary and a nation-builder, Hinrich van der Smissen was fond of looking backwards. The Hamburg-Altona pastor, who at the end of the First World War was nearing his seventieth birthday, had presided for more than four decades over the unification of Germany's Mennonites. Editing newspapers, heading educational institutes, and chairing national conferences, he worked tirelessly to inspire cooperation among the far-flung congregations of the German Empire. As he told it, these efforts had begun in 1871—the same year that Germany became a country. "Prior to this time," van der Smissen recalled, "we [Mennonites] had only banded together in loose and scattered groups." A modest conference had formed in the Prussian east. Some contact was growing between the northwestern congregations. And there were stirrings in the south, among Mennonites in Baden, Bavaria, and Wurttemberg. But it was only in 1871, with "the new establishment of the German Empire, that these efforts in our congregations received a more promising outlook." Inspired by the larger political unification of the German states, "we, too, in our Mennonite circles, initiated the first attempts to utilize the newly created situation to our own purposes, and to forge the weak ties that had developed between us into a Union that would span the entire empire."[2]

Not until the late nineteenth century, according to van der Smissen, did some Mennonites begin to associate their confession with Germanness. Prior to this time, few members drew on the language of German nationalism to describe their religion. In part, this reflected the geographic and cultural barriers separating the congregations in German-speaking lands. Members in these areas were generally divided into three separate populations—east,

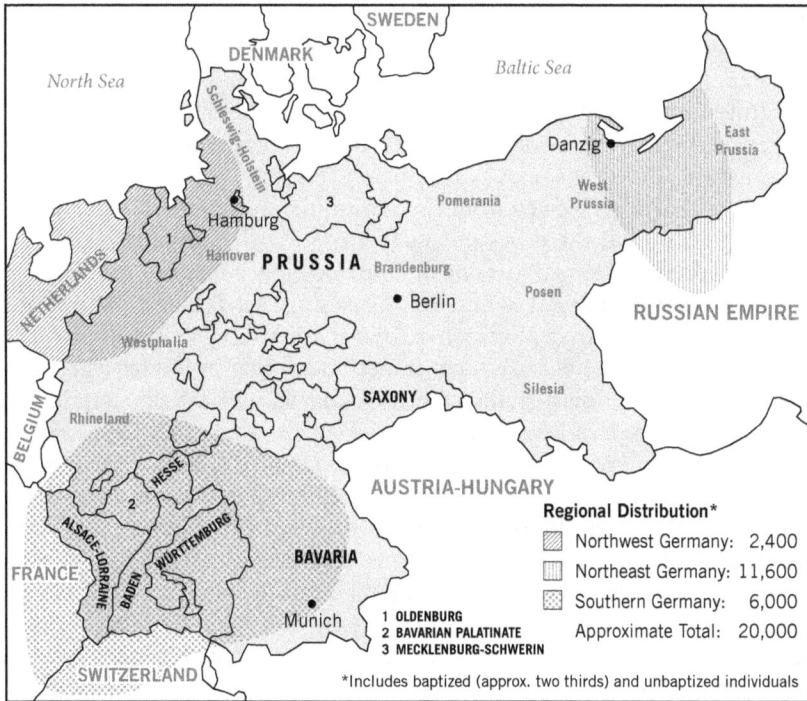

Mennonites in Imperial Germany, 1871

northwest, and south—each with vastly different histories, theologies, rituals, and legal codes. If they took spatial appellations at all, individual communities were more likely to identify as Prussian, Bavarian, or Palatine than as German. When they did cooperate with coreligionists beyond their own regions, they typically engaged populations outside German lands, whether in France, Imperial Russia, the Netherlands, or elsewhere. In fact, as van der Smissen recalled, a majority of Mennonites in the German states, especially those in the east and northwest, believed they had Dutch origins and were not "native Germans" at all. Similarly, most of those in the south held collective memories of "Swiss" ancestry. It was only through the passionate, painstaking work of activists like van der Smissen that a common narrative based on German nationality began to emerge. Influenced especially by German nationalist Protestants, as well as by broader Enlightenment notions of citizenship obligations, proponents of this account began to distance themselves from coreligionists in the Netherlands. Although the Low Countries had long provided Mennonitism's cultural and intellectual center, activists in German lands aimed to furnish a new global capital. Claiming that most members of the confession had radiated outward from these regions, they identified German-speaking congregations in other countries as representatives of a worldwide German Mennonite diaspora.

While German nationalist Mennonites such as Hinrich van der Smissen portrayed the growing association between their religion and their nationality as natural and almost inevitable, this process was in fact contingent and highly contested. As viewed from the beginning or even the middle of the nineteenth century, the development of a specifically German-Mennonite nexus would have seemed just one of many possible outcomes, and in later years, observers continued to find it as surprising as it was new. Even steadfast supporters like van der Smissen expressed astonishment at their project's successes, lauding the pervasiveness of an outlook that would have been inconceivable to their own grandparents. Of course, such self-congratulatory sentiments offered too clean a picture. Despite the grandiose terms in which these nationalists touted the emergence of a German Mennonite "imagined community," this idea always held more power for a few dedicated activists than it did for the majority of its alleged members. Far from a unique and monolithic outgrowth of modernization, nationalism offered merely one new means of conceptualizing collective belonging.[3] It joined regionalism, localism, religion, and many other forms of affiliation that had been available to Mennonites for centuries and that continued to exist alongside and even within nationalism over the ensuing years. Just as all of these categories were themselves fluid, the concept of German Mennonitism held various meanings for different observers. Interpretations of Mennonites' nationality were always subject to negotiation, and individuals adapted and modified them, supplemented them with other loyalties, or even rejected them outright.

SHIFTING ALLEGIANCES

In 1851, the year Hinrich van der Smissen was born, there was no German nation-state. A patchwork of principalities, kingdoms, and coalitions dissected the vast expanse between the Netherlands and the Russian Empire that two decades later would unite to become the German Empire. These lands formed the rough shape of an inverted triangle. Had anyone thought to plot the location of Mennonite congregations in this territory, they would have discovered three distinct clusters, each located at one of the triangle's distant corners: northwest, northeast, and south. The northwest was home to the wealthy city congregations. Established in the aftermath of the Reformation by refugees from the Low Countries, they retained close personal and trade ties to the Netherlands. Many people still spoke and preached in Dutch, and members were often highly integrated into the business life of Atlantic port cities.[4] Far to the east, in the former crown lands of

Poland and Lithuania, lived the largest of the three communities. Known as the Mennonites of East and West Prussia, they had also arrived from the Netherlands in the sixteenth century. Policymakers along the Vistula and Nogat rivers, where the majority of the region's Mennonite settlements developed, favored these migrants for their water engineering abilities. While early settlers in Poland retained religious and commercial relations with friends and extended family members in the Low Countries (Menno Simons even visited the area on at least one occasion), most eventually entered agricultural professions. Employing Dutch-style windmills and canals, they drained the swamps of the Vistula Delta and cultivated the newly won land.[5] The third and final population, also primarily agrarian, lived in the south. Largely descendants of immigrants from Switzerland who had helped to repopulate the south German states after the Thirty Years' War, their small congregations faded in and out with related clusters across the Swiss and French borders.[6]

While these three communities would eventually find common ground within the territory of a united Germany, it would be misleading to speak of their earlier iterations as pre-national, as though they were destined to achieve a single preordained outcome. Mennonites in seventeenth- and eighteenth-century Europe inhabited a vastly different political landscape, and contemporary political geography structured congregations' engagement or non-collaboration with other communities. Although the first Anabaptists had preached and baptized indiscriminately across official boundaries, early Mennonite populations quickly became concentrated in a limited number of states. Because intolerant Catholic and Protestant rulers considered Anabaptists both politically threatening and religiously idolatrous, they condemned practitioners to incarceration, torture, and death. "Whoever persists in his error," the cities of Bern, St. Gall, and Zurich wrote of Anabaptism in 1527, "becomes a preacher or leader of the sect, or, having sworn to amend his ways and to desist from his error, backslides, shall also be drowned."[7] Two years later, an Imperial Diet pronounced adult baptism a capital offense across the entire Holy Roman Empire. As the news of burnings and dismemberments emanated from places like Amsterdam, Alzey, and Strasbourg, Anabaptists learned to steer clear of these areas. Thousands fled to more lenient countries, where they found relative religious freedom in exchange for curtailed civil rights or special taxes. In 1573, for example, the Polish-Lithuanian Commonwealth vowed that it would "not for a different faith or a change of churches shed blood nor punish one another by confiscation of property, infamy, imprisonment, or banishment."[8] Mennonite immigrants built on such assurances, further lobbying rulers for expanded property rights and privileges, such as exemption from military service. By avoiding unfriendly states while settling in more tolerant ones, members delineated their religious space with political borders. Just as some countries were officially Catholic, Lutheran, or Calvinist, the boundaries of Mennonitism could also be drawn on a political map.[9]

Nevertheless, certain forms of mobility—including migration, trade, and interregional marriage—kept Mennonites' spatial distribution in flux. Some Anabaptists' theology also placed them on a temporal continuum, positing an eternal community of God that stretched from the ancient Israelites to the second coming of Christ. By invoking their spiritual homeland in heaven, in addition to their earthly residences in Europe, these individuals imagined their place in a Christian tradition that transcended both worldly temporality and state borders. It was in part for this reason that later writers spoke so frequently about their Reformation-era ancestors, many of whom had faced persecution in Switzerland and the Netherlands. The influential *Martyrs Mirror*, first published in 1660 by the Dordrecht elder Thieleman J. van Bracht, became widely known among Mennonite families throughout Europe and the Americas. Its graphic accounts of more than eight hundred Anabaptist martyrs fostered a transnational sense of Mennonite peoplehood.[10] Influenced by this and other works, most Mennonites in German lands—especially in eastern Prussia and the northwestern states—possessed strong narratives of emigration from the Low Countries. According to one 1841 history book, all the congregations in Prussia "originate from those who emigrated from the United Netherlands."[11] A variety of traditional practices—farming techniques, for example, or certain dishes and baked goods—as well as inherited material objects seemed to confirm such accounts. The congregational library of the Danzig church contained far more books in Dutch than in any language besides German; the number of Dutch versus German books for the years prior to 1800 was nearly equal.[12]

By the beginning of the nineteenth century, the Netherlands had become Europe's progressive capital of Mennonite culture and theology. Persecution had largely ended by the close of the sixteenth century, and local Mennonites acquired significant religious and economic freedoms. Spurred to innovate by their relative outsider status and insulated by a tight-knit communal safety net, they soon became disproportionately wealthy per capita. Newfound riches, generated especially by the textile and shipping industries, provided the funding for elaborate churches, mutual aid societies, printing presses, and in 1735, a seminary in Amsterdam.[13] Unlike most of their coreligionists in the Prussian east, France, Switzerland, North America, the south German states, and later, the Russian Empire, Mennonites in the Netherlands were primarily urban and had less hesitancy about participating in "worldly" spheres, including art, literature, politics, shipping, and banking. By contrast, Mennonites in German lands—especially those in the south and east—were usually more rural, less wealthy, and emphasized values like simplicity and humility. Such differences laid the groundwork for cultural clashes with coreligionists in the Netherlands, who sometimes caricatured intra-confessional tensions in dramatic or spiritual literature. In 1713, one poet criticized the "corrupt manners of many Dutch Mennonites" through the eyes of "Sister Simplicity," a fictional Amish Mennonite girl from Switzerland.[14] Yet despite strains, works produced in the Netherlands regularly traveled east. In 1766, the Hoorn preacher Cornelis Ris published *Articles of Faith of the True Mennonites or Anabaptists*, a doctrinal handbook that inspired discussion among all three communities in the German states.[15]

Among these populations, Mennonites in the northwest were by far the best acquainted with their counterparts in the Netherlands. It was here that Menno, like many early Anabaptists, spent the most active years of his life—finding refuge and fertile recruiting ground across East Friesland, the Lower Rhine, and southern Denmark. Eventually securing privileges similar to those in the Netherlands, Mennonites in these areas enjoyed comparable wealth. In Krefeld, one of Prussia's most successful export cities, the manufacturing family von der Leyen amassed fabulous riches through the production of silk and linen. One commentator ascribed Krefeld's eighteenth-century boom "to the linen trade of the Mennonites."[16] The von der Leyens exercised broad political influence and even hosted Frederick the Great in their lavish home. During the same period, Mennonites in Hamburg, despite comprising less than 1 percent of the harbor city's population, controlled an astounding 18 percent of its merchant ships and nearly half its whaling industry.[17] Well into the nineteenth century, common religious convictions, intermarriage, and economic ties continued to link Mennonite congregations in the northwest German states with those in the Netherlands. Members read Dutch-language sermons, newspapers, histories, and theological treatises, and supplied ministerial candidates to the Amsterdam seminary. Institutional affiliations provided another bond; several congregations were members of the Netherlands' General Mennonite Conference, founded in 1811.

Congregations in other German states likewise maintained ties with coreligionists in non-German regions. Those in the Prussian east enjoyed frequent visits and letter exchanges with their relatives in the Russian Empire. And in the south German states, Amish and Mennonites maintained contact with migrants to North America, or cooperated with neighbors in Switzerland and France. But within German lands, interregional ties were comparatively weak. An average distance of more than five hundred miles separated the three groups, and leaders rarely invited delegations from other areas to discuss matters of church doctrine, discipline, or mutual aid. That most members lived in rural settings further complicated exchange. Intermarriage was rare. One study found 454 distinct surnames among Mennonites in the Prussian east, 660 among those in the northwest, and 478 in

Mennonite industrialists exhibiting their wares to Frederick the Great during his 1763 visit to Krefeld. Merchant and manufacturing families like the von der Leyens in the Netherlands and northwest German states achieved wealth and power beyond the means and preferences of coreligionists to the south and east.

the south—few with significant regional overlap.[18] Congregational address books provide one window onto the limitations of cooperation. During the first half of the nineteenth century, the most expansive of these booklets included congregations only in "East and West Prussia, Lithuania, Poland, and in the German colonies of the Russian Empire." Those west of Berlin were not "sufficiently well known."[19]

It was mission work that in the 1820s first induced cooperation between all three regions. Some Mennonites had already engaged in evangelism by sending donations to organizations like the Prussian Main Bible Society. But only through contact with a Baptist preacher from England named William Angas did proselytism emerge as a pan-confessional undertaking. A former sea captain turned mission advocate, Angas traveled extensively among continental Mennonites. Invoking similarities between Baptism and Mennonitism (the first Baptists had been influenced by Anabaptist writings), he hoped to win support for a recently established mission in India. In 1821, Angas convinced Mennonites in the Netherlands to form a "Dutch branch of the Mission Society of the English Baptists to Serampur."[20] He then visited congregations across Prussia, the Palatinate, Switzerland, and

Alsace. In the south German states, Angas found willing ears among the most progressive communities, which in 1824 formed an evangelically oriented Conference of Palatine-Hessian Mennonite Congregations. Listeners in West Prussia also took up collections for the Baptists, eventually founding their own regional institutions, including the semi-ecumenical Danzig Missionary Association.[21]

Evangelism signaled a theological revolution. Congregations in German lands had long banned proselytism, considering it a threat to their special state privileges. When the Polish-Lithuanian Commonwealth had granted Anabaptist refugees asylum, freedom of religion, and exemption from military service, authorities stipulated that they refrain from growing through conversion. Violation invited steep consequences. In 1720, when Protestant farm hands joined one community in ducal Prussia, King Friedrich Wilhelm I expelled the entire group. "I will not tolerate such a rogue people," he wrote, "that cannot become soldiers."[22] But with the advent of the European Enlightenment, Mennonites began to encounter new ideas about social and legal egalitarianism. Often, they experienced these as negative, external pressures. When an expansionist Prussia absorbed most congregations in the Polish-Lithuanian Commonwealth, leaders struggled to preserve for their military exemption. Friedrich Wilhelm II issued a "Mennonite Edict" in 1789, guaranteeing Mennonites' nonparticipation in military service but limiting their ability to acquire new land.[23] While this law prompted mass migration to Imperial Russia, it also began to inculcate—among those who remained—notions of universal civic duties.

Broader social patterns emerging across Europe reinforced these norms. Following the French Revolution, a general rise in mobility and cultural exchange acquainted Mennonites in German lands with the Enlightenment and philosophy of the new French Republic. In 1795, a guest from France in the home of Christian Möllinger, a Mennonite peasant merchant in Rhineland-Hesse, referred to his host as "a valued citizen of the state," invoking ideals like fraternity, egalitarianism, and liberty.[24] The Napoleonic wars only magnified such ideas, and it was during the French occupation that many congregations first received political emancipation. In 1803, one assembly of church leaders in Rhineland-Hesse had reaffirmed their commitment to pacifism: "All who voluntarily take up arms fall under our congregational punishment and will have no spiritual fellowship with us but will instead be expelled."[25] But when Napoleon brokered a wartime Confederation of the Rhein, Mennonites in the new member states fell under the Napoleonic code. While this legal system granted them full citizenship rights, it revoked their exemption from military service. A delegation to Paris failed to change Napoleon's mind, and by 1815 men from these congregations had fought in Spain and the Russian Empire. Mennonites in provincial Prussia faced similar pressures. During the French invasion, they refused conscription, instead gifting 30,000 thalers to Friedrich Wilhelm III and providing horses, clothes, and foodstuffs. Young men served as fire-fighters and in other noncombatant roles.[26]

The Napoleonic experience prompted reform across the German states. Remembering defeat at the bayonets of France's new citizen soldiers, authorities sought to transform their own subjects into nationalized citi-zens. Mennonites were often unable to regain recognition of their pacifist beliefs. "Every Hessian is required to take part in the regular military obli-gations," the Grand Dutchy of Hesse's new constitution proclaimed. Baden, similarly, insisted that "religious difference does not constitute an exemp-tion from military service," while Bavaria singled out "Mennonites and Jews" for inclusion.[27] Although draftees could secure replacements for a large fee, they remained, as under Napoleon, emancipated citizens. Congregations in Prussia, by contrast, retained or renegotiated their exemption, fulfilling ob-ligations through tax payments. Nevertheless, Enlightenment ideas contin-ued to flourish in all German lands. Buoyed by the onset of industrializa-tion, members of the middle classes developed new interests in fraternities, choirs, gymnastic societies, and other voluntary associations. These held appeal for progress-minded Mennonites, who joined groups ranging from the professional to the ultra-patriotic. Relationships with new Protestant and ecumenical organizations were particularly significant. A spiritual awaken-ing helped produce Christian mission societies, alms houses, and orphan-ages, as well as larger movements for evangelical unity throughout Europe and the world.[28]

This was the context in which Mennonites began engaging overseas mis-sions. Evangelism expanded members' religious horizons, allowing them to envision relevance for their faith across the globe. Individuals contrib-uted spiritual and monetary resources with the aim of Christianizing the world. But if the Baptist Mission Society's main objective—according to its Mennonite-run Amsterdam branch—was to "spread the kingdom of truth and of peace," the conversion of colonized peoples did not threaten Men-nonite eurocentrism.[29] To the contrary, evangelism provided an early vehi-cle of its production, helping establish a still pervasive distinction between white, wealthy Mennonites and poor neophytes of color. Mission enthusi-asts positioned themselves at the center of a set of concentric circles from which the gospel should radiate along lines representing both geographic distance and decreasing levels of civilization. Missionaries' task was to carry the light of Christianity to "uncultivated nations" at the far extremities of the globe. Both men and women participated in missionary societies, trav-eling long distances to attend festivals or hosting their own events, where speakers read inspirational reports from faraway lands. Listeners fantasized about the conversion of "heathen" populations, consummating their de-sires with donations to "missionaries serving in the East Indies or the West

Indies or one of the islands of Australia."[30] Such geographic imprecision was typical. Contributors were often less concerned with their money's exact destination than the more general knowledge that they were saving non-white, non-Christian souls beyond the margins of their own privileged context.

Amid this globalizing worldview, Mennonites theorized their own coordinates. If mission work encouraged participants to trace the flow of their financial and spiritual aid across an apparently Christianizing planet, it also prompted them to think about more local conditions. "During our council on the promotion of Christianity among the heathens," one mission conference recorded in 1826, "our focus turned as if of its own accord to the condition of our own congregations." Upon self-examination, the delegates concluded that their community had become fragmented, and they resolved to promote evangelism as a "middle point through which all will be renewed, ordered, and held together."[31] Efforts to export their faith thus directly induced European Mennonites to articulate their own commonalities. The language of "awakening" and "rebirth," employed by advocates like Angas, promoted revivalism; ministers promoted evangelism as a blessing "not only for the conversion of the heathens, but also for the donors themselves."[32] As mission societies gained steam—often literally, expanding their reach through new technologies of travel and communication—they simultaneously found new means of entering Mennonite households. Pamphlets detailing organizational activities, including exact counts of souls saved, circulated widely, both praising donors' contributions and requesting increased funds.

Drawn to the excitement of missionary activities, some young Mennonite men began seeking higher education. Most members considered advanced learning and reason in general highly suspect. Especially in the southern and eastern German states, congregations had a long-standing tradition of lay leadership. Believing that all people could understand the Bible without recourse to scholarly training, they elected preachers for life. These men usually balanced ministerial duties with full-time farming. But by the mid-nineteenth century, a small number had begun to study at universities or mission schools. Theology students further exposed their confession to evangelical thinking, both through letters home and, following their training, as educated pastors. In 1837, Carl Justus van der Smissen, a recent graduate of the Basel Mission Society's institute, accepted a pastorate in Holstein's Friedrichstadt congregation, where he made his name as a proponent of overseas evangelism. Educated and salaried pastors like van der Smissen helped erode traditional distinctions between Mennonites and Protestants, pushing their congregations to adopt Protestant-style worship materials, catechisms, and hymn selections. The introduction of instrumental music, which conservatives considered prideful and ostentatious, followed a similar trend. In the 1840s, one rural visitor was scandalized to hear a Beethoven sonata in the home of a city pastor.[33] Already in the eighteenth century, the Altona congregation had installed an organ, a decision emulated over the following decades by progressive communities to the south and east. Conservative Heubuden, by contrast, held out until 1890.[34]

Mennonite revivalism, engendered and compelled by mission activities, inspired interregional integration. Congregational address books illustrate the pattern. The authors of one 1835 directory hoped its use would encourage letter writing and visits, prompting disparate communities to "sling the band of love around each other."[35] Compilers also discarded the descriptors Frisian, Flemish, and Old Flemish, which stemmed from a sixteenth-century altercation over proper forms of dress, business, and orientation toward the external world. At a time of missionary cooperation, the schism appeared to have lost its relevance. Revealing the fluid nature of Mennonite collectivism, these changes demonstrate how notions of citizenship, evangelism, and ecumenicalism could alter the ways that congregations interacted with each other. As members adopted positions on the issues of their time, they recast acceptable modes of religious belonging, ultimately reshaping what it meant to be Mennonite in the first place. Just as new citizenship requirements could prompt debates about nonresistance, opportunities for inter-continental evangelism enabled increasingly global outlooks. Such developments reflected a constant evolution of confessional allegiances; as leaders became acquainted with rising nationalist discourses, the language of Germanness would provide one additional means of negotiating these relationships.

ARTICULATING NATIONALISM

Not until the mid-nineteenth century did prominent Mennonites in German lands begin calling for interregional cooperation based on common German nationality.[36] Among the earliest was Jakob Mannhardt, pastor of the progressive Danzig congregation. The first university-educated minister in the Prussian east, Mannhardt was well situated to introduce change to a conservative Anabaptist setting. His father was a Protestant schoolteacher from Wurttemberg and his mother a Mennonite from the wealthy van der Smissen merchant family of Hamburg-Altona, a background that lent him both worldly authority and in-group authenticity. Throughout his long career, Mannhardt drew on his studies at Protestant institutions in Tübingen and Bonn to advocate for Mennonite consolidation across German lands. In a widely read 1854 article, he decried confessional disunity: "our various congregations in Germany ... stand apart from each other, without a close relationship or connection and without a feeling of solidarity."[37] Over the following years, other leaders—especially ministers from the urban northwest, those with theological education, or individuals raised in mixed-marriage households—echoed Mannhardt's critique of regionalism. Hamburg-Altona pastor Berend Roosen lamented his own community's "isolated position in northwest Germany," noting that members had little contact with the "more tightly connected German Mennonite congregations in the south and east."[38] Pointing less to a revival of old ties than to the formation of new relationships, such sentiments signified an emerging belief that Mennonites in German lands necessarily belonged together.

The outlooks of Mannhardt and Roosen tracked with attitudes among Protestant counterparts. Nationalist activists had recently begun advocating the political consolidation of German lands, arguing that these countries should merge into a single nation-state. Some proponents adopted a religious lens, attempting to organize this movement around the principles of Protestant Christianity. According to their vision, the new state would be led by the Kingdom of Prussia and would exclude predominantly Catholic Austria. Such selective corporatism lent focus to progressive Mennonites' desire for religious unity. Members in both urban and rural areas followed closely, often through Protestant newspapers, as popular reformers agitated for widespread institutional change, including political unification, freedom of the press, and democratic rights. The writings of Carl Harder, elder of East Prussia's Königsberg congregation, demonstrate the influence of Protestant-mediated German nationalism. In 1846, Harder—who had studied Protestant theology at the universities of Danzig and Halle—unveiled the first confessional paper for Mennonites in the German states. Entitled *Monthly Journal for the Evangelical Mennonites*, his periodical aimed to "unite our [Mennonite] people in a league of brothers."[39] In addition to providing news from congregations in multiple countries, it championed involvement in select Protestant endeavors. Harder tolerated intermarriage with other Christians, favored participation in military service, and recommended ecumenical aid organizations. Above all, he encouraged his coreligionists to "emerge from their secluded position, and without giving up their convictions ... come into lively intercourse with all other Christian confessions."[40]

The wider German nationalist movement came to a head in the spring of 1848. Following a European-wide wave of revolutionary violence, German lands stood on the brink of cultural and political reconfiguration. Along with a broad cross-section of participants—from peasants to military commanders, communists to monarchists—Protestant nationalists hoped to harness the revolutionary spirit for their own agenda. In May, several months after the revolts' outbreak, representatives from multiple German countries convened a National Assembly in Frankfurt. Intending to forge a new national state, the parliament drafted a spirited constitution that, while never successfully implemented, laid the groundwork for debates about unification until the establishment of the German Empire a quarter century later.[41] Many Mennonite observers embraced the conceptual geography codified at Frankfurt. Carl Harder, for example, promoted his country's integration into a larger German state: "The inhabitants of Prussia speak the same language that is spoken ... in the other German lands, and their character aligns so perfectly with no other national tribe as with the German. The Prussians are Germans and can only protect and develop their particular characteristics if they join with the other Germans in a great whole, in a united Germany." According to Harder, all Prussian subjects—including the state's Mennonites—would remain stifled, doomed to cultural fragmentation and political entropy, until they set aside their differences with other German-speakers from Hamburg to Wurttemberg and joined to form a new "German Empire."[42]

Mennonites were well represented at the Frankfurt Assembly. Hailing from the northwestern cities of Emden and Krefeld, delegates Isaac Brons and Hermann von Beckerath were both liberal, nationalist Mennonites. "O God! O God! Germany!" Brons wrote his wife, "We must now come to an end, to unity."[43] Epitomizing the progressive front edge of Mennonite thinking across German lands, both Brons and von Beckerath favored civil equality for religious minorities in the proposed nation-state. They envisioned a country in which all Mennonites would enjoy the same duties and privileges as other citizens. Von Beckerath, who had recently advocated Jewish emancipation in Prussia, emerged as a major figure at the parliament, which proposed him as Germany's first finance minister. When the topic of military service arose for debate, von Beckerath argued against Mennonite exemption. Acknowledging that members possessed a legitimate claim in previous centuries, he reasoned that universal conscription had rendered nonresistance obsolete: "since a free state is to be established, a state whose very authority rests upon the equality in rights and duties of all citizens, such a special favor can have no justification."[44] Traditionalist Mennonites, unsurprisingly, resented this position. Unlike the urbanites Brons and von Beckerath, rural conservatives desired minority privileges. Leaders from both Baden and the Prussian east dispatched petitions to Frankfurt, requesting exemption from military service and from the obligation to swear oaths. "Our religious principles," the Baden petitioners insisted, "require us to act with patience and to defend ourselves without the use of arms, and not to swear formal oaths, but rather to affirm our testimony with a simple explanation of the truth."[45]

The Frankfurt Assembly was the first governmental body to which Mennonite spokespersons from all three areas of settlement represented themselves. Although they expressed their opinions separately and did not agree on content, each community hoped to influence the parliament's religious policy. Even those opposed to equal rights were willing to accept or at least

debate the merits of entering a German national state. In their request for
military exemption, leaders from Prussia named the Frankfurt delegates
"German brothers," while those in Baden lauded the "power, greatness,
and unity of our beloved fatherland"—attitudes revealing a newfound read-
iness to collaborate with non-Mennonites.[46] Conservatives had long disparaged ecumenical engagement as a betrayal of Anabaptist convictions,
but as the Frankfurt episode demonstrated, nationalism offered an avenue
of pan-Christian solidarity. Even the torture and martyrdom of so many of
the confession's early members, ordered by Catholic and Protestant rulers,
seemed to fade from memory or were recast as an argument in support of
cooperation. In Carl Harder's estimation, the first Anabaptists, despite en-
during the cruelest persecution, witnessed to Christ's faith through their
undying love. "If we wish to be worthy of them," he admonished, "we cannot attend to the work of our Menno halfheartedly."[47]

Ecumenical participation and German national consolidation seemed increasingly self-evident. Six years after the Frankfurt Assembly, Danzig pastor
Jakob Mannhardt initiated the first popular movement for a nationally
based German Mennonite collectivity. Through the establishment of a bi-
monthly *Mennonite Journal*, Mannhardt appealed to "members of our Mennonite congregations of the German tongue, in East and West Germany,
in Russia, and America."[48] This audience was global in scope, but limited
to German speakers. Readers encountered a number of initiatives that earlier had been the prerogative of individual congregations or regional conferences, including the study of Anabaptist history, debates about church
practice and theology, mission work, and the exchange of news. By providing a central forum, Mannhardt and his collaborators hoped to awaken a
"feeling of solidarity" among German-speaking Mennonites, offering a nationalized locus for intra-confessional exchange. In the *Mennonite Journal*'s
first issue, one column stressed members' common origins in the Reformation, "from the feet of the Alps in Switzerland and Tirol, to the coasts of
the ocean in the Netherlands," while another sought to build theological
unity by printing excerpts from the writings of Menno Simons.[49] If not as
polemical as Carl Harder's now defunct *Monthly Journal*, Mannhardt likewise situated his periodical within a broad political and religious context,
providing sections of non-Mennonite news and advocating certain elements
of Protestant faith.

Mannhardt intended, in part, to unify Mennonites across German lands.
As a nationalist who grew up in the northwest, attended university in the
south, and lived in the Prussian east, he was eager to bring his far-flung
coreligionists together. An 1857 congregational address book, also published
by Mannhardt, reveals this goal. While earlier directories had stopped firmly
at the Oder River, his volume took an expanded view, also encompassing
congregations "in West (north and south) Germany." Specifically, this meant

the areas of "the Eider, Elbe, Rhine, Bavaria, [and] Baden"—that is, all Mennonites within the borders of the German state proposed at the Frankfurt Assembly. Locating his Danzig congregation on the plane of a contiguous landmass stretching westward to the edges of France and the Netherlands, Mannhardt posited the natural coherence of a single German Mennonite collectivity. He was well aware that listing a group of otherwise unconnected names under a single heading like "Germany" could bridge entrenched geographic and theological divides. Just as the compilers of earlier address books had alleged cohesion among proximate congregations by organizing them under common subheadings, Mannhardt grounded his notion of German Mennonitism in the physicality of a bounded territory. "This booklet intends to be a greeting," he wrote in the directory's introduction, "from the congregations to the congregations. It is admittedly only a book of names, but may the names be seen not simply as dead letters, but rather … words of living fellowship."[50] Anyone who used this directory would themselves be furthering national consolidation.

As striking as Mannhardt's desire for unity across German lands was his disinterest in the Netherlands. He published the *Mennonite Journal* for nearly all Mennonites of the world—except those in the land of Menno Simons' birth.[51] On one hand, this reflected a general issue of language barriers. The fact that Mannhardt's *Journal* was a German-language paper at all signaled the near completion of a linguistic shift among a majority of the world's Mennonites. Members in the south German states had shed their earlier Swiss dialects for local German after the Thirty Years' War, while in the Prussian east, congregants stopped printing and preaching in Dutch by the mid-eighteenth century. Because of its strong trade ties to the Netherlands, the Danzig congregation transitioned unusually slowly; its first German-language sermon occured in 1762. Yet two decades later, linguistic change necessitated the printing of a German hymnal. Similar evolutions were slower in the northwestern states, where communities regularly intermarried and exchanged preachers with counterparts in the Netherlands. German became the predominant language of worship in Krefeld only in 1818. Friedrichstadt transitioned a decade later. Some congregations, like Hamburg-Altona, continued using Dutch for some purposes until the 1880s; Gronau conducted Dutch-language services until 1922.[52] But the overall trend was disengagement. Marriage, finance, and education no longer connected Mennonites between Germany and the Netherlands as in previous years. "During the last century," one pastor commented, "the divisions between our [Dutch and German] branches have grown somewhat sharper."[53] Another noted that while exchange still flowed, it no longer "has the character of border-traffic."[54]

Nationalized understandings of geography facilitated the rift. Its dynamics were particularly clear in mission work—the area where Mennonites in

Dutch and German lands were most likely to cooperate. By the century's midpoint, Protestant theorists had begun dividing the spectrum of evangelical activities into two main categories, known as "inner" and "outer" missions. As Carl Harder explained, "one calls *outer* mission that which spreads Christianity among foreign nations, and *inner* that which cares for Christian life among one's own nation." While outer missions encompassed traditional forms of overseas evangelism, practiced by institutions like the Baptist Missionary Society, inner missions drew especially on the work of Protestant organizations focused on strengthening their own confession within German lands. Inner missions included alms houses, orphanages, widows' and veterans' services, and traveling ministry. Presuming a geography of bounded nationalities, commentators further distilled this binary into the language of "foreign" and "domestic."[55] Through outer missions, leaders like Harder were willing to partner with coreligionists in the Netherlands. The *Mennonite Journal*, for example, called readers to support an Amsterdam-based organization called the Mennonite Society for the Spread of the Gospel in the Dutch Overseas Colonies. Founded in 1847, this was the first association to send Mennonite missionaries abroad. While congregations in the Netherlands had maintained their branch of the Baptists' India mission for more than two decades, they now prepared to spread Anabaptism on the island of Java in the Dutch East Indies.

Because outer missions focused on converting members of foreign nations, inter-national cooperation within the Mennonite Mission Society itself was also acceptable. Already by the 1850s, Carl Justus van der Smissen and his Friedrichstadt congregation had begun supporting the endeavor. Van der Smissen encouraged coreligionists across German lands to lend further aid. "I recommend the work of our brethren in Holland," he wrote, extending a broad "invitation to participate in tending the vineyards of the Lord."[56] Just as Mennonites of various backgrounds had earlier worked with "English" Baptists, they could combine forces to promote their own religion overseas. Collaboration, however, prompted invocations of national difference. When the Amsterdam mission received its first donation from Holstein, the board commended this aid from "beyond the borders of our own [Dutch] fatherland." Believing that cooperation would "wrap a band around the Mennonites of various countries and show them a work through which they can support and reach out to each other," spokespersons from each side defined their own nationality against images of the other, in turn depicting their partnership as an alliance between two very separate communities.[57] Despite sharing the same faith, they remained separated by language, culture, and geography (and of course, all emphasized their difference from the "heathens" they hoped to convert in Indonesia).

Given the perceived inter-nationality of this relationship, the two populations were unlikely to collaborate on inner, "domestic" missions. Indeed,

Dutch-born evangelist Pieter Jansz with schoolchildren on a Mennonite mission station on Java. Collaboration between congregations in Germany and the Netherlands to save "heathen" souls in the Dutch East Indies helped generate a discourse of global Mennonite peoplehood, while simultaneously constructing notions of national difference.

in the 1880s, when Mennonites in Germany instituted a network of traveling preachers, their expansive itineraries—which ranged well into German-speaking areas of France, Switzerland, and the Russian Empire—ended abruptly at the Dutch border. When one pastor from the Netherlands offered advice for the project, leaders in Germany took his suggestions because his position "as a Dutchman" rendered him relatively impartial.[58] Rather than patterning their program directly on a Mennonite organization in the Netherlands, however, planners opted to more closely follow Protestant models in Germany. True collaboration between self-described Dutch and Germans remained restricted to inter-national engagement—such as the outer mission to Java. "How wonderful it is," one evangelist marveled, "that different nationalities have little meaning in matters of faith, that we Germans and Dutch are one in the Lord, and have in mind only the spread of His Kingdom."[59] In reality, this statement demonstrated that national difference possessed far from small consequence, and that to the contrary, Mennonites were constantly wrestling with its influence. At least for this writer, such distinctions fell away only in the context of overseas evangelism; "Dutch" and "German" congregations no longer found mutual ground within nationally divided Europe. By the mid-nineteenth century, cooperation entailed a boat trip to colonial Indonesia. This gulf would only grow. "Our hearts beat warmly for our Mennonite brethren, regardless of which nation they belong to," one Dutch citizen wrote at the *fin de siècle* to a friend in Germany. "Your German heart and my Dutch heart."[60] Coreligionists on either side of the border became not only culturally distinct, but anatomically different.

INVENTING THE MENNONITE DIASPORA

German nationalism was not uniformly xenophobic. At the same time that progressive Mennonites in German lands were beginning to distance themselves from counterparts in the Netherlands, many simultaneously sought closer relations with other German speakers across the globe. Jakob Mannhardt's address book, for example, included groups in Galicia and the Russian Empire, while his *Mennonite Journal* catered to congregations as far away as Ontario. In one wide-ranging article, Mannhardt's paper issued an "Appeal to all the Mennonite congregations in the Old and New World," proposing the creation of a global mutual trust fund for "*all* our congregations, from the state of Iowa to the Volga." Visionary as it was ambitious, this piece imagined a cooperative edifice girded by "the building blocks of the Prussian thaler, the Russian ruble, the Rhineland gulden, and the American dollar." It also took pains to link global Mennonite unity with militant German nationalism, invoking the enmity harbored by many German speakers toward post-Napoleonic France: "Germany will soon need soldiers to fight the wretched archenemy of the German nation; our congregations likewise need soldiers, warriors of Christ." Just as men across German lands would mobilize against French aggression, young Mennonites should rally behind their own confessional flag. Educated in the German "fatherland" and coordinated by a central organization, new generations of pastors would spread out across the Atlantic or to the Sea of Azov, defending their faith from dangerous influences and bringing the word of God to less cultured peoples.[61]

According to contemporary terminology, German speakers outside German borders were members of a national "diaspora." This expression first gained prominence among nationalists in the early nineteenth century, when Protestant activists used it to refer to members of their own confession living in Catholic lands. Often, Protestants "in the diaspora" were insufficiently concentrated to form their own churches, and coreligionists worried that without proper spiritual care, they would waver in their faith, eventually assimilating into the Catholic fold. In 1832, Protestant leaders founded the Gustav Adolf Association to minister to scattered members. They named their organization after the famous seventeenth-century king of Sweden, Gustav Adolf, because of his timely intervention in the Thirty

Years' War, which, according to tradition, had saved the faltering coalition of Protestant princes from their papist enemies. Portraying Gustav Adolf as the first military champion of a free Protestant Germany, they contrasted his supposed vision for German national independence with the machinations of contemporary Catholics who, they suggested, wished to tether Germany like a dog to the Vatican. As Gustav Adolf developed into a potent symbol of German national unification—at least in some circles—the notion of a "Protestant diaspora" simultaneously metamorphosed into the broader concept of a German diaspora. While the phrase "in the diaspora" could still refer to Protestants living in Catholic lands, even in areas like Baden and Bavaria that eventually fell within the borders of Imperial Germany, it also came to mean German speakers—and especially German-speaking Protestants—in non-German lands. German-speaking settlers in the Russian Empire counted as diasporic nationals, for example, as did those in North America.[62]

Diasporic ideas and rhetoric entered Mennonite discourse quite early. Some members began participating in the Gustav Adolf Association within the first sixteen years of its founding, and leaders like Jakob Mannhardt and Carl Harder directly patterned their most important ideas about Mennonite space and identity on German diasporic models. "My great love of the Mennonites," Carl Justus van der Smissen wrote in 1838, "encouraged me to acquaint myself with as many of our congregations as possible. I have therefore made many trips and am in correspondence with many of our brethren." Van der Smissen's interest extended not only to the German states, however, but also to coreligionists across Europe and even overseas. In a letter addressed "To the Mennonites in Canada," he requested information on their beliefs and practices. "I love my brethren wherever they may be scattered throughout this world, and it gives me great pleasure when I receive a letter from a brother in faith, whose face I will first learn to know in heaven before the throne of our God."[63] Van der Smissen considered Mennonites members of a scattered fellowship who because of their common faith would eventually reassemble in heaven. Moved to learn all he could about his coreligionists while still on earth, he inquired whether they performed the same rituals, read the same books, and worshiped Jesus in the same ways he did. Just as German nationalists courted German-speaking communities from China to Brazil, he envisioned diaspora in a specifically Mennonite vein.

Van der Smissen's curiosity was driven, in part, by an increasingly mobile world. The same forces that allowed him to receive letters from beyond the Atlantic soon enabled him to traverse it himself. In 1868, the pastor accepted a call from the United States to teach at an institution of Mennonite higher education. Shortly after emigrating, the newly minted professor traveled to Canada, where he beheld with his own eyes the settlements that just a few years earlier he had not imagined seeing in his earthly life.[64] Within the span of three decades, technological progress transformed Mennonites' thinking about diaspora. Where previously it had been difficult or impossible to meet distant members, relatively high-speed global travel allowed groups to form closer linkages than ever before. Yet technology alone did not determine cultural change. External commentators also worked to reshape Mennonites' diasporic thinking, actively constructing distant communities as bastions of Germandom. During the 1840s, the political economist and German nationalist August von Haxthausen visited the recently established Mennonite colonies in the Russian Empire. "We felt as if we had suddenly been transported to West Prussia," von Haxthausen noted upon arrival in Chortitza, the oldest settlement, "so familiarly German was everything around us!" Not just the people, but also their "character, their language, their costumes, the houses and their decoration, every pot and pan, even the pets, the spitz and the poodle, cow and goat were German." Under Mennonite care, nature itself seemed to have acquired a German look; had a painter immortalized the colonies in oil and canvas, viewers might easily have mistaken them for settlements somewhere in German lands. Employing the language of order and labor, von Haxthausen dubbed the colonies a measuring stick for imperial administrators. "In the entirety of Russia," he wrote, "there is no other stretch of land where such a comparatively high culture pervades the agriculture and the population." After examining fields, gardens, and well-laden tables, it was with remorse that he finally left the "flowering German settlements."[65]

If von Haxthausen's nationalism and taste for fresh produce left a glowing impression of Mennonite colonialism, it obscured the reality that emigrants left German lands for good reason. Often seeking to escape rather than promote Germanness, most settlers remembered their old homelands as places of economic hardship and religious repression. And yet, German nationalist writers saw these emigrants not merely as unpatriotic draft dodgers (although this was certainly a common sentiment), but as heroic pioneers. The confession's high rate of mobility even allowed some interpreters to argue that they had led the German people on their journey across the world. The story of Mennonites' arrival in the New World was particularly well known. In 1683, after a meeting with the Quaker state-builder William Penn, several families from Krefeld traveled to Pennsylvania, where they became the "first Germans in America."[66] Settling just north of Philadelphia, they named their community Germantown, and their descendants, along with those of later Mennonite immigrants, counted among the continent's most numerous and best-known German speakers. Tales of Mennonites' cultural integrity and demographic prowess were so persuasive, in fact, that by the early twentieth century, theorists suggested that their primary sociological role was as "German outposts." Shortly before the First

World War, one official from the Association for Germandom Abroad proposed dispatching Mennonites en masse to nationally contested borderlands, such as the eastern regions of Austria-Hungary. In those contexts where the German nation had not yet won a foothold, "we can especially use the Mennonites—with their efficiency (particularly in agriculture), their bustle and integrity, domesticity and sobriety—as groundbreakers for Germandom."[67]

The life and writings of Wilhelm Mannhardt demonstrate the growing association between German nationalism and Mennonite diasporic thinking. Born in 1831, the only son of Adriana Thomsen and Danzig pastor Jacob Mannhardt, Wilhelm was the first Mennonite in German lands to receive a doctoral degree. A prominent folklorist, nationalist, and territorial irredentist, he wove geographic politics into his extensive scholarly work, which proved influential not only for thinkers like Friedrich Nietzsche, James George Frazer, and Claude Lévi-Strauss, but also for Mennonite congregations throughout German lands.[68] Already as a child, Mannhardt had developed a fascination for German folk literature and national myths. "The stories of my venerable great-grandmother and of my mother," he recounted, "instilled within me at an early age an interest for folktales." These women's religious convictions impressed young Mannhardt, while in their capacity as cultural door wardens—a role that allowed them to control his access to formative material—they steered him firmly in the direction of celebrated national works. Books such as Jung Stilling's *The Longing for Home*, the writings of Schiller, and *Grimms' Fairy Tales* formed the basis of Mannhardt's boyhood pantheon. Just as his mother and great-grandmother helped him imagine his place within the Mennonite community, they fostered a patriotism tied to wider German nationality: "In our house the relationship with the old homeland, Schleswig-Holstein, was heartily maintained, and it was therefore natural that when in 1844 the people of Schleswig-Holstein began struggling for their territorial rights, which had come under attack from Denmark, I inwardly took part and dreamed with glowing longing of the reestablishment of a *united German Empire*." This atmosphere shaped Mannhardt's self-described "German national pride."[69]

As a professional folklorist, Wilhelm Mannhardt drew his views on diaspora from his immersive studies of German national mythology. His first essay on diasporic Mennonitism appeared during the same year he was conducting research for a book entitled *The Gods of the German and Nordic Nations*, in which he drew parallel conclusions about the broader German diaspora. "For centuries we [Germans] have wandered in foreign lands," he wrote. "Our nation has thereby become great."[70] Mannhardt considered Germanness and diasporic experiences intimately related. By cataloguing and analyzing peasant myths, he thought that folklorists, linguists, and historians could discover the origins and essential characteristics of German nationality. "The spring of the Germanic, as well as every other true mythology," he explained, "is simply and alone the oral tradition that descends from the highest peak of primeval human life, still streaming ever young and fresh in a thousand rivulets through our mountains, valleys, and plains."[71] Mannhardt ascribed his passion for folkloristics to the writings of Jacob and Wilhelm Grimm, to whom he dedicated his 1858 volume, *Germanic Myths*. Jakob Grimm in particular represented a scientific "Columbus," pioneering previously unchartered areas of knowledge.[72] The invocation of the great explorer was appropriate, as Mannhardt was especially drawn to the Grimms' methodology of collecting fairy stories from across German lands. The spatial breadth of their approach, in addition to their scientific and literary brilliance, impressed Mannhardt, for whom mythology became a nationalist calling.

Through his own research, Mannhardt radically expanded the Grimm brothers' approach. In 1863, he began amassing oral agrarian traditions from across Europe. Composing a detailed questionnaire, he asked respondents to describe local customs and superstitions, including folk festivals, tales of mythical creatures, harvest rituals, and funerary rites. Mannhardt translated this form into multiple languages and dispatched 150,000 copies to newspapers, folklorists, rural communities, and interested persons across the continent. He eventually received responses from some 2,000 locations, representing almost every country in Europe. Using the data thus generated, he planned to evaluate the geographic distribution of particular myths—a process he believed would reveal their national origins. To discover the ancient sources of Germandom, Mannhardt proposed to "compare the surviving vestiges of mythic traditions from ancient periods of our nation or from the closely related tribes."[73] Charting the prevalence of myths in various locations, he attempted to use each tale's sphere of geographic influence to determine its original site and date of genesis, thereby separating inherently Germanic tales from those belonging to other European nations. Mannhardt considered this the first step toward compiling a *Monumenta Mythica Germaniae* that would catalogue and diagram all German myths.[74]

While most Mennonites knew little about Mannhardt's academic writing, it nevertheless shaped discussions of diasporic peoplehood. In the early 1860s, when the Prussian parliament briefly debated Mennonites' military exemption, a group of concerned congregations commissioned Mannhardt to write a historical account of their relationship to pacifism. Intended for circulation among Prussia's lawmakers, *The Military Exemption of the Mennonites of Provincial Prussia* appeared in the same year Mannhardt began composing his questionnaire on agrarian myths. Echoing his claims about the transmission of German folktales, the book's central conceit was that pacifism belonged to a traditional canon of essential Mennonite characteristics, handed down from generation to generation since the Reformation. Mannhardt's method was twofold. First, he outlined the early history of Anabaptism, concluding that "the principle of nonresistance is substantiated in the innermost nature of the Mennonite experience and that it was therefore considered inalienable by the entire sect in former times." Second, he examined the state of pacifism among contemporary communities across a vast geographic spectrum. Not all Mennonites remained nonresistant. It was in the Netherlands as well as the southern and northwestern German states—ironically those regions where the religion first arose— that members tolerated military service. By contrast, opposition to war remained strong in the Prussian east, Galicia, Hamburg, Imperial Russia, and North America. Mannhardt's argument, then, was that immigrant groups provided better indicators of Anabaptism's original essence than did those who had remained behind. While the most traditionalist Mennonites "considered emigration as a religious duty and have settled down in new territories where their faith was tolerated," those unwilling to be uprooted "have changed the essence of their confession of faith, and cannot be cited as precedent for those persisting in the old doctrine."[75] True Mennonitism had been preserved not at home, but in the diaspora.

Running through Mannhardt's geographic and genealogical nexus was the ever-present green thread of agrarianism. In an article on "Mennonites in the diaspora," published in his father's *Mennonite Journal*, the folklorist attributed the confession's scattered nature to its talent for farming and cattle raising. Agricultural acumen, he wrote, "led our forefathers to Prussia; this occupation ... called in our days so many members of the confession to Russia; this occupation served the Palatine congregations; the Lord has once again given this occupation into the hand of our brethren who have immigrated to America."[76] Associations between Mennonitism and ruralism were not new. Indeed, by Mannhardt's day, the stereotype that agronomy was a religious duty for Mennonites was long established. "We are well aware," Władysław IV of the Polish-Lithuanian Commonwealth declared in 1642, "of the manner in which the ancestors of the Mennonite inhabitants ... were invited here ... to areas that were barren, swampy, and unusable.... With great effort and at very high cost, they made these lands fertile and very productive."[77] Much like this seventeenth-century monarch, later commentators summoned quasi-mystical images of bounty, referencing Mennonites' agricultural prowess as well as their many children. Diasporic congregations, in particular, seemed to invite ripe descriptors like "blooming" or "flourishing." From Virginia to south Russia, they were said to infuse their spirit with the ground to call forth new life. Wherever Mennonites set foot, "there the desert bloomed again, there swamps and morasses were transformed into fertile land, there the fields again bore rich golden harvests."[78]

In Wilhelm Mannhardt's view, agrarianism had the added benefit of separating Mennonites from the "ignorant and half wild peoples" they encountered.[79] This too was an old trope. Imperial rulers had long linked farming with conquest, justifying agricultural imposition as a means of taming "wild" lands and their "savage" inhabitants. In the classic formulation, civilized peoples cultivated the soil and herded animals, thereby ensuring a stable social order, while uncivilized groups hunted and gathered as the whim took them, leading a primitive, wandering existence. Mannhardt placed the farming-savvy Mennonites squarely within the former category—the same class that contained the peasant storytellers from whose myths he hoped to distill the essentials of German nationality. But if Christian farmers stood in triumphal opposition to heathen nomads, they nevertheless retained for Mannhardt some ambivalence. Agrarians were certainly the (unwitting) bearers of historic traditions, but they also instigated odd superstitions. Although hearty farmer folk had supposedly preserved aspects of German nationality in an original form, they had also introduced unfortunate customs. Undisciplined Germans, Mannhardt admonished, had "taken up more of the foreign than we can blend with our own national spirit."[80] The germs of this injurious crop, either accumulated in the diaspora or planted by infiltrators, inundated the entire national yield.

Separating the chaff from the true German wheat would require the toil of expert mythologists. In order to help his alleged co-nationals winnow the alien elements from their lives, Mannhardt recommended the preservation of all extant myths: "Because the old traditions disappear in rapidly growing proportions beneath the storm march of modern culture, it appears that the holy imperative of our generation to collect [myths]—being that we alone can bring real benefit to science—comes too late. We load a heavy guilt upon ourselves, and posterity will accuse us bitterly, if despite knowing better we neglect forthrightly to turn our hand to this task."[81] While isolated peasant groups had kept ancient traditions alive through oral storytelling, the lightning pace of industrialization threatened to break or at least muddle these chains of knowledge. New technologies were extracting farmers for the first time from their rural villages, while simultaneously pumping new ideas in. As agricultural practices became mechanized, antique harvest rituals disappeared; as fashion magazines promoted new styles, traditional costumes rotted in attic trunks; as railroads brought international literature into previously secluded valleys, old tales appeared lackluster and anachronistic. For Mannhardt, in short, the inevitable and all-pervading force of modernity—itself necessary for the culmination of

OVERVIEW (OF MENNONITES AROUND THE WORLD)

Germany approx.	22,000 Souls	
Switzerland	1,500	"
France	1,000	"
Netherlands	52,000	"
Russia	41,000	"
Austria	500	"
United States	130,000	"
Canada	10,000	"
Argentina	1,500	"
In all approx.	289,500 Souls	

This 1889 table resembled nationalist charts depicting German-speakers around the world. Notably, only white Mennonites are included, despite the detailed statistics that missionaries compiled on indigenous converts in the United States and Dutch East Indies.

German national teleology—threatened to sweep away eons of agrarian culture, and with it, the final possibility of determining, once and for all, what was German and what was not.

Mannhardt's interpretation of agronomists, both in the diaspora and in the German homeland, as protectors of fundamental knowledge, helps to explain why urban and well-educated German nationalist Mennonites expressed such interest in their rural coreligionists, despite the theological chasm that often separated them. It clarifies, for example, why Carl Justus van der Smissen derived such pleasure from reading about the traditional practices of Mennonites in Canada, and also why Jakob Mannhardt chose to print news from the Russian Empire and North America in his *Mennonite Journal*. These intellectuals' newfound search for global unity, modeled in part on German nationalist projects, necessitated the cataloguing and mapping of every known Mennonite group, as well as an evaluation of the ways they expressed their faith. Just as the folklorist Wilhelm Mannhardt envisioned a *Monumenta Mythica Germaniae*, so might his father have longed for a *Monumenta Mythica Mennonitiae*. Once congregational address books included precise information on each congregation in the world, and once a copy of the *Mennonite Journal* lay on every kitchen table, leaders would be able to track the basic elements of their religion—to weed out the syncretisms that had crept in over the centuries or that had always been present in an imperfect confession.

Slowly, the outlines of a global Mennonite community began to crystalize. Especially through the *Mennonite Journal*, leaders in German lands corresponded with coreligionists around the world. Letters, settlement reports, and aid requests from Switzerland, France, Galicia, Canada, Imperial Russia, and the United States appeared in the periodical, solidifying the idea of an inter-continental fellowship. Writing in 1884, one historian described the paper's legacy: "It established a connection across the ocean, carrying congregational news back and forth from Germany, Russia, and the other foreign congregations, as well as requests and advice in congregational matters.... From this journal, the Palatine congregations once again began to receive news from their daughter congregations in Pennsylvania, Virginia, Illinois, Minnesota, and Canada, and the Russian mother congregations from their settlers in Canada, Nebraska, Dakota, and Kansas."[82] Entrepreneurs beyond German borders copied this model, establishing new forums for the publication of letters, articles, and news across Europe and North America. If copies of the *Mennonite Journal* failed to reach a given pocket of German-speaking Mennonitism, another paper soon filled the void. Leaders in Germany applauded this network, observing that while Mannhardt's periodical had "broken the ice," other journals "in Baden, in Switzerland, and in America have opened further ground and apparently exhibit a much greater number of readers."[83]

The development of this worldwide informational web inspired yet more ambitious collaboration. Writing from Hamburg-Altona in the 1850s, Pastor Berend Roosen invited "the Mennonite brethren in Pennsylvania" to support the Amsterdam-based Mennonite Mission Society. Such calls—particularly those involving overseas evangelism, which enthusiasts like Roosen identified as "the middle point, around which the love of the far-flung brethren has assembled"—found supporters in both Imperial Russia and North America.[84] In the words of one Palatinate-born immigrant to the United States, mission work could strengthen the "bond of fraternity" between congregations "not only from the Atlantic far into the western prairies, but even from the northern climes of Europe to this land of the setting sun."[85] Such phrasing evoked a contemporary American discourse of Manifest Destiny as well as the expansionist language of German imperialism. In both the United States and Imperial Russia, congregations instituted their own inner mission systems, complete with German-style traveling preachers. And, in addition to more local "outer" missions (among American Indians and Russian Orthodox, respectively), they also prepared to enter foreign mission fields. The Mennonite Mission Society soon received its first US candidate and sent its first Russian-born evangelist to Indonesia.[86]

If visions of Mennonite collectivism evolved rapidly across the world, this was no less true in German lands. On January 18, 1871, when the victorious parties of the Franco-Prussian War assembled in Versailles Palace to proclaim Wilhelm I emperor of a new German nation-state, they placed 20,000 Mennonites together in one country. The congregations united that winter day—if only by a few fresh cartographic strokes—represented three vastly different populations. That their members now held common German citizenship was neither inevitable nor a deeply felt desire of most individuals affected. Rather, a small cohort of progressive interpreters assigned the event confessional significance. Drawing on the language of German nationalism—often in a distinctly Protestant guise—they reformatted religious narratives to align with political unification. All peoples of the earth, according to their understanding, belonged to discrete demographic units best described by labels such as "German" or "Dutch," a belief that presupposed egalitarian citizenship obligations and other Enlightenment ideals that had been percolating through Central European society for more than a century. While these writers generally associated national categories with contiguous geographic regions, they also believed them to be interspersed with "diasporic" minorities. Mennonites in Canada or Galicia could thus hold non-German citizenship yet still be labeled Germans.

This outlook was the property of a modest number of people at a particular historical moment. It represented a contingent and often contradictory process of ideational invention, in which Mennonite intellectuals across German lands alternately mimicked and sparred with actors ranging from German nationalist Catholics to Dutch nationalist Mennonites, not to mention one another. Most congregations, after all, remained conservative, preferring older systems of autocratic rule and special minority charters. Yet despite the persistence and even prevalence of alternate opinions, for the first time it had become possible to see Mennonitism as a German-centric faith and its scattered members as diasporic Germans. "From these homelands," one pastor wrote, "they only later arrived through expulsion or emigration in Russia, Poland, Galicia, and America, where they have meanwhile everywhere almost entirely preserved their German character."[87] Just because some Mennonites came to think of themselves and their coreligionists as German, however, does not mean this story has reached its conclusion. Rather, the reverse is true. By accepting German nationalist ideas, a small but influential cadre provided themselves with a powerful set of tools. Nationalism lent them security: as long as they could prove their German credentials, these visionaries believed they could protect their confession against the stunning barrages of hate leveled against Catholics, national minorities, Jews, and other potential non-Germans. And just as nationalism acted as a shield, it equally proved an offensive weapon. Activist Mennonites now had access to a potent discursive palate with ready-made arguments as well as an audience attuned to the language of nationalism. They would harness this power over the following decades, waging a linguistic war on the detractors of their faith and advocating new forms of identity that transcended established notions of both Mennonitism and Germanness.

CHAPTER 2

FORGING HISTORY

ANABAPTISM AND THE *KULTURKAMPF*

Just as a whole nation is compromised when it loses the
knowledge of its past, so is it also with a single confession.

—ANTJE BRONS, *ORIGINS, DEVELOPMENT, AND FATE
OF THE ANABAPTISTS OR MENNONITES*, 1884[1]

In 1878, the German nationalist playwright Ernst von Wildenbruch
published a tragedy entitled *The Mennonite*. Set during the Napoleonic
Wars in a village in East Prussia, Wildenbruch's drama portrayed Mennonites as nationally apathetic cowards, unwilling to take up weapons for the
German cause against French invaders. Loosely based on historic events,
the play connected some Mennonites' traditional separatism to *Kulturkampf*
ideas of national primacy over religious loyalty. During the "cultural struggle" that dominated Germany during the 1870s and 1880s—in which confessional rivals competed to chart the course of the new state—nationalism
and faith became inextricably linked. Would Germany be an officially Protestant country? To whom would Catholics owe their primary allegiance—
the Kaiser or the Pope? Which parties would control Germany's church
policy, and to what degree would the political sphere exercise control over
religion? Just as other confessional spokespersons strove to align their traditions with German nationalism, Mennonites' beliefs became barometers of
their collective patriotism. For many onlookers, the refusal to bear arms on
the part of most of the country's Mennonites provided sufficient grounds
to cast them from the nation. As Wildenbruch's hero proclaimed, "Here in
the sun's holy majesty, I renounce forever that disgraceful word 'Mennonite.' Curse the day that I was born among you! Curse all the days that
shackled me to your confession! May lightning destroy your houses and ex-
tinguish you from the German soil, which you defile; and if the lightning
fails, live and wither in your own squalor!"[2]

The *Kulturkampf* pushed Mennonite leaders to articulate their relationship to German nationalism. Emerging from the formation of the German
Empire, including the abolition of military exemption in Prussia, spokespersons disagreed over the appropriate response. While conservatives found
military service and by extension German nationalism incompatible with
Mennonite faith, progressives argued that such logic only confirmed the

charges from patriots like Wildenbruch. Torn between the poles of non-resistant theology and nationalist ideology, Mennonite communities descended into chaos. Sons defied their parents, congregations deposed their elders, and ministers excommunicated entire families. Defending the sanctity of human life, pacifists argued that it would be un-Mennonite and un-Christian to support a militarist Germany. Without exemption from the draft, they consigned to damnation all who remained in the country. For them, emigration was the only option. "However hopeless it appears among us," one elder wrote, shortly before leading a small exodus to Kansas, "the Lord will nevertheless fulfill his word so that the gates of Hell do not engulf his people; and if the judgment of reprobation should fall upon the congregations in provincial Prussia, morning simultaneously begins to dawn over other areas [where] new congregations arise entirely according to old Mennonite, or better said, biblical and apostolic principles."[3] Abandoning their homeland, Germany's pacifists would make a new life on distant shores.

For those left behind, the challenges of the *Kulturkampf* remained. Faced with rising nationalism and the demise of nonresistance, they were forced to regroup. Emigrants had charged that absent a unifying commitment to pacifism, Germany's Mennonites would no longer be Mennonite at all; pressured by nationalist agitators, they would soon give up their distinctiveness and assimilate into a hegemonic German nation. And yet, it was not assimilation but contestation that defined Mennonitism in the empire over the following decades. Far from accommodating themselves to Protestant or Catholic agendas, progressive Mennonite leaders advanced a specifically Anabaptist version of German nationalism. Interpreting politics through a religious lens, they embraced the new strategies of the *Kulturkampf*, seizing the opportunity to reorganize both their congregations and their public persona. According to the struggle's logic, if one side could prove that its convictions most perfectly embodied German nationality, it could command the public's allegiance, forever marginalizing its confessional competitors.[4] Progressive Mennonite activists relished the opportunity to outmaneuver the fledgling state's other confessions, not only recasting Mennonitism in a German mold, but also advocating a uniquely Mennonite Germany. By refocusing attention from military service to early Anabaptist history, these writers reconstructed their political theology around the doctrine of separation of church and state. True Germanness, they argued, was not embodied by Catholic or Protestant state churches, but rather by the independent Mennonite congregations.[5]

MILITARY SERVICE AND NATIONAL BELONGING

In 1871, Mennonites' entry into the German nation-state was mediated by issues of military service. The empire had formed on the heels of three wars, in which Prussia and its allies acquired territory from Denmark, Austria, and France. Many of Germany's new citizens considered participation in these campaigns synonymous with national commitment. Imperial ideology favored veterans' associations, and patriotism meant celebrating historic victories. Mennonites in East and West Prussia had lost their military exemption four years earlier, when Chancellor Otto von Bismarck's North German Confederation introduced universal male conscription. This law directly challenged congregations' pacifism, the "central tenet of their faith."[6] Writing to the confederation, regional leaders requested that they remain outside the draft. Along with the royal Hohenzollerns and the ruling families of other German states, this was one of three potential exemptions considered in 1867. While parliament upheld the royals' military freedom, it easily defeated Mennonites' proposal. Liberal delegates maintained that conscription was "only a great and holy principle if it really allows no exceptions at all," while rightists denied that patriotism was separable from service: "Whoever will not defend his homeland should leave it! Whoever will not defend his fatherland does not have one!"[7]

Mennonite leadership responded with a deputation to Berlin. Their representatives gained audience with the House of Lords, the Finance Minister, the War Minister, the Crown Prince, and King Wilhelm I. "We are willing to lay down our lives for our brothers," spokespersons explained, "but we cannot kill them. Our Lord and Savior commanded 'Love your enemies,' and we wish to obey."[8] At Bismarck's suggestion, the king issued a cabinet order, allowing Mennonite draftees to perform noncombatant roles. Rather than bearing arms, they could serve as medics, clerks, artisans, or wagoners. This was less generous than many had hoped but nonetheless represented a concession far greater than in other German lands. Mennonites to the south had lost exemption decades earlier—although it was eventually reinstated in Baden. During the Franco-Prussian War, one southern paper printed letters from Mennonite soldiers and denounced France as the seedbed of atheism. "German brothers!" a column read; "Away with the whole despised French land! We want to be German and Christian throughout our life!"[9] Such language linked faith and nationalism, suggesting that by supporting the war, Mennonites struck a blow for Christianity. When Prussia and its allies emerged triumphant, interpreters claimed divine favor: God "has allowed our German warriors, through their many victories, to successfully cast our enemy, who brought such great consternation over us, far from our borders."[10]

If the Franco-Prussian War helped nationalize some Mennonites, memories of the conflict continued to inform their self-identification as Germans. A young Hinrich van der Smissen, studying at the University of Göttingen, broke away to serve in the medical corps. For the rest of his life, the pastor, who regarded volunteering as his "earthly duty," remained close with his former regiment; on special occasions, he wore a dark jacket with medals pinned over his heart.[11] During the early 1870s, discussions of religion and nation coalesced during Sedan Day, the empire's de facto national holiday. Like other citizens, some Mennonites commemorated the North German Confederation's victory against France at the Battle of Sedan. Bavaria's Eichstock congregation, for example, gathered at their church on one Sedan Day for a morning service. Pastor Jakob Ellenberger praised the German nation's ability to transcend religious and political boundaries. Quoting the poet Ernst Moritz Arndt, he asserted that "Not we alone, but millions of our German brothers unite today to light a fire of friendship for the purpose of remembering and giving thanks for what God the great Lord has done *through our nation and for our nation*. Today we want to prove that our fatherland is greater than Bavaria; today we want to festively celebrate that, 'So long as the German tongue sounds, and God sings hymns in heaven,' we have become 'a united nation of brothers.'"[12] Afterward, the congregants moved outdoors where they shared a feast of pork cutlets, sausage, eggs, bread, beer, and cigars. In this merry atmosphere, they mustered three cheers for the Kaiser, three for the princes, and three for the warriors—including several of their own—who had won the war.

If few Mennonites in the Prussian east were as overtly patriotic as their coreligionists in Eichstock, most were nonetheless willing to accept noncombatant service. Channeling the militarism that undergirded the Wars of Unification, a growing number called their congregations to embrace equal citizenship. In 1869, one observer concluded that "only a very small minority is actively and consciously devoted" to pacifism, while the "vast majority clings to this article of our forefathers' faith through the force of tradition or because of the advantages it offers."[13] Disparaging these attitudes as unprincipled and cowardly, nationalist Mennonites promoted patriotism. One voice belonged to the folklorist Wilhelm Mannhardt, who shortly before the Franco-Prussian War entreated his coreligionists to "defend the endangered fatherland."[14] He argued that taking up arms would allow Prussia's Mennonites to assist their homeland and elevate their own second-class status. Invoking Immanuel Kant's doctrine of "perpetual peace," nationalists like Mannhardt insisted that universal conscription was prerequisite for a stable international system. Militarism, in their telling, was more peaceful than pacifism. Thus draftees would not need to discard the ideal of "total peace on earth"; they would simply have to "change the *method* by which one participates in the defense of the fatherland."[15] While Prussia's congregations had previously contributed a tax for the training of soldiers, now they would personally serve.

Progressives increasingly saw conscription as an opportunity. In their thinking, pacifist intransigence could result only in emigration and the end of the confession in Prussia. But acquiescence could revitalize the congregations, providing new legal protections as well as the goodwill of the nation. Those who fought for king and country would support not only their fatherland, but also "the interest of our entire confession."[16] Elder Carl Harder of Elbing, in particular, hoped the draft would enable Mennonites to leave behind their quiet sectarianism. He portrayed military service as the first step in a nationwide renewal movement. Without pacifism as a unifying principle, Germany's congregations would need to identify "the principles unique to the Mennonite confession," articulating everything "that differentiates Mennonites from *other* religious societies."[17] In early 1870, Harder's congregation was the first in the Prussian east to revise its church statutes. Rather than mandating military nonparticipation, the new constitution substituted "hope for a universal peace."[18] Several months later, the progressive Danzig congregation followed suit. Although its members conceded that "every war is a sin that springs from great evil," they affirmed the "law and the preservation of the state."[19]

By championing military participation, communities like Danzig and Elbing achieved leverage with German policymakers. At the same time that conservatives were agitating for reinstated exemption, nationalists petitioned Berlin for an end to all special privileges, taxes, and restrictions on Mennonite economic and religious life. One lay-led petition gained signatures from 1,278 men willing to perform either combatant or noncombatant service. In exchange, the authors requested full civil liberties.[20] Lawmakers acquiesced in 1874. Five years after Jewish emancipation in the North German Confederation, Mennonites received formal liberation. New laws lifted restrictions on property acquisition, as well as the old military exemption tax. Churches were also allowed to incorporate, placing them on comparable legal footing with Protestants, Catholics, and Jews. As state restrictions crumbled, so did local constraints. Occupations open to Mennonites in Danzig had once been confined to textile manufacturing and brandy distillation; by the late 1870s, the Danzig congregation boasted doctors, teachers, architects, and city council members.[21]

Nevertheless, a small number of Prussia's Mennonites continued to oppose military service, even in noncombatant forms. Their nonresistance was nonnegotiable. In one petition, conservatives proposed to exchange suffrage for military exemption. "Why allow us to vote?" 1,800 signatories asked. "We do not demand it and would be more than happy to give it up at any time." Desiring only their traditional privileges, they demanded neither "equality before the law along with other Prussian citizens, nor an end to the discriminatory laws aimed at us."[22] But such efforts failed, and increasingly, conservatives turned to emigration. Despite generally opposing emigration as a means of draft dodging, the State Ministry agreed to provide exit visas for young Mennonites motivated by conscience. Anyone in possession of an exit permit was expected to renounce citizenship, although when some men remained longer than officials wished, new rules limited them to a six-month grace period. Those who overstayed the deadline were charged with draft resistance. In 1872, the Mennonite Johann Dyck was still in Germany when his visa expired. Forcibly conscripted, he soon landed in prison for refusing to wear a uniform or swear loyalty to the Kaiser. Dyck's arrest inspired outrage among Prussia's most conservative Mennonites, who wrote to Berlin, condemning "the coercion the military employs against our brother to force him to swear an oath and to deny his faith."[23] But even with this support, Dyck was unable to reverse his sentence.

In May 1873, Bismarck's government passed a statute declaring it illegal for religious leaders to excommunicate members for obeying German legislation. Known as the May Laws, these regulations targeted Catholics, whom the country's more numerous Protestants often believed followed the Vatican over Berlin. Yet they could also be applied to non-Catholics perceived to undermine national objectives. In at least one instance, they were used against Mennonite pacifism, embodied by elder Gerhard Penner of Heubuden, Germany's largest congregation. When three Heubuden youth accepted military service, Penner considered this a repudiation of the faith and revoked their membership. He denied the servicemen communion and barred one from using the church building as a wedding location. Following a complaint from the disgruntled groom, a county prosecutor accused Penner of violating the May Laws. Sentenced to a week in jail or twenty-five Reichsthaler, the elder appealed to Berlin. Stating that pacifism was an inalienable tenet of Anabaptism, he argued that the May Laws illegally legislated Mennonite theology. Prussia's High Court upheld his conviction. "The state does not demand," its opinion read, "that religious communities adjust their confessions according to the law, the state demands only that all citizens regardless of confession obey the laws."[24] Rebuffed not only by the legislative but also the judicial system, nonresistance seemed to have no place in the German Empire.

As support for pacifism flagged among Prussia's Mennonites, a small number of members prepared for emigration. Without complete exemption, they saw "no other way than to leave the fatherland."[25] Conservative elder Wilhelm Ewert chastised the majority of his coreligionists for compromising with the state. It was a poor exchange, he argued, to abandon Jesus' teachings for "incorporation rights, legal equality with other confessions, [or] safeguarding property." Ewert did not merely wish a return to old ways, however. He was equally critical of the claim that pacifism belonged specifically to Mennonites, labeling it a foundational Christian doctrine. That Germany's congregations had allowed themselves to become marginal and sectarian, defined more by opposition to certain practices than by their witness for the gospel, signaled a failure indeed. "Our congregations have long ceased to be what they should," Ewert wrote; "for fear of crucifixion, they limited themselves to a certain size or a particular number of people and therefore also allowed the light of the true discipleship of

Christ to be hidden under a bushel, and ceased to win souls for the Kingdom of Peace and the peace-gospel of Lord Jesus; so that our congregations
are not built from living stones, a spiritual house and holy priesthood
erected out of all nations, but rather restricted their continuation to the
corporeal descendants of Mennonite parents." A mass exodus would be
preferable. By the end of the decade, around two thousand heeded Ewert's
injunction to "take up the walking stick and go to a place where we are free
of such terrible deeds," leaving for Imperial Russia or the United States.[26]

Although only a small minority of Prussia's Mennonites chose emigration, they were joined by a much larger group from the Russian Empire.
Just as Germany was undergoing nationalization, politicians elsewhere in
Europe implemented similar measures. Seeking to catch up with its west-
erly rivals, perceived as more economically and militarily advanced, Imperial Russia was among the most aggressive. The tsarist state issued its own
draft law in 1874. Mennonites in the Russian Empire—unlike their coreligionists in Prussia, who were fewer in number and less valuable to the
government—negotiated the right to alternative duties. As forestry workers,
conscripts remained outside the military. Nevertheless, 18,000 pacifists—
approximately one-third of the total population—chose to depart for North
America. Fearing the loss of their best agriculturalists, Russian authorities
sent a German-speaking general named Eduard Totleben to southern Russia to dissuade the migrants. After visiting the settlements, Totleben reported that conscription was not the only cause for departure. He informed
the Ministry of Internal Affairs that most Mennonites considered alternative service "completely fair." Indeed, during the Crimean War two decades
previously, many had volunteered in noncombatant roles. "The real cause,"
Totleben concluded, was "the spreading of rumors by officeholders and by
private individuals of the impending russification of the colonies."[27]

The formation of the German Empire had generated a wave of anti-
Mennonite sentiment among Russian nationalists. Believing the new German state posed a military and cultural threat, Slavophiles targeted settlers
as German agents. The "threatening force of Germanism," one nationalist
wrote, "is moving over our fatherland like a dark cloud from the West, and
our German colonies serve it as an obedient and willing instrument."[28]
Some Mennonites feared that tsarist officials intended to assimilate them
into Russian national culture. Rumors circulated about the erection of Orthodox churches and the forced baptism of babies. "We are currently in the
same predicament as Joseph's descendants were in Egypt," one colonist
wrote, envisioning that Russian-speaking farmers would be settled in Mennonite villages and that language instructors would be sent to their schools;
"we are supposed to be intermixed with the Slavs, to assimilate into them
and disappear without a trace."[29] Russian nationalists fed such anxieties.
After a visit to south Russia, one Slavophile claimed that Mennonites and

other German speakers had effectively robbed their peasant neighbors, raising commodity prices and improving farmland only for themselves. Through the "systematic occupation of our best land," Mennonites posed "a greater and more serious threat than would bloody and noisy wars."[30] Faced with such animosity, thousands felt they had only one option: "Leave Russia!"[31]

Ironically, the mass migration of Mennonites from Imperial Russia helped to advance German nationalism among their coreligionists in Germany. Although few Mennonites in Russia felt strong attachment to the German nation-state, observers from both empires frequently categorized them as Germans. While Slavophiles denigrated the settlers as Western infiltrators, German nationalists praised them as hearty cultural outposts. In this light, the relocation of thousands to North America appeared to be yet another victory for Germandom. Progressive Mennonites in Germany—at the same time they opposed emigration from Prussia over military service—lauded the "power of conviction" of those who departed Russia for the same issue. Even Hamburg-Altona pastor Berend Roosen, in whose home hung portraits of Bismarck, the Kaiser, and Field Marshal Moltke, opined that "we here in Germany may not begrudge" their adherence to "a very important component of the old-Mennonite faith."[32] Roosen and others followed their coreligionists' transplantation to southern Canada and the American Great Plains with enthusiasm. When discussing the migration, they spoke of "German settlers" and of "colonization," words that invoked the growing movement for German overseas territories.

Both within the confession and in Germany's wider society, Mennonitism became synonymous with trans-Atlantic migration and German-speaking settlers abroad. Popular literature on encounters with exotic non-Germans featured Mennonites in foreign contexts, such as the American West, where they could meet gunslingers and Indians. In Theodor Fontane's 1890 novel *Quitt*, a young criminal flees Silesia for the New World, where he takes up residence near a Mennonite mission station in the Oklahoma Indian Territory. When Fontane's protagonist arrives in the "Mennonite colony," he is emotionally overcome by the sight of their dwellings, whose German character had been "maintained with so much affection." And while these Mennonites, "delighted to have another German in [their] house," could shelter a lawbreaker exiled from his homeland, they remained intimately connected to Germany. The children of one congregational elder had "returned to Prussia, to Danzig and Dirschau."[33] This family, spread across two continents, exemplified a confession separated in space yet united by nationality and faith. Fontane researched his novel through contacts in West Prussia, from whom he solicited information on Mennonites in the United States. Affirming the colonialism of their North American coreligionists, progressive leaders could influence how writers like Fontane portrayed Mennonite geography, helping to reinforce nationalized interpretations of their diasporic confessional structure. These activists did not only imagine German Mennonitism as a spatial entity, however. They also projected it backward, into the realm of history.

REWRITING THE PAST

In the waning days of winter 1888, schools across Germany prepared for their upcoming Easter pageants. Students memorized lines and sewed costumes in anticipation of an event that would demonstrate their schools' commitment to Christian values and German honor. In the northern port city of Emden, gymnasium teachers distributed programs for the festivities that listed each student and their respective religions. One boy, who hailed from a rural Mennonite family and was now living with his grandmother so he could attend an urban school, noticed that on his playbill, there were only four confessions listed: "Protestants, Catholics, Dissidents, and Jews." His name appeared in the third category, under Dissidents—as did those of every other Mennonite student. Returning home to a stately townhouse in Emden's wealthy harbor district, the boy showed the program to his grandmother, a seventy-seven-year-old Mennonite historian named Antje Brons. When Brons read how her grandson had been labeled, she "felt urged to speak out against this expression." Writing to the school's director, she explained that the Mennonites were not a ragtag group of freethinking spiritualists, akin to atheists, Monists, and Hegelian pantheists, but rather the noble descendants of "Old-Evangelical pre-Reformation congregations."[34]

When Antje Brons found herself holding a paper that called her grandson a Dissident rather than a Mennonite, she felt she clutched a manifestation of the threat pressing in upon her confession from every side. By relegating Mennonite youth to a category of undefined nonconformists, the Emden gymnasium's Easter playbill seemed to eviscerate Anabaptist identity. Brons feared that, if left unchecked, such prejudices could lead to the demise of the religion. Mennonite youth, educated in state schools that offered only Protestant and Catholic religious instruction and in which the very name of their own confession proved inconsequential, could forget Anabaptism's distinctive principles, becoming "lost in the great mass of other confessions."[35] As Emden pastor J. P. Müller characterized the dilemma, "the great majority of German Mennonites themselves hardly knew their history"—a diagnosis compounded by the fact that most non-Mennonites considered them "entirely without history."[36] In 1884, Brons had sought to provide a corrective with her *Origins, Development, and Fate of the Anabaptists or Mennonites*, the first comprehensive study of Mennonite history from the Reformation to the nineteenth century. She compiled her book with the intent, "above all, to convey to the young generations in the Mennonite congregations the knowledge of what their righteous forebearers endured

The consummate activist. Affluent, articulate, and well-connected, Antje Brons (1810–1902) became a household name among Mennonites in Germany through her historical writing and advocacy for confessional solidarity.

under terrible persecution for the sake of their religion, what they have testified and achieved with their blood." Armed with their history, Brons hoped that a new wave of Mennonites—her many grandchildren among them—would renew the confession's "warrant for existence in the German fatherland."[37]

Persuaded that only a major excavation of their past could resuscitate the faith, activists like Brons and Müller embarked on a campaign to popularize Mennonite history. Preachers, university students, and concerned grandmothers ransacked archives, pilfered attics, and pored through rare book collections. From Hutterite colonies in the Dakotas to manuscript libraries in Dublin and Prague, they searched for centuries-old decrees, letter collections, and crumbling documents in forgotten languages. From children's literature to scholarly tomes, they published an array of historical pamphlets, treatises, and polemics. New volumes, aiming both to refute antagonists' "many false and deficient judgments" and to strengthen Mennonites' "inner solidarity," flew off printing presses.[38] Fueled by weekly sermons, consumer demand justified second or third printings, revised editions, and sequels. In 1886, Berend Roosen sparked a series of congregational histories with his two-volume account of Mennonites in Hamburg-Altona. "Only after thorough treatment" of each community, Roosen argued, will a "complete history of our confession in Germany become possible."[39] In the same year, Hinrich van der Smissen, the *Mennonite Journal*'s new editor, began restructuring his periodical from a congregational newsletter into a formidable academic organ. Collaborating with Protestant church historians, van der Smissen solicited the newest scholarship on Anabaptist history and theology, envisioning a literary force reminiscent of established forums like the *Journal for Church History*.

In Germany's high-stakes *Kulturkampf*, Catholic and Protestant activists wielded history as both a stick to savage their competitors and a carrot to woo undecided spectators. The most contested historiographical battleground proved to be the eventful years of the sixteenth-century Reformation. Biographies of Luther, treatises on past papal policies, and volumes of primary documents proliferated as never before. Because the Reformation was generally presumed to delineate the original break between Protestants and Catholics, sixteenth-century texts became the much-studied (and much-contested) rulebooks of the *Kulturkampf*. For many, the struggle became a reprise of the Reformation and the resulting wars of religion. The Vatican Council's 1870 proclamation of papal infallibility and Bismarck's May Laws afforded Germany's confessional rivals an opportunity to revisit their premodern conflict on modern terrain. By framing the *Kulturkampf* as a reincarnation of the Reformation, combatants could impose their historical interpretations on the present, justifying positions with the empiricism of centuries past.

Catholic historians typically located the German nation's greatest epoch in the medieval Holy Roman Empire: before the Reformation, all German speakers from the Alps to the North Sea had been united in a magnificent Catholic state that had nurtured and protected the nation—that is, until Luther and his upstart church incited decades of bloodshed and prompted the humiliating invasion of foreign powers. A return to Germany's heroic past, ultramontanists asserted, would require a nationalist revival styled after the lost Catholic empire of the late Middle Ages. Protestant historians spun a different tale. According to these writers, pre-Reformation Germandom had been only a shadow of its potential self, shackled to a corrupt institution and beholden to the arbitrary rulings of non-German popes. Luther and his followers, then, were liberators who had freed the nation from its papal bondage, and in so doing, had created a new Christian church grounded in the essential characteristics of German nationality. According to this telling, the Reformation was an inspired people's movement in which God's chosen nation had righteously wrested power from an imposter church. Doubters of Germany's debt to the Reformation need only listen each Sunday to the semi-archaic words of the beloved Luther Bible, resounding like a national hymn from every Protestant pulpit in the empire. When Luther translated the gospel from Latin into the vernacular, he had empowered German speakers to take ownership of Christianity as a national priesthood of believers, allowing them for the first time to read, quote, and cherish scripture in their own worthy tongue.[40]

In most narratives of the Reformation, as recounted by either Protestant or Catholic authors, Mennonites received harsh—if any—treatment. When church historians did discuss the early Anabaptists, they often focused on the violent "re-baptizers" of Münster, whose brutal rule of the conquered Catholic city during 1534 and 1535 had long provided a shorthand for the evils of sectarianism. Interpreters who did delineate between the apocalyptic Münsterites and their more peaceful cousins were usually no more compassionate. In their apostolic communalism, some conservatives (as well as several prominent Marxists) divined "the Social Democrats of the sixteenth century"—radical revolutionaries who threatened the primacy of the state.[41] Mennonite activists like Antje Brons, attributing much of their faith's identity crisis to such accusations, linked historiographical revival with the politics of the *Kulturkampf*. "We are confronting a confessional high tide," she wrote, calling her coreligionists to unite in order to weather the inundation.[42] If Germany's formation truly had provided the grist for a new Reformation, Anabaptists did not at first glance possess an advantage. Religious upheaval in the sixteenth century had left thousands bound to fiery stakes or wrapped in chains at the bottoms of riverbeds. More than three hundred years later, a fresh outbreak of persecution seemed possible. "As in generations previously," one observer noted, "the struggle against the 'sectarians,' among which one also counts the 'Mennonites,' now again stands in bloom."[43]

Kulturkampf Mennonites were not in the same predicament as their fore-bearers, however. By achieving legal equality with other confessions and by watching both Catholic and Protestant activists, leaders had acquired strategies that could help them not only avoid persecution, but even stage an ambitious run at a new Reformation. Employing the political and cultural "resources that stand to hand," they hoped to assert a confident public presence.[44] In 1888, Mennonite spokespersons began a campaign to prevent the Royal Theater in Berlin from staging Ernst von Wildenbruch's play, *The Mennonite*, with its unflattering portrayal of Napoleonic-era Anabaptists. Wildenbruch's critique was directed more at Catholics—whose papal allegiance he parodied through the metaphor of pacifism—than at Mennonites, about whom he in fact knew little. His source material was more than six decades old, and his title included a spelling error, "Menonite," missing an "n." Congregational leaders were well aware of Wildenbruch's anti-Catholic intent, and when they contacted the playwright, he confirmed that he "did not intend to attack contemporary Mennonites." Nevertheless, spokespersons felt the obviousness of his anti-Catholicism could not "prevent countless readers and viewers of *The Mennonite*, who will be inspired with revulsion by the Mennonites in his play, from applying their condemnation of our confession to the Mennonites of today."[45]

When Wildenbruch refused to withdraw his drama, leaders sensed an opportunity. As one put it privately, the issue provided a platform "first to stimulate many indifferent members in our own circles, and second to disabuse the outside world of many misconceptions about our confession."[46] On one hand, activists felt the *Kulturkampf* had revived old dangers. Readers of Wildenbruch's play had already begun to question Mennonites' patriotism, and for those who had staked their careers on wedding Anabaptism with German nationalism, such attacks cut to the bone. But by providing an attentive audience and a readymade framework for religious polemics, the *Kulturkampf* also opened intriguing new doors. In the summer of 1888, seven high-profile leaders, representing populations in the south, northwest, and Prussian east, dispatched a "Public Explanation" to theatrical journals, literary reviews, and daily papers around the empire. The effort was unprecedented: while Mennonites in German lands had a long tradition of sending petitions and delegations to secure favorable legislation from governments, they had rarely engaged the more ticklish politics of convincing a broad public. The issue's national nature required spokespersons to represent their confession to a politicized readership that—as demonstrated by widespread animosity toward Catholics and Jews—was on the lookout for religious scapegoats.

In their declaration, the authors denied that their forebearers had ever refused to serve the state in times of need. Earlier generations had perhaps payed war taxes rather than serving on the battlefront, but they had never been unpatriotic: "Such a Mennonite congregation has at no place and in no epoch ever existed in our German fatherland." Participation in the Franco-Prussian War demonstrated their loyalty. Just as many had already proven allegiance on the battlefields of France, "So will those of us, who belong to the military, at any time in the future, if, God forbid, the fatherland is attacked."[47] Opponents of *The Mennonite* took their fight to the highest authorities. In June, a terminally ill Friedrich III temporarily thwarted their objective, writing "Stage *Mennonite*" to the director of the Royal Theater.[48] But by dying four days later, the emperor inadvertently reversed his own ruling. During the period of official mourning, the play was deemed unseemly and was struck—not in deference to its namesakes, but to the memory of their monarch. Despite its inglorious conclusion, the campaign fulfilled two of its major purposes: first, to rewrite Mennonites' history in a visible space, and second, to reiterate their status as loyal Germans. In a reversal of Wildenbruch's logic that they should be banished from German soil because of their refusal to fight, Mennonite leaders invoked the recent conflict with France to portray themselves as protectors of that very soil. In each instance, military participation defined Mennonites' relationship to the nation.

Leaders realized that whoever controlled the narrative of the past could mediate the present. As long as they knew their own history better than anyone else, confessional historians held a stacked deck, and they anticipated enemy forays so they could play their hand. Just as some celebrated Wildenbruch's anti-Mennonitism because it allowed them to "develop a polemic" on the national stage, Antje Brons seized upon the ill-conceived categories in her grandson's Easter playbill to institute her own reforms in the Emden gymnasium.[49] To label Mennonites as Dissidents, she admonished the school's director, had not only made an "unpleasant impression upon the students," it was also historically inaccurate. Brons requested that in the future, the school refer to its Mennonite pupils as "Old-Evangelicals."[50] To justify this choice, she enclosed a pamphlet *On the History of the Old-Evangelical Congregations*. Upon leafing through its contents, the director discovered an unorthodox interpretation of the Reformation that conformed to neither prevailing Protestant nor Catholic narratives. According to the booklet, not two but *three* major parties had striven for dominance, each representing a different "form or mold" of Christianity. The first two contenders—the "priestly church" of Catholicism and the "constitutional church" of Protestantism—bore familiar faces.[51]

It was the third that took the director by surprise. "The *third* form of Christianity," he read, "lies not in priesthood or hierarchy" but "is marked by the basic principles that constitute the character of the *Old-Christian congregations.*" While still on earth, the tract explained, Jesus had established an apostolic community, a "voluntary league of brethren," which by emphasizing personal conversion transmitted Christ's teachings from each generation to the next through a grassroots process of "apostolic succession." Letters and visits united the scattered early Christians into an "Over-Congregation" that remained their predominant organizational structure until the fourth century, when Emperor Constantine corrupted the movement by transforming it into a state church. During the sixteenth-century Reformation, Anabaptists had sought to rebuild this apostolic model, agitating for a new "Over-Congregation." Members of this third confessional party ostensibly comprised a variety of radical groups and their descendants, including Mennonites, Hutterites, Bohemian Brethren, Schwenkfelders, Quakers, Puritans, and Baptists, as well as, surprisingly, German Freemasons. All of these denominations fell under the appellation "Old-Evangelical," which signified both unity in Christ and commitment to an apostolic lifestyle. While sixteenth-century Catholics and Protestants had been distracted with determining which of their perverted institutions was preferable to the other, the Old-Evangelicals had meanwhile resurrected Jesus' own blueprints for the kingdom of heaven on earth. Had the Reformation played out differently—had history progressed as God intended it—millions of German citizens would now belong to Old-Evangelical congregations, and the main topics of the *Kulturkampf* would be laughably moot.[52]

Mennonite researchers adopted the Old-Evangelical thesis during the 1880s as their primary method of asserting an Anabaptist-friendly interpretation of the Reformation. But in a surprising twist, their trump card lay not in Reformation historiography itself—which remained controlled by Protestant and Catholic church historians—but in the centuries preceding it. As heirs to the earliest Christians, Mennonite interpreters reasoned that their Old-Evangelical theology must predate the sixteenth century. Seeking historic ties between Reformation-era Anabaptists and earlier reformers, confessional sleuths traced a cautious line from Menno Simons, who had renounced Catholicism in 1536, to Conrad Grebel and Hans Denk, who had been active at the Reformation's start. From there the trail led to Jan Hus in the fourteenth century and Petrus Valdes in the twelfth. Even further back then, through a dizzying array of medieval heretical groups, historians tracked their beliefs past the early Middle Ages and well into the waning Roman Empire until, finally, their search terminated in Christianity's original "Over-Congregation" and the life of Jesus himself.

With a little publicity, this narrative blossomed from a tentative genealogical trickle into a torrent of unbridled apostolic succession. The tradition of Christian self-sacrifice ran from its inception on Golgotha through

Mennonite writers had long portrayed Waldensians as their spiritual forebearers. While earlier depictions—such as this seventeenth-century illustration from the *Martyrs Mirror* of the burning of 224 Waldensians in Toulon—served to counteract charges that Anabaptism had emerged with the violent Münsterite uprising of 1534, assertions of kinship with pre-Reformation dissenters now bolstered claims that Mennonites were better Germans than either Catholics or Protestants.

Roman gladiatorial arenas to the torture chambers of the inquisition and the pyres of the Reformation. Similarly, from Jesus' own anointment down to the present age, the practice of adult baptism surged as full and true as the River Jordan. Historians especially touted the connection between Reformation-era Anabaptists and their earlier incarnation in a medieval heretical group called the Waldensians. Founded—according to legend—in the twelfth century by Petrus Valdes of Lyons, a wealthy merchant turned wandering apostle, the Waldensians promoted an ascetic lifestyle modeled on that of Christ. They eschewed worldly goods and valorized poverty, an orientation in pointed contrast to medieval Catholic ostentation. Other tenets included nonresistance, refusal of the oath, and a decentered church structure. In 1215, the Vatican pronounced Waldensians anathema, and sixteen years later it convened the Inquisition to root out heterodoxy through organized violence. Despite brutal persecution, Waldensianism survived as a people's movement. Holding secret meetings from town to town and preaching in local dialects, adherents gained inroads across Central Europe. By the Reformation's outbreak, Waldensian influence stretched from Bohemia to Piedmont and north through the German states.[53]

Mennonite historians in Imperial Germany considered this group their spiritual forebearers, claiming direct connections between sixteenth-century Anabaptists and earlier Waldensian communities. In the words of pastor Carl Harder, Mennonitism—as the "continuation of the original Christian church" and a locus of "principles far older than the Reformation"—owed a significant debt to the Waldensians, who already in the Middle Ages had broken with Catholicism and thrown in their lot with the "repressed Christian confession of saints."[54] A vital link in the Old-Evangelical chain, Waldensians also supposedly played a "very great role in the history of the German nation." One historian identified their rise with the "first flowering" of German national religious life.[55] While Protestants crowed over Luther's famed vernacular bible of 1522, students of the Old-Evangelical school revealed that Waldensians had produced German-language bibles centuries before. One translation, a fourteenth-century manuscript known as the *Codex Teplensis*, had exercised enormous influence across Central Europe, inspiring further versions in both High and Low German and helping to lay the groundwork for the Reformation. Lengthy passages of Luther's own Bible, in fact, had been lifted nearly word for word from this earlier work. Mennonite historians also claimed ownership of the *Theologia Germanica*, another nationally significant text associated with Luther. One pastor argued that the fourteenth-century treatise, which Luther had popularized with a print edition in 1516, was actually the work of an Old-Evangelical whose legacy belonged less to Protestants than to Mennonites.[56]

Some weeks after Easter of 1888, when the director of the Emden gymnasium finished reading the booklet on Old-Evangelical history sent by Antje Brons, he wrote to the tenacious septuagenarian, informing her that he had found it of great interest, and that "in the future, Mennonite students *would not again be presented as Dissidents.*"[57] Echoing the conventions of German nationalist storytelling, Mennonites like Brons used their history as an anchor point for external observers. Drawing on the most emotionally evocative elements of German master narratives—a glorious ancient past, centuries of victimization, a romantic destiny—they reformatted their confessional image into an attractive public persona. In fact, much of their account was already familiar. Its arc followed the same progression and formula as the beloved German national hymn; it possessed the same rhetorical high points and valleys, the same invocations of time-honored tradition, the same final heart-warming call to collective action. A typical German citizen, hearing this Mennonite tale for the first time, would know just where to nod, where to shake his or her head in commiseration, and where to smile with empathetic pride. Antje Brons had counted on exactly this preexisting knowledge when she sent the pamphlet on Old-Evangelical history to the director of the Emden gymnasium. Because he was literate in German nationalist narratives, the director had understood exactly how to interpret this variation on the theme. Writers like Brons relied on their audiences to read history in a certain way. For both parties, the process of recounting the past was not so much a one-way transfer of previously unknown knowledge, but rather a contractual conversation, in which the hearer supplied a predetermined framework and the teller filled in the blanks.

THE MENNONITE UNION

Mennonite leaders' historicizing was, at heart, motivational. By demonstrating that the German nation's natural telos lay in a return to the ancient principles of Old-Evangelical Christianity, they hoped that millions would join their cause. The movement's "ideal future outcome," according to Hermann Mannhardt—the new pastor of the Danzig congregation and a rising star in the church, dapper as he was eloquent—would be the formation of a "German Christian National Church" based on Old-Evangelical principles.[58] The equally visionary but more seasoned Carl Harder clarified that although members of other denominations "should not be expected … to call themselves 'Mennonite,'" all confessions would eventually recognize the "truth of the pure Christian principles of the Mennonite congregations."[59] Inspired by Mennonites' apostolic devotion, the remainder of Christendom would supposedly adopt Anabaptist-style baptism, refuse to swear oaths, and develop a symbolic interpretation of the sacraments. Already, some observers pointed to the rise of Free Protestant churches in Germany, Switzerland, and Scotland. Even in the empire's powerful state churches, Anabaptist ideas seemed to have taken root. "Does not the call for separation of church and state sound louder than ever?" a hopeful Mannhardt wondered. "Do not weighty voices struggle against infant baptism and the oath?"[60] Proponents conceded that their project might take centuries, but the German Empire had already been a thousand years in the making. At such a critical juncture, their calling to make straight the way of the nation held paramount.

Activists framed their efforts in the competition-saturated terminology of the *Kulturkampf*. Just as the Protestant League, formed in 1886, had provided a "bulwark against Catholicism," Mennonite agitators hoped to "stand firm against the papal church" as well as against orthodox Protestantism.[61] They believed the success of an Anabaptist agenda hinged on the formation of an Old-Evangelical Alliance, modeled on the London-based Evangelical Alliance, in which progressive Mennonites had participated since mid-

century. To promote their own coalition, spokespersons began corresponding with Quakers and Baptists, Freemasons, and a group of Waldensians
in northern Italy. Organizers planned to rally these factions around a common historical mission. If they could set aside minor differences and stand
together—fulfilling their Reformation-era forebearers' goal of "reestablish-
ing the old Over-Congregation"—Old-Evangelicals could form a new religious counterweight to shift the balance of power among Germany's war-
ring confessions.[62] As essays on Old-Evangelical history appeared in major
journals across the country, church historians, theologians, and politicians
began to roll this program into their own *Kulturkampf* cosmologies. One
observer remarked that researchers were not examining their past "out of
historical interest," but were forming the "beginnings of a Mennonite propaganda in Germany."[63]

Non-Mennonite theologians and historians took increasing interest in
Anabaptism, even championing elements of this third confessional route.
By the mid-1880s, one scholar could identify an entire "class of portrayals
that allow Anabaptism to shine in an essentially more favorable light."[64]
Among the dozens of academics who began engaging Anabaptist ideas,
three Protestant writers stood out. These were Friedrich Nippold, co-founder
of the Protestant League and professor of church history at the universities
of Bern and Jena; Ludwig Keller, head of the state archives in Münster; and
Friedrich Fabri, chief inspector of the Rheinish Missionary Society at Bar-
men. Each of these men met and corresponded with Germany's leading
Mennonites, forging ties between an emerging Old-Evangelical coalition
and the country's elite Protestant milieu. Fabri, for example, assessed congregations' archival holdings and promoted the formation of a Mennonite
historical society. And Nippold, who provided insider tips on Protestantism's palace intrigue, mentored a number of Mennonite theology students
during his tenure at Jena.

Fabri and Nippold both arrived at Anabaptism through their interest in
decoupling Protestantism from the new imperial state. They saw in Mennonitism a model for Christian society predicated on a division between
religious and civil governance, and they hoped to convince policymakers
to institutionalize the two-kingdom aspect of Mennonite theology. In 1880,
as the University of Bern's newly appointed president, Nippold delivered an
inaugural address on *The Theory of the Separation of Church and State*. Nippold's speech identified Anabaptist principles as the solution to the *Kulturkampf*. "History gives us the answer," he suggested, "in the development of
those churchly associations, which due to the symbolic borders of the major
[Catholic and Protestant] churches found room for their conviction in neither one nor the other."[65] These nonconformist groups, namely Anabaptists, Remonstrants, and Quakers, survived to the present day and provided

a resource for state leaders. In a similar 1887 work entitled *Where Next? Ecclesio-Political Observations at the End of the Kulturkampf*, Friedrich Fabri outlined his vision for a post-*Kulturkampf* Germany. A longtime proponent of the separation of church and state, Fabri had once, in the early 1870s, pitched his vision for state church autonomy to Chancellor Bismarck. More than a decade later, he recognized the emerging Old-Evangelical coalition as new clout for his unfulfilled dream. In *Where Next?* Fabri noted that countries that separated church and state, such as the United States, Belgium, and the Netherlands, had "remained free of a *Kulturkampf* and of other significant ecclesio-political upheavals." He ascribed such tranquility to the principle of confessional independence "that in the age of the Reformation was already vocalized by the Anabaptist movement."[66]

Ludwig Keller, the Münster archivist, shared his coworkers' longing for a revitalized and self-governing Protestantism. Like Nippold and Fabri, he invoked Anabaptism to advocate a dismantling of Bismarck's state church apparatus. As he explained to the chancellor, his studies of Mennonite history had convinced him that "the concepts 'church' and religion" were not identical.[67] Through his exposure to Reformation-era texts in the Münster archives, Keller had become attracted to Anabaptist structures and practices, which, by allowing adults to freely choose their faith, offered a way around the "sinister collusion between politics and religion."[68] Significantly younger than both Nippold and Fabri, Keller had not yet become a national figure. With fewer obligations than his better established counterparts, as well as a greater incentive to take risks, Keller escalated his flirtation with Anabaptism into a full-fledged affair. In 1880, he published a provocative volume on the sixteenth-century Münsterites, suggesting that Anabaptism arose not during the Reformation but centuries earlier.[69] In 1882, a second book, titled *An Apostle of the Anabaptists*, located the Reformation's high point in the teachings of the pre-Münsterite Anabaptists.[70] Throughout his work, Keller espoused a thesis of "historical continuity," tracing broad lines of causality across the ages.[71] The Roman and the medieval periods, he maintained, bore heavily on the Reformation, which in turn had set the backdrop for modern European politics. The tragedy of the sixteenth-century Münsterites, notably, had caused the "downfall of Anabaptism" as a mass phenomenon and ensured the predominance of Protestantism and Catholicism "until the present time."[72]

Protestant activists like Keller, Nippold, and Fabri helped to popularize the Mennonite movement's most controversial positions among Germany's academic and political elite. Their polemicizing appeared in popular newspapers, secret society circulars, and the pages of major literary, theological, and historical journals. One reviewer praised those who had "broken ground for an entirely new outlook" on church history, while another predicted that Anabaptist historiography would "have much to offer for theological researchers as well as friends of objective historical portrayals."[73] But by deemphasizing Luther and by carving Christianity along tripartite rather than dual confessional fault lines, pro-Mennonite books also tempted bitter, torrential criticism. One Catholic historian was particularly outraged at the suggestion that the German nation owed its earliest Bible translations not to medieval Catholic priests, but to "heretics, the Waldensians."[74] Protestant historian Theodor Kolde was equally dismissive. Rejecting the hypothesis of the Reformation's Old-Evangelical origins as well as the link between Anabaptists and Waldensians, the Luther biographer disparaged Mennonites' defenders.[75] As its most public proponents, the movement's Protestant allies were also its most visible targets. "Now, after the Mennonites have begun to reconnect to their distinctive character," Keller confided to a friend, "a great hate is aligning against those who supported them—including Nippold and me.... You cannot believe how significantly the Mennonites in Germany are repressed, underappreciated, and ignored. They are entirely excluded and isolated. Even today, excepting Nippold and me, no one concerns themselves with them."[76]

Progressive Mennonite leaders, for their part, were deeply appreciative. Antje Brons was among the earliest to contact Ludwig Keller. In 1883, her first letter to the archivist began by praising his *Apostle of the Anabaptists*. She confided a personal experience his book had evoked: "It was as though the martyrs, killed for their faith more than three hundred years ago, and now made to live again as if through the touch of God, were looking around to ask, 'Do we find recognition among the current generation?'" Brons felt that Keller's work challenged all Mennonites to "acknowledge and atone for the debt committed to us by our forebearers." Convinced that he had experienced this same imperative, Brons proposed a partnership. Already, Mennonites in East Friesland and the Netherlands had supplied Keller with research materials, including books, articles, and testimonies from baptismal candidates. But Brons envisioned an even closer relationship. For her, Anabaptist history entailed wholesale renewal. She saw Germany's Mennonites as standing "unfortunately alone," squeezed between aggressive state churches. Even if other confessions "are not openly hostile," she told Keller, "they nevertheless perceive us as only marginally Christian." But Brons countered her own diagnosis with news that across Germany, Mennonites were beginning to wake from their ahistorical sleep. For the first time since the Reformation, Anabaptism was ripe for a revival that could challenge both Protestantism and Catholicism as the nation's premier form of Christianity. If Keller would lend his support, Brons could assure him "participation from Mennonite circles."[77]

Already inclined to interpret the *Kulturkampf* as a continuation of the Reformation, Keller needed little convincing. By tapping into what appeared to be the makings of a major confessional movement, Keller hoped

to harness Mennonite resources for his own goal of remaking Protestantism in an apostolic guise. He launched his experiment by trying to fashion
Germany's mass of disunited congregations into a useable coalition. "At the
beginning of the 1880s," he later wrote, "when I became acquainted with the
Mennonites, I discovered that *the spirit of the old Anabaptists* ... had largely
disappeared." Although a number of well-intentioned activists were attempting to awaken and rally their coreligionists, they could not agree on any
one theological basis or direction of attack. "Some leaned (unfortunately!)
toward the Protestant Association"; others applauded the writings of the
Moravian Brethren, while yet a third group favored the Baptists.[78] In 1885,
Keller composed a letter offering his services: "it is my duty, with all of my
modest abilities, to stand on the side of the descendants of the [sixteenth-
century] congregations whose guiltless suffering I have seen."[79] The archivist was willing to invest his career in the innermost affairs of an obscure
sect, in which he sensed a dormant greatness. "The Old-Evangelical Anabaptists, ancient and older than Menno," he declared, "possess a vital task
for the future construction of God's kingdom, and for them a new epoch
appears to be dawning."[80]

But if Keller was going to sacrifice for Mennonites' cause, he requested
they meet him halfway. The full-scale reintroduction of Anabaptism's most
important values—which for Keller included the separation of church and
state, an emphasis on personal conversion, and the re-creation of early Christianity's Over-Congregation—would require the cooperation of all Mennonites in Germany. Convinced that they could most effectively "emerge from
their fragmented state ... through the immediate formation of a *general
conference*," the archivist threw his weight behind their fledgling unification movement.[81] Working closely with Hermann Mannhardt, Antje Brons,
and other leaders, he attended conferences, wrote editorials, and exchanged
letters with both conservative and progressive ministers. Keller believed the
new organization should emphasize youth education: "Above all, raise young
men in the spirit and through the writings of the old Anabaptists and the
old martyrs."[82] Rather than training their children in the style of other
confessions, parents should use the works of Menno Simons, Hans Denk,
and other early reformers. He especially encouraged the excision of "foreign elements." Borrowing too heavily from Baptists or Moravians would
separate Mennonites from their roots, while turning to the state churches
would allow assimilationists to swallow Anabaptism whole. Protestant ideas
"have won much ground in your confession," he wrote to one pastor. "The
inner rebirth of your congregations will be accomplished much more easily" given a wariness "against the intrusions of state church influence."[83]

The archivist's call for a nationwide conference found favor among Germany's most progressive Mennonites. Already, several leaders had formed

an exploratory committee, having sent a proposal in 1884 to all of the empire's congregations. "Never before have the necessity and the duty of the Mennonite confession in Germany to take common steps for the security of their future lain as close together as at this moment," the appeal read. "The point in time has come for us to confirm our true foundational principles and to strive, even sacrifice, for their preservation."[84] Organizers adopted the title "Union of Mennonite Congregations in the German Empire," drawing on conceptions of spatiality coalescing since the early nineteenth century. The word "Union" evoked the language of unification surrounding the formation of Bismarck's state, while "in the German Empire" demonstrated geographical precision. Conceived as the logical conclusion to a decades-long solidarity movement, proponents intended the new Union to provide a centralized organ. Its mission was to coordinate resources, advocate on behalf of all congregations, and initiate projects including a Mennonite seminary, a network of traveling preachers, a publishing firm, and a mutual aid fund. Daily operations were the responsibility of a Directorate, consisting of rural as well as urban members from the south, northwest, and east.[85]

Union headquarters were in Berlin. Organizers had convened their first exploratory conference in the city, which was located approximately equidistant from all three major areas of settlement. "Berlin is the right location," Hermann Mannhardt explained, "because Berlin is the most comfortable to reach from all sides for our widely scattered congregations."[86] It was therefore an appropriate place for an assembly of "brethren from east and west, north and south."[87] As a rendezvous point, it was also territorially neutral. At no previous time had any Mennonite congregation existed in Berlin, so no group could lay more claim to the city than another. Delegates to the first meeting agreed that collective institutions should not be based in regions dominated by any one community, as this would lead to the establishment of parallel organizations in the other areas, in turn risking "spiritual isolation."[88] Berlin also had much to offer in its own right. It boasted an excellent transportation system, archives for religious research, and "a great university with capable theological teachers" who could prepare young Mennonite men for ministry.[89] Above all, it was Germany's capital. Where better to locate a national institution than at the focal point of the empire? To choose the city where the emperor made his home and where parliament passed legislation would be to adopt an aura of sophistication, worldliness, and patriotism.

By naming Berlin their metaphorical capital, unionists carved out a space in the city. "In the capital of the German Empire," Hermann Mannhardt wrote in 1886, when he and his peers formally commissioned the new Union, "in the middle of all the tremendous hustle and bustle that surrounded us there, in the middle of so much greatness and importance of brilliant things, of so many of the forces which move world history, a small unimposing presence saw first light."[90] Attendant was the formation of a new congregation—a permanent and sovereign body that would represent Mennonites' interests in the city. According to the 1880 census, ninety-five Mennonites lived in Berlin, enough for a healthy congregation. But these individuals had no pastor and no nearby support networks; they were functionally in the diaspora. Concerned that the absence of a congregation rendered the critical city a blank spot on the Mennonite map, unionists considered it "of the greatest importance that a Mennonite congregation now exist in Berlin."[91] In their estimation, it was Germany's modernization—so perfectly symbolized by its greatest metropolis—that was responsible for the presence of Mennonites in the city at all. And as industrialization transplanted more members to urban areas, they intended to capitalize on this trend.

Throughout the Union's formation, Ludwig Keller provided assistance. In addition to traveling across the country, the archivist hosted an exploratory meeting in his home city of Münster and edited a draft of the organization's constitution. But while he promoted the Mennonite Union as a preliminary step, Keller's ultimate plans were much broader. Lauding the semi-ecumenical Evangelical Alliance of European Protestantism, he hoped to forge a comparable "*alliance* between the denominations ... whose origins derive from the *Old-Christian and Old-Evangelical* congregations of earlier centuries."[92] In addition to Mennonites, this coalition would include a variety of other Old-Evangelicals: "It is my wish and my hope that earlier or later it will be possible to bring all those denominations that since the sixteenth century have grown out of the so-called Anabaptism and that still do *not* believe in predestination into an alliance modeled on the Evangelical Alliance (which excludes the Quakers, etc.): Anabaptists, Remonstrants, General Baptists, Quakers, Schwenkfelders, possibly even Congregationalists and Unitarians. Thereby, a new life could be awoken among all these denominations."[93] Carl Harder, who of all Keller's associates most closely identified with his vision, clarified that Mennonites and similar groups should "give up their special customs and unite into a new *unified church* under the name 'Old-Evangelical.'" This umbrella institution, liberated from hierarchy, would find "ever greater general recognition in the evangelical world."[94] As it drew new converts from other confessions, the Old-Evangelical Church would permanently weaken state control over religion.

In the short term, progressive Mennonite leaders hoped their confession would gain prominence. "For us," Hermann Mannhardt predicted, "the time of great dependence on ... churchly circles is past." While imitating state church practices had once offered an escape from social alienation, Mennonites' new trajectory pointed away from Protestant orthodoxy. "That is not to say," Mannhardt cautioned, "that a new time of exclusion has arrived for us." Members would still enjoy close relationships with Protestant neighbors, but "we will do so with the conviction that we do not stand there like those, who beg for bread crumbs at the master's table." Rather, Anabaptists would engage other confessions from a position of friendship and council. Armed with assurance in their God-given task, they would guide the country's Christians until "the priestly churches are transformed into congregational churches, and the state churches *into a German National Church*."[95] In 1888, when a journalist for Berlin's *Imperial Messenger* attended a service at the city's newly formed congregation, he spoke with pastor Hinrich van der Smissen—the Mennonite Union's first chairman—who had traveled from Hamburg for the occasion. Van der Smissen presented his confession with the still unfamiliar language of unionism: "The Mennonites, so named after Menno Simons, prefer to call themselves 'Old-Evangelical Congregations' because they believe in a spiritual and historical connection between their confession and the first pre-Roman Christian congregations." Readers of the *Imperial Messenger* learned that the Mennonites "place their main emphasis on the 'freedom of the congregations,' and therefore reject the form of the state church."[96]

By identifying the separation of church and state as Anabaptism's primary characteristic, activists like Harder, Mannhardt, and van der Smissen recast their theology in a nationalist mold. Like other nationalists across Germany, they had discovered that by privileging the good of the nation above that of the state, they could justify positions at odds with Bismarck and his policies.[97] Certain Protestants, interpreting their imperial ties as a burden, advocated the decoupling of church and state as a method of reorienting the nation around their own religion. Mennonite spokespersons, sensing that the coming "German National Church" would be characterized by its independence, seized the opportunity to assert that such a confession would by definition be Mennonite in nature. This ability to harness certain forms of German nationalism explains the movement's magnetism for scholars like Keller, Nippold, and Fabri. If Mennonite scholars could defend their history as one among many equally German stories, they had already accomplished the minimum task necessary to claim a place in national culture. And if they could contend that their history was *the* German history—that it represented the German national character more perfectly than did Protestants, Catholics, or any other group—then they could enter the fray to determine the future course of the nation. If their logic held true—if the Waldensians were responsible for awakening both Mennonitism and Germanness, if religious affiliation was the truest expression of national identity, if the *Kulturkampf* was a chance to refight the Reformation and achieve a new outcome—their historical narrative held a power whose potential influence far exceeded the size of their confession. Activists' vision of a non-state national church "in which all subdivisions and parties will be abandoned" was one of complete assimilation.[98] But it was not Mennonites who would abandon their distinctiveness and move into a subsuming German whole; it was the German nation, rather, that would become Mennonite.

And yet, however appealing they found this vision, confessional leaders still had to enlist the majority of their coreligionists.

CHAPTER 3

RAISING THE FAITH

FAMILY, GENDER, AND RELIGIOUS
INDIFFERENCE

Whoever has the youth has the future.
— ERNST GÖBEL, 1885[1]

When the Union of Mennonite Congregations in the German Empire formed in 1886, only a fraction of the country's seventy-one congregations joined. Despite hopes that all Mennonites would grasp the necessity of supporting a national association, enthusiasm among rural conservatives—especially in southern Germany and the Prussian east—proved elusive. Two years later, membership remained at a paltry seventeen, less than one-fourth the desired total. Determined to pry coreligionists from their separatist ways, organizers portrayed the Union as a confession-wide association that represented all congregations, whether members or not. According to Hermann Wiens, a lay leader in the newly formed Berlin church, its "main concern and primary desire" was that "those congregations which have not yet joined the Union will gradually enlist."[2] Unionists like Wiens justified their objective through a discourse of paternalism, evoking certain understandings of home and family life. Founders framed themselves as "wise parents," who while procuring clothes for a young child had cut the garment long "because they know the child will soon grow to fit the over-large dress." The implication was that although rural conservatives still lived in a state of organizational immaturity, modernization and the threats it heralded would force them to outgrow their childlike reservations.[3]

In unionists' parlance, a majority of Germany's Mennonites exhibited "religious indifference."[4] Not only were they uninterested in the Union; they allegedly cared little about their confession at all. It was indeed true that few were invested in the creation of a politically significant collectivity. Yet resisting incorporation into an aggressive national organization was not synonymous with irreligiosity. In fact, those most adamantly opposed to the Union counted among the country's most conscientious, strictly observant members. Invocations of indifference, then, represented less a dispassionate interpretation of religious mood than a normative claim about what it meant to be Mennonite. The concept's true function was not to illuminate but to obfuscate. Like other nationalists, unionists aimed to collapse difference, obscuring a pluralistic field in which individuals practiced their faith in diverse ways. Placing Mennonitism on an evolutionary continuum, they denigrated alternative modes of religiosity as pre-modern indifference, suggesting these "older" forms could and should be replaced by a more up-to-date form of Mennonite modernism. The language of "parents" and "children," in particular, constructed an intra-confessional hierarchy according to which those who embraced unification stood above the unaffiliated. Just as the strength of a single family was believed to grow with the maturation of its children, unionists argued that Mennonitism would progress as members tightened their interregional bonds.

By charging kinship words with overtly religious dynamics, unionists simultaneously depicted their confession as a biological organism. During Bismarck's *Kulturkampf*, some liberal commentators had framed inter-confessional conflict with the language of Darwinism, drawing on rising scientific discourses of heredity, competition, and speciation.[5] In this context, Mennonitism appeared to compete in a larger struggle of natural selection with Germany's other confessions. Just as state governments and national spokespersons worried about their respective demographic trajectories, progressive Mennonites generated anxieties about their potential extinction in Germany. Unless they could adapt to meet the challenges of modernization and secularization, the congregations would allegedly succumb to falling birthrates, shrinking membership, defecting youth, and intermarriage. Unionists hoped to perfect group competitiveness. In 1889, when Hermann Wiens noted that "Our Mennonite Union continues work on its eventual consolidation," he argued the confession could be saved by exposing its youth to a proper upbringing: "Major advances can only be expected with the development of a new generation."[6] Such sentiments disclosed a concerted effort to reorganize the Mennonite domestic sphere. As activists like Wiens inscribed their program within progressive assumptions about parenthood, childhood, marriage, and gender, they hoped these ideas would be reproduced in congregants' most intimate relationships. Identifying the family as an appropriate site of contestation, unionists leveraged anxieties about stability and propriety, calling coreligionists to reorganize their households, their congregations, and the entire confession.[7]

MENNONITE INDIFFERENCE

Nationalism can be a disappointing pastime. Populations rarely express as much enthusiasm for their supposed identity as proponents would like. In the years after Germany's establishment, nationalists lamented the persistence of regionalist attitudes. Among the most damning charges was "national indifference." Anyone whose patriotism or commitment to German customs appeared lackluster could find themselves categorized as indifferent. Speaking Polish, French, or other non-German languages could draw this epithet, as could any other manner of perceived "ambivalence," "side-switching," "amphibianism," or "hermaphroditism." Throughout Central Europe, nationalists of every background employed similar terms, all designed to guilt purportedly apathetic co-nationals into robust participation. In the same way, German nationalist Mennonites decried their congregations' general disinterest or even opposition toward unification. Regional bodies, for their part, preferred provincialism, citing social and theological differences with coreligionists in other parts of the empire. A particularly deep gulf loomed between rural and urban congregations—tensions that further inflamed regional fault lines. City communities dotted northwest Germany and the Baltic coast, while rural Mennonites clustered across inland Prussia and the pasturelands of the southern states. Differing opinions on scriptural interpretation, church discipline, intermarriage, education, dress, and music quickly derailed interregional dialogues.

Like the self-appointed spokespersons of other populations, German nationalist Mennonites sought to root out indifference. Sponsoring conferences across the empire, they promoted the Union through sermons and personal testimonies. But success was limited. Rural members remained wary, fearing that the organization would privilege urbanites. Opponents especially decried a clause in the Union's charter assigning voting power based on financial contributions. While poor churches would only carry one vote, urban congregations, if they donated 1,000 marks per annum, could wield up to six. Rural commentators found this hireling democracy "no longer brotherliness, but naked worldly morals." One preacher suggested that "If the new Union were seated in a house of worship, the rich city congregations would sit in the front with six votes, and behind, the poor rural congregations would be stuck in the corner."[8] His remark encapsulated an anxiety of urban members' hegemony as well as a critique of their worldliness. Many congregations had adopted a fund-raising policy, long used in state churches, allowing wealthy families to purchase permanent seats at the front of the sanctuary. Just as conservative Mennonites accused urban coreligionists of buying their faith with elaborate churches, salaried ministers, Protestant-style pastoral robes, and theological education, some saw this system as a metaphor for the dynamics of the new Union.

Another concern was the absence of a Union-approved confession of faith. Many rural leaders were unwilling to commit to an organization that did not articulate its religious principles. "If all congregations in Germany unite," Baden elder Ulrich Hege informed one ministerial assembly, "there must be something that can serve as a foundation for all." Hege's position belied a deeper suspicion of urban coreligionists' theological soundness.

When Pastor Hinrich van der Smissen of Hamburg-Altona toured south Germany to garner support, several rural listeners found his sermons inappropriately worldly. Van der Smissen was affronted. "I have preached all over the Palatinate," he replied, "and one could know I have always taught the word of Christ." Hoping to deflect criticism, the pastor steered conversation toward more "practical issues." He portrayed the Union, regardless of theology, as rural Mennonites' best hope of preserving legal freedoms, such as exemption from oaths, noncombatant military service, and immunity from church taxes. But van der Smissen's logic did not dispel his audience's apprehensions. One skeptic, a lay leader named Samuel Blickendörfer, apologized for offending the pastor. He admitted that he was not well educated and "cannot articulate my reasons [for opposing the Union] nearly so well." But however elusive those reasons might be, Blickendörfer reiterated: "I am mistrustful."[9]

Unionists sought to substitute an entirely different set of anxieties. Rather than wading into a morass of theological nitpicking, they hoped to generate a powerful common enemy, the fear of which could drive all Germany's Mennonites to emphasize their commonalities. Central to this project was the notion of indifference, a potent yet amorphous category to which Union leaders could attach all manner of alarming attributes. In their telling, indifferent persons were largely responsible for isolation and atomization within the confession, outcomes understood as antithetical to the organization's offer of spiritual unity. Commonly recurring words and phrases in unionists' lexicon reinforced this binary. Derogatory terms like "scattered" and "fragmentation" stood in opposition to positively connoted ideas like "solidarity" and "great entirety." Proponents often placed these concepts in direct proximity to each other, constructing a rhetorical polarity that pulled readers or listeners in a clear direction. Echoing other nationalist storytellers, they called for the recreation of a long lost, idyllic past. During the days of the Reformation, "all our congregations were entirely of one mind on issues of Christian faith and life."[10] Yet over the following centuries, indifference had crept in, smothering the true light of Anabaptism. Both ideas were necessary for the narrative to function: the conjuring of primordial coherence cast indifference as a fall from grace, while the specter of disunity justified activists' pleas for Mennonites to come closer together. Of course, portrayals of unambiguous unanimity among early congregations represented less an accurate portrayal of the past than an admonition to motivate separatists in the present. Such historicizing was intended to bring sixteenth-century Anabaptists into a contemporary state of being, not the other way around.

Conservatives' opposition paralleled the Union's nationalization attempts. Far from ignoring changing conditions, rural spokespersons followed developments closely, reacting against the recently invented concept of German

Mennonitism. Their disapproval of unionists' relationship with Protestant church historians, especially the Münster archivist Ludwig Keller, is a case in point. Already leery of progressivism, they contested Keller's authority among the Union elite. As one skeptic asked, why should Mennonites bow to "one who does not belong to *our* religious confession?"[11] Most labeled Keller an "outsider" and refused to tolerate his pontificating. Even in liberal urban congregations like Krefeld, Emden, and Danzig, few bought Keller's books or promoted his mission. Krefeld pastor Ernst Weydmann had to beg the archivist's pardon for his own congregants, who remained "uninterested in these scholarly endeavors."[12] Unionists like Weydmann requested Keller's patience. They believed that the congregations "must first be consolidated, and a younger generation with a more clear-headed outlook must first grow up."[13] Only after indifference had been cleared away would Mennonitism be ripe for his grandiose plans. But conservatives' disinterest permanently jaded Keller. "The defect of this confession," he scrawled angrily on a piece of scratch paper in 1902, "lies in the spiritual *darkness* which engulfs the majority; this Pharisee-ism crops up at every opportunity. Although the condition in which I found them in 1882 was most miserable, there was never a call for improvement. Nowhere have I found people who are more *thin-skinned*." His final, bitter conclusion: "Great reforms with this confession are impossible."[14]

REFORMING THE FAMILY

While they shared Keller's frustrations, Union leaders were more persistent. Long after the archivist had given up on Germany's rural congregations, unionists strove for universal membership. Among their favored tactics was a narrative of declension. Mennonitism, they claimed, faced a demographic crisis of frightening proportions. Employing the language of youth, childhood, and family, unionists invoked new ideas about population biology to predict confessional extinction. Unless conservatives recognized the indifference in their midst and moved beyond it, they would never transition from static traditionalism to dynamic modernism. As Germany industrialized, so the story went, young Mennonites were being confronted with opportunities and pressures their parents had never experienced. Signs of modernization were everywhere. Changing business, agricultural, and educational practices incentivized youth to leave their ancestral homes. As young people studied at distant universities or accepted jobs in distant cities, they moved to places without congregations. Admittedly, urban communities had long experienced mobility. But demographics had recently begun to change across the empire. "Even in rural congregations," unionists explained, "it is no longer an entirely typical custom that the sons simply follow in their fathers' occupations and become farmers, but instead they often take on other jobs, becoming merchants, technicians, tradesmen of all sorts, civil servants, doctors, teachers, etc." Young women, likewise, often "marry in the city or enter jobs that carry them away from their home congregations."[15] Unionists alleged that in the coming decades, it was precisely non-member communities that would be most affected.

The ultimate, unsettling implication was that the confession would cease to exist. Concerned leaders collected statistics. From year to year, they compared rates of growth and decline within individual congregations, between regions, and for the confession as a whole. After synthesizing congregational records with census data, writers concluded that their outlook was bleak. Over the last half of the nineteenth century, the number of Mennonites in Germany remained constant, hovering around 20,000 baptized members and children. But while Anabaptism stagnated, the empire's total population increased by 2 percent annually. Lack of growth could be partially attributed to emigration to Imperial Russia and the United States—areas where communities were admittedly healthy and expanding. But other factors indicated that even if no further emigration occurred, those remaining faced a "slow but certain demise."[16] Several city congregations— allegedly early predictors—were quickly losing ground. In Altona, the population had fallen from 320 in 1780 to 125 in 1840. In 1887, it stood at a meager 65.[17] "In fifty years," pessimists predicted, Germany would have "no more Mennonites."[18]

Commentators regarded decline first and foremost as a familial crisis. Not only were young people leaving in greater numbers than ever before; the confession was supposedly producing fewer children with each generation. Comparing the country's major confessions, one researcher found that Mennonites married less often than Protestants, Catholics, or Jews. In Prussia, one Protestant marriage occurred annually per every 114 souls. Among Jews, one marriage happened per every 122 souls, and among Catholics, one per every 125. For Mennonites, the ratio was one per 143. Birth statistics allegedly demonstrated a similar trend. Catholics in Prussia had one birth per every 27 members; Protestants had one per every 28; Jews had one per 29; and Mennonites, one per 33.[19] In reality, these numbers are highly suspect; they were drawn from a hodgepodge of sources representing varying degrees of reliability and extrapolated to make assertions about populations far larger than initial sample groups. To even pose such questions presupposed a clarity of confessional divisions, through which all individuals could be meaningfully categorized as either Mennonite, Catholic, Protestant, or Jewish—terms that, as demographers knew perfectly well, were never entirely clear. But when artfully presented, such statistics painted a frightening picture. They implied that Mennonites were less fertile than their competitors and that they were falling behind in the race for proportional growth.

Unionists intended this data to foster confessional solidarity. Appropriating preexisting discourses of education and parenting, they portrayed families as the most essential loci of Christian instruction: a properly functioning household was not simply a credit to its members, but "a blessing for the entire congregation."[20] To invert the maxim, congregations likewise served as symbolic extensions of individual families. Indeed, many communities literally consisted of complex kinship networks. Regionally—and, toward the end of the nineteenth century, interregionally as well—Mennonites were closely intertwined by marriage, ties reflecting centuries of legal prohibitions against accepting new converts as well as internal restrictions against marrying outsiders. In eighteenth-century Prussia, for example, rulers had discouraged congregational growth by preventing members from acquiring new farmland. Military exemption, meanwhile, was offered on an increasingly tenuous basis, prompting elders to keep a low profile by banning proselytism. A century later, the folklorist Wilhelm Mannhardt described how such decisions, largely by accident, had turned Mennonitism into a "hereditary caste." Membership became "an act of inheritance based exclusively on the purity of the bloodline rather than on an inner consensus based on conviction."[21]

In addition to genealogical linkages webbing the Mennonite world, leaders described spiritual bonds through the metaphor of family. Early Anabaptists had depicted their confession as a priesthood of believers, each person capable of scriptural interpretation. Familial language provided a key means of representing this decentered structure. By referring to each other as "brothers," "sisters," or "brethren in faith," members emphasized their equality before God. In many areas, they addressed each other with the familiar "thou," usually reserved for family and close acquaintances, rather than the more formal "you." Ministers also used kinship as a cipher to elucidate the divine. Just as the spiritual "bond of the family" joined human relatives, it could unite "God with the people, the heaven with the earth." The connection mortals felt "with the eternal Father" found approximation in the intimacy with which "the child nestles against the father." And just as Jesus had loved his "siblings and his mother," Mennonites were called to honor their own relations.[22] Interweaving kinship with Anabaptist theology, members permanently blurred distinctions between the earthly and the spiritual; between human and confessional families; and between God and the Mennonite male. Thus, when preachers utilized words like "parents," "children," and "brother"—as well as corporeal terminology such as "heart," "organs," "blood," "eyes," and "limbs"—they always evoked multiple meanings.

The rhetoric of "mother congregations," "sister congregations," and "daughter colonies," for instance, drew on traditional understandings of Anabaptism as feminine. Menno Simons and other early theologians had conceived of Jesus and the church as two participants in a holy matrimony. The messiah, celibate during his earthly life, awaited the church as an expectant bridegroom, while his followers collectively formed the "bride of Christ," ready to submit to her divine lover.[23] This language resonated throughout the nineteenth century; just as Mennonites portrayed their congregational units as female, they continued to think of Jesus as a powerful lord who courted their devotion and whose masculine authority they should obey. If the confession constituted Christ's bride, each member was responsible for performing his or her own integral function. Writers constructed male gender, for instance, in relation to the outside world. Men were expected to oppose oaths, military service, and public office. It was their responsibility to fill leadership positions, both for group guidance and to bargain with external organizations. By contrast, women's roles were theorized as internal and domestic. Just as the bride of Jesus was supposed to follow his teachings and await his triumphal return, Mennonite women were to remain loyal, deferential, and unadulterated. Yet they also possessed representational functions. While formal leadership remained an explicitly male domain, women participated in both Mennonite and Protestant missions, staffed alms houses and orphanages, and joined voluntary associations. State authorities frequently used gender as a political instrument, targeting marriage and women's inheritance rights to control demographics and force Mennonite compliance with policy. These laws politicized women—especially widowed property holders—sometimes prompting them to support immigration to Imperial Russia or to appeal directly to Berlin.[24]

Among the most likely reasons for low marriage and birth statistics was Mennonites' high rate of intermarriage with other confessions. "The greatest danger," historian Antje Brons assessed in 1883, "threatens our congregations through mixed marriages."[25] Some attributed the rise of extra-Mennonite mingling, occurring "ever more frequently," to economic success.[26] According to Brons, the daughters of respectable and affluent families were much sought after by suitors from different backgrounds; young women were especially likely to marry civil servants who would resettle in distant towns without Mennonite congregations. Mobility thus often resulted from intermarriage. Children of these unions were usually baptized into state churches and raised Protestant or, less often, Catholic. Since confessional affiliation was patrilineal by law, those born to non-Mennonite fathers were typically baptized at infancy. Even in marriages between Protestant women and Mennonite men—which theoretically resulted in Mennonite children—husbands frequently came under their wives' influence and raised offspring in state churches. In 1877, Arthur Roosen, the two-year-old son of a Mennonite father and Protestant mother, was baptized along with nine cousins into the Protestant faith. "My father did not consider it desirable," Roosen reported years later, "to let me become Mennonite, as this tiny faith confession existed only in very few places in the world."[27] Antje Brons lamented that nearly all families had similar experiences. One of her own sons had married an "extreme Protestant" who insisted that their children receive infant baptism.[28]

Congregations across Germany took different stances. A majority forbade inter-confessional mixing altogether, excommunicating anyone who disobeyed. In East and West Prussia, matrimony was tied to pacifism. Although royal decree allowed conscripts to perform noncombatant service, this applied only to "members of the old-Mennonite families," and not to new converts.[29] Most elders cited the regulation as grounds to continue banning mixed marriages even after state restrictions had been lifted. They argued that draftees of non-Mennonite heritage would necessarily perform combat duties—and anyone who took up weapons was by definition not Anabaptist. Conversely, congregations that allowed full military service generally also tolerated mixed marriages. In 1870, when Mennonites in Danzig agreed to abandon complete pacifism, they simultaneously struck their intermarriage moratorium: "Along with the revocation of our earlier privilege of military exemption, which has changed our relationship to other citizens of the state, we will not from this point forward revoke membership from those members of our congregation who feel compelled to enter into marriage with members of other Christian confessions."[30]

Opposition in southern Germany rested less on nonresistance than on theological purity. Conservative leaders in Baden, for example, considered matrimony not simply a personal affair, but a sacrament integral to the entire congregational family. Elder Ulrich Hege expressed a typical view when he called mixed marriage a "cancer in the congregation." For Hege, intermingling with "Jews and heathens" was obviously unthinkable and merited little comment.[31] But even in cases where the non-Mennonite partner belonged to one of the state churches and was a believing Christian, he found it indefensible. Unlike pure Mennonite marriages, a mixed couple would never be one in flesh, heart, soul, spirit, faith, love, hope, or bliss as commanded by scripture. Partners would be unable to share the same communion, the same baptism, or the same articles of faith. Their fervor for God would invariably diminish. Hege considered intermarriage a product of "religious indifference," which he believed directly caused "the shrinking of our congregations."[32] In the words of Christian Schmutz, also a conservative elder in Baden, "Those who marry people outside the confession generally already exhibit coldness and indifference toward the congregation." Because young people's faith was not yet mature, they easily succumbed to the allure of external marriages. Ministers especially cast non-Mennonite women as temptresses, whose seductive beauty or worldly wealth pulled weak-willed men into a sinful "lust for mixed marriage."[33] For traditionalists like Hege and Schmutz, intermarriage produced a "mixed faith" and a "mixed creed," in turn generating a "mixed community"—"a diseased congregation that is degenerate, limping from both sides, half biblical, half state church."[34]

Progressive leaders held looser views, and although few looked favorably on intermarriage, some—mostly urban—congregations accepted them. It "is better if the couple belongs to the same confession," elder Carl Harder wrote in 1848, "but from a Christian standpoint, a marriage in which both partners do not belong to the same confession should also be tolerated."[35] Harder's position tracked with his larger commitment to ecumenical dialogue. He saw marital toleration as one means of aligning Mennonitism with a changing world. But, to the chagrin of Harder and his followers, this would remain a minority view in East and West Prussia for decades. Only with the demise of military exemption and the founding of the Mennonite Union would such ideas gain traction. In northwest Germany, however, the practice had a long history. Hamburg-Altona pastor Berend Roosen went so far as to suggest that without intermarriage, his own congregation "would have almost died out."[36] Between 1820 and 1850, only 20 of 93 marriages performed in Hamburg-Altona were unmixed. Between 1868 and 1875, the number fell to 3 in 26. But even in tolerant communities, intermarriage did not always increase membership, since Mennonites frequently converted to their spouses' faith. Roosen had once even married two Protestants with sentimental ties to Anabaptism but who had no intention of joining.

Proponents of the Mennonite Union, including both Harder and Roosen, identified mixed marriage as one method of reversing their confession's population slump. Rather than disparaging those who fell in love with non-Mennonites as indifferent, they suggested that the truly indifferent act was to exclude otherwise valuable members. They saw modernity, not spiritual antipathy, at the root of inter-confessional unions; and modernity marched ever on. "Part of the damage caused by the enormous exodus of young members," argued Danzig pastor Hermann Mannhardt, himself a convert from Protestantism, "can be recouped through the recognition of mixed marriages." Mannhardt illustrated the point by showing how his own congregation had grown since dropping its intermarriage ban. Of 240 Mennonites baptized in Danzig between 1881 and 1895, only 20 of the 67 who had already entered marriages chose Mennonite partners. But because none had been excommunicated, all 47 in inter-confessional relationships retained their membership. Further, 25 had convinced their spouses to convert, so now a majority of couples were "entirely Mennonite."[37] With intermarriage on the rise in rural as well as urban areas, Mannhardt recommended open-mindedness across the country. By asking rural conservatives to welcome outsiders, unionists like Mannhardt hoped, in turn, to convert intransigents to their own cause.

REMAKING CHILDHOOD

Echoing their support for mixed marriage, spokespersons constructed the Union as a new mediator of familial relationships. In an 1889 letter dispatched to every congregation in the empire, its Directorate outlined concerns over the "inclination among our young members to leave their home territories." Growing urbanization and ease of transportation continued to pull Mennonite youth—especially those interested in scholarly, business, or technical training—from their homes. According to the Directorate, young people were not themselves at fault. Progressives had long believed the confession would benefit from greater access to education. Twenty years earlier, Wilhelm Mannhardt—still the German states' only Mennonite to earn a doctorate—had argued that "it is simply wrong when some among us, including even wealthy landowners, still shy away from letting their children receive an education that would go beyond the most meager elementary knowledge."[38] Like Mannhardt, the Union Directorate found young members' desire for education understandable. But the resulting loss "of this young strength from our congregations" was regrettable indeed. As youth spent years far from the nearest congregation, their membership—and their faith—was likely to lapse. Sooner or later, these "scattered" Mennonites turned away from Anabaptism, joining one of the state churches and allowing their children to be baptized as infants.[39]

Childrearing had been a common theme in Anabaptist writing since the sixteenth century. Traditional accounts held that childhood ended at baptism. While children were too young to accept Christian discipleship, adults could follow Jesus of their own volition. Baptism, usually performed at age fourteen or fifteen, thus symbolized the transformative moment between childhood and adulthood. During the Reformation, detractors had cast believers' baptism as a particularly heinous form of child neglect, one that doomed anyone who died before baptismal age to eternal fire. Early Anabaptists, consequently, wrote extensively about childrearing, encouraging coreligionists to treat kin with love. "If anyone does not provide for his relatives, and especially for his own family," Menno Simons maintained, "he has disowned his faith, and is worse than an unbeliever." Separating home life from worldly temptations, parents were to raise children "in the nurture and admonition of the Lord."[40] The views of Menno and of other early leaders colored the thinking of their inheritors across Imperial Germany. "The home," one pastor in south Germany suggested, "is the foundational pillar upon which all religious life, as expressed both in individuals and in the entire congregation, rests and grows." To a greater degree than state church members—who relied largely on state-run schools to educate their young people—Mennonite families possessed "the high priestly calling to raise children to be true youth in Jesus and to be active members of the congregation."[41]

Although elders, preachers, and deacons could convey basic beliefs, the final responsibility for children's education lay with the most irreducible unit of congregational life. "Everywhere there is talk of raising children," one elder put it, "the *family* has the most important role."[42] Mennonite parents were to say dinnertime prayers, attend church regularly, and protect their children from wicked influences. As with church life generally, childrearing duties were to be divided by gender. It was the father's role to assemble the family for morning and evening devotionals, and to cultivate discipline. By contrast, the mother was to instruct her children in the rituals of everyday piety: "It is the mother who teaches the children to pray and the meaning of prayer, she who teaches the world's holy history, who put many a hymn, which she treasured and valued, in your heart and mouth. It is the mother, who plants the delightful seeds of God's word in the receptive heart of the child, so that in time it may bear fruit."[43] Women bore responsibility for passing memories from one generation to the next. By inducting children into the mystery of prayer, mothers mediated their relationships with God; by relating history, they connected them to centuries-old traditions; and through song they handed down a creative, performative manifestation of their religion. Parents, in short, were responsible for the healthy development of their offspring's faith, so that when they received baptismal training, young persons would commit themselves to Christ.

In the decades before the Union's formation, congregants in German lands had begun to expand their thinking about childrearing. New words to describe different stages of childhood were entering everyday vocabularies across Europe.[44] For Mennonites, "child" still referred to the pre-baptismal period, but other terms meaning "youth" could apply to baptized men and women well into their twenties. In 1869, Carl Harder founded a *Journal for Religion and Parenting*, which printed treatises on Christian pedagogy, news about changing German school policies, and comparative studies of Mennonite educational systems around the world. Harder's periodical reflected an increasingly popular belief among confessional leaders that "a society that does not strive to awake an inner piety in its youth has *no future*."[45] If Mennonites were to save their confession, they needed to secure the allegiance of coming generations. Authors published reading material geared toward children at an unprecedented rate. New catechisms appeared in 1877, 1880, 1888, and 1893. In 1878, a preacher in south Germany named Jakob Ellenberger issued the first-ever collection of Mennonite children's stories, *Images from the Pilgrim Life*. Intended to "sharpen the consciousness of solidarity and to help weave the band of unity more and more around us," Ellenberger's anthology included a biography of Menno Simons, a chronicle of Mennonite experiences during the Napoleonic wars, and childhood reminiscences from several ministers.[46]

Mennonite newspapers began printing columns for young readers. In 1870, the first article "For Children" in one Baden-based monthly opened, "Dear Children! The *Congregational Paper* will also bring something for you with every issue, either an educational story or something else instructive and useful that will have blessed results for your entire life in this world, and especially for the salvation of your soul in the next world."[47] Other articles included stories of children doing good deeds—fortunate children helping those in need, for example, or unfortunates maintaining their faith in harsh circumstances. There were tales of children in the Bible, of children on overseas mission stations, the youthful remembrances of wise elders, and accounts of Reformation-era martyrs. Readers were supposed to identify with these characters and to internalize their Christian values. In 1885, Carl Justus van der Smissen, editor of a Mennonite mission paper called *News from the Heathen World*, restructured his publication to appeal to children as well as adults, adding the subtitle "For Old and Young" to its banner head. Writers for van der Smissen's journal adopted an informal and conciliatory style, sometimes personifying the periodical itself. "Hello!" began its first children's column. "It is a long-treasured wish of mine to spend time among you and to bring you news of your brothers and sisters in faraway places. Surely you are very excited! But first let me lie down in your middle; I have grown weary during my many travels, which have brought me through many lands and cities."[48] The article aimed to excite young readers with oriental descriptions of non-white heathens and ultimately to instill a passion for Christian evangelism. Mennonite youth were to discover the global dimensions of their faith; their coreligionists might be missionaries in Indonesia or the Oklahoma Indian Territory, but they belonged to the same confessional family.

Authors of literature for young Mennonites hoped their stories would instruct not only children but "every member of the family."[49] Books and articles were to be read aloud by the whole household, perhaps at bedtime or on Sundays after returning from church. By addressing youth directly and in a familiar tone, authors used the language of a hypothetical father or mother—an approach designed to make children think of their faith in familial terms. And because it was parents who most likely read such literature aloud, this process was also supposed to transform their conceptions about childrearing. Stories for young people employed linguistic conventions designed for normalization in the home. By putting words into parents' mouths, they taught adults how to speak to their progeny—which cadences to adopt, the preferred distribution of biblical quotations, appropriate use of terms and metaphors. Occasionally, they even supplied the responses children should give to particular texts, teaching parents how they should expect their offspring to act. The article in *News from the Heathen World*, for instance, provided audiences' ideal reaction. "Oh! Stay among us," children were supposed to say, "and tell us of the American Indians with whom our dear missionary brothers and sisters work, and also of the Chinese, Indians, Africans, and islanders."[50] A proper Mennonite child would be fascinated by these topics—and proper parents would answer knowledgably and with love.

Mennonites' heightened focus on childhood education tracked with contemporary trends among faith communities across the industrializing world. Evangelical Christians especially—who from the massive revival meetings of D. L. Moody in the United States to those of Charles Spurgeon in Great Britain experienced a heyday during the late nineteenth century—were highly concerned with children's instruction. Baptists, Presbyterians, Methodists, independent Lutherans, and Pentecostals, as well as Germany's state churches, all developed a barrage of new educational curricula, Sunday school programs, and literature for young Christians. Mennonite observers followed these movements, quoting innovators in their sermons and circulating articles from evangelical presses. When Germany's Baptists formed a general conference in 1884, the *Mennonite Journal* reprinted their keynote address as "An Admonition to the Mennonites." Editor Hinrich van der Smissen drew readers' attention to the Baptists' focus on childhood education and unity by italicizing a section that read, "*the Publication Association and the school have contributed to our unity throughout* [Germany], *so that wherever I have been in the country, the Baptists there are one. They feel together, they think together, they work together, they believe together, and they love together.*"[51] Other ministers were likewise interested in non-Mennonite traditions. In 1889, Pastor Christian Neff of the Palatinate proposed a Sunday "children's service," to be held parallel to adults' worship time. Originating in eighteenth-century England, this practice had arrived in German lands shortly before unification. Neff believed that children's services would bring students and teachers closer together, strengthening young people's faith through specialized lessons, while allowing adults to read and recount scripture in new ways.[52]

Leaders like Neff reworked such borrowed educational strategies for Mennonite contexts. They increasingly scrutinized the materials to which they exposed their youth. "*Where it is at all possible,*" Carl Harder cautioned, "the Mennonites must make sure their children no longer receive religious instruction from the teaching booklets of other confessions." While parents were often familiar with non-Mennonite literature—especially works aimed at turning children into good Germans or good Protestants—ministers like Harder hoped for an explicitly Anabaptist canon. As Jakob Ellenberger introduced his collection of Mennonite children's stories, "Of the numerous good and Christian writings of German *national literature*, many a book has already found approval among our families." These volumes were certainly a boon, Ellenberger admitted. He recalled that as a child, his own faith had profited from writers like Gerhard Terstegen, Ernst Moritz Arndt, Thomas von Kempen, and Jung-Stilling. But such texts could speak as intimately to Protestant sensibilities as to a specifically Anabaptist consciousness. "Do we not also want," Ellenberger asked, "a *Mennonite booklet of this type?*"[53]

Commentators especially questioned the religious education young people received in non-Mennonite institutes. At the elementary level, almost all youth attended state schools, where they received Protestant religious instruction. Thousands of Mennonite families thus permitted public schools to provide a basic foundation in biblical history and Christian values. Although schools did teach prayers and religious songs, as well as scriptural passages and parables, they did not promote traditional Anabaptist articles of faith such as adult baptism, pacifism, or the refusal of oaths. Reformist leaders expressed doubts about Protestant instructors, charging that they approached pupils with detached, critical, and secular attitudes. "For the majority of teachers," Christian Neff criticized, "religious instruction is not a matter of the heart.... Thanks to their modern university training, they view the matter with high-nosed disdain and obvious indifference." Ministers could thus favor some forms of education while at the same time remaining suspicious of others. Just as conservative Mennonites had long opposed the "worldly" philosophy taught at Protestant universities, Neff did not believe that state-provided elementary educators—even Protestant pastors and Catholic priests—could be trusted to impart the true spirit of the gospel. "Is it then to wonder," he asked, "that [our children] enter baptismal training with a frightful ignorance?"[54]

Unlike coreligionists in Switzerland, North America, and the Russian Empire, Mennonites in German lands did not develop a strong parochial school system. A handful of Mennonite elementary schools had once operated in the Palatinate, Bavaria, and West Prussia, but few functioned past the 1850s. A number of leaders did become involved with educational projects of a philanthropic nature. In Emden, Antje Brons helped open a kindergarten; Carl Harder established a girls' school in Elbing; and several congregations even collaborated to finance a school in France for disadvantaged children. But such ventures had more to do with good Christian works than with reshaping the confession. Participants considered them comparable to the orphanages and alms houses they supported. The sole exception came in 1867, when fifty leaders in the south German states formed a Mennonite Educational and Schooling Association, establishing a small academy for boys in Weierhof, Palatinate. Founders hoped the academy would eventually become a ministerial training institute. But despite initial enthusiasm, coreligionists outside the region gave it little backing. Those in Baden, Wurttemberg, and Bavaria proper felt excluded from the planning process, while congregations in the Prussian east and northwest were too geographically removed. By 1879, the number of pupils had fallen from a onetime high of forty-five to a meager nine. While the Weierhof School remained in operation and under Mennonite control well into the twentieth century, it never became the seminary its founders had envisioned.[55]

Absent a strong educational grounding, leaders from both progressive and conservative backgrounds projected anxieties about Mennonite youth onto familial environments. "Apart from individual persons," wrote the Mennonite Union's Directorate, "many families live scattered across our fatherland, distant from congregations and without connections to them. They move out from their congregations with warm interest, but it cools due to lack of contact."[56] As single families became separated from religious support networks, they ran the "danger of becoming indifferent."[57] Christian Hege, a traveling minister from southern Germany who worked especially with scattered Mennonites, ascribed the phenomenon to atomization. Isolated from spiritual kin, "the communal consciousness planted in the heart of the youth gradually begins to grow cold."[58] And while some young people eventually did move back to their home communities, many exhibited the tell-tale signs of weakened faith. In the words of one preacher old enough to have watched several generations come and go, the youth "move out as good Mennonites; most return as half-Mennonites."[59]

As in the case of mixed marriage, proponents of the Mennonite Union utilized fears about young people's retention to win new membership for their organization. The Directorate informed church boards across the country of their "solemn duty" to maintain ties with "the migratory young male and female members [who are] often the best educated of our congregations."[60] Since this demographic was most likely to comprise future leaders and major financial contributors, their allegiance was critical. The Union outlined several recommendations for local ministers. Sending Anabaptist reading materials, for example, would keep scattered members up to date with confessional news. If individual communities could not afford postage, the Union was willing to supply copies of its yearly reports as well as free subscriptions to the *Mennonite Journal*, its primary organ. The *"Journal* must have greater readership in all congregations!" Hermann Mannhardt declared. "Why are there thousands of German Mennonites who do not even know its name?"[61] The Directorate further suggested that young people move to cities with functioning congregations. Union member communities were preferred. Such interregional efforts would be difficult to organize piecemeal, however; only a centralized body like the Union could ensure smooth coordination. In this spirit, the Directorate requested regular reports from each church on births, baptisms, marriages, and deaths, as well as the number of members who joined or left.[62] Unionists portrayed these initiatives and more broadly their organization, "which has pursued no other goal than the preservation and strengthening of our congregations," as Mennonites' best hope of saving their confession.[63]

MENNONITE MANHOOD

Beyond reforming childhood and familial life, the Union's third major objective was to reshape Mennonite masculinity. Because men held responsibility for congregational leadership and formally represented the confession to external actors, unionists most directly proposed to reform their gender. If Mennonitism was to adapt to the changing landscape of modernity, allegedly heralded by the formation of the German Empire, a cadre of modern men should guide it. The types of manhood required could be summed up in two words: soldiers and pastors. In Hermann Mannhardt's thinking, the confession most vitally needed to transition "from nonresistance to *complete* military service, and ... from lay preaching to the appointment of salaried pastors." Only after turning these corners could Anabaptism keep pace with its competitors. Disassociating themselves from pacifism, Mennonite men would renounce the prime symbol of their one-time national indifference, thereby winning neighbors' respect. And by adopting salaried pastorship, they would build an educated elite, capable of defending their faith in the public sphere. These efforts were linked: some soldiers would go on to receive theological training, while educated pastors would promote military service from the pulpit. Already, a few communities had completed the evolution. "Our Danzig congregation," Mannhardt explained, "has this period behind it and has arisen from it invigorated." But the rest would emerge only with difficulty. Especially in rural areas, many "are still in the middle [of this process], while others are just at the beginning."[64] Only when every congregation championed the same modernist vision, Mannhardt believed, would the metamorphosis of German Mennonitism be complete.

From its inception, the Union's most prominent initiative was the establishment of a seminary in Berlin. Intended to educate a new generation of pastors, the seminary—potentially affiliated with the University of Berlin—would be administered by a professor of Mennonite theology. How such an institution might function, or who might be qualified to run it, were matters of debate. Although coreligionists in the Netherlands had maintained a seminary for more than one and a half centuries, leaders in German lands had no such experience. Any young man seeking pastoral training—unless he knew Dutch or was willing to learn it at the Amsterdam seminary—had to turn to non-Mennonite establishments. Of all ministers active in the German states during the nineteenth century, only forty-eight received any form of higher education. Most were concentrated in the urban northwest. While a few studied in Amsterdam, the majority attended German-language universities or mission schools.[65] By contrast, rural congregations—financially and theologically averse to salaried pastorship—usually practiced lay ministry. These communities often had a three-tiered system with one "elder" and multiple "preachers" and "deacons." Men were typically called to the ministry from within the congregation. Each candidate, after a short training course with his elder, would hold a trial sermon, and if the wider assembly deemed him acceptable, he would receive ordination for life. Because lay preaching was not remunerated, ministers were expected to earn through other means, usually farming. Rural congregations could thus have five or six preachers simultaneously. At the time of the Union's founding, approximately three hundred were serving across Germany.

Unionists hoped a seminary would help reverse demographic decline. Rural congregations, especially, faced an unprecedented shortage of preachers. As fewer young men remained on family farms, candidate pools shrank. Of those who did stay, many began refusing ministry calls, despite promises made during baptismal training. One congregation in the Palatinate had to hire a Baptist because no suitable Mennonite could be found. In West Prussia, three men in a row declined to serve another community.[66] Some practicing ministers even opted to step down, feeling unable to preach at a sufficiently modern level. "I myself have been present, when faithful men, trembling, tears running from their eyes, asked to relinquish this office," one minister reported. They "did not feel equal to the ever advancing levels of education of the times."[67] By the 1880s, many congregations in southern Germany had been forced to abandon lay ministry. Smaller groups sometimes joined forces to hire a single preacher, who would hold services in each church once or twice a month. Others disbanded altogether. Unionists thus promoted their seminary as a matter of survival. "Among all the Christian confessions," Hinrich van der Smissen claimed, "there is not a single one that up to now has been more ambivalent about the education of its future preachers than our Mennonite confession in Germany."[68]

Beyond eliminating the ministerial shortage, unionists hoped a seminary would foster new forms of leadership. Unsalaried ministers, saddled with employment elsewhere, could not effectively serve their congregants. "We should not just be preachers but also stewards," Hermann Mannhardt entreated; "we should know our congregation members, the grown and the young, we should go in and out of their homes, should visit the sick and the frail, console the mourners, give strength to the weak, warn the reckless, correct the errant."[69] Trained and salaried preachers could dedicate full attention to their flocks. One vital function would be caring for scattered families. "The Mennonites are birds of passage; where large and powerful congregations once stood, now there are only a few families," educator Ernst Göbel wrote. "It is easy to understand what a difficult situation these lone Mennonites are in, if they wish to retain a proper connection with their congregation. At most, the costly trip to the mother congregation can only be undertaken once a year for participation in the communion celebration. How can they be helped? Only through the *traveling ministry*."[70] Disproportionately understaffed communities in Hesse and the Palatinate lauded these plans. "Where the Sunday service is absent," one leader explained, "absent also is the focal point of our spiritual life."[71]

Nevertheless, most rural congregations remained suspicious of the Union and its proposed seminary. Conservative elders had long viewed theological training as a threat to pacifism, finding it "difficult to convince the educated world that a Christian must be nonresistant." They observed how young men, filling their heads with academic knowledge, allowed pacifist convictions to be "outflanked by worldly philosophy."[72] Believing that education twisted scripture, the large Conference of East and West Prussian Mennonite Congregations declined to support the Union, noting that it "could have no reason to join an association that makes the education of preachers its main task."[73] Conference decisions exercised a coercive force over more progressive member communities. Although two of West Prussia's rural congregations initially backed the Union, they ultimately remained unaffiliated in order to uphold regional consensus. In Baden and Bavaria, conference leaders adopted similar stances, explaining that while they shared the Union's goals, they disapproved of its methods. "If it established new congregations, found new preachers, and had helped with the lack of Sunday worship services," one minister clarified, "we would have greeted it with joy. But instead the emphasis is placed on the professor idea."[74] Considering isolation a means of protecting traditional beliefs, rural conservatives further opposed sending youth to cosmopolitan Berlin.

With such little support, unionists abandoned seminary plans in 1897. But while this project never came to fruition, it did facilitate the expansion of confessional education. In lieu of administering its own institution, the Union chose to fund students at approved Protestant seminaries and universities. Scholarship recipients were required to pass examinations on biblical, church, and Anabaptist history as well as Christian ethics, philosophical history, and practical theology. Each candidate wrote a thesis and delivered a sermon before the Union Directorate.[75] This program produced several influential pastors. They represented Mennonite interests in ecumenical contexts, became members of the Directorate, or advocated Union initiatives among reluctant congregations. Phillipp Kieferndorf, for example, utilized his education to promote modernization in his native Palatinate. Emil Händiges, another stipend holder, became a longtime Union chairman. In addition to scholarships, the Union instituted a number of

Faith and patriotism intertwined in kinship. Oriented around the Bible, yet adopting the trappings of German modernism—from buttons, mustaches, and military uniforms to the worldly technology of photography—this Mennonite family in West Prussia embodied the Union's dual religious and national objectives.

other policies to stabilize congregational leadership. In 1897, the organization provided pensions for the widows of deceased preachers; in 1905, it established a fund to finance ministers of struggling congregations; and in 1911, leaders began discussing preachers' pensions.[76]

But reforming congregational leadership was only half the Union's campaign for the new Mennonite man. If salaried ministry would change the confession from within, it also needed a fresh face for the external world: unionists hoped not only to turn lay preachers into educated pastors, but also conscientious objectors into soldiers. Transforming coreligionists' orientation toward military service necessitated the development of a militarist masculinity. Unionists frequently disparaged pacifism, calling it a "rigid dogma that has banished thousands to Kansas and Nebraska and a small flock to Central Asia." They assured coreligionists as well as the non-Mennonite public that "We have come to believe that the principle of nonresistance is untenable in a modern state. It is incompatible with the requirement that the state—which provides its citizens with the same rights regardless of confession—also makes of its military-age youth." Such claims were bolstered by new readings of early Anabaptist texts. Militarist interpreters revealed that pacifism had been only a minor point among

Reformation-era theologians, while some had never advocated it at all. Moreover, the very nature of warfare had ostensibly changed since the sixteenth century. This narrative held that while early church leaders correctly eschewed physical force as a means of spreading religion, they would not have opposed modern defensive wars to protect nation and fatherland. Armed service was thus "in no way a deviation from the original [Anabaptist] idea of *peaceful tolerance.*"[77]

Pacifism proved difficult to eradicate. Even though full military exemption was no longer possible, conservative elders continued to instruct young men to choose noncombatant service, guaranteed in Prussia and, once again, in Baden. Draftees who disobeyed could be stripped of their church membership and refused communion. Conscripts occasionally wrote statements defending their right to choose. One from West Prussia called it an "inherited advantage," encouraging others to make the same decision. A study of Mennonites in Germany's armed forces during 1901 found that two-thirds conscripted from these regions had done so. The other third likely came from urban congregations, such as Danzig and Elbing, or retained minimal ties to their home communities. Exact policies varied between regions. In Bavaria, Wurttemberg, and northwestern Germany, many congregations deemphasized pacifism. But even here, collective memories were long, and nonresistance evoked fondness. One soldier from Bavaria, for whom noncombatant service had been denied, feared for his soul in the event of war. He urged all congregations to collaborate so that "no Mennonite youth would enlist in the infantry, cavalry, or artillery."[78]

Unionists considered noncombatant duties simply cowardly—and not pacifist at all. "Military service is military service," one pastor reasoned; "there is no such thing as soldiers without weapons, and train conductors, medics, etc., are as little nonresistant as other soldiers; in whatever form one accepts the military law, the old Mennonite principle of nonresistance is unquestionably abandoned."[79] Other critics blamed pacifism for the confession's "constant decline," casting it as weak and effeminate. They charged that while opposition to weapons had not stopped a single war, "it has had the consequence that those congregations most strictly attached to it *could not find a single sympathetic ear for their true ideas.*"[80] By foregoing military service, Mennonites had made themselves into second-class citizens, in turn squandering the social capital needed to attract new adherents. Just as members could increase numbers through evangelism, they could supposedly also do so by fighting for Germany. Alongside intolerance of mixed marriage, uninvolved parenting, and poor education, pacifism thus became understood as a form of religious indifference. Predictably, the Union invoked demographic crisis to pressure conservatives. Although many rural elders refused membership to men who had undergone combat training, the Union considered this tantamount to excommunication. Unwelcome at local congregations, mobile young men joined Protestant churches. "We encourage the board of each congregation," the Directorate resolved, "to prepare a certificate for all of those members who move into the area of another congregation and to mandate that they register themselves, with the assurance that the newly admitted member will be granted full rights."[81]

One method of undermining pacifism was to normalize military partic- ipation. By lavishing attention on draftees—whether in combat positions or otherwise—unionists hoped to shift confessional focus. Instead of think- ing about how to oppose state service, members should ask how they could support their troops. In 1899, leaders in south Germany established a Sol- dier Commission to provide Mennonite conscripts with spiritual aid. While this was not formally a Union program, Chairman Hinrich van der Smis- sen and his allies strongly approved. On one hand, the commission encour- aged noncombatant roles. "If today the principle of nonresistance is given little notice," its founders wrote, "this is worth decrying." But their larger mission—and the area most supported by van der Smissen and the Union— concerned demographic integrity. The Soldier Commission sought to en- sure that conscripts remained Mennonite during and after their service. Draftees who left home for the first time encountered "all sorts of elements" that could lead them astray.[82] Asking congregations to submit current ad- dresses for each serviceman, the organization provided them with religious literature, petitioned army administrators to station soldiers to towns with Mennonite congregations, and introduced recent arrivals to local families.

The Soldier Commission secured draftees' confessional loyalties by polic- ing their masculinity. Each was to comport himself according to expecta- tions of proper Mennonite manhood. The "best equipment for a good Chris- tian soldier," spokespersons explained, "is a pious mind, which is firmly grounded in faith in Jesus Christ." This counsel was all-encompassing. From their manners of speech (boasting was discouraged) to bodily move- ments (no strutting!), the commission sought to influence every aspect of soldiers' conduct. Just as the larger German military disciplined conscripts' bodies, fashioning docile instruments of the state, church leaders attempted to produce specifically Mennonite soldiers. Mirroring army instruction manuals, the Soldier Commission provided its own directions from the first mustering to the final week of garrison life. One handbook assured draft- ees that service was a transformative part of life. "It is an honor to wear the Kaiser's uniform," they learned. But while former soldiers often looked back with pride, the military could also prove a graveyard for youthful in- nocence. Too many had "laid the seed of a disease that cannot be healed, which they continually carry through life like a chain of sin." Surrounded by atrocious language, unsavory characters, and depravity beyond imagina- tion, even the purest hearts could descend into an "abyss of moral and reli- gious corruption." The worst of these evils—unseemly even to mention—

was extramarital sex. In the unfortunate event they should be approached by a prostitute, conscripts were encouraged to slap her and walk away. On Sundays, they should go to church.[83]

Between the formation of the German Empire and the outbreak of the First World War, nonresistance eroded steadily. At the same time that secular pacifist movements were gaining modest traction, Mennonites distanced themselves from peace witness.[84] Urban churches, especially, censured the tenet. "In relation to the old Mennonite principle of nonresistance," northwest Gronau resolved, "the congregation is in consensus with a great number of other German Mennonite congregations that the earlier justifications concerning the fulfillment of military duty in Germany, which essentially promotes the protection of the fatherland, no longer stand."[85] Even conservatives increasingly tolerated weapons. When West Prussia's rural leadership adopted a common confession of faith in 1895, they admonished congregants to "avoid the abomination of war" but did not tie membership to any particular form of service.[86] Constituent groups were free to make their own rules. Schönsee, for instance, designated noncombatant roles as most "consistent with the nature of our congregation," but acknowledged that "according to God's word and the laws of our country, we do not have the right to revoke the membership of congregational members who perform full military service."[87] Pacifism had become less as a corporate doctrine than a personal choice. By the twentieth century, it was little more than a historical inclination among Germany's Mennonites—a matter widely understood but rarely discussed, best left to individual conscience. Some men did continue to avoid arms. Yet with flagging support from parents and preachers, nonresistance became increasingly difficult. In 1914, a remarkable two-thirds of conscripts performed full military service.[88]

As rural conservatives moderated their positions on a host of issues—intermarriage, childrearing, education, and pacifism—many joined the Mennonite Union. Whether because they absorbed the organization's ideology or saw it as a strategic partner, opposition crumbled. Already by the fin de siècle, unionists were hailing the culmination of their German Mennonite movement. As Hinrich van der Smissen assessed, the deepest antipathies had dissipated. Members had risen to the challenge of modernity, exchanging indifference for solidarity. Admittedly, a majority of congregations had not yet filed for membership. But with the exception of south Germany's Amish Mennonites, the largest conferences seemed ready to join. Even the barrier between urban and rural communities was losing prominence. Designating the nineteenth century the first great epoch of German Mennonitism, van der Smissen lauded his coreligionists for stepping beyond their regionalism. Having recognized power in numbers, many had embraced a centrally administered Union, capable of supporting the needy, caring for scattered families, engaging the state, training new preachers, and fostering relationships with coreligionists outside the homeland. At long last, this organization would utilize "the strength of the whole for the general good."[89]

Van der Smissen's appraisal was prescient. With the addition of West Prussia's large Heubuden congregation in 1914, the number of rural Mennonites in the Union outnumbered urbanites for the first time. And while the organization still represented less than half of all congregations, the combined population of its twenty-seven member churches now comprised 70 percent of all Mennonites in the empire.[90] Conservatives were undoubtedly swayed by fears of demographic decline, which unionists continued to portray as a confession-wide calamity. "Only when the distance between our various groups is overcome," Hermann Mannhardt reiterated, "can our congregations be saved from their steady demise."[91] This refrain lost none of its potency in the years before the First World War. Especially with Europe's budding arms race—in which nationalists across the continent raised the stakes in their game of comparative demographics—unionists redoubled their commitment to evolutionary ideas like species fitness and group perfectibility. Treating Mennonitism as a coherent population, they tied the fate of individual families to the destiny of the confession as a whole; if the loss of even one person adversely impacted coreligionists everywhere, each congregation should join the common struggle. While the stream of youth leaving rural villages did flow on, unionists often turned it to their advantage. Fostering contact with scattered Mennonites—both through the distribution of periodical literature and the appointment of traveling preachers—they created a nationwide network of sympathetic individuals and families. And as young people moved to urban areas, new congregations formed in cities like Munich and Hannover. Several even joined the Union, further expanding its influence.

The Union's success represented less an epistemic rupture, however, than one moment in an ongoing and highly contested debate about the nature of Mennonitism. Broader political and economic processes may have provided stimuli for some members to leave their homes, pursue technical training, or marry outside the faith. But macro-events like industrialization and universal conscription were not indicators of a coherent modernity. Rather, they constituted a shifting cultural backdrop against which modernist claims could be understood. In this context, religious indifference was less an accurate characterization of individuals' personal outlooks than a motivational strategy, designed to produce certain types of action. Unionists combined the concepts of indifference and modernity. Categorizing certain modes of Mennonite-ness as indifference, they mapped them onto one end of a temporal continuum stretching from a problematic past into a bright future. Insisting that all members should gravitate from pre-modern disunity toward a single teleological outcome, these leaders employed indifference as a tactic of demographic control. At its most effective, this strategy induced widespread change, pushing parents to behave differently toward their children, congregations to reverse their stances on interconfessional marriage, or young men to perform full military service.

During the first decades after Germany's formation, progressive Mennonite leaders consolidated ranks within national borders. But with the outbreak of the First World War, their gaze would turn outward. As the empire became entangled in a worldwide conflict, unionists extrapolated new understandings of religious kinship across oceans and continents, developing a truly global program.

CHAPTER 4

WORLD WAR, WORLD CONFESSION

INTERNATIONAL VIOLENCE AND
MENNONITE GLOBALIZATION

The distress that the World War brought over the
nations ... has drawn Mennonites across the entire
world more tightly and inwardly together.

—MICHAEL HORSCH AT THE FIRST MENNONITE
WORLD CONFERENCE, 1925[1]

On a September day in 1915, Emil Händiges arrived at a German prisoner of
war camp called Bütow. As the Mennonite pastor entered the compound,
hundreds of faces surrounded him. "I saw the various types of Russians and
Poles," he recalled; "the Jews, many of whom spoke German, showed a particularly lively and vocal interest." But it was neither Jews nor those he labeled Russians or Poles whom Händiges had come to see. He sought the
thirty-six Mennonites in the crowd. All were conscientious objectors from
Imperial Russia, who had been serving as medics on the front when German troops captured their train. For Händiges, these Mennonites were not
enemies. Their pacifist beliefs meant that none had ever fired a shot against
Germany, while their supposed German characteristics set them apart from
other denizens of the tsarist empire. "How admirably our brethren stuck
out from their surroundings! Already outwardly from their different clothing: they wear their leather medical smocks; and how German they are in
their entire being!"[2]

Händiges considered the prisoners members of a worldwide Mennonite
diaspora, scattered geographically but united by nationality. While persecution and migration might long ago have separated their congregations, the
pastor found it only natural to spend the afternoon with his coreligionists,
worshiping in the camp chapel, singing, and reading the Bible. Händiges'
visit to Bütow was not merely an acknowledgment of Mennonite globalization, however. It was a globalizing act in its own right. During the following weeks, the story of his encounter made its way into Mennonite homes
across the world. The event symbolized confessional indivisibility: even

during "this terrible time of war, with the dreadful enmity and unholy divisions that it brings between nations," Mennonitism could not be fractured.[3]

Such claims of wartime solidarity owed less to long-standing legacies than to the conflict at hand. For progressives in Germany, the war had generated new possibilities. Having spent the prewar years asserting their Germanness at home while cultivating relationships with coreligionists abroad, leaders like Händiges saw international violence as a means of unifying these objectives. At one level, they hoped military service would enable Germany's Mennonites to overcome decades-old accusations of cowardice, thereby securing their place in the nation. More broadly, they saw the conflict as a Mennonite "holy war." Depicting the Central Powers as protectors of vulnerable congregations in France, Germany, Austria-Hungary, and Imperial Russia, they cast victory as a pan-Mennonite imperative.[4]

Yet if the war provided a vehicle for narrating Mennonite globalization, it also generated new forums for dissention. While leaders in Germany encouraged draftees to fight and die for their homeland, few Mennonites abroad—especially in Entente countries—had strong incentives to praise German war aims. Moreover, most were pacifists. Like the medics interned at Bütow, draft-aged men throughout the Russian Empire, Canada, and the United States largely refused to take up arms. Conscientious objection further prompted disavowals of Germanness; considered German sympathizers by local nationalists, many insisted that they eschewed killing for religious reasons and not because they supported Germany. Perhaps the most explicit rejections came from the beleaguered colonies in Imperial Russia. Denying they were German at all, spokespersons asserted Dutch nationality.

The Bolshevik Revolution of 1917, however, did more to spur a global Mennonite consciousness than leaders in Germany had dreamed possible. As formerly tsarist lands spiraled into famine and civil war, an international welfare community began to mobilize. Leaders across Europe and North America developed plans to extricate all 100,000 of their coreligionists. Comparing their confession to other persecuted minorities, such as the Armenians in the Ottoman Empire, they exploited a postwar climate saturated with Wilsonian notions of self-determination and racist predilections for white agriculturalists. By the early 1930s, they had relocated 24,000 Russian-born migrants to the Americas and established a semi-autonomous "Mennonite State" in Paraguay.[5]

GERMANY AT WAR

In August 1914, the most common image used to describe the conflict engulfing Europe was that of storm. A whirlwind of violence, commentators agreed, had shattered the fair weather of peace. Such language resonated with Mennonites in Germany who described the arrival of "the terrible storm of war" like "a bolt of lightning from the placid sky."[6] Authors struggled to render the catastrophe meaningful. "We are experiencing the judgment of God," one preacher wrote, blaming Europe's "godlessness and ambivalence, presumptuousness and cultural pride, sins and vice of all kinds." Just as brimstone destroyed Sodom and Noah's flood had drowned the world, "so is it with the storm that has broken over us."[7] The natural imagery of water, wind, and fire, especially when bound to visions of an angry God, bolstered calls for mobilization. One Mennonite portrayed God as a discerning farmer. Winnowing fan in hand, the deity would "sweep his threshing floor and collect the wheat into his barn; but he will burn the chaff with eternal fire."[8] More prosaically, God would grant victory to Christian Germany.

Interpreting the war as a divine contest of the nations, patriots considered participation a holy prerogative. "We German Mennonites bind ourselves to the fatherland," Union chairman Hinrich van der Smissen declared. "All will do their duty."[9] While women and girls volunteered with the Red Cross, their husbands, sons, and brothers would perform military obligations. Anabaptism itself became linked to the war effort. Ministers identified sixteenth-century martyrs as models for Mennonite soldiers. Just as Felix Manz, Michael Sattler, and Balthasar Hubmaier had gone singing to the grave, their spiritual heirs were expected to give their lives for Germany. The doctrine of nonresistance received little support. Although some conservative elders promoted weaponless service—still a right for conscripts in Prussia and Baden—neither the Mennonite Union nor the Mennonite Soldier Commission put their weight behind it. In a nod to rural traditionalists, Union leaders did tout the confession's long-standing separation from the state, especially encouraging draftees to refuse oaths of fealty.[10] But noncombatant privileges, by contrast, were depicted as the last barriers to "truly equal citizenship."[11]

Discussions of pacifism once again drew accusations of cowardice. As theaters around the country booked nationalist plays, several chose Ernst von Wildenbruch's 1878 drama, *The Mennonite*. By late 1914, this critical portrayal of nonresistance had debuted twice in southern Germany and was scheduled for Berlin's Royal Theater. Unionists protested its resurrection. "The damage [its performance] will cause in the hearts of many Mennonites who are loyal to Germany," spokespersons wrote to the Royal Theater's director, "are far greater than any resulting upswing in patriotism."[12] After meeting with a Union delegation, the director agreed to strike the play. In part, his decision signaled a change in national culture. *The Mennonite*'s anti-Catholic overtones no longer flamed the passions they had during Bismarck's *Kulturkampf*. But decades of confessional propaganda had also reshaped the religion's image. Even non-Mennonite journalists reported that "German Mennonites now perform armed service with the same enthusiasm as Catholics and Protestants."[13] Indeed, of the approximately 2,000 members in uniform, only one-third chose noncombatant service.[14] Unionists were pleased with these numbers. But they continued to ask, "What can and must we do in order that we do not lose this first zeal?" It would not be enough to sing patriotic songs and to cheer outgoing troops: "We must grasp the holy earnestness of the moment in all its greatness. We will only achieve this if in the violent roar of the storm of the times, we learn to listen to *the voice of God*."[15]

If the interweaving of environmental and eschatological imagery helped orient Mennonites toward German nationalism, it also prompted internal consolidation. When ministers spoke of lightning and floods, they evoked not just the collapse of a larger European peace, but also the battering of their own religious garden. Commentators had long cast their "little nation" as an idyllic farming people, living close to the land and blooming with the earth they cultivated. It was appropriate that this myth, crafted through the rhetoric of ordered nature, would invite counter-images of climatic disorder. From Hinrich van der Smissen's perspective, the only comparable travesty in living memory was the "devastating flooding of the Vistula Delta twenty-six years ago." In 1888, a raging Nogat River had broken its protective dams, emptying across Baltic Prussia to ravage seven of the region's largest congregations. Flooding thus held a particular terror for Mennonites in these areas. According to tradition, the first Anabaptists to arrive in the low-lying delta had received toleration because of their water engineering abilities. Fleeing Western Europe's bloody Reformation, they settled on barely habitable soil. But they had drained, dammed, and diked until their holdings counted among the richest in Europe. As they staked their reputation on the transformation of the Baltic landscape, inundations became anti-Mennonite phenomena. It was a religiously specific charge, then, to portray the 1888 flood as but a rain shower in comparison to the "misery already wrought by the war's ghastly tempests."[16]

That Noah's flood emerged as a potent descriptor was no accident. A cataclysm submerging the earth beneath waters of judgment, the Bible's first apocalypse evoked the situation of Germany's congregations. In the *Mennonite Journal*'s telling, prewar harmony had facilitated global connections. "How often we rejoiced," its editors wrote, "when some piece of news we published reappeared in another of the confessional papers, perhaps in Holland, then in America, and then again in Russia or Galicia. In this way our paper ... made it possible for us to share the most important stories with our readers in all countries where Mennonites live." But as war severed these ties, Germany's congregations found themselves cut off, floating in a rising sea. The *Journal* maintained contact with Switzerland and Austria-Hungary, but for weeks, there was no word from France, North America, or Imperial Russia. When a single Mennonite periodical finally arrived from the United States, staff received it "with the same joy as the olive leaf that the second dove brought Noah on the ark."[17] Channels of communication slowly reopened. By 1915, newspapers carried reports from Mennonite pastors, soldiers, and refugees in both enemy and allied states, keeping readers well informed about conditions across the Atlantic world. With more Mennonites underway than ever before, small populations were even discovered in Luxemburg and Macedonia. As their knowledge of coreligionists abroad grew, many learned to see the war through confessional geography. Journalists fused the course of the conflict with the fate of their faith, structuring their reports around the effects of battles, treaties, and troop movements on local congregations. Trench warfare became an emergency for Alsatian Mennonites; fighting in Galicia threatened the Lemberg church; US neutrality fortified nonresistance overseas.

If the war created a distinctly Mennonite crisis, observers perceived peril to be external, not intra-confessional. Hinrich van der Smissen, for one, defended the relationships "that in the last generation have been cultivated with so much energy and love between our congregations across the entire globe."[18] That these ties straddled geopolitical divides did not dictate their disintegration. The Union chairman admitted that each population would remain loyal to its respective government. Mennonites in British Canada or tsarist Russia should not be expected to defect to the German cause. But, as van der Smissen happily added, the chance that any would meet in battle was negligible. The only substantial community outside Germany to favor military service lived in the Netherlands, which was likely to remain neutral for the duration. Otherwise, the vast majority were nonresistant. Pacifists, for their part, generally criticized their militant coreligionists, although some were willing to overlook the point, framing them as victims of a larger tragedy, coerced by the German state to defend their homes, families, and nation. Especially in the United States, where most Mennonites spoke German and held collective memories of Central Europe, commentators did sometimes look favorably on the Kaiser's war aims.[19] There, as well as in neutral Switzerland and the Netherlands, well-wishers collected humanitarian aid for families in Alsace-Lorraine, East Prussia, and Habsburg Galicia. Leaders in Germany thus credited the war with strengthening the "threads of love between our coreligionists hither and thither across land and sea."[20]

THE RUSSIAN CRISIS

Overshadowing this hopeful picture were developments in Russia. An Allied belligerent locked in deadly struggle with the Central Powers, the tsarist state possessed the overwhelming majority of Europe's German-speaking

Mennonites. Observers in Germany were used to thinking of these colonists as intrepid pioneers, but now their fortunes had fallen. Since the war's onset, tsarist officials had revived old Russianization efforts. Maintaining that "every German in Russia is a spy" and that "every German village is a strategic point for Kaiser Wilhelm," policymakers waged a campaign against perceived enemy aliens.[21] Regulations prohibiting German-language use struck at the heart of communal Mennonite life, including schooling, worship, and the press. And in 1915, land liquidation laws threatened farmsteads with state seizure. Authorities in Volhynia cleared a "safety belt" to protect the front, deporting approximately 400,000 individuals to the country's interior.[22] Although most Mennonites fell outside this zone, fears of expropriation caused a run on the market, depressing land and livestock values.

Spokespersons asserted their loyalty to Russia, distancing themselves from Germanness. They dispatched delegations to the Duma and wrote petitions to the tsar. "The Mennonites have never, nor will they ever forget what they owe Russia," one booklet assured, casting Germany's aggression as an attack on their own colonies, "for no other European state has given them what Russia has."[23] Although most of the empire's Mennonites did not perform armed service, young men accepted noncombatant or alternative duties. Some 6,000 undertook forestry work, while an equivalent number joined the medical corps. But despite this participation, their position remained tenuous. With rights sharply curtailed and the repossession of their land seemingly imminent, some began to contemplate "mass emigration."[24]

The plight of coreligionists in Russia became the defining disaster of the war for many of Germany's Mennonites. Palatinate pastor Christian Neff depicted the colonies at the heart of a clash of civilizations. "The struggle of states," he predicted, "will become a struggle of the races." No longer in a tolerant, multiethnic empire, this literally defenseless German minority was being "throttled" by "racially withdrawn, deceitful, and cunning" Slavs.[25] Prewar narratives of Mennonites as diasporic Germans provided a familiar repertoire. One author retold the story: long ago, settlers had arrived in south Russia to find the soil rich and black, "lacking only diligent hands and progressive agricultural knowledge." As they dug their plows into the virgin loam, flowering villages arose, filled with neighborly families and many children. When the first colonies became too crowded, "daughter colonies split off, moving to the east and south. They traveled to Crimea, to the other side of the Volga and across the Caspian Sea, finally sending their offshoots as far as Siberia." Already within this triumphalist depiction, however, lay a dark inverse. If the settlers had been intelligent enough to cultivate the "fecund and fertile" land, the implication was that previous inhabitants had failed to do so—that they were culturally, technologically, and racially inferior. Just as other Europeans spoke of civilized explorers traveling into the African "heart of darkness," Mennonite writers portrayed their colonies as "blossoming islands in the middle of Russian barbarianism."[26] With the coming of the war, these islands faced dissolution from the surrounding Slavic sea. Images of flooding once again signaled confessional danger.

Leaders like Neff advocated the colonists' repatriation to Germany. At the same time the Ottoman Empire and other states were deporting, exchanging, and murdering minorities, these activists promoted a "population transfer" of their own. Attempts to move entire communities based on nationality—whether Armenian, Jewish, or Mennonite—helped normalize the fledgling discourse of "ethnic cleansing," whose consequences would prove so tragic over subsequent decades.[27] Unless the settlers rejoined their original mother congregations, observers feared that they would be annihilated: "If the Mennonites remain in Russia, then they are lost for our Germandom and for our confession. A tremendously promising branch of our confession will disappear without a trace."[28] Despite their century-long separation, the two communities allegedly remained connected by cultural traits like modesty, industriousness, and piety. Just as any German might travel for a week through Eastern Europe without transforming into a Slav, Mennonite colonists had preserved their nationality across multiple generations—or so the argument went. The critical term "repatriation" suggested that because they had once emigrated *from* Germany, it was now possible to *return* to it.

Already in 1912, an organization called the Welfare Agency for German Remigrants had approached Russia's Mennonites about relocating to Germany.[29] At the time, spokespersons had rejected the idea. Their colonies were prospering, and as pacifists, they could not comply with German conscription. "We have imbibed the notion of nonresistance with our mothers' milk," one teacher observed. "*It is a Mennonite dogma.*"[30] Even following wartime anti-German legislation, there was little chance of a change in opinion. And besides, as some nationalists in Germany noted, the issue of military nonparticipation might outweigh any benefits. Hermann Mannhardt contended that although the colonists were "admittedly of Low German heritage and have a German essence and German character, they possess not the slightest political affinity for the German Empire." Under no circumstances, he cautioned, should a substantial number resettle. Mannhardt and his associates had spent the last half century ridding pacifism from their own congregations; at the very moment that charges of cowardice were finally dissipating, it would be madness to import 100,000 colonists who would "shirk their duty to defend the fatherland." As for the potential immigrants, Mannhardt expected they would want little to do with their militarist coreligionists: "In no way do they perceive us German Mennonites as their equals. In their eyes, we are no longer Mennonites."[31]

Indeed, Russia's congregations were not only unimpressed with Germany and its inhabitants; many were skeptical that they themselves possessed any German "essence." Through speeches, editorials, and petitions, spokespersons identified their origins not in provincial Prussia but in the Low Countries of the Reformation. Emanating from Friesland and Flanders, they had spent three centuries migrating across northern Europe in search of religious freedom. "Our blood is purely Dutch," some Mennonites argued—sounding much like their Protestant neighbors, who claimed they were more Swiss than German. "Among ourselves we speak either Russian or Dutch (the Frisian dialect) and not German. Our first names and family names are all Dutch. We cultivate religious relationships to Holland and not to Germany."[32] Although they had "never paid much attention" to their Dutch past, as one writer put it, Russia's Mennonites had supposedly always claimed this heritage; they were not simply repudiating older pro-German sentiments now that the Kaiser was violating their country's western flank. During the 1899 Boer War, they were said to have followed events in Africa with great interest and "often spoke of their Dutch origin and their kinship with the Boers." This Dutch creation myth became well-polished and widely disseminated. One estate owner, hoping to protect his property, wrote to Tsar Nicholas II: "The Mennonites are native citizens of Great Russia, ready to sacrifice everything for their beloved tsar and fatherland. How wrong are those who consider Mennonites to be the so-called 'colonists from Prussia'! They ignore the truth that our *ancestors came from the Netherlands, contemporary Holland and Belgium, and belong to the Dutch nationality.*"[33] Another petition concluded: "*Not a drop of German blood flows in our veins. ... We reject everything 'Germanic'!*"[34]

Despite minimal encouragement from Russia, leaders in Germany continued to advocate mass repatriation. Brushing aside claims of Dutch ancestry, they reasoned that the settlers had become German over the centuries. "German was the place from which they migrated to Russia," Hinrich van der Smissen noted. "German is their language, their customs until this very day; German education has trained their younger generations for decades and has effected a great blossoming in their colonies."[35] If they were so Dutch, the Union chairman quipped, why couldn't a single one of their preachers hold a Dutch sermon? Hoping for state backing, van der Smissen's organization drafted a letter to German Chancellor Theobald von Bethmann-Hollweg. In the name of the "entire German Mennonite community," it implored the chancellor to support repatriation, portrayed as a potential victory for Germany. Leaders explained that the only requirement would be to extend those privileges enjoyed by current Mennonite citizens—namely, exemption from oaths and freedom to choose noncombatant service. Pacifists would not come without these rights. But once on

German soil, their objections would fade. "We German Mennonites," the Union assured, "have become ever more supportive of full military participation, as we have proven in the present war."[36] It was only a matter of time until Germany similarly modernized their coreligionists.

The Mennonite Union was not the only body interested in Russia's colonists. Confessional leaders across Europe and North America proposed various settlement schemes. Outside Germany, it was usually assumed the settlers would have to leave the continent, as all conceivable European destinations, including the German Empire, Austria-Hungary, England, and the Netherlands, required military service. Some commentators, persuaded by assertions of Dutch ancestry, suggested that they resettle to Dutch Indonesia or potentially to Australia. Others talked of South America, Africa, and Ottoman lands. Perhaps the most serious option was North America, where some 18,000 Mennonites had resettled from Imperial Russia in the late nineteenth century. Many congregations in Canada and the United States, eager for reunification with their relatives, hoped to bring the remainder across the Atlantic. Activists in Germany opposed this solution, arguing that the colonists would be as lost in English-speaking North America as in Slavic Russia. "We German Mennonites are convinced," the Union's Directorate explained, that a transatlantic move "would not be in the best interest of our German-Russian coreligionists." Once they entered America's "melting pot," immigrants' German characteristics would slip away, and they would be lost to the nation.[37]

Colony leaders continued through the final days of tsarist rule to assert Netherlandic origins. They even enjoyed fleeting success: in January 1917, Tsar Nicholas recognized his Mennonite subjects as Dutch.[38] Yet within weeks, social upheaval forced the monarch's abdication. With the Russian Revolution, and especially during the Civil War that followed the collapse of a short-lived Provisional Government, settlers had to parley with new groups. As coreligionists in Germany pieced events together, political change had not improved their situation. If possible, it was drastically worse. Promises of a communist utopia threatened dispossession just as surely as tsarist liquidation laws. More immediately, the Civil War wove a horrific tapestry of robbery, rape, and cold-blooded executions. Witnesses told of mass graves and villages burned to the ground. "Bolshevik hordes" reportedly gutted south Russia in a "rage of plunder and destruction against the Ukrainian population and above all against the German colonists."[39] By 1918, reports circulated of a counterrevolutionary White Army, heavily armed and fighting pitched battles with bandits, brigands, and Bolsheviks. In May, the first personal letters arrived in Germany since the second, Bolshevik Revolution. "For the last three months, we have lived in constant anxiety, literally trembling for our lives. Robbers and murderers became our rulers," one colonist wrote. "Revolvers were pressed to our foreheads at the slightest provocation."[40]

With Russia's disintigration, Germany emerged as Eastern Europe's unparalleled military power. The Central Powers soon invaded eastward, capturing much of the Baltics and the Black Sea region. Local Mennonites saw the German army as a liberating force, and they prayed for its arrival. "A great unrest pervades the German colonies," one Mennonite wrote, "and we hope that in the next days the German troops will come as far as the Chortitza Mennonite colonies. From there it isn't far to the Molotschna region."[41] When the two largest settlements of Chortitza and Molotschna came under German control, colonists greeted the first trainloads of soldiers with jubilation. "The day will remain unforgettable," one eyewitness wrote; "our station has never—even during the mobilization—seen such a crowd of people.... It was a miracle! First of all they were Germans, and second they were our saviors from the greatest need and danger of death."[42] Mennonites quartered soldiers in their homes and sponsored patriotic festivals. The German military, meanwhile, organized Mennonites and other German speakers into paramilitary Self Defense forces. Despite local traditions of nonresistance, pro-German enthusiasm and a desire for protection led many to abandon pacifism. Providing machine guns and other munitions, army officers trained members for combat on the steppes.[43]

For the first time, Mennonites in tsarist or formerly tsarist lands considered immediate exodus to Germany. "These years have effected among us Mennonites—even among us—a great transformation, not only in relation to the religious principle of nonresistance, but also in our relation to Russia," one leader wrote. "Now we are, thank God, no longer in Russia, but in Ukraine, and it remains to be seen how this state will take form and if it will succeed. But I have little desire to wait and see, as we are dealing here with the Slavs, and that says enough."[44] When the Central Powers and Soviet Russia signed the Treaty of Brest-Litovsk, the repatriation of German nationals became a formal right: "For a period of ten years after the ratification of the peace treaty, the members of every participating country of the treaty who originate in the territory of another participating country shall be allowed ... to remigrate to their land of origin."[45] Although a majority of Russian-born Mennonites already lived in German-occupied territory, the agreement offered the remaining colonies—mostly located in Siberia—access to the German state. It did not specify whether repatriates would be exempted from military service, but spokespersons wrote to Germany, hoping to settle the matter quickly.[46] The Mennonite Union worked to facilitate their move. Union officials partnered with coreligionists in Siberia to form a Settlement Society for Mennonite Remigrants. Based in Berlin, the new organization cooperated with the Imperial Office for German Remigration and Emigration to facilitate the "settlement of ethnically German Mennonites from former Russia."[47]

Throughout the spring and summer of 1918, the Union Directorate discussed logistics with leaders from Siberia and Ukraine. While some delegates continued to propose settlement in North or South America, most favored locations within Imperial Germany. Hinrich van der Smissen encouraged the establishment of colonies in Posen and West Prussia. The government had for years offered cheap farmland in its northeastern provinces for German-speaking settlers, including those returning from abroad. By the war's midpoint, the Royal Prussian Settlement Commission—intending to bolster German populations in predominantly Polish-speaking areas—had resettled more than 130,000 people in six hundred farming villages.[48] Proponents argued that the return of Russia's Mennonites would counteract the racial threat of Germany's Polish minority. "Would not the danger posed by the Poles," one local asked, "have been significantly decreased, if the hundred thousand Mennonites who settled in Russia had been retained for us West Prussians?"[49] In this way, colonists' reintroduction promised both to prevent their own demise and to strengthen anti-Polish initiatives at home. Relocating several refugee families to rural areas, Union activists prepared destination points for a coming migration.

Others favored resettlement to Germany's overseas colonies. Although most of the African territories—including large parts of the continent's eastern and western coasts—had been lost to Allied troops, optimists predicted their reintegration into a victorious German Empire. With its warm climate and fertile soil, East Africa would supposedly allow Mennonitism to flourish. Another perceived benefit was that white Christian immigrants would make good missionaries. Evangelists from the tsarist state had long provided the backbone for Anabaptist missions to Indonesia, a partnership hindered by the war. Settling 100,000 in the tropics would recoup wartime losses, while benefiting Africa's "primitive natives."[50] Still others advocated the creation of an autonomous "colonial state" in Eastern Europe.[51] If the conflict had frustrated German overseas imperialism, it simultaneously enabled a colonial drive to the East. There, dictators Paul von Hindenburg and Erich Ludendorff administered a brutal military state, known as Command East, in lands conquered from the Russian Empire. Hindenburg and Ludendorff intended much of this region to become a puppet country, a strategic buffer zone whose Jewish and Polish residents could be expelled and replaced with German-speaking colonists from the Soviet Union. The plan held appeal for Mennonites since it would allow them to retain large-scale farming techniques developed in south Russia.[52]

Had it not been for the war's end, one of these schemes may well have come to fruition. But while Mennonite leaders worked with army and civilian officials to influence enormous territories and populations in Eastern

Europe, events to the west thwarted their plans. Military defeat in autumn 1918 forced the Central Powers' capitulation. In the face of a November 11 armistice and the subsequent Treaty of Versailles, repatriation halted. In addition to mandating German troops' withdrawal from Command East and all occupied areas of the Soviet Union—including the Mennonite colonies along the Black Sea—negotiators stripped away large regions belonging to Germany before the war. Allied mapmakers transferred its western rim to France and portions of its eastern provinces to a reconstituted Poland and the new Free City of Danzig. After the reshuffling, Germany's Mennonites discovered that far from bolstering their population with transfers from the old Russian Empire, the war had drastically reduced their numbers. Two of the densest areas of settlement, Alsace-Lorraine and West Prussia, were no longer German. Not only had four hundred Mennonite soldiers died, but whole congregations were metaphorically amputated, reduced to German-speaking minorities in foreign states.

INTERWAR MIGRATION

Punitive peace terms set a bitter stage for interwar relief. "Only a month ago," Hinrich van der Smissen lamented at the end of 1918, "who among us could have dreamt that our nation and army would face without recourse such an oppressive ceasefire!"[53] Perhaps the greatest travesty for leaders like van der Smissen was the distance that the armistice created with colonists to the East. They anticipated that with Germany's dismemberment, the creation of a new Polish Corridor, and Soviet Ukraine's increasingly rigid border, the question of repatriation would recede. Once a near certainty, it now seemed impossible. Van der Smissen recalled how the war's first years had led coreligionists in "Poland, Galicia, the Ukraine, and Siberia to actively seek fellowship with our German Mennonites. It was more than a dream for the future that these brethren would come and ... establish a safe home on the soil of an expanded Germany."[54] Still holding onto memories of Eastern victories, defeat felt sudden, depressing, and complete. Now, there was little choice but to turn to the reconstruction of their country, a project that paralleled the necessity of confessional rebirth. Just like Germany, Mennonitism would rise from the rubble: "Difficult work has always been the fountain of youth for our Mennonite people; the strength we derive from our persecution has always been able to pull us together."[55]

Yet while Germany discussed postwar plans, the conflict in the East raged on. Far from returning the former Russian Empire to peace, armistice in Western Europe unleashed a new phase of paramilitary violence. As German troops withdrew from the Black Sea, they left a power vacuum in their wake. Bolsheviks, monarchists, Ukrainian nationalists, and anarchists of every sort sensed an opportunity to assert their claims. Independence fighters declared two separate Ukrainian people's republics, as well as an anarchist Free Territory; local warlords waged their own offensives; and communist revolutionaries sparred with counterrevolutionary Whites over plans for two mutually exclusive multinational empires.[56] As Red, White, and Black armies washed over the Mennonite colonies like a vindictive tide, they left a gruesome residue of starvation, disease, and death. In this chaos, Mennonites were not merely victims or onlookers. While some continued to tout nonresistance, a rising number—hoping for a return to the prewar order—embraced violence. Hundreds were conscripted or volunteered with the White Army, serving as drivers, gunners, or infantrymen. In one battle, a joint Mennonite-Cossack battalion captured the small city of Tokmak with five hundred soldiers and two tanks. Other fighting-aged men remained in Self Defense militias, taking up arms alongside neighboring Protestant and Catholic German speakers. The largest predominantly Mennonite force, composed of 2,700 men in twenty companies, operated around the Molotschna colony. Commanded by officers left by the retreating German military, these soldiers fought a variety of enemies, including Bolsheviks, army deserters, and above all the anarchist leader Nestor Makhno. Mennonites won some minor victories, especially as they concentrated forces around Halbstadt, the colony's administrative center, swollen with refugees from outlying towns.[57]

But the Self Defense units provoked as many attacks as they prevented. Already tainted by their association with the German army, whose dismal treatment of non-German speakers had alienated much of the population, Mennonite involvement in the Civil War generated further antipathy and cast them in the doomed camp of the reactionary Whites. At the same moment that their legendary abundance of food, wagons, and animals became targets for underequipped anarchist and communist forces, Mennonites' wealth, religion, and perceived Germanness combined to signify the antithesis of the revolutionary ethos. Many Russian and Ukrainian speakers, having worked on Mennonite farms or in their factories, were predisposed to see them as foreign parasites and abusive employers. Nestor Makhno himself had begun work on one estate at age eleven. In his memoirs, the anarchist later identified the ill treatment he received as the origin of his "anger, envy, and even hatred" toward the landowning classes. With disgust, he recalled the children of his Mennonite master, "those young slackers who often strolled past me sleek and healthy, well-dressed, well-groomed and scented; while I was filthy, dressed in rags, barefoot, and reeked of manure from cleaning the calves' barn."[58] If men like Makhno welcomed turmoil as means of reversing power relations, most Mennonites preferred the old order. Leftists were unwelcome in their villages, and when Red or Makhnovite troops sought to requisition supplies, the Self Defense militias labeled them "bandits" and escalated encounters. Zealous young men as-

A Mennonite mass grave in Blumenort, Ukraine, 1919. Coreligionists across Europe and North America followed the Civil War with horror, particularly the retributive massacres committed by followers of the anarchist Nestor Makhno.

sassinated local revolutionaries and reportedly shot peasants who came to beg for food.

Although Mennonite casualties were lower than those of other populations near the Black Sea—an estimated 3,000 colonists, roughly 5 percent, died of war, famine, or disease between 1914 and 1923—commentators in Germany presented the situation as a systematic attack against all things German.[59] Reports told of "whole families butchered," of bodies "found with arms and legs hacked off, their ears cut off and their eyes stabbed out."[60] Mennonites across Europe and North America spoke of the rape of women and children, of men shot down in the streets, prisoners hacked to death in cellars, and whole villages put to the torch. As external observers tried to take stock, letters flew across the Atlantic with news—always several weeks belated—of the latest battles and atrocities. "Our Russian coreligionists cry to us in terrible pain," one assessment read. "Nameless is the distress that the World War has caused. The flourishing colonies are largely destroyed, laid in ruins and pillaged. Everything is destroyed: commerce and trade, industry and agriculture. Many villages are fully depopulated.... The typhus epidemic rages horribly. Whatever is not taken by the sword and the bullet falls to this ravishing disease."[61] In early 1920, four prominent Mennonites escaped the carnage, beginning a speaking tour across Germany, the Netherlands, Canada, and the United States. Abraham Friesen and Benjamin Unruh, two surviving leaders of the Molotschna colony, led the group. "My colleagues and I are traveling only because of the need of our congregations," Unruh informed his audience. Their "situation harkens to that in the book of Exodus."[62]

With the Bolsheviks' conclusive victory, many Mennonites hoped to abandon their homeland. "Boys, if you can emigrate," one dying mother told her children, "then go, even if you have to leave everything behind."[63] A number who had fought against communism were already gone, fleeing south or west with the remnants of the White Army. Although few of those remaining welcomed the Civil War's outcome, most tolerated the ceasefire with mixed relief and trepidation. An uneasy peace returned. While the poorest, most religiously conservative, and vehemently anti-Bolshevik prepared for emigration, their wealthier and more accommodationist neighbors began reconstruction.

In the newly formed Ukrainian Soviet Socialist Republic as well as the larger Russian Soviet Federative Socialist Republic, Mennonite leaders cultivated relationships with powerful government offices, securing greater autonomy than comparable populations. Despite their official atheism, Soviets' policies toward religious groups were not uniform, and small nonstate confessions fared much better than did Russian Orthodoxy. Under Vladimir Lenin's relatively liberal New Economic Policy, Mennonites experienced unusual latitude in establishing emigration agencies, religious advocacy groups, and interregional agricultural cooperatives. Authorities allowed conscientious objectors to seek military exemption, although the bitter legacy of the Self Defense militias caused difficulties for Mennonite applicants. Some later chroniclers even wrote of the 1920s as the "golden years" of Anabaptist church life and evangelism.[64] A subset joined the Communist Party, and several committed themselves to combatting religiosity. In a searing tract entitled *Anti-Menno*, one Chortitza native attempted to foment class struggle among his former coreligionists.[65] But such opinions were in the minority. Bolshevik agents reported that "Mennonites are the strongest sect in Ukraine. They conduct strong religious propaganda ... so as to minimize Soviet influence."[66]

The outbreak of famine in 1921 helped cement ties between Ukraine's Mennonites and the Soviet bureaucracy, particularly the agricultural ministry. Following seasons of bad weather, crop failure combined with the devastation of the Civil War to yield miserable harvests. Although paramilitary violence had subsided, mass hunger now cost the region six million lives. "The torture of starvation," one Mennonite wrote, "haunts the population worse than all the experiences of war and the terror of banditry we have undergone."[67] Unable to feed its dying citizens, the Soviet state opened Ukraine to foreign aid workers and struck tariffs on humanitarian goods. Concerned governments and welfare organizations across Europe and North

America launched a massive relief campaign. The international Mennonite community, likewise, formed several new institutional bodies. In the United States, previously quarrelsome factions reconciled to form a Mennonite Central Committee, or MCC. Leaders in Canada established a Canadian Mennonite Board of Colonization, while those in the Netherlands created a General Committee for Foreign Relief. In Germany, the Mennonite Union reformed its wartime aid programs into German Mennonite Aid, designed to unify "all the members of our faith to provide significant, effective, and long-term assistance for our Russian brethren in need."[68] While this organization sent food packets, clothes, and bibles, its better funded counterpart in the Netherlands delivered entire shiploads of foodstuffs, clothing, medical supplies, seeds, and farming equipment. Mennonite Central Committee signed its own bilateral contracts with the USSR. According to their first agreement, "American Mennonites desire to participate directly in this humanitarian service of relief for the needy in a spirit of love, peace, and goodwill, regardless of race, religion, or social status," although they preferred "the regions where their co-religionists are suffering."[69] Rural congregations in the United States' Midwest, many of which hailed from Imperial Russia, shipped fifty Ford tractors to the colonists. MCC established some 140 soup kitchens across Ukraine, serving 75,000 individuals, including virtually all of the area's 60,000 Mennonites.[70]

Meanwhile, Germany's economic collapse handicapped German Mennonite Aid. "A peace reigns today that has not created any real state of peace," Hermann Mannhardt complained. "And all peace work is hindered to no end by the sad political conditions in which we live."[71] Runaway inflation slashed currency values, making it difficult for the organization to buy relief materials or to send them abroad. The ruin wrought by war and the penalties imposed at Versailles nearly bankrupted all of Germany's most prominent Mennonite institutions, including the Union and *Mennonite Journal*, as well as many congregations. Continuing to hope for large-scale repatriation from the USSR, leaders kept establishing refugees on pilot settlements, particularly in Mecklenburg and Bavaria. But these efforts bore scant fruit. Few migrants chose to farm the poor land available, and most who tried eventually gave up and moved to Canada. Conditions in the Weimar Republic were so bad that ministers struggled to preserve their own congregations. With their prewar population already redistributed into four different countries, they feared further demographic erosion. Young Mennonites, discouraged by the democracy's low employment rate, sought opportunities in other parts of the world. Leaders attempted to prevent a mass emigration from Germany similar to the one they simultaneously promoted in the Soviet Union. "Remain true to your homeland!" they reprimanded; "just as the fatherland still needs you, so too do our congregations."[72]

With little money flowing from Germany, the burden to fund Ukrainian relief fell on North America and the Netherlands. Founders of German Mennonite Aid acknowledged their helplessness without Mennonite Central Committee, and they dubbed themselves a "German branch office" of this organization.[73] Nevertheless, they portrayed the Weimar Republic as a key staging ground. In 1925, the country's significance was formally confirmed when local ministers planned a Mennonite World Conference, inviting counterparts from across the globe to return to their confession's "birth place" in northern Switzerland. Over the following decades, further summits would continue to shape aid operations in the USSR.[74] A healthy public interest also cemented the German-centric character of these ventures. One "thinks especially of [Mennonites], when one speaks generally of the German colonists," commentators noted, rendering their plight symbolic of the larger crisis of Germandom in the East.[75] Some members capitalized on this sympathy, fleeing the Bolshevik state and requesting asylum from Germany. In one instance, the arrival of sixty refugees at the Polish border sparked a minor international crisis. Fearing for their safety if returned to communist lands, coreligionists from the United States, Switzerland, and the Netherlands traveled to Germany, where they pooled funds and negotiated custody of the migrants.[76]

This incident seemed to confirm claims of German nationality. The statutes of German Mennonite Aid insisted that Germany "is the homeland of the Russian Mennonites. Although they left it one hundred years ago, they remain bound to it by the unbreakable bonds of history, language, faith, culture, family, and friendship. The German occupation of south Russia already saved the colonists once from a sure demise, and the indescribable memory of this liberation lives in the heart of every Mennonite in Russia."[77] The assertion was partially true. For many colonists, the war had indeed created a sense of German identity. "Remaining in Russia under Slavic or Jewish-Slavic rule among an overwhelmingly racially alien people," argued a local leader named Peter Braun, "would mean the destruction of our national character."[78] Utilizing anti-Slavism and anti-Semitism, writers like Braun encouraged emigration.[79] The end effect was to further alienate colonists from their Russian- and Ukrainian-speaking neighbors. One Mennonite explained that before the war, congregations in Imperial Russia had not seen themselves as particularly German. But when hostilities commenced, "it became ever more apparent to us whose national children we were, where we really belonged, for whom our hearts beat." Assistance from Germany solidified this process: "We had been awakened out of our blissful childhood slumber to a [German] national consciousness."[80]

And yet, assertions of Dutch ancestry remained very much alive. Given the global prevalence of anti-Germanism, the weak state of Germany's economy, and restrictions on German nationals' mobility, some Mennonites in or from Soviet territories once again found it advantageous to present themselves as Dutch. Only after six weeks of negotiation, for example, did Benjamin Unruh and Abraham Friesen gain exit from Constantinople, receiving French travel permits as "Mennonites originating in Holland."[81] Others seeking emigration saw little prospect in Germany's overcrowded rump state, and they turned to other options, including royal Dutch holdings. Leader J. J. Hildebrand of Siberia wrote to Amsterdam in 1921, requesting the "repatriation" of 25,000 coreligionists to the Dutch colony of Suriname in South America. Hildebrand explained that since leaving the Low Countries, Siberia's congregations had remained distinct from surrounding non-Dutch populations "through language, culture, and religion, as well as through the purity of blood."[82] Leveraging racial kinship, he solicited military exemption and one square kilometer per family. A year later, spokespersons in Ukraine contacted the Netherlands' Queen Wilhelmina, proposing settlement in their "old homeland."[83] Analogous appeals to Canada and the United States likewise portrayed hopeful immigrants as Dutch.

Efforts to relocate minorities wholesale were increasingly common. The rising rhetoric of national self-determination lent spokespersons unprecedented authority on the global stage. After forming in 1920, the League of Nations became an arbiter of minority protection treaties, guaranteeing rights in multinational areas—such as the ability to school children in their alleged mother tongues—as well as organizing population transfers between states. Beginning in 1923, the League famously brokered the exchange of 350,000 Muslims in Greece for approximately one million Turkish subjects believed to be of Greek origin. Despite the violence that invariably accompanied national un-mixing, observers generally considered it a means of peacebuilding that would minimize inter-ethnic strife over the long term.[84] Yet such projects rested on an unstable foundation, namely the self-evidence of national affiliation. As nationalists everywhere knew full well, ethnic categories could be easily manipulated. The case of Mennonitism in the USSR provided an extreme example. Confessional leaders considered national ambiguity both an asset and a liability. On one hand, they could plausibly claim membership in a variety of collectivities. Yet the hybrid nature of their language use, origin stories, and cultural practices also underscored the tenuousness of their position. Slight shifts in international mood, state laws, or bureaucratic discretion could radically alter how they presented themselves or how the world saw them. While the League of Nations categorized members as "Russian refugees of German origin," others perceived them as Dutch or simply Mennonite.[85]

Narrating nationality was complicated by colonists' efforts to simultaneous lobby German and non-German actors. In 1922, when leaders in Ukraine renamed their flagship relief organization Association of Citizens of Dutch Heritage, they drew ire from coworkers in Germany. As Benjamin

Unruh fumed from Berlin, "that title will cause us great difficulties." He explained that German politicians were beginning to speak of a "Judas disposition" among the Mennonites and warned that "Our Dutch ancestry" should not be "so publicly inscribed as on a flag for all to see."[86] Just as important, however, was that the settlers retain independence of action. If word spread that the Netherlands or any other country was willing to accept migrants, they should be ready to cut ties with Germany.

In fact, it was Canada that finally opened its doors. This represented a major victory. Since the start of the World War, Mennonites in the British Dominion had experienced harsh discrimination. Patriotic Canadians decried their German-language use—especially conservatives' refusal to school their children in English—as well as their pacifism. At a time of national crisis, racial and religious prejudices were quickly institutionalized. By 1916, the government had disenfranchised conscientious objectors; all Mennonites were denied suffrage a year later; and in 1919, an Order-in-Council barred entry to Mennonite, Hutterite, and Doukhobor immigrants. "Owing to results of the war," lawmakers explained, "a wide-spread feeling exists throughout Canada ... that steps should be taken to prohibit the landing in Canada of immigrants deemed undesirable owing to their peculiar customs, habits, modes of living, and methods of holding property."[87]

The escalation of nativist, anti-Mennonite sentiment in Canada demonstrates how seemingly bounded events shaped global relief efforts. By denying entry to refugees from the USSR, Ottowa forced Mennonites on multiple continents to articulate appealing national narratives. Leaders courted Canadian policymakers by asserting their assimilability into North American culture and stressing colonists' agricultural value. Only in 1922, after years of pressure, did the country repeal its ban on Mennonite immigration. But even so, mobility remained highly regulated. The Minister of Immigration and Colonization stipulated that refugees could enter only if extant congregations guaranteed housing and employment. The Canadian Mennonite Board of Colonization contracted with the Canadian Pacific Railway for more than $1 million to transport migrants from Ukraine to Manitoba. Health stations in Latvia inspected passengers' medical suitability, and through German Mennonite Aid, any who failed these tests waited out their ailments in German transit camps. Between 1923 and 1926, 20,000 settlers—one-fifth of all Mennonites in the Bolshevik empire—relocated to Canada. Until the Soviet-Nazi population transfers of the late 1930s, this was the most substantial legal emigration of a national or religious minority out of the USSR.[88]

Before running its course, however, Bolshevik authorities turned against the exodus. Although political and economic stabilization dissuaded most colonists from leaving, Party officials became troubled by the drain into capitalist Canada. Mennonitism became a category of police surveillance in 1924, and over the next half decade, the Central Committee's Secretariat discussed it a dozen times, never favorably. Echoing tsarist Russianization campaigns, officials denounced colonists' "closed-off nature" and accused them of rejecting communism for "the interests of Mennonites world-wide." Such charges acquired new gravity in 1928 with Joseph Stalin's "Revolution from Above," a violent process of class warfare and social collectivization. Decrying the continued power of "kulaks"—a derogatory term for wealthy farmers and industrialists—the dictator called for their "liquidation as a class." Qualities that once made Mennonites attractive to Soviet leaders, including international ties and agricultural expertise, now rendered them suspect. While Stalin did not officially target national minorities, local prejudices enabled disproportionate abuse. German speakers were considered "fascists" or "kulak colonizers to the marrow of their bones."[89] As Mennonite land was seized and reorganized into collective farms, leaders experienced imprisonment, banishment, and execution. By 1933, 2.1 million Soviet citizens—including an unusually high number of Mennonites—were deported to Siberia, Central Asia, and the Far North.[90]

THE MENNONITE STATE

With violent demonstrations against collectivization igniting across the USSR, thousands of Mennonites demanded emigration. Abandoning their possessions, colonists from Siberia, Ukraine, and elsewhere descended on Moscow, requesting passage to Canada. By late 1929, 13,000 refugees—mostly Mennonites—were encamped in the capital. Fueled by Western journalists in Moscow, Riga, and Berlin, the story swept the international press. "At a single blow," Emil Händiges marveled, "the whole civilized world was made aware of the small religious confession of the Mennonites."[91] Germany's government initially took little notice, but popular outcry forced it to act. The "return of the settlers to Siberia is not politically acceptable," the Foreign Office determined. "German public opinion is already strongly interested and will not understand if the farmers of German origin are ... abandoned to certain demise."[92] For eight tense weeks, diplomats, reporters, and League of Nations officials struggled to extract the refugees. Benjamin Unruh helped form Brethren in Need, a new aid association sponsored by Protestant, Mennonite, Jewish, and Catholic relief agencies, as well as the German Red Cross. The organization initiated a nationwide pledge drive. "A catastrophe has befallen Germans abroad!" its plea read. "Starvation, economic distress, and political events have driven thousands of German farmers from their homes in Siberia. A German hunger march has begun in Russia!"[93] President Paul von Hindenburg set an example by donating 200,000 reichsmarks, and by late 1929, the Soviet Politburo agreed "to let Mennonite kulak elements from the USSR emigrate in separate groups."[94]

Although more than half were ultimately refused exit, 4,000 Mennonites, along with a smaller number of Catholics and Protestants, arrived in German transit camps. The whole event was deeply unsavory for the USSR, and German-Soviet relations emerged severely tarnished.[95]

Where the 4,000 expatriates would ultimately settle remained unclear. At the same time the League of Nations debated the future of other religious minorities, such as Assyrian Christians in Mesopotamia, a host of actors argued over the Mennonite refugees. Receiving food, clothing, and medical attention in the German camps, they waited for a new home. Canada, most migrants' first choice, had once again closed its doors. Just as the Soviet Union erected barriers to keep Mennonites in, Canada did so to keep them out. The influx of 20,000 during the middle of the decade had led some critics to speak of a Mennonite "invasion." Nativists charged that they were racially undesirable and complained that they took the country's best land. "If we cannot obtain British and good northern European settlers," one trade association argued, "it would be better to have no new immigrants at all." The Canadian Mennonite Board of Colonization defended migrants' racial worth, insisting that they had refrained from miscegenation with Slavs and were positioned to "become assimilated with the Anglo-Saxon race."[96]

Germany emerged as another alternative. Several nationalists developed a short-lived plan to colonize wasteland in East Prussia. "The German farmers," one diplomat told Hindenburg, "have distinguished themselves through outstanding diligence and efficiency and would be extremely well suited to populate ... the border regions."[97] But few found this option desirable, and the government preferred to relocate them to Brazil, already home to some 600,000 German speakers. Co-sponsored by Germany and coreligionists in the Netherlands, 1,200 refugees settled in Brazil, while another 1,000 managed to enter Canada.[98]

Yet because Brazil would not guarantee military exemption, the North American Mennonite Central Committee opposed additional transports. Instead, MCC proposed the formation of a "Mennonite State" in Paraguay. Anabaptist statism had been on the rise since the first land liquidation laws in tsarist Russia. As thousands in Eastern Europe either were forced from their land or immigrated to Canada, they developed narratives of a lost homeland. Tales of ruin at the hands of anarchists and Bolsheviks emphasized their colonies' previous affluence, retroactively constructing a prewar golden age of Mennonite colonialism, culture, and self-governance.[99] MCC adapted such discourses, imagining Paraguay as the site of a new theocracy—despite the absence of historic connections to the country. Just as some Zionists considered a return to British-controlled Palestine impractical, instead advocating Jewish resettlement to Uganda or Argentina, Mennonite nationalists believed Paraguay's Gran Chaco could provide a new place of refuge.[100] "One and a half million hectares," according to the project's architects, "stand in a block entirely unpopulated and at our disposal." With a temperate climate and rich alluvial soil, the Chaco appeared to be one of the largest undeveloped lowlands in the world. Although it remained "economically very backward," MCC ascribed this to its extreme "lack of inhabitants."[101] In fact, the Chaco was already home to some 60,000 indigenous people.[102] Their alleged primitivism, which Paraguayan politicians contrasted with enlightened Europeanism, helped confirm for Mennonite observers the land's availability.

Paraguay already possessed a small Mennonite population. In 1921, the country's government had carved out a semi-autonomous region in the Chaco for conservative immigrants from Canada. Since the wartime enactment of anti-German legislation, these traditionalists had sought a new homeland where they could teach their children German and practice pacifism unmolested. While some settled in Mexico, others requested colonization rights and religious freedoms from Paraguay. Local nationalists initially opposed the inflow, charging that without exposure to wider society, the migrants would remain outsiders. One detractor feared that in fifty years, the country would be entirely overrun: "the official language would be German, all of the inhabitants of Paraguay would be Mennonite." Others opposed their conservative beliefs. "Logically and legally," they argued, "we should consider superior the last Indian of the Chaco to a foolish people like ... the Mennonites."[103] Proponents eclipsed such concerns by depicting the settlers as bearers of culture, claiming that they would build bridges and railroads or bring values like honesty, progress, and hard work. Paraguay eventually allowed entry to all Mennonites, regardless of age, physical health, or mental capacity. It also granted special freedoms, including the right to German-language schools and exemption from oaths and military service.[104] When the first 1,700 migrants arrived from Canada in 1927, commenters hailed them as the vanguard of a pioneer army.

Confessional leaders portrayed the Chaco as a haven for persecuted coreligionists across the globe. Measuring half the size of Belgium, it was large enough to accommodate "all the Mennonites of the world." MCC imagined that every member in the Soviet Union could be transferred to this "state within a state." Mass settlement would serve political as well as religious purposes: while Paraguay's government hoped white Christian colonists would "civilize" the natives, MCC saw indigenous inhabitants as targets for evangelism. Once these peoples were converted or driven out, the Chaco would become a uniquely Mennonite space. "The fact is," advocates explained, "no culture exists there. There is no danger that the Mennonites with their German culture will disappear into a foreign culture. The little Mennonite nation, with its culture and its faith, can live in peace under the best conceivable conditions."[105] Hard labor and international aid

Colonial encounters in the "Mennonite State," 1931. Although settlers found the Paraguayan Chaco far from uninhabited, they generally viewed indigenous populations as primitive and non-threatening, targeting them for civilizing and evangelization efforts.

could transform the wilderness into a garden, comparable to Russia's prewar colonies. During 1930 and 1931, 1,600 refugees arrived from the Weimar Republic, joining those already in residence from Canada. A smaller number came from Poland. And in 1932, a fourth wave—under the co-sponsorship of MCC, Germany, and the League of Nations—sailed from a refugee camp in northern China.[106] While North American observers characterized the settlement from Canada as a "pure theocracy," administered by elders and preachers, they considered the newer community an "amalgamation of church and state." Organized "on identical lines after the pattern of the ancient Mennonite autonomous organization in South Russia," each village possessed an elected magistrate, or *Schulz*, while the entire settlement had a general superintendent, or *Oberschulz*.[107] A colony assembly served as legislative body, and although delinquents received corporal punishment, there was no militia or standing police force.

Echoing MCC, many immigrants portrayed themselves as state-builders. "The Chaco is more than the South Russian steppes were for our forefathers," one colonist wrote. "I am convinced that this will be the place where our Mennonite people come together from all parts of the world." Another reasoned, "We are all of Dutch-Prussian origin but have been separated for 150 years. We nevertheless feel that we belong to the same tribe, the same people." But high rhetoric belied material realities. Despite MCC's claims of agricultural paradise, arrivals found the Chaco hot, dry, and brutal—threatening to confirm fears that white Mennonites were ill suited to tropical climates. Living in tents until they constructed mud brick huts, refugees suffered heat during the day and frost at night. Disease ravaged the villages. One hundred kilometers of bush separated them from the closest railway station, making consumer goods difficult to obtain. Food was short and labor difficult, while fresh water was nearly impossible to find. "We were sold to South America like sheep," one settler charged; "the preachers always said that they left [the Soviet Union] for religious reasons. I'll tell you how it is. The capitalists of Germany bought the preachers, and then they had to travel around in Germany to criticize our Russia.... Everyone wants to leave [the Chaco], because if we stay here, we'll all die." Dissatisfaction ran so deep that MCC feared the project would be abandoned. "Your struggles are our struggles," it reassured the colonists. When some agitated for exodus, aid workers disparaged them as "disloyal settlers," arguing that they were damaging the organization by reneging on land and travel debts. "Please continue to keep in mind," Benjamin Unruh wrote, "the eyes of the world—especially the eyes of us Germans—are upon you. If you succeed in proving that the Chaco can be colonized, this will be of great importance to future emigrants."[108]

If the establishment of a "Mennonite State" in Paraguay seemed advisable and even natural to some activists in the early 1930s, it in fact reflected a contentious, ongoing debate about the confession's nationality. The rise of a Zionist-like movement among some Mennonites neither was inevitable nor did it enjoy universal support. That only 4,000 colonists arrived by the decade's midpoint suggests that for most members, it had limited appeal. Those who did participate generally saw the Chaco as a refuge from persecution rather than as a destination in its own right. And given their greatly divergent theologies and backgrounds, settlers' interactions were characterized as much by discord as solidarity. Nevertheless, the project was not anomalous. It presupposed a long history of Mennonite nation-building. Just as nationalist discourses pushed other minorities to articulate their positions toward larger collectivities, Mennonite spokespersons in Germany, Russia, Canada, and elsewhere engaged discussions of national belonging. As the World War inflamed tensions on a global scale, questions of Germanness, Dutch nationality, and Mennonite ethnicity became significant at a truly transnational level. The actions of congregations in Manitoba held relevance for colonists in Brazil or Siberia, while the language used by settlers in Ukraine affected the efficacy of coreligionists in Germany. International violence globalized these relationships, providing justification for cross-border and even inter-continental population transfers. Mennonite leaders throughout Europe and the Americas discovered new power in claims for territorial control and autonomous governance, gaining backing from the League of Nations and multiple national governments.

It was no unanimity of opinion, however, that characterized Mennonites' actions. To the contrary, transatlantic migration was only possible because members' nationality was *not* self-evident. Activists in Canada and the United States maneuvered by emphasizing their compatibility with neighboring Anglo-Saxons. Their coreligionists in Imperial Russia retained property by stressing Dutch provenance, a claim that again proved useful as they sought refuge from the USSR. And in Germany, the Mennonite Union facilitated an archipelago of transit camps by presenting their confession as exclusively German. Without these disparate and clearly contradictory narratives, the mass exodus of nearly one-fourth of all Mennonites in the Soviet Union would never have occurred. Only by telling different nationalist tales could spokespersons win the support they needed.

Yet while leaders in various countries argued over the best means of self-presentation, their disagreements also helped to build a transnational consensus, however tentative, about the nature of Mennonitism. While they split hairs over the details of their history, faith, culture, and destiny, it was exactly these equivocations that helped create a belief—both within and beyond Mennonite circles—that the confession constituted a cohesive transstate entity. After all, it was on this basis that Paraguay offered special privileges to all Mennonite immigrants, regardless of their countries of origin. As much as it revealed members' dissimilarities, the First World War and its aftermath consolidated the idea of a global Mennonite community. The conflict, in the words of one pastor in the Netherlands, "created a momentous bond between all Mennonites of the world."[109] A colleague in Germany agreed: "the suffering and the blood of their countless martyrs has created a band of unity around all. They feel themselves to be *one* tribe, yes even *one* great family dispersed across the whole world."[110] As they carried this new visage into the 1930s, leaders' increasingly racial outlook would give them much in common with a rising Nazi power.

CHAPTER 5

THE RACIAL CHURCH

NAZIS, ANTI-SEMITISM, AND THE
SCIENCE OF BLOOD

> The Mennonites, dispersed across the globe, are the
> corporeal descendants of the "Anabaptists" of the
> Reformation—they constitute a tribal community; all are
> united by the undeniable bond of family, immediately
> recognizable whenever two or more Mennonites come
> together, may they hail from different positions in life or
> from different countries or corners of the earth.
>
> —MICHAEL HORSCH, 1934[1]

In early 1930, a young Mennonite woman posed for a camera. She was thin, perhaps still undernourished from the long journey from Ukraine. Her blouse hung loosely about her shoulders, and she kept her hair woven at the nape of her neck. The photographers, visiting from the Anthropological Institute at the University of Kiel, did not record her name. She was just one of thousands of Russian-born Mennonites in a series of north German transit camps—a data point in a larger sample group. Along with hundreds of her fellow inmates, the unnamed woman submitted to their attentions. She held still as they pressed rulers to her face and pincers to her temples. Turning on cue, she enabled them to calculate the length of her nose, the width of her head, her facial length, nose, ear, and eye height, and the breadth of her forehead. She allowed color charts to determine the tint of her eyes and the hue of her hair.[2]

Since the fall of the Third Reich, histories of Nazism have oscillated between interpretive poles of coercion and consent. The earliest studies, written in the context of denazification, presented race-based nationalism as a socially pervasive force, dominating people's private lives and restricting their ability to resist.[3] On one hand, the subjects of racial testing were indeed at their examiners' mercy. Mennonite refugees examined by the Kiel anthropologists hailed from rural farming communities; they likely knew little about the techniques and purposes of racial science. Hoping to leave for the Americas, they sought camp administrators' goodwill and cooperated with the visiting scientists.

 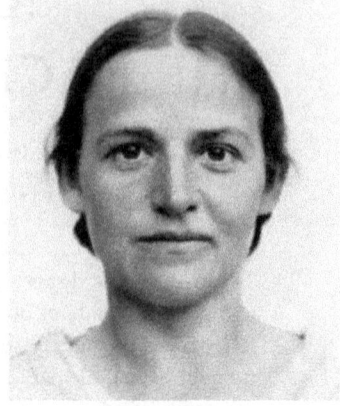

37   38

Scientists in Germany used photography and anthropometry to construct Mennonitism as a category of racial analysis. Such pictures demonstrated the pigmentation and cranial features of racially "pure" Mennonites or the physiological defects of those thought to be tainted with Slavic heritage.

If racial nationalism was unquestionably coercive, it was less predicated on force than some would have us believe. Theories of totalitarianism have done little, for example, to explain the appeal of racial science prior to fascist rule, or how racism helped produce fascism in the first place. More recently, scholars have argued that popular backing for racial nationalism helped facilitate Hitler's rise. Emphasizing spectacle, ritual, and mythology, revisionists insist that "ordinary Germans" underwrote his horrific achievements.[4] Indeed, Mennonites and others often were not merely the subjects of Nazi racism, but also its authors. The racial testing of Mennonite populations, beginning during the Weimar Republic and continuing through the end of the Third Reich, enjoyed broad support. Spokespersons portrayed their confession as a "racial church" years before Hitler became chancellor.[5] Conflating Anabaptism with Germanness, they provided biologists, anthropologists, and eugenicists with access to their bodies and their congregational record books. Researchers generally concluded that Mennonites were more Aryan than the average German. For these scientists, the 500,000 members outside Germany became emblematic of "ethnic Germans," a term referring to millions of people without German citizenship but considered racially German. While they differed over whether to categorize Mennonitism as a unique "race" versus a consanguineous "clan" or "tribe" within the larger German nation, most Mennonite and non-Mennonite researchers conceived it in racial terms.[6]

Although historians emphasizing popular consent for the Third Reich have accurately identified the fluidity of racial nationalism, they problematically assume a distinction between Nazism as ideology and Germans as people. Such approaches imply a relatively self-contained German national community, whose continuity was fundamentally interrupted by fascism's arrival. Yet, as demonstrated by some Mennonites' production of racial knowledge, it would be inaccurate to think of "ordinary Germans" as merely accommodating themselves to racial nationalism. Their actions were often constitutive of it. Studies of Mennonite language, nomenclature, genealogy, and disease, for instance, popularized the notion of a racial church while also providing new means of articulating members' relationships to other confessions. As quintessential Aryans, Mennonites simultaneously became understood as "anti-Jews"—an idea denoting their confession as an Aryan version of Judaism as well as an antidote to Jewish degeneracy. Many observers found the parallels obvious. Both Mennonites and Jews were considered historic religious minorities defined by racial ancestry. Both lived in a global diaspora. And both allegedly possessed characteristic physiologies. But although Nazi scientists cast Jews from the boundaries of the German "racial community," they placed Mennonites at its center. Helping to justify anti-Semitic laws, such narratives implicated the confession in policies of internment, expropriation, and genocide.[7]

MENNONITES IN THE THIRD REICH

In 1933, as the Swastika replaced the republican tricolor over Germany, Mennonites generally welcomed the new Nazi government.[8] Few had been strong supporters of the Weimar Republic. Many associated it—and democracy more broadly—with Germany's defeat at the end of the First World War. Disproportionately affected by the Versailles Treaty, their population had been dissected and redrawn within Poland, France, the Free City of Danzig, and a shrunken Germany. These new borders disrupted economic and cultural relationships, generating support for irredentist politics. Critics further denounced Weimar for its weak stance on the Soviet Union. While Germany refused to re-arm, tens of thousands of coreligionists in the USSR faced dekulakization, collectivization, imprisonment, banishment, starvation, and death. Attuned to Bolshevik violence, some Mennonites thus interpreted Hitler as a messianic figure. Shortly after he achieved power, the Conference of East and West Prussian Mennonite Congregations wrote to the Führer, expressing their "deepest thanks for the mighty revolution, which God has granted our nation through your energy."[9]

Mennonites began joining the Nazi Party well before Hitler took office. In Munich, the cradle of National Socialism, members appeared on Party rosters as early as 1920, the first year of its existence. Participation was likely most robust in East Prussia and the Free City of Danzig, where the injustices of Versailles and threat of Bolshevism seemed particularly evident. Of seven elders in the Danzig area, five were reportedly Party members.[10] According to Harold Bender, a US Mennonite familiar with the region, "in Eastern Prussia at first the party made its progress largely on the basis of Mennonite participation."[11] While Bender's assessment was overstated, Mennonites did exercise moderate influence in regional politics. After 1933, several members or former members with long-standing ties to National Socialism served as county commissioners, including for the districts Marienburg and Stuhm in East Prussia, and for Großes Werder in the Free City of Danzig. Others headed Party chapters, funded Nazi cultural houses, or ran regional agricultural organizations. Ernst Penner represented the Nazi Party in the Prussian Parliament.[12] And Otto Andres rose to the lieutenant governorship of Danzig-West Prussia, acting as Albert Forster's second in command. While not all these men held congregational affiliation, they generally maintained informal ties and advocated policies favorable to Mennonite interests. When Hitler requested information on the confession, Commissioner Walter Neufeldt helped ministers gather materials for the Führer. "Future founders of religions," Hitler reportedly told Neufeldt, "should take Mennonite traits as examples!"[13]

Given their congregations' rightist orientation, church leaders anticipated little trouble from the Nazi state. "Our political loyalty is impeccable," the aid worker Benjamin Unruh assessed. "That is because the overwhelming majority of German Mennonites were always nationally oriented and welcomed Hitler's project with open arms."[14] If they followed voting patterns among neighboring Protestants—a demographic likely to support Nazism at the poles—large numbers of Mennonites probably cast ballots for National Socialism in the elections leading up to the "seizure of power."[15] Nevertheless, the Mennonite Union and other conferences worked to ensure independence. As Hitler and his allies took control of the country, they expected all organizations to align their agendas. Religious institutions came under special scrutiny. In a climate favoring muscle, hierarchy, and centralization, confessional leaders worried about their freedom. The banning of political parties, as well as a broader wave of paramilitary violence, demonstrated the situation's gravity. Jews, communists, Jehovah's Witnesses, homosexuals, and anyone considered hostile to the regime suffered rising discrimination. In March, the first concentration camp appeared. Mennonite observers imagined a worst-case scenario in which Nazi bureaucrats would merge their congregations, along with other small churches, into a Nazified version of the Protestant Church.[16]

Leaders convened a series of emergency conferences. Their first goal was to forge "a national Mennonite Union that the German state will legally recognize."[17] Protestant Nazis, who argued that religious diversity fractured the racial community, stoked fears of assimilation. One pastor in East Prussia suggested a nationalized "Third Church" for the Third Reich, in which "The various sects and church groups must be set aside to create space for a unified faith community!"[18] Local Mennonites were incensed. *"Hands off our German Mennonitism,"* they retorted. "We ... reject every attempt to infringe upon the existence of our religious confession." Spokespersons sympathized with the proposal's nationalistic pathos but felt it ignored their faith's unique cultural contributions. Convinced that Germany's "oldest Free Church" deserved its own place in the sun, they initiated an overhaul of their national Union, streamlining its (increasingly authoritarian) Directorate while reengaging the old drive for comprehensive membership.[19] Framers unveiled an updated and Nazi-friendly constitution in June 1934. Re-christened the Union of German Mennonite Congregations, its statutes read, "Honoring worldly authority and human order, [the Union] considers it Christian duty to faithfully serve nation and state."[20]

The reformers' second objective was to shore up loyalty within their confession. Already, the Union had lost a number of young people, including pastoral candidates, to Nazi populism. Its leadership feared a greater exodus. Commentators worried especially about the "German Christian" movement, National Socialism's religious wing. Influenced by the anti-Semitic writer Alfred Rosenberg, the German Christians advocated the elimination of all "Jewish" elements, such as the Hebrew Bible, from Christian practice. Most Mennonites condemned these efforts, preferring to worship Jesus in his historical context. "Whoever discards the Old Testament," one pastor warned, "also discards Christ."[21] Individuals occasionally found the German Christians' veiled neo-paganism grounds to repudiate Nazism outright. The movement's founding in 1932 prompted discussions of the question "Can a Christian be a National Socialist?" As one skeptic responded, "The National Socialist promotes Christian culture only as far as it is in his own interest. He knows only one goal: race! Everything else is subordinated to this. Even Christianity is cut away, and only the 'positive Christianity' that can serve the German race is kept. We must reject that. It is idolatry and therefore godlessness. For us there is only one goal: to erect the Kingdom of God among all nations. As Mennonites we reject National Socialism."[22]

But such opinions were the exception. Although few Mennonites were sympathetic to German Christianity, most expressed greater dismay at its ability to attract converts than toward its theology. It was to prevent losses within their own ranks that leaders resolved: "The 'Religious Movement of German Christians' must be seen as a religious current within the Protestant Church, and therefore the members of our faith are asked to refrain from joining."[23] Spokespersons simultaneously emphasized their overall support for National Socialism, hoping that despite selective criticism, they would be allowed to preserve confessional autonomy. "Our duty is to build up our congregational life," Benjamin Unruh explained. "In this, we have not been disturbed. We have regular church services and not once have they been disrupted. Neither have our meetings, with the exception of our conferences."[24] As long as they were held in church buildings, large gatherings could occur without police presence.

Institutions deemed inessential were sacrificed. In 1936, leaders sanctioned the transformation of the Weierhof School, Germany's last surviving Mennonite educational establishment, into a "Napola," one of forty-three elite Nazi training academies. Although the Weierhof School had retained ties to the Mennonite Union, it served a mostly non-Mennonite constituency. Policymakers were attracted to the academy in part because it was one of only a handful of "Jew-free" schools in the Palatinate. While it had once enrolled a disproportionately high number of Jews, the board expelled all Jewish students in 1890.[25] Four decades later, overseers offered little opposition to nationalization. "School policy is being unified throughout the Reich," one leader remarked. "The Mennonites are stepping into line."[26] If young members opposed such changes, congregational authorities were willing to silence their voices. Youth groups around the country had long debated controversial topics through circular letters. While many were openly pro-Nazi, some questioned the Party's totalitarian claim to stand above biblical teachings. When Party censors discovered these sentiments in 1937, a group of elders in southern Germany pressured the adolescents to end their correspondence. Acknowledging that it could prompt "state intrusions into the life of the Mennonite congregations," organizers agreed to strike "political" content.[27]

For members seeking Nazi posts, swearing supplied the only formal hindrance. Congregants in German lands had historically refused oaths of fealty, holding allegiance to God paramount. Through the First World War, conscripts in Prussia had been allowed to affirm loyalty through a verbal "Yes," followed by a handshake. Other states enacted similar policies. But when Hitler resurrected Germany's military in 1935, recruits were required to say: "I swear before God this holy oath that I will render unconditional obedience to the *Führer* of the German Reich and nation, Adolf Hitler, the Supreme Commander of the armed forces, and as a brave soldier I will be prepared at any time to give my life for this oath."[28] Reich law and Party regulations provided similar formulas for anyone in the justice system, the bureaucracy, or the Party's paramilitary or youth subsidiaries. Church leaders objected to the words "swear" and "oath" as contradicting Anabaptist principles. "Many Mennonites have experienced a severe conflict of conscience," the Union informed Nazi executives. "It cannot aid the intentions of the Reich government nor the principles of the Party if Mennonites are advised to controvert to their baptismal vows."[29] In reality, most were willing to swear. Nazi official Martin Bormann noted that "only in isolated and exceptional cases have the members of the Mennonite congregations refused."[30] A majority of relevant organizations nevertheless exempted them by 1938—although oaths remained required for leadership positions.[31]

More controversial, if less supported by confessional spokespersons, was nonresistance. During a decade when millions of German citizens supported rearmament, especially to reconquer territories lost through the Treaty of Versailles, opposition to military service signaled a rejection of common goals: "There can be no place in our fatherland for people whose religious beliefs directly undermine the nation's military objectives."[32] Mennonite leaders sought to reassure themselves, the government, and the wider public that their pacifism was dead and buried. "Through the constitution of the 'Union of German Mennonite Congregations,' the principle of nonresistance has been fully *abandoned*," Chairman Emil Händiges informed Nazi bureaucrats. "*Today* the German Mennonites perform military duties without any qualifications. Already before the reintroduction of universal conscription, many Mennonites from the Reich and the partitioned territories voluntarily joined the army."[33] As in earlier years, armed service remained tied to national belonging. Jews—who had long faced accusations of "stabbing Germany in the back" and causing the Central Powers to lose the First World War—attempted to prove that a proportional number of their members had died in battle.[34] Mennonites, similarly, provided statistics on their own war heroes. Although less than 2 percent of their population had fallen (an embarrassing third below the national average), spokespersons emphasized that hundreds had served as officers or received war medals. Some congregations, the Mennonite Union proclaimed, lost 6 percent.[35]

Young people were more likely to treat pacifism as a museum object than a living creed. "Hasn't the entirety of our German Mennonitism capitulated in the face of this problem?" one boy asked.[36] Some were willing to defend the tenet as part of an honorable past. According to Emil Händiges, "we do not need to be ashamed of our forefathers, not even of their nonresistance."[37] Echoing critiques of peace theology from the *Kulturkampf*, this position assumed that modernity had fundamentally transformed warfare. Sixteenth-century Anabaptists allegedly did not protest fighting per se, but rather fighting for religious goals. Unlike Hitler's pan-German objectives, Reformation-era Catholics and Protestants had killed fellow Germans simply for following a different creed. Only Anabaptists abstained from this Aryan fratricide. "No German can deny the true German character of these people, whose forefathers endured torture, prison, and death for this principle," an amateur ethicist exclaimed. "No, these were no cowards! They were heroes." But these were heroes of the Reformation, not the Third Reich. Here, a new heroism held sway. One girl summarized her coreligionists' mood: "The majority of young Mennonites feel indebted to Adolf Hitler; they unconditionally support military service because, if the need should arise, they wish to defend their fatherland."[38]

This was, in some ways, a new turn of events. Pacifism had experienced a minor resurgence during the Weimar Republic. Some observers connected the doctrine to a wave of anti-militarism sweeping interwar Europe, often transmitted through contacts outside Germany. US delegates to the 1925 Mennonite World Conference called for a common Anabaptist "opposition to all war," while in the Netherlands—where pacifism had long fallen from grace—ministers once again proclaimed it "a special Mennonite principle."[39] These ideas took tentative root in war-devastated Germany, surviving in isolated instances into the Third Reich. Unionists even considered adding pacifist wording to their revised statutes. "It is a matter of individual conscience," an early draft read, "which form of state-approved military service one chooses to perform."[40] Although this language never made it to press, the organization was willing to contemplate "relevant steps" should any "conscripted individuals oppose service for reasons of conscience."[41] A few did join the medical corps—later a point of evidence in claims of Mennonite resistance to Nazism—but no more prominent test case ever arose.

In 1935, the propaganda film *Frisians in Peril* briefly entangled the confession in a public debate about pacifism. Directed by Reich dramaturge Willi Krause and distributed by the Nazi Party, critics hailed *Frisians in Peril* as Germany's most important picture of the year. Joseph Goebbels labeled it "highly valuable for the state and race," and Party functionaries arranged screenings for the Hitler Youth. Set in Ukraine after the Bolshevik Revolution, the film followed a small Mennonite colony's struggle against the new Soviet government. Portraying Bolsheviks as Semitic and Asiatic brutes, the film cast Mennonites as their Germanic antithesis. Termed "Frisians" in accordance with Nazi racial terminology, they appeared as a heroic pioneering people whose hearty Aryan stock gave them the strength to withstand communism. Nonresistance provided the film's moral dilemma. When young Mennonite men plan to take up arms in self-defense, their congregational elder implores them to forgive their tormenters. "Even those," the men ask, "who have stolen our horses? Who rob us? Who take our women?" "Yes," the elder replies, "Even them." This stance only emboldens the Soviets, however, and the futility of pacifism becomes increasingly clear. In the final scenes, the once peace-loving elder loads his revolver and organizes the colony's men into a militia. They surround their house of worship, which the Bolsheviks have turned into a drinking hall. Guns blazing, the Mennonites slaughter everyone inside and burn the church to the ground.[42]

Mennonites' onetime pacifism rendered them uniquely useful to Nazi propagandists. Overcoming their historic opposition to war made the colonists of *Frisians in Peril* all the more heroic. On one hand, such depictions

The 1935 Nazi film *Frisians in Peril* depicted Mennonites in the Soviet Union as Aryans under attack by Bolshevism and racial defilement. Following Germany's wartime invasion of the USSR, Propaganda Minister Joseph Goebbels rereleased it as *Village in the Red Storm*.

confirmed the confession's induction into the German racial community. Readers and filmgoers across the Third Reich learned about members' harrowing experiences under Bolshevism, their escape from Russia's "red hell," and their travels to Canada and Latin America. Images of Mennonites and other "ethnic Germans"—conjured with angular faces, blond braids, and quaint peasant costumes—became as recognizable as Jewish stereotypes. In addition to *Frisians in Peril*, several of the era's most influential films, including *Refugees* (1933) and *Return Home* (1941), featured Mennonite themes. Novels, short stories, and histories depicted members from the earliest days of the Reformation to the latest clash between Bolshevism and fascism. These accounts fetishized German speakers in conflict: militiamen battling communists in south Russia; schoolteachers fighting anti-German legislation in Canada; pioneers taming the wilds of Paraguay; families overcoming impossible odds to return to their German fatherland.[43] Writers portrayed colonists in the Soviet Union, especially, as victims of martyrdom and genocide: "Through execution, deportation, exile, through sickness and forced racial mixing, the entirety of Germandom in Russia is being systematically annihilated."[44]

Yet pacifism remained a live and dangerous charge. With sectarianism considered as grounds for racial repudiation in Hitler's Germany, violence in the cinema could easily spill off the screen and into everyday life. After watching *Frisians in Peril*, one reviewer erroneously concluded that Mennonitism was "forbidden in the Third Reich."[45] Church leaders responded hastily with a public relations campaign, alternately downplaying their relationship to nonresistance and trying to turn it to their advantage. Benjamin Unruh advised Nazi officials in one letter not to confuse the tradition with "any kind of modern pacifism."[46] Spokespersons like Unruh sometimes argued that, by refusing military duties, coreligionists in other countries positioned themselves to offer more valuable agricultural services. Nonresistance thus bolstered a broader narrative of Mennonite pioneering. Others suggested that pacifism abroad was in fact a form of German nationalism. In the old Russian Empire, military exemption had "luckily spared [Mennonites] the pain of having to bear weapons in the World War against the German motherland and against their racially German brethren."[47] As soon as the enemy shifted, however, the colonists had shed their reticence, taking up arms against communist oppression. Commentators in Germany were keen to point out that in 1918, it had been their coreligionists "and not the Protestant or Catholic Germans in Russia, who organized the Self Defense militias against the Red Army."[48]

Mennonites outside the Third Reich contested such representations. Especially in North America and the Netherlands, pacifists questioned whether their militarist coreligionists, having lost "fundamental Mennonite principles, conscience against war, against religious oppression, against a totalitarian state which demands loyalty to the state above loyalty to God," were even still Mennonite at all. C. Henry Smith, a leading confessional historian in the United States, admonished that "Menno Simons would find himself ill at ease, today, among his namesakes in Germany were he to return to his familiar haunts around the Baltic; in fact he would find himself, in all likelihood, in a concentration camp."[49] Others, however, were more supportive. "We thank the Almighty," the leadership of Paraguay's "Mennonite State" proclaimed, "that He has sent men who will form a strong force against communism; we could not understand why the previous governments did not bring the scourge of communism to an end."[50] Likewise in Brazil and Canada, many congregations cheered Hitler as an antidote to Bolshevism. They imagined that with communism extinguished, Russian-born Mennonites now scattered across the globe could return to Eastern Europe. "We old advocates of *Adolf Hitler*," a Self Defense veteran explained, "believe one day the time will come, when the rightful claim of our fatherland will find realization on colonial soil."[51] For some, Nazism thus symbolized the culmination of international Mennonite relief efforts.

BIRTH OF A RACE

Mennonite activists' most successful strategy for courting Nazi patronage lay in the idea of the racial church. Appeals to Party authorities or government ministries nearly always mentioned the confession's purportedly racial composition. "Mennonitism was an originally *German* ... reform movement," one essay read. "In the world, there are a half million Mennonites. Without exception, they are of German heritage.... Scientific research has conclusively demonstrated that the ethnically German Mennonites, through their church discipline and religious-racial defense system, have protected one hundred percent against the dilution of their blood through the infiltration of foreign elements.... There is likely no other confession in the world that demonstrates such a racially uniform character as the Mennonites."[52] Such narratives were strikingly new. While scholars of Anabaptism had long depicted the faith as a familial entity, unified through Germanic origins and global diaspora, it became linked to explicitly racial discourses primarily during the interwar period. This transition reflected changing scientific and political agendas, academic funding mechanisms, and state interests. Mennonite studies became a subdiscipline during the 1920s within new fields like "East Research," racial science, and the study of Germandom abroad.[53] The two establishments most responsible for pioneering Mennonite race exploration, the Kiel Anthropological Institute and Berlin's Kaiser Wilhelm Institute of Anthropology, Human Heredity, and Eugenics, were founded in 1923 and 1927 respectively.[54]

Scientific interest in Mennonitism intensified during 1929 and 1930, when 4,000 refugees from the Soviet Union arrived in northern Germany, bringing the confession global attention. With these migrants contained in three transit camps, anthropologists seized the opportunity to examine a diasporic group firsthand, comparing them with coreligionists across Germany and the Free City of Danzig. "In the case of the Mennonites," one analyst wrote, "we are confronted with isolated parts of the same racial body, which live in very different environments. It is thus possible to perform a comparison of 'biological twins'—not of two genetically identical individuals, but of two genetically similar populations."[55] Convinced that it constituted "an organic racial community, almost a clan or a large family," researchers treated the confession as a nearly perfect microcosm for testing racial theories.[56] The comparison of migrants from the USSR with their "twin" population along the Baltic seemed particularly compelling, given that most of the refugees' ancestors had once lived around Danzig. The temporary re-convergence of these groups, separated for nearly 150 years, provided an unprecedented opportunity to explore the utility of race as a biological analytic. The results did not disappoint. Upon completing their studies, researchers proclaimed Mennonites to be among Germandom's most genetically distinctive and anatomically impressive specimens. Even those from the Soviet Union, surrounded for generations by Slavic and Central Asian cultures, supposedly possessed a "heredity quotient" of more than 98 percent.[57] Both males and females were prone to light hair, eyes, and skin. Of all Aryans, another study concluded, Mennonites were the tallest outside Scandinavia.[58] In addition to illuminating their anatomical characteristics, genetic researchers claimed to detect a commonly held set of psychological tendencies. One compendium identified members' innate qualities as "simplicity, orderliness, diligence, integrity, detachment, stamina, but also stubbornness, insularity, and severity."[59]

Mennonites' racial uniqueness was typically attributed to their "strict prohibition against marrying outsiders."[60] By emphasizing endogamous marriage, congregations had supposedly maintained biological continuity from the sixteenth century to the present. Even though the first Anabaptists were thought to hail from different parts of Germanic Europe—usually identified as Switzerland and the Netherlands—a dense network of interregional marriages had ostensibly woven these bloodlines into a single genetic pool. While most racialist explanations located the origins of Mennonitism in the Reformation, some went farther back, suggesting that Anabaptism had emerged from Germanic tribes whose patterns of interrelation were already intact. Especially popular was the idea that Mennonites—or at least those with "Dutch" heritage—belonged to the "Frisian" tribe, the oldest and noblest of all Germanic groups, whose racial character could be traced back for millennia.[61] While earlier generations had distanced themselves from coreligionists in the Netherlands, writers now favored such accounts, noting that the "Dutch are a true Germanic tribe, and so among [Dutch] Mennonites, one can still recognize many pure Germans."[62] Others suggested that although they came from Dutch stock, their sojourn on German soil had transformed them into racial Germans. "Previously, when we spoke of being Dutch," the scholar Horst Penner wrote, "it was only in the sense of being a Low German tribe, which through the centuries since 1550 has become racially different from the people in the Netherlands." The first Anabaptists around Danzig may indeed have arrived from the Netherlands, but their descendants emigrated to Imperial Russia and the Americas "not as Dutchmen, but as Mennonite east Germans."[63]

A new center of Mennonite research emerged during the Nazi period at Stuttgart's German Foreign Institute, which, in addition to full volumes, featured the confession in its periodicals, including *Germandom Abroad* and *Yearbook for the Genealogy of Germans Abroad*. Studies of Mennonite economics, society, and culture were especially common. These projects presupposed that "Mennonites in various regions, directly *because* of their Mennonite character, have been phenomenally productive—whether as pioneers of agriculture, as industrialists, as businessmen, or as tradespeople."[64] Academics asserted that congregations abroad offered a glimpse of Germany's past. Cut off from changes in modern Europe, diasporic groups functioned like time capsules. "You are no longer true Germans," one researcher quoted a Russian-born Mennonite as saying; "the authentic German speaks Low German."[65] Long lists of surnames in Germany, the Soviet Union, and elsewhere elucidated interrelation between various groups.[66] Or statisticians focused on Mennonite dialects as a linguistic method of determining links (or lack thereof) with other German speakers.[67] Scientific institutions dispatched specialists across Europe and the Americas. Equipped with cameras and measurement devices, they trekked through prairies, deserts, and jungles in search of remote settlements. The German Foreign Institute's Karl Götz described his visit among conservative "Old Colony" Mennonites in Mexico. "We sat in many houses and took notes," Götz recalled. "We sketched and photographed and tried time and again to trace the genealogical lines back through Canada and Russia to West Prussia and the Danzig area." Researchers like Götz attempted to untangle the "many wandering paths of German blood," systematizing and pinpointing diasporic communities within the larger space of "German fate and history."[68]

Racialist narratives were not simply imposed on Mennonites, however. Anthropological studies could never have occurred without subjects' cooperation. During the 1930s, the Mennonite Union and other organizations facilitated research among their congregations. Individuals willingly submitted to the pokes, prods, and flashes of racial testing. And ministers provided centuries-old birth and marriage registers so heredity specialists could calculate rates of fertility and racial mixing. One biologist praised the "gracious participation of the Mennonites themselves," extending thanks to several elders, including Union chairman Emil Händiges.[69] These leaders relished the attention, attending films, speeches, and museum exhibitions that treated the confession favorably.

More fundamentally, Mennonite activists made such depictions conceivable in the first place. They produced their own Aryanism.[70] Beginning in the Weimar Republic, confessional scholars and leaders popularized the notion of a racial church, especially through the burgeoning field of genealogy. Although earlier generations had drawn family trees and occasionally published genealogies, it was only in the late 1920s that these became objects of serious scholarly study. "Until now, our circles have concerned themselves only marginally with historical family research," one enthusiast lamented.[71] It was a novel idea when another German-born Mennonite, writing in the newly founded US *Mennonite Quarterly Review*, argued that "Mennonite family histories furnish basic material for practically all the objects in view," and that "Mennonite history *per se* would gain a good deal if such researches were taken up systematically."[72] Existing in a realm between science and mysticism, genealogical studies drew on new racial disciplines arising on both sides of the Atlantic. In 1926, the first journal of Mennonite genealogy aimed to marry "the young science of family studies to the cultural as well as the natural sciences." It positioned the "clan," defined as "those who share the same blood," as a subject of biological and historical inquiry. "The same common ancestor lives in you all," the editors explained. "The ancestors *live*, although they are dead, in some little drop of blood—perhaps in a brain cell or a heart chamber—within your body."[73] Notions of racial continuity and group hygiene worked their way into Mennonite theological doctrine. A handbook by Berlin pastor Horst Quiring discussed the God-given "racial-biological differences between peoples and nations." Quiring's volume encouraged ministers to teach "the preservation of the purity of blood, the care for a healthy race" and to "promote genealogical research" among their congregants.[74]

The Mennonite Union incorporated genealogical research into its mandate in 1933 when it helped established a confessional Historical Society. Publishing scholarly books as well as a yearly journal, this organization intended "especially to promote the research of Mennonite family history."[75] In the following years, independent genealogical associations sprang up across the country. They sponsored semi-regular "reunions" and printed volumes of family history as well as, occasionally, their own periodicals. Most were regionally oriented or focused on a single surname, although in 1937, several collaborated on a Consortium for Mennonite Genealogy, providing a unified platform for the study of populations in Germany, Poland, the Soviet Union, and the Free City of Danzig.[76] Genealogists encouraged broad participation. "Listen to parents, grandparents, uncles and aunts—as much as you can get out of them," one practitioner advised. "Hold it fast, write it down, and put it in a dignified form." For the most authentic accounts, "it is best when grandmother, father, or aunt writes down their remembrances in their own word and own script."[77] Family research could also provide a spiritual outlet. The pages of genealogical periodicals, in addition to quotations from Hitler, Goebbels, and other Nazis, featured poetry, religious reflection, and art. One genealogist composed a racialist love poem to an unborn fetus. Entitled "Embryo," it read in part: "How peaceful you lie there. Within you stream the powers and patterns of centuries, fluids and forces of all ancestors who already found form in your father and in your mother.... And this blood, it brings you all that which earlier generations have assembled for you, o unborn child.... For nine months, centuries course through your tiny growing body, and every century forms you further."[78]

Genealogy in the Third Reich became directly linked to citizenship rights. The 1935 Nuremberg Laws established four racial categories for German residents. Based on their number of Aryan versus Jewish grandparents, they were either Aryans, Part-Jews, Half-Jews, or Jews. In order to receive employment, enter a marriage, or pay taxes, self-identified Aryans compiled their own "racial passports." The necessary forms, sold in any paper shop, allowed filers to enter birth, marriage, and death dates for their parents, grandparents, and children. For agencies requiring unusually pure blood, such as the SS, applicants detailed their ancestry as far back as 1750. Many individuals kept going. Enthusiastic researchers developed intricate personal archives. These collections helped produce Aryanism at a tactile level. The crafting of genealogical lists—often with dozens, even hundreds, of ancestors—created an impression of racial continuity, while the physical ordering and reordering of clan members into card catalogues normalized Nazi policies of hiring, relocating, or interning people based on their race. Mennonite genealogists typically linked their work to the larger goal of creating a German racial community, in turn receiving approval from Nazi officials. When one periodical asked Joseph Goebbels to introduce an upcoming issue, the Propaganda Minister called it "extraordinarily valuable."[79] Another received funding through the Treasurer of East Prussia.[80]

Family research solidified the concept of a racial church. When assembling "racial passports," individuals consulted church record books, which Nazi race offices recognized as authoritative sources on Aryan identity. At least one congregation sponsored a formal event for members to complete their ancestry papers together.[81] Deacon Gustav Reimer of Heubuden calculated that without these registries, "proving Aryan ancestry—especially for dates before 1800—would never have been possible."[82] Tying Mennonitism to Aryanism also helped promote favorable attitudes toward coreligionists abroad. National Socialists were more likely to advocate for members in Poland or Paraguay if they were known to possess valuable blood. Proving the collective Germanness of colonists in the Soviet Union seemed particularly critical, since the Russian Civil War had destroyed much relevant documentation. Although émigrés from the USSR sometimes entered Germany without papers, they could verify purity by identifying as "Mennonite." In one case, Benjamin Unruh vouched for a young girl, testifying that her parents were "unquestionably Aryan-German because the strict religious regulations of the evangelical Mennonite congregations strictly forbade mixed marriages. The racial integrity of the Russian-German Mennonites is universally scientifically recognized."[83]

THE ANTI-JEWS

The concept of racial Mennonitism was irresistible for Germany's race researchers—not least because Anabaptism supposedly constituted a Germanic equivalent of Judaism. During a moment when the "Jewish antirace" and its alleged peculiarities were of paramount interest, scholars competed to explain its relation to other collectivities. Nazi philosopher Alfred Rosenberg described Judaism as homeless, drifting, and parasitic in his 1930 bestseller, *The Myth of the Twentieth Century*: "For 2,500 years, we see the same recurring practice. Greedy for the goods of this world, the Jew moves from city to city, country to country, and remains where he encounters the least resistance to his bloodsucking business operations."[84] Had these images been inverted, their connotations would have corresponded with contemporary depictions of Mennonitism. Indeed, commentators frequently likened Mennonites to the "chosen people" of the Old Testament. Like the ancient Israelites, they had survived long centuries of persecution primarily through procreation. "Instead of proselytizing," as one author put it, "Mennonitism had to produce children."[85] Ever on the run from their tormenters or in search of new land, they too had become a wandering, semi-nomadic people. "For four hundred years," wrote a German Foreign Institute researcher, "the roots of these colonists have been ripped out time and again to be replanted in foreign soil." Authors talked of "migration without end," explicating Anabaptist history through litanies of exotic place names: Mennonites had lived "in the Vistula Delta, in the south Russian and Siberian steppes, in Caucasia, in the Ural, in the Canadian prairie, in the Mexican highlands, in the Brazilian jungle, and most recently in the endless bush desert of the Chaco." Emphasizing continuity as well as movement, such accounts echoed the structures of Rosenberg's anti-Semitism: "Exceptional are the centuries-long paths of these world-wide wanderers through countries and continents, from west to east, from east to west, from north to south—an unbroken and persistent struggle for Germandom, faith, and soil."[86]

Just as Jewish migrants had spread across the world, Anabaptists formed their own "Mennonite diaspora."[87] These travels became symbolic of the German nation's global movements, uniting far larger populations into a single, centralized narrative. "The migrations of the Russian German Mennonites belong to the most spatially impressive population movements of the postwar period, perhaps even of the history of the German race overall," one book on Germandom abroad asserted. "If the group at issue is in fact relatively small, it can nevertheless serve as an allegory for the entire fate of Germandom; it can teach us ... to think about all members of the German race across the entire earth."[88] Cartographers pictorialized the Mennonite diaspora through new charts, atlases, and diagrams. One 1938 map, which inspired imitations well beyond the Nazi period, depicted the confession both chronologically and spatially. Working backwards, viewers could trace a series of arrows, each labeled with dates of historic migrations, to their point of origin in Germany. Rather than a series of isolated colonies, mapmakers portrayed Mennonitism as a complex network; decades or even centuries after their occurrence, migrations continued to form linkages between groups in Canada, Siberia, and Brazil, and above all with their common fatherland.[89]

Mirroring such documents' originality was the novelty of their anti-Semitism. Prior to the twentieth century, Mennonites in Germany rarely indulged in extreme denunciations. While everyday anti-Semitic prejudices were common, some liberals felt kinship to Judaism as a similar religious minority. "As long as the Jews are not free," the politician Hermann von Beckerath declared in 1847, "we ourselves are not free."[90] Practitioners of both faiths had long experienced social antipathy and state-sponsored violence, as well as occupational, marital, and landholding restrictions. Governments classed them together for surveillance and legislative purposes well into the nineteenth century; Prussian law enforcement included the policing of "Jewish and Mennonite matters," while Mennonites received military exemption on the same basis as Jews.[91] During the First World War, some pastors compared violence against their coreligionists in Galicia and south Russia to Jewish pogroms—and it was certainly no accident that Zionism provided a model for Mennonite nationalists. Nevertheless, until the Weimar years, Judaism remained an under-theorized element in Mennonite ideology. Leaders rarely discussed contemporary Jews in their periodicals or mentioned them in their sermons. Although entrepreneurs regularly conducted business with Jews, they did not proselytize. Congregations in the Prussian east had supported Jewish missions in the 1830s, but a century later, this was thoroughly forgotten. "It is a scandal we have so much to do with Jews," one farmer commented shortly before Hitler's rise, "yet through us not a single Jew has come to believe in Christ."[92] Intermarriage

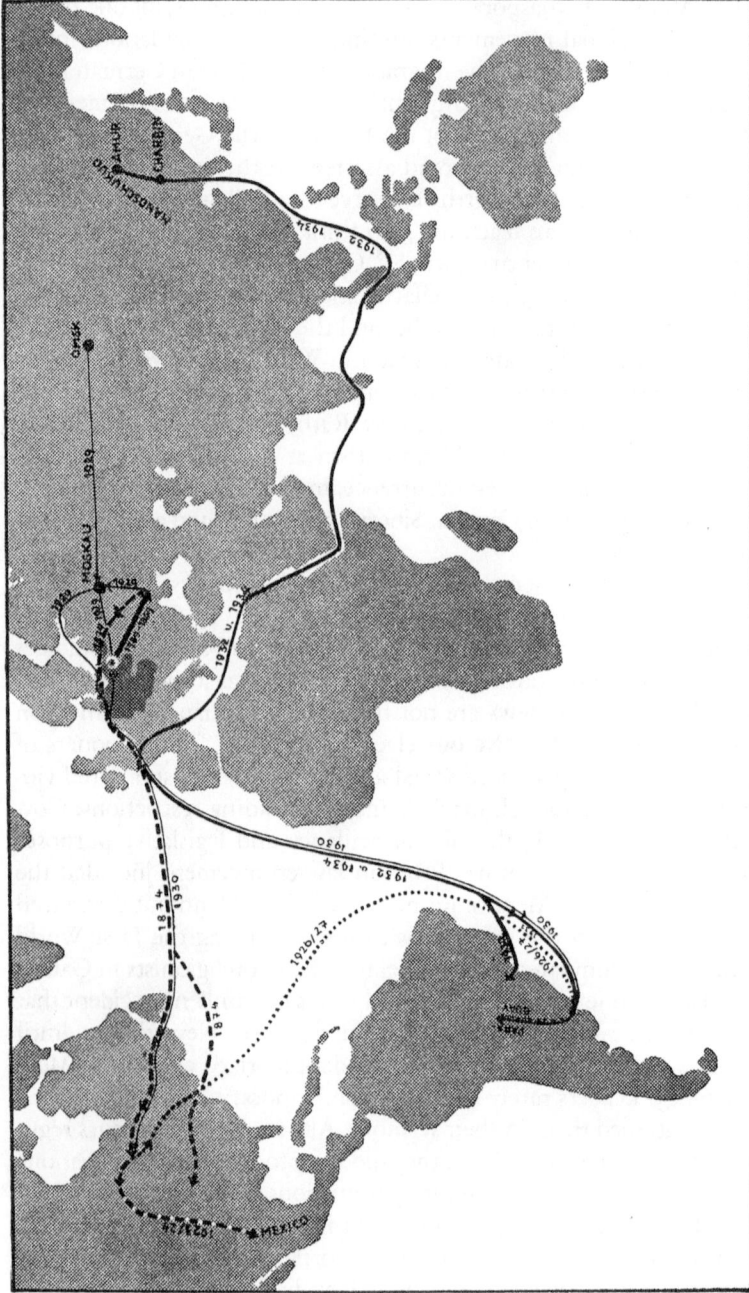

"The worldwide migrations of the [Mennonite] Germans from Russia." Produced by an employee of the German Foreign Institute, this 1938 map portrayed Germany as the homeland of Mennonites around the globe, alleging interconnection through common heritage and diasporic ties.

was virtually nonexistent. The division between Mennonites and Jews could be so clearly drawn that in 1936, one ministerial group noted, "Until now, a Mennonite was considered Aryan without question. A single case would ruin our reputation."[93]

Strongly articulated anti-Semitism did not enter Mennonite discourse until the 1920s. Prejudice was greatest among members connected to the Nazi Party. Danzig pastor Erich Göttner talked of "racially alien Jewry," decrying the "damages of Jewish infiltration," including "a stifling of [non-Jewish] business, an inner degeneration of morals, and the ever increasing mixing of races." Insinuations that Jews had killed Jesus, that Jews were ruining the economy, and that they were responsible for Germany's military defeat in the First World War became common. Some tempered these sentiments, cautioning: "we cannot identify 'Jewification' as the only source of misery in our national life."[94] But not all were so discerning. "Let this race be pure!" a Munich-based activist wrote to the *Mennonite Youth Observer*. "Away with all racial aliens, such as the Jews."[95] The Mennonite Nazi propagandist Heinrich Schröder asserted that a "nation that does not take control of the fate of its blood in the world ... *loses its right to exist*."[96] Informing young people about the dangers of racial defilement, Schröder implored them "to be careful when *choosing a spouse*."[97]

Mennonite institutions offered no formal opposition to anti-Semitic legislation in the Third Reich. Sometimes, they even used these laws to denounce their enemies. In 1937, when the Propaganda Ministry approved a performance of Ernst von Wildenbruch's anti-Anabaptist play, *The Mennonite*, the Union launched an inquiry into the playwright's allegedly "Jewish" past, attempting to have his drama banned once and for all. "If one makes these laws," Emil Händiges wrote, "then we should be allowed to make use of them."[98] Pastors rarely protested when their Jewish neighbors were deported, beaten, or otherwise harassed. "I am sorry about the fates of individuals," Gustav Kraemer told his congregation in Krefeld. "But are the parents who lost their sons during the war any guiltier—or the children who lost their fathers, the women their husbands? ... Not to mention the millions in Russia who the Bolsheviks and their Jewish leaders torturously martyred!"[99] The alleged betrayal of colonists by Jews in the Soviet Union served as a specifically Mennonite "stab in the back" myth. "In Russia, thousands of our families have been butchered," Benjamin Unruh charged, blaming the massacres on "Jewish commissars."[100] Such notions were bolstered by ties to the Anti-Comintern, a Nazi organization dedicated to the eradication of communism worldwide. Headed by Adolf Ehrt, a scholar of Mennonitism, the Anti-Comintern conflated anti-Bolshevism with anti-Semitism, constructing a general fear of "Judeo-Bolshevism." The organization's propaganda alleged that Jews had orchestrated the Bolshevik Revolution and now administered the Soviet Union. Blame for the destruction of

German-speaking colonies, including many Mennonite settlements, sup-posedly lay with the Jewish race.[101]

In addition to Ehrt and other non-Mennonite propagandists, a good percentage of Germany's Mennonite intelligentsia spent the interwar years producing anti-Soviet literature. Exiles from the USSR helped solidify mili-tant anti-communism—suffused with anti-Semitism—as a core tenet of the Mennonite Union's interwar agenda. Several operated an independent press in Wernigerode. Others worked for the German Foreign Institute or as Party propagandists.[102] Their scholarship on Mennonite racialism appeared in journals ranging from *German News from the East* and *German Archive for the Research of Countries and Races* to Mennonite papers throughout Can-ada, the United States, and Latin America. Harrowing quotations embel-lished their articles. As letters arrived, however sporadically, from Siberian work camps and the Russian Far North, readers learned of coreligionists' travails. "We were brought here to be sacrificed," one woman wrote from the icy village of Grosowetz. "Does anyone abroad think of us, the ban-ished? Do they know that our brethren are sent here, in order to annihilate them?"[103] Chilling accounts of collectivization and the Great Terror pro-vided yet more links on the chain of supposed Mennonite oppression at the hands of Jews. The Mennonite "is the king of German farmers, a proven colonist for a century and more," one book began. "Therefore he must be obliterated: Soviet Russia can only use slaves, crowds, collectives, and mass labor under Jewish order."[104] The freedom and German will of Mennonite farmers in the USSR became symbolic targets of—and sites of resistance against—"Judeo-Bolshevism."

Judaism thus appeared to be the frightening antithesis of Mennonitism, its dark inverse. Rather than pushing the confessions conceptually apart, the exacerbation of Mennonite anti-Semitism reinforced their parallels. If Jews were the scourge of Germandom, Mennonites were anti-Jews. Tell-ingly, pro-Nazi scholars adapted descriptions of Mennonitism directly from anti-Semitic theories. Just as Judaism's diasporic structure supposedly influ-enced its racial character, for example, Mennonites' culture reflected their own globalism. Adolf Ehrt posited "internationalism" as a source of "the special Mennonite feeling of solidarity"; imagining themselves part of a worldwide Anabaptist community, members purportedly held themselves apart from surrounding groups.[105] While thinkers like Ehrt or Alfred Rosen-berg emphasized ideological underpinnings, anthropometric sciences al-lowed racial categories to be read back into individual bodies. Physiological metrics presupposed the existence of ideal types, against which specimens could be measured. Comparing Mennonitism's racial integrity to that of Jews, anthropologist Friedrich Keiter presented the confession as a consan-guineous minority capable of self-preservation in alien environments. "De-spite close local symbiosis," Keiter wrote of Eastern Europe's congregations, "the chasm between Mennonites and natives was without doubt very great." But as with Jews, not all Mennonites were pure. Mingling with other racial communities, they could also absorb foreign qualities: "Just as the Jews adapted somewhat to their host populations through infiltrative mixing, a similar result must be expected among the Mennonites."[106]

Anabaptism deviated from its Jewish analogue in several critical respects. Unlike Jews, for instance, Mennonites possessed a homeland. Although most resided outside Germany and had for centuries, their alleged country of origin continued to exist, a point spokespersons constantly reiterated by calling upon coreligionists abroad to "return home." Jews, by contrast, lived in perpetual exile. The perceived statelessness of the Jewish people—by evoking images of invasion—provided much of their supposed danger for anti-Semites. Partly for this reason, Nazi politicians promoted quasi-Zionist Jewish states in Madagascar, Latin America, and Eastern Europe.[107] Another difference was Mennonites' supposed agrarianism. If the "international Jew" usually appeared as an urban figure, researchers associated Mennonitism with farming and soil, suggesting that rural settlement had enabled cultural preservation while imbuing their bloodlines with distinctive traits. In his study of Baltic colonization, Horst Penner portrayed the confession as inseparable from the region's meadows, waterways, and marshes. "The breed of people that once immigrated here has changed the landscape, but it has also been transformed by the landscape," he wrote. "Not with the sword but with the plow and watermill, they secured this land for Germandom for all time."[108]

Of course, the Jewish analogy invited certain dangers. The idea that Mennonitism constituted a separate—and potentially non-German—race proved threatening to some Nazi ideologues, as well as to Mennonites anxious for Aryan credentials. In 1936, Heinrich Schröder argued against using the word "Mennonite" in racial contexts, given that global membership encompassed groups of "Swiss" and "Dutch" heritage. "It is untenable," Schröder explained, "to speak of the entirety of Mennonitism as a 'racial tribe' or a 'race,' as unfortunately so often occurs in the Mennonite press."[109] A year later, historian C. Henry Smith drew criticism in Germany for suggesting that the "term Mennonite might almost as well be applied to a special race, as to a body of religious beliefs."[110] Smith's position was becoming increasingly common in North and South America, where many supported Nazi racism but preferred a confessional variant. "I am a German Mennonite," these members were likely to insist, "not a Mennonite German."[111] Concerned Nazis tracked the spread of Mennonite nationalism. Geographer Herbert Wilhelmy, for example, claimed that all members, secretly or overtly, longed for citizenship in a theocratic Mennonite state. "Centuries of isolation and an astounding genealogical tradition have awakened in the Mennonites the notion that they are an independent 'race' or an independent 'tribe,'" Wilhelmy assessed. "Everywhere in the world ... observers count the Mennonites not among the German racial groups, nor among the Russians or Canadians, but rather consider them members of their own '*Mennonite nation.*'"[112]

Mennonite nationalism held a bad reputation among National Socialists. Propagandists were prepared to commend congregations abroad, but only if they shared an equal admiration for the Third Reich. When Herbert Wilhelmy traveled to Paraguay's Gran Chaco, he held pro-Nazi lectures in Mennonite villages. The geographer was pleased to note listeners' enthusiasm for Germany. But soaring rhetoric and slide projectors appealed to only some. Allegiance to Anabaptism often outweighed interest in the Third Reich, which for many was simply too militarist and too worldly. Wilhelmy complained in his report to the German Foreign Office that those "settlers who limit themselves to 'Mennonite' thinking are the ones who years earlier migrated to a remote wilderness to establish an ideal Mennonite state." He criticized their isolationism, arguing that they had been spoiled by extraordinary privileges: "The group of religious fanatics consider [pro-Nazi Mennonites] as being traitors to the Mennonite cause. They consider them to be rebels who would soon lose their Mennonite identity if they were to live scattered among other Germans or Paraguayans."[113] Most damning of all, Wilhelmy classed his hosts with Judaism, insinuating they were better followers of Abraham than of Hitler. "Like the Jews," he wrote, "Mennonites believe the bonds of blood make them not just a *single* race, but the 'chosen race' of God. Jewish history dominates the Mennonites in all details; through the giving of Jewish first names, they seek to compare themselves to the Jewish race."[114]

Pro-Nazi Mennonites repudiated these claims. In a response to the Foreign Office, educator Fritz Kliewer of Paraguay insisted that Judaism "sickened every upstanding Mennonite." He explained that the colonists favored Old Testament names—such as Sara and Isaac—not out of sympathy for Jews, but for biblical reasons. Settlers were increasingly giving their children good Aryan names. And far from denizens of a separatist "Mennonite State," they were the truest of Germans. Kliewer denied that the confession was more religious than racial, noting that missionaries could spread Christianity, but never Anabaptism: "That an Indian could become a Mennonite is a thing of impossibility." Kliewer—who in 1933 had co-founded a fascist youth organization in the Chaco, complete with paramilitary marches—defended his coreligionists' anti-Semitism. "Regarding the position of the settlers toward the Jewish question," he wrote, "it is the same as that of any people who have come from the East and experienced communism firsthand. Self-evidently: one knows the Jews as a deceitful and corrosive element that must unquestionably be avoided."[115] Kliewer's opinions were certainly far from representative of Mennonite thinking, either in Paraguay or elsewhere. Having written a doctoral dissertation in the Third Reich, he was unusually well acquainted with Nazism, and of all members in the Americas, his politics fell to the extreme right. Nevertheless, other Russian-born Mennonites were also likely to position themselves as anti-Jews. The Canada-based C. F. Klassen, for instance, aligned himself with Hitler's Germany, railing against "social-democratic rot, the Communist insanity, and the machinations of the Jews."[116]

And yet, charges of Mennonite nationalism were not unfounded. Most spectacularly in 1933, J. J. Hildebrand, another Russian-born resident of Canada, promoted the establishment of a fascist Mennonite state in Australia. Writing to the country's government, he requested "complete treaty independence" for a "white settlement of a religious group … now scattered all over the world." As imagined by Hildebrand and his supporters, the state's official languages would be High and Low German; a centralized conference would regulate religious matters; and the *Menno Gulden* would be the primary currency. The settlement's flag was to be blue, green, and white, with a dove bearing a peace palm. Hildebrand's was probably the world's only pacifist fascist movement. Although Australia informed the dreamer that his plan was "quite impossible," religious fascism continued to flourish.[117] Others in Canada promoted a Mennonite free trade zone to cement kinship ties with an economic union, while in Paraguay, 145 families formed a new racialist colony, dubbed "Friesland" after their allegedly Dutch origins.[118] A number of fascist or fascist-friendly periodicals supported such causes. The Canada-based *Mennonite Racial Observer*—influential for Mennonite publishing well beyond the Nazi period—provided news from an ethnic perspective beginning in 1935. "The *Racial Observer* intends to be 'Mennonite,'" its first issue declared, "and stands in the service of all who are born to Mennonite parents." Fostering a confessional literary and artistic culture, its goals were "to strengthen our racial group-consciousness and to fortify the desire to remain what we are: Mennonites."[119]

Spokespersons in Germany sought to root out religious nationalism. "Since the National Socialist revolution," propagandist Walter Quiring informed the Foreign Office, "there has been a newspaper war in the American Mennonite press … regarding German identity and the issue of becoming German among the foreign Mennonites. A substandard racial education had nurtured among the Russian and American Mennonites the idea that they are nearly their own, special race."[120] Leaders like Quiring intervened in this discussion, attempting to prove their confession's Germanness with cutting-edge racial scholarship. During 1935 and 1936, Quiring alone contributed more than 160 articles to this debate.[121] Benjamin Unruh published more than 180 in the same period.[122] A quantitative analysis of one Mennonite newspaper in Canada found 2,484 column inches of "Germanism content" in a single year, of which 83 percent was "favorable."[123] Much of this material, produced in the Third Reich, sought to counteract the notion that some Mennonites had originated in the Netherlands and were thus of Dutch, not German, heritage. The majority of "Dutch" Mennonites, Quiring maintained, "originated in *Eastern Friesland*, which has always been German."[124] Unruh went a step further: "German science has fully and clearly delineated between political versus national-racial distinctions.... It has nothing, absolutely nothing to do with political boundaries!"[125] Whether they liked it or not, all Mennonites were racially German.

Despite the efforts of Unruh and Quiring, some Nazis continued to criticize congregations abroad—especially the most traditionalist communities. If for different reasons than their more progressive counterparts, conservative Mennonites and Amish held little admiration for Hitler. Although most spoke some form of German, their theologies were staunchly anti-political; they were pacifists and practiced humble living. Racialist observers, for their part, ridiculed anyone who refused to drive automobiles, use electricity, or "maintain a living relationship with Germany."[126] After his visit to Mexico, researcher Karl Götz labeled the country's Old Colony Mennonites "probably the strangest, spiritually and culturally insane splinter of the German nation."[127] While some Nazis developed an agrarian-romantic fondness for bonnet-wearing, buggy-driving conservatives, most pronouncements were similarly severe. Among Canada's congregations, scholars identified many "fully ossified groups whose world views and religious beliefs have not advanced since before 1800."[128] Discourses of "inbreeding" and even "incest" provided scientific vectors for race-based anti-Mennonitism. In the same way that anti-Semites depicted Jews as racially diseased, the language of degeneracy could also target traditionalist Anabaptists. Some members had criticized their confession's inbred nature already in the 1920s, citing the "danger of bodily and spiritual sickness through the perpetual intermarriage of relatives."[129] Comparable to certain houses of the European aristocracy, commentators argued that each was "related to all the others, direct kin or in-laws." But even among those with immaculate pedigrees, unchecked intermarriage "invited the danger that such unmixed blood will eventually become sterile."[130]

Pacifism, in particular, seemed not just a religious foible but also a racial affliction. After watching *Frisians in Peril*, one Catholic polemicist characterized Mennonitism as "a schismatic element of the racially corrosive sect of the Anabaptists." For this reviewer, members were anything but virile pioneers of Germandom. A majority lived abroad, he reasoned, because pacifist inbreeding had made them "unfertile for their nation."[131] Others agreed; it was "self-absorbed religious insularity" that led them to "turn their backs on the German homeland."[132] When viewed from a clinical perspective, however, nonresistance sometimes appeared a boon. According to the physician Werner Zimmermann, it had actually strengthened members' blood by preventing the loss of military-aged men: "Because they enjoyed freedom from military service, the negative process of sifting out through war did *not* affect the Mennonites until the start of the nineteenth century." Moreover, the confession was relatively young. Formed *"only* in the *sixteenth century*," its stock could not have degenerated in so short a time. Noting the rarity of marriage between first cousins as well as low rates of schizophrenia, epilepsy, and retardation, Zimmermann concluded that "Genetic infertility has certainly not appeared among the Mennonite families."[133] Nevertheless, individuals sometimes claimed the opposite stance, arguing that generations of cowards had weakened their constitution. "In our veins, we have relatively little soldiers' blood," genealogist Fritz van Bergen wrote, "but we promise our nation we will create it. I myself am the first soldier in my lineage since 1500." Van Bergen—for whom only a "living deed of blood" could overcome the "dead word" of pacifism—fell on the Eastern Front a year later.[134]

As in van Bergen's case, racial nationalism was often a matter of self-fashioning. Not simply imposed by scientists or politicians from without, racial categories could be generated by those they purportedly described. Without support from within the confession itself, Mennonitism would likely never have emerged as a significant rubric of racial classification. Only through the efforts of pastors, genealogists, and aid workers did the notion of a "racial church"—an essentially German collectivity whose worldwide membership remained linked through blood—gain salience among congregations in Germany and beyond, as well as among a wider non-Mennonite public. Unquestionably, such depictions were highly contested. The global nature of this story demonstrates how racial nationalisms espoused in the Third Reich reflected events far from German borders. Whether commentators regarded congregations in Paraguay, Canada, or Mexico positively often depended on local attitudes toward Hitler and his projects. By claiming Mennonite nationality, denigrating Nazi dogmas, or failing to exhibit sufficient anti-Semitism, these communities could draw National Socialists' ire and, in turn, racial condemnation. Only if Nazi policymakers regarded faraway populations as loyal did they extend their racial umbrella, with promises of international protection and development assistance. Traditional tenets like pacifism proved volatile missiles in this struggle, serving to justify all manner of contradictory measures.

And yet, by the outbreak of the Second World War, public perception had so tightly intertwined Mennonitism with Aryanism that members were commonly understood as anti-Jews, an association that drew many into the machinery of an anti-Semitic and increasingly genocidal regime. The symbolic dichotomy between Mennonites and Jews would be horribly reified over the following years as Hitler's armies worked to reengineer Eastern Europe's racial landscape. As the German drive for "living space" linked repatriation and Holocaust, images of Mennonitism helped propel the internment, dehumanization, and slaughter of much of Europe's Jewish population.

CHAPTER 6

FATHERLAND

WAR AND GENOCIDE IN
THE MENNONITE EAST

The greatest chapter of our aid work is at hand:
the restoration of our colonies in Russia!
—BENJAMIN UNRUH, 1938[1]

On New Year's Eve 1942, Benjamin Unruh arrived at SS headquarters in East Prussia. As the train brought him eastward through German-occupied countryside, the professor had drawn closer to the land of his youth. Born in Crimea six decades earlier, Unruh had been exiled to Germany after the Bolshevik Revolution. There he had advocated for coreligionists in the Soviet Union, helping tens of thousands migrate to Canada, Paraguay, and Brazil. After 1933, he served as the Third Reich's foremost consultant on Mennonites. Collaborating with government agencies, Unruh promoted Nazism across Europe and the Americas. In return, he expected support for ambitions in the East. "It is clear to me," he wrote shortly before the war, "that everything, *everything*, comes from politics." Identifying Hitler as "a German William of Orange, a Wilhelm Tell, and a Washington," he believed that the Führer would bring about the "collapse of Stalin's tyranny."[2] No one else seemed capable. While the Weimar Republic and Europe's western powers had tolerated Bolshevism, Hitler declared his hostility from the beginning. In Unruh's thinking, a stable future for Mennonitism depended on the annihilation of communism. Anticipating the advance of Nazi tanks, he envisioned a resurrected Ukraine—a flourishing German protectorate that could become a new fatherland for the world's Mennonites.

With the outbreak of the Second World War, Unruh's moment arrived. German forces surged across Stalin's border in the summer of 1941, driving the Red Army deep into the Soviet heartland. Much of Ukraine came under German control within weeks. Located far to Germany's east and possessing a largely "expendable" population, Nazis found this territory perfect for racial engineering. For two years, they reshaped Ukraine. Drawing on discourses of Manifest Destiny, Hitler dubbed his largest colony—officially the Reich Commissariat Ukraine—a new American West. "There's only one duty," Hitler announced in October 1941: "to Germanize this country by the immigration of Germans, and to look upon the natives as

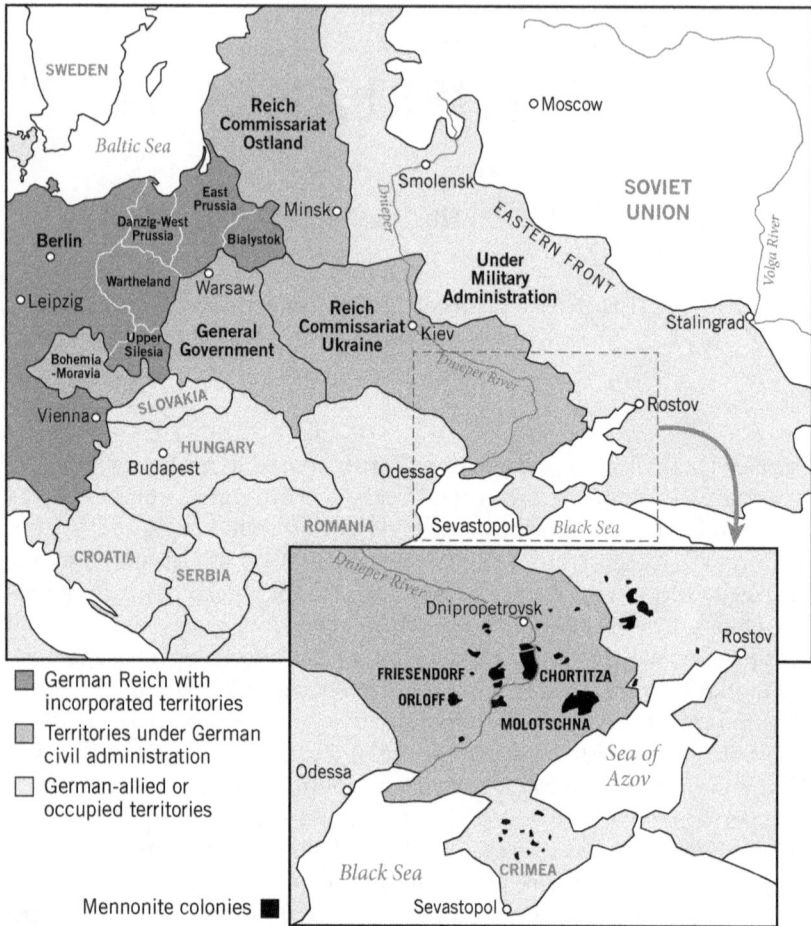

Nazi-occupied Eastern Europe, November 1942

Redskins."³ Mennonitism seemed ready-made for this project. Nazi scholars portrayed it as a global confession of Aryan farmer folk that directly linked Ukraine with the "enormous wheat region" of the Canadian and American prairies. There, 40,000 Mennonite immigrants from the Black Sea had performed "outstanding colonial work."⁴ In the same way their relatives had pioneered the Great Plains, Nazis expected Mennonites in Ukraine, along with other so-called ethnic Germans, to transform the steppe. From a Bolshevik wasteland, it was to become the "granary of Europe."⁵ This was a program of expansion, conquest, and genocide. Emulating the displacement of American Indians, Ukraine's Mennonites were supposed to seize Jewish and Slavic-held land. Understood as anti-Jews, they were considered ideal for reconstructing territories supposedly ravaged by Jewish Bolsheviks. "The Jew, that destroyer, we shall drive out," Hitler explained. "I don't see why a German who eats a piece of bread should torment himself with the idea that the soil that produces this bread has been won by the sword. When we eat wheat from Canada, we don't think about the despoiled Indians."[6]

Benjamin Unruh's train pulled into the station. As he stepped into the winter sun, men in SS uniforms greeted him. Heinrich Himmler, head of the *Schutzstaffel*, Chief of German Police, and the second most powerful man in the Third Reich, had invited Unruh for three days of meetings. It was Himmler who, following Germany's invasion, had begun Ukraine's racial reconstruction. Under his command, elite death squads, called *Einsatzgruppen* or "Task Forces" swept the territory, sifting the total population of 16.9 million for its remaining 1.2 million Jews. Aided by local volunteers, the Einsatzgruppen identified Ukraine's Jews, forced them to dig mass graves, and shot them. Fewer than 2 percent survived.[7] Unlike the majority of European Jews, who would die in mechanized extermination camps in Poland, the Jews of Ukraine experienced improvised, chaotic killing. It was here, in makeshift ghettos and rural farmyards, that Himmler's units initiated the process that would become known as the Holocaust. At the same time, a separate team called Special Command R, also under Himmler's orders, combed Ukraine for Mennonites and other "ethnic Germans." On the surface, Special Command R appeared the antithesis of the Einsatzgruppen. It provided German speakers with all the services denied to Jews. But welfare and mass murder were two sides of the same coin. Those believed to possess German blood received the clothes and shoes of murdered Jews, and thousands moved into their vacant homes. Sometimes, the distinction between Special Command R and the Einsatzgruppen fell away altogether, as when Einsatzgruppe C registered German speakers in Zhytomyr, or when Special Command R, along with dozens of "ethnic German" charges, helped murder 52,000 Jews in Transnistria.[8]

Himmler's staff led Unruh to the commander's field wagon. "There he is," Himmler reportedly exclaimed, "this pope of the Mennonites!" As Unruh made himself comfortable, Himmler opened a bottle of wine. "Do you drink red or white?" the SS chief asked. "Both," Unruh replied, causing his host to laugh.[9] Over lunch, they discussed Mennonitism and Ukraine. Unruh had long awaited such a meeting. Since leaving the Soviet Union in 1920, he watched anxiously from afar as his coreligionists faced disaster upon disaster. The end of the NEP era spelled the end of their relative independence in the USSR. Dubbing Mennonites a "kulak" community, Soviet officials had shipped thousands to Siberia, bundling their property into collective farms. Preachers were targeted and church buildings shuttered, sometimes to be repurposed as dance halls or cinemas. By 1938, nearly half of all Mennonite men in Ukraine had been arrested. If prisoners were not shot, they faced slave-like conditions in Stalin's gulags. Social turmoil and government mismanagement combined to catastrophic effect. Collectivization brought poor harvests, and poor harvests brought famine. Of approximately 11,000 Mennonites in the Chortitza colony in 1914, more than 20 percent were murdered, banned, starved to death, or deported by 1941.[10] The number was far higher in other colonies. Molotschna, the largest and most famous settlement, was now only sparsely inhabited; farm machinery lay broken or unused, and livestock wandered ownerless in the fields.[11]

With Himmler's help, Unruh intended to recreate Mennonitism's lost glory. In part, this meant repopulating the colonies. He hoped that emigrants from the former Russian Empire, now scattered throughout the globe—in Canada, the United States, Mexico, Brazil, and Paraguay—would return to their old homeland. "Today," Unruh claimed, "the vast majority of ethnically German Mennonites across the whole world stand on the side of Adolf Hitler."[12] It was not a complete exaggeration. In 1940, a summit in Brazil had voted unanimously to "repatriate to the German motherland," confirming that their draft-age men would join Nazi military organizations.[13] One spokesperson explained: "our settlers wish nothing more ardently than to become German citizens and if possible once again to live under German sovereignty."[14] Nearly half of all Mennonites in Paraguay desired the same.[15] Even in Allied Canada, talk of repatriation was in the air.[16] Unruh had promoted a global return since before the war. "I have always spoken of a *temporary* emigration," he told the executive secretary of Mennonite Central Committee in 1939, "and never a total abandonment of Russia."[17] For many immigrants, German pride recalled refugee assistance from Weimar and Nazi governments. "When we lay before the gates of Moscow," one member in Paraguay recalled, "it was Germany that offered us a saving hand."[18] Encouraged by letters from the Third Reich, entire colonies believed that Hitler would enable their resettlement on the steppe. The German consulate in Paraguay reported local Mennonites' hope that the *"Führer might conquer Ukraine for Germany,"* so they could once again become "wheat farmers on the beloved Russian soil."[19] "We too want to help build the great Reich," proponents asserted. "When all is settled in Russia ... we want to return there. Heil Hitler!"[20]

By the mid-1930s, SS leader Heinrich Schröder had begun drafting remigration plans. Since Ukraine remained under Soviet control, he envisioned one hundred "racially-pure frontier colonies" in Germany, a concept adapted from Hitler's *Mein Kampf*.[21] Schröder concentrated on the northwest region of East Friesland, which he considered the origin point of Russian-born Mennonites. He found enough East Frisian land for an initial settlement, and in 1935, fifty families volunteered to relocate from Paraguay. The plan fell through, however, when Berlin declared its opposition. "As long as the settlements of ethnic Germans can be preserved," Nazi officials told Benjamin Unruh, "they should not be weakened or abandoned."[22] These communities provided leverage with governments abroad. Just as the existence of "ethnic Germans" in Czechoslovakia helped justify Hitler's seizure of the Sudetenland, the presence of Mennonites in Poland or Latin America could aid German ambitions. But by the end of the decade, as the Third Reich prepared for war, sympathy for repatriation increased. "The enormous need for technical expertise and agricultural skills in the Reich," the German Foreign Office determined, "requires the abandonment of the previous position that German racial groups abroad are not to be numerically weakened."[23] Mennonites in the Americas seemed to fit this need.

Aided by the Foreign Office and Himmler's new Ethnic German Office, Unruh and Schröder arranged several pilot transports. In June 1939, five young women and twenty-eight men from Paraguay landed in Germany. Similar groups—probably totaling in excess of one hundred individuals—arrived from Canada and Brazil.[24] As Unruh confided to an MCC colleague, "a small settlement of young people in Germany can only help improve our relationship" to the state. Nazi leaders would look more favorably on Mennonitism if diasporic groups sent some members "home." These micro-migrations were intended as forerunners of a larger return. "Sooner or later," Unruh believed, "the question of the reacquisition of our settlements in Russia will be put on the order of the day." At that time, all "who left to their old temporary homeland will return." From the persecution of the Reformation to Weimar's economic woes, Mennonites had long been driven out of Europe. Hitler would allegedly reverse this trend. Under the Führer's guidance, a majority of the confession's members would finally make permanent residence in the lands of their origin. But full-scale resettlement would have to wait. In its current form, Germany was too crowded to house the bulk of the world's Mennonites. There was simply not enough space. "Should more become available," however, "the question would naturally present a different face."[25]

The conquest of the East provided just this opportunity. For Nazis, these vast lands promised the nation's much needed "living space." Much of the soil, in fact, was supposedly already German, tilled for centuries by Mennonites and other German speakers. Maps of Poland and Ukraine shaded vast swaths in "German" colors, claiming them as rightfully German. One chart of Chortitza identified Mennonite villages with swastikas—each crooked cross asserting not only Germanness but also political orientation.[26] Scholars of Germandom abroad touted colonists' racial characteristics. Their studies, conducted primarily among Mennonites, revealed that German speakers in the Soviet Union possessed a higher "Nordic blood quotient" than the average Reich German.[27] Biological purity had ostensibly facilitated cultural and agricultural wonders. "Before the World War," another report found, "the tsarist empire was home to more than 2,000 flowering German settlements, testament to German diligence and order in the East."[28] In the Black Sea region alone, 55,000 initial immigrants had multiplied to 400,000. And, as some enthusiasts pointed out, this number doubled when including emigration to the Americas. Perhaps the most significant rubric for racial success was land ownership. Prior to 1914, German speakers owned 3 million hectares of south Russian soil, a landmass equivalent to the combined area of Baden, Wurttemberg, and Alsace-Lorraine. Total agricultural holdings approached those of England.[29]

Specifically Mennonite tallies were, if anything, more impressive. Nazi ethnographers placed the confession "at the pinnacle of all German settlers in Russia."[30] "Wherever they settle," scholars maintained, "the Mennonites are the unquestioned leaders of the Germans." One researcher determined their "colonial potential" was fourteen times greater than Protestants' and an astounding fifty times that of Catholics.[31] The strictness of their religion had supposedly fostered an unparalleled sense of group cohesion, in turn generating a deep colonial temperament. Theorists explained that by the time they left Prussia, members were *already* a closed tribal group."[32] Between 1789 and 1861, immigrants to south Russia had founded four "mother colonies." From there, they spread throughout Siberia and Central Asia, producing an additional thirty-six "daughter settlements." Across the tsarist empire, Mennonites' four hundred villages, with a total population of 100,000, had acquired nearly 1.5 million hectares.[33] This was well beyond the average for "ethnic Germans." Visitors from Germany had long marveled at the confession's accomplishments. Their villages, one traveler wrote, "resemble each other like eggs in a basket." At a distance, they were easily distinguished from other German-speaking towns. Tree-lined avenues set them apart, as did the richness of their orchards, flower beds, and vegetable gardens. Even Mennonite homes were supposedly "larger and better built than the houses of the Protestant and Catholic Germans."[34]

When Himmler's SS units reached the Dnieper in autumn 1941, they confirmed these findings. Special Command R praised the colonists' Low German and their Dutch-Prussian surnames. Whole towns seemed transported from the Vistula Delta. In organization and culture, "Mennonite villages rose above the other German communities."[35] The Third Reich's highest officials expressed immediate interest. Figures like Fritz Todt, Erich Koch, and Fritz Sauckel visited the communities not only to inspect their infrastructure, but also to see the settlers for themselves. When Alfred Rosenberg, Reich Minister for the Occupied Eastern Territories, toured Ukraine in 1942, he described his visit among the "Frisians" of Chortitza as the "most moving moment of the entire trip." The colony had planned an elaborate rally. "For many kilometers before we arrived," Rosenberg re-

Alfred Rosenberg, Nazi philosopher and Reich Minister for the Occupied Eastern Territories, speaking in Chortitza, 1942. Occupation officials praised the agricultural achievements and German-language use of Mennonites in Ukraine, lauding their settlements as model colonies.

called, "cordons of German colonists with their whole families and swastika flags in their hands formed a passage to our goal." The cavalcade rolled past waving bands of schoolchildren, all shouting "Heil Hitler!" Rosenberg addressed the crowd, emphasizing that "for more than one hundred and forty years," they had "defended Germany."[36]

Nazi leaders hoped to duplicate the Mennonite model throughout Ukraine. According to a secret project called General Plan East, the colonies of Chortitza and Molotschna were to be incorporated into a new German province called Goth Land.[37] Planners envisioned a dense network of closed agrarian communities. At the cross points of roads and railways, small cities of 20,000 inhabitants would form. Villages would then surround each node at a ten-mile radius, like protective cocoons.[38] Less fertile spaces would be given to "subhumans." Unlike Poland, Ukraine was not intended for complete Germanization. It would function as a traditional European colony. "What India was for England," Hitler expounded, "the territories of Russia will be for us." Alongside anti-Semitic treatises, East Ministry officials read books on Indian and African colonialism. They considered Russian and Ukrainian speakers fit neither for self-rule nor for assimilation. With a handful of "scarves, glass beads, and everything that colonial peoples like," a single German could supposedly subdue 100,000 "natives." The best land, of course, would remain in German hands. Agricultural prowess seemed to confirm settlers' racial right to the soil. "The German colonists ought to live on handsome, spacious farms," Hitler remarked. "The German services will be lodged in marvelous buildings, the governors in palaces."[39] In three hundred years, Ukraine's black earth would become "one of the loveliest gardens in the world."[40]

Creating such a model state required massive resettlement. To the Nazis' chagrin, not all German speakers lived in idealized soldier-farmer strongholds. For one thing, only half remained. In August 1941, the Soviet Politburo had ordered the entire population eastward. As gunfire crackled in the distance, the Red Army loaded whole villages into boxcars or wagon trains. When the *Wehrmacht* arrived, this process was half complete. Across Ukraine, only 200,000 of 400,000 individuals believed to be of German descent, including 35,000 of 60,000 Mennonites, escaped deportation. Many of these were highly dispersed. "Ethnic Germans" often lived in predominantly Ukrainian-speaking villages, where—Nazi activists believed—they were in danger of losing their Germanness. Some had already "gone native," speaking Ukrainian in the home, or marrying spouses categorized as Russian. Even worse were the urban German speakers. Many of these had adapted to Bolshevik life, working in the Soviet civil service or other suspect positions.

In the summer of 1942, Himmler prepared for demographic reconfiguration. Nazi organizations had already settled hundreds of thousands of "ethnic Germans" in other parts Eastern Europe—most coming to occupied Poland. Now it was Ukraine's turn. Some settlements, like the Hegewald colony in Zhytomyr, sprang up overnight. Although few people of purportedly German heritage had lived in the area, thousands of local Russian and Ukrainian speakers were violently evicted. Ten thousand bewildered "ethnic Germans" arrived in truck beds to replace them. No one had been given more than a few hours' notice, and the arrivals' limited possessions had to be supplemented with spoils from Auschwitz.[41] In other cases, Nazi leaders strengthened extant colonies. Molotschna received 6,300 German speakers from Mariupol, Grunau, and Kharkiv.[42] And Himmler ordered that "ethnic Germans" from Kryvyi Rih be relocated near Chortitza.[43] To aid this process, the Reich Commissariat Ukraine decreed that members of the German race receive use of land approximating their holdings from January 1, 1914—that is, before the First World War. Intended as a forced reparation, territory allegedly stolen by the Soviets was "returned" to its previous owners. Redistribution varied from region to region. In the joint Protestant-Mennonite area of Kronau-Orloff, SS leaders compared old land records to village genealogical lists, attempting to give families the same properties farmed by their parents and grandparents. In Chortitza, land was simply seized and dispersed to any Mennonites capable of farming it.[44] Previous tenants were often moved elsewhere. Many were shipped to the Reich for forced labor.

As they dined, Himmler told Benjamin Unruh of his recent visit to Molotschna. The SS chief had traveled Halbstadt in October, where he reviewed the activities of Special Command R and met with local leaders. "I have been in the Ukraine and seen the people there," he reportedly said. "Your Mennonites are the best."[45] Unruh agreed that the colonists' blood was purely German. He attributed this to their historic prohibition against intermarriage—an argument he had used for years to push for mass remigration. "Unions with Jews were forbidden," he expounded. "Biologically and racially, the question of the resettlement of Russian-Germans generally and of the Mennonites in particular is therefore very favorable."[46] Unruh hoped that after the war, the North America-based Mennonite Central Committee would help relocate Mennonites to Ukraine. As MCC's official representative in Germany since 1936, he had facilitated the organization's collaboration with the Nazi government. Through the 1930s, they had negotiated the finances of the Latin American colonies. Between 1939 and 1941, MCC deepened its partnership with Hitler's government, providing relief to war-ravaged congregations in occupied Poland and France. After the invasion of Ukraine, MCC even contemplated aiding Nazi population transfers. A "very large part of our future work," wrote its director of European operations, would involve locating "Mennonites in different parts of Russia and ... getting them resettled."[47]

Himmler was pleased with Unruh's report. He assured the professor his activities were contributing to the war effort. While the United States' entry into the conflict had put MCC's operations on hold, this partnership could be rekindled later. Himmler had been especially impressed with the colonists in Halbstadt, where he had met many of Unruh's friends and relatives. He was cautious, however, about the confession's unusual traditions. It was the "stiff-necked adherence to their religious faith," some scholars argued— the "shunning of oath and sword"—that had prompted immigration to south Russia in the first place.[48] Church leaders in Germany now distanced themselves from pacifism, and they encouraged their eastern coreligionists to do likewise. But the oath was a different matter. Unruh and his allies insisted that Ukraine's Mennonites, including those inducted into the Wehrmacht and the Waffen-SS, should not be forced to swear. An honestly spoken word, he assured Himmler, would be stronger than any oath: "The Mennonite soldier will be loyal to our Führer unto death, even when he, as Menno Simons clearly requires in matters regarding the state, 'solemnly promises' according to the form of his forefathers."[49] This response satisfied Himmler. "Whether 'solemnly promise' or 'swear,'" he said, "we will not stumble over this piece of straw."[50]

Upon finishing their meal, Himmler and Unruh exchanged final pleas-antries. Unruh was just rising to leave, when the SS chief's voice grew seri-ous. "Take a guess, Herr Professor," he said. "How many political dissidents would you say I have imprisoned?" Unruh was suddenly ill at ease. He ex-cused himself, saying he could not name a number. "Yes, well, what have you generally heard from others?" Himmler insisted. His gaze did not waver. "Very many," Unruh hazarded. He waited, unsure of himself. Finally, a smile crossed Himmler's face. "Well then, I'll tell you," he said. "Less than a *thousand*."[51] This exchange stuck with Unruh. On his return trip, it played repeatedly in his mind, and when he arrived home, it figured prominently in a report to his children. For Unruh, the scene demonstrated the intimate connection between Mennonite resettlement and Nazi policies of intern-ment and extermination. Leaders like Unruh knew full well that Ukraine's Jews were gunned down, often just outside Mennonite villages; they knew that Mennonites received goods taken from murdered Jews; and they cer-tainly knew that Himmler's prisoners numbered not in the hundreds but in the hundreds of thousands.[52] These realities left a psychological toll—hence Unruh's insistence on recounting Himmler's final question. But the Nazi commander's assurance that the count of political prisoners was low seemed to provide absolution. Despite their unquestionable complicity in Hitler's industry of death, Unruh and fellow Mennonite activists learned to see the issues separately, compartmentalizing genocide from the ways it benefited their own objectives.

MENNONITES AND THE HOLOCAUST

In November 1941, Heinrich Hamm, a Mennonite from Dnipropetrovsk, Ukraine, told his life story to Special Command R. His tale began with the coming of the Bolsheviks. In 1917, Hamm had six siblings, each of whom, during the intervening years, met a terrible fate. His eldest brother, Abram, had been hacked to pieces in the Civil War. Peter, his youngest brother, had fought for the Whites and been shot by the Reds. Others were beaten, tor-tured, starved, imprisoned, and expelled. Hamm's third brother, Wilhelm, had managed to become a factory owner, only to be labeled a "kulak." He had been sent to the Urals, where he died in a coal mine. The last of Hamm's siblings fled to the countryside. There they lived in abject poverty, hiding among Ukrainian speakers and hoping to avoid deportation. But this was in vain; just days before the Nazis' arrival, Soviet agents had apprehended and shipped them eastward. No one had seen them since. Why had the Mennonites experienced so much suffering? "It was not the Russian people who despised Germans," Hamm told his interviewers. Rather, he blamed "Jewish hatred for all that spoke German." Hamm explained how Jews plotted their extermination. Across the Soviet Union, Jewish communists had allegedly engineered famine, dispossession, and murder. "This is how the Jewish-Bolshevik beasts liquidated German families," he concluded. "The term beast is not even appropriate in this case since animals kill for the sake of food, but these hordes of Jews and misbegotten bastards kill and destroy for the pure joy of it."[53]

In Hamm's telling, Mennonites were anti-Jews. Understood as hard-working, noble, and righteous, they were the quintessential victims of "Judeo-Bolshevism." Delivered at the height of the Einsatzgruppe killings, Hamm's story was suited to the condition of local Mennonites. It fit a pattern both expected and encouraged by Nazi occupiers. For Mennonites, as for other inhabitants of Ukraine, expressing anti-Semitism was a method of showing loyalty to Hitler. When German troops first arrived, most of the population viewed them as liberators. "It was a joy for us all," one Mennonite wrote, "as we greeted the German soldiers for the first time and were able to speak of our sufferings and express joy to them in the German language."[54] With the entire USSR seemingly poised to fall, not just "ethnic Germans" but also Ukrainian and Russian speakers offered their support. In this context, anti-Semitism was self-serving. By disparaging Jews, Mennonites and their neighbors could focus occupiers' anti-Bolshevik measures against a limited population, while simultaneously cementing a belief in their own superiority. As spokespersons learned to narrate their history into racially acceptable scripts, they imbued their collective image with connotations of anti-Semitism. Notions of Mennonites' agricultural acumen thus systematically enabled or subsequently justified the murder of neighboring Jews. Individual Mennonites sometimes joined Nazi killing squads, personally executing Jewish men, women, and children. More often, it was the broader idea of Mennonitism—a joint racial and spatial construct—that helped facilitate genocide.[55]

Mennonites and Jews had a long history of coexistence in Ukraine. Jews "had always lived among Mennonites," one Chortitza resident later wrote, recalling that they were "never unfriendly toward us during Soviet times."[56] The similarity of Yiddish and German eased daily communication. Business relationships were common, and during pogroms, some Mennonites opened their homes to asylum-seekers.[57] Limited intermarriage occurred. Jews residing in Mennonite colonies were usually concentrated in large towns such as Chortitza. In 1941, Einlage had nearly half as many Jews as Mennonites—633 versus 1,390. Numbers were smaller in outlying villages. In Nikolaifeld, there was only one Jewish family. Osterwick had six. Kronsweide, none.[58] At least one colony, known as Stalindorf, had been jointly settled by Mennonites and Jews. Established in the 1840s in Kherson province, the original settlement had six villages, each with around five hundred inhabitants. Only a small number of Mennonites participated initially—the Russian government recruited eight per village to serve as model farmers—

but others soon arrived, bringing the population to eight hundred. Despite maintaining separate religious and educational systems, Mennonites cultivated good relations, lest they become a "mockery to the Jews."[59] Anti-Semitism was nevertheless common. Prejudices of Jews as backward and lazy dated at least to the nineteenth century.[60] By the early 1920s, some Mennonites conflated Bolshevism with Judaism. Both inside and outside the USSR, leaders utilized anti-Semitism as a means of encouraging emigration.[61]

Nazi occupiers sought to exacerbate these prejudices. The first step was to "Germanize" local Mennonites, who did not always meet expectations. Some, thought to be Soviet agents, were shot. Those remaining were vetted, categorized, and reeducated. Among the first to arrive in German-speaking villages, close on the heels of the Wehrmacht, were Nazi anthropologists. Especially in Romanian-occupied Transnistria and Ukraine's military-administered zones, Himmler's Special Command R catalogued "ethnic Germans," sifting them through a so-called German Racial List. Their general rubric: "no drop of German blood may be lost." Individuals were assigned one of three levels of Germanness. Those believed to possess untainted heritage were placed in the first category. Anyone thought to have partial Ukrainian or Russian lineage, biologically "pure" individuals who had married outside the race, and those with suspect political backgrounds found themselves in one of the lower two. Only in cases of mixed German-Jewish families was German blood to be rejected, as this had been "jeopardized by the foreign content."[62] Alfred Rosenberg's East Ministry deployed a similar team of eighty researchers, known as Special Command Stumpp, to catalogue "ethnic Germans" in civilian administered areas. Headed by ethnologist Karl Stumpp—himself a former Russian citizen from the Odessa region—the Command documented hundreds of villages, including dozens of Mennonite settlements. Stumpp's group distributed questionnaires, asking individuals of German heritage to provide full genealogical information. By completing these forms, Mennonites aligned their personal histories with Nazi conceptions of blood inheritance and diasporic peoplehood. "From which province and place in Germany did your ancestors emigrate?" one questionnaire asked. Many responded: "Danzig." Others, "Holland."[63] While narratives of Dutch ancestry had once distanced Mennonites from Germanness, they now signaled Aryan blood.

Nazi occupiers gained support for genocide through anti-Semitic propaganda. Locals received a foretaste during the invasion, when German planes dropped leaflets over Ukraine. "Beat the Jew-Commissar," one sheet read, "his mug asks for a brick!"[64] Beyond genealogical information, ethnologists took detailed statements on Mennonites' experiences under Soviet rule. "How many German families are without a head of household?" they asked, noting the number of colonists banned, starved, or murdered since the First World War.[65] Such studies helped construct a narrative of suffering under "Judeo-Bolshevism." Mennonites learned to emphasize Jews' supposedly degenerate characteristics, conjuring the "criminal and grotesque faces of Jewish bureaucrats" or mimicking the "sneering," "curse-laden" speech of Jewish secret service agents.[66] Antipathy toward Soviet police ran deep. It had not been atypical for Bolshevik agents to claim that "Mennonites had been the main base for the carrying out of counter-revolutionary fascist activities," or that "They are the most reactionary part of the German population."[67] These and similar arguments were used to justify the exile and execution of tens of thousands of preachers, businessmen, and families. In the words of one Mennonite, this was "true Bolshevism," under "rule of the Jews."[68]

Nazi recruiters deployed such logic to grow their murder squads. At least one Mennonite was already serving with the Einsatzgruppen. Heinrich Wiens, a Molotschna native who had immigrated to Danzig in 1930, now returned to Ukraine as a sub-commander for Einsatzgruppe D. Operating throughout German-occupied territory, he and his soldiers forced Jews to strip naked before climbing into gas vans, where they were asphyxiated. Wiens made other Jews pull bodies from the vehicles before killing them too.[69] Units like Wiens's employed local Russian and Ukrainian speakers as well as "ethnic Germans" as auxiliary policemen. Beginning in October 1941, one to two dozen Mennonites from Chortitza, along with another fifty volunteers, reportedly joined Einsatzgruppe C, helping massacre the area's remaining 30,000 Jews—as well as thousands of communists, partisans, Roma, and mentally or physically disabled persons. Murderers transported victims to a ravine south of Zaporizhia and slaughtered them. One Mennonite later recalled how in early 1942, these perpetrators—men he had known since childhood—"celebrated the completion of the extermination of the Jews in the Zaporizhia region."[70] Fewer killing actions occurred in the immediate area around Molotschna, which Einstazgruppe D described as "always nearly Jew-free."[71] Partly because of the colony's purity, Himmler saw fit to raise a private Mennonite army. In addition to a larger regional Self Defense militia, consisting mostly of Russian and Ukrainian speakers, he ordered the formation of several all-German cavalry squadrons. Rather than serving on the front, these show troops protected the settlement. "I forbid," Himmler wrote, "that the three ethnic German cavalry squadrons be taken out of the Halbstadt area."[72] Remaining outside army jurisdiction, they were eventually inducted into the Waffen-SS.

Like most Mennonites in Ukraine, policemen and soldiers were not long-time church members, as no congregations had been operational since the mid-1930s. Contemporaries nevertheless would have understood them to be Mennonites, widely considered an ethnic as well as a religious appellation. Not all volunteers identified themselves as Mennonites. Some claimed to be "Protestants," or simply "believers"—a Nazi term indicating a pared-down form of Christianity. Others said nothing about the matter. For these, Mennonitism may have carried undesirable sectarian connotations. Many young people simply lacked information about the faith, which no one in the USSR had practiced publicly since their youth. They may also have worried about the confession's historic association with pacifism. Echoing interwar discussions of Mennonite racial degeneracy, one rumor suggested that Nazis would treat members as "white Jews."[73] But a pacifist background could also prove valuable. When Viktor Fast of Crimea joined the army, authorities commented that "His voluntary registration to the German Wehrmacht is interpreted to be a commitment to the German people, as the old Russian Mennonites in the past were exempt from military service."[74] Fast's childhood nonresistance made him more desirable for National Socialism, not less.

Like other populations, Mennonites experienced the war as a religious revival. Christianity flourished across Ukraine as locals sought to demonstrate their repudiation of atheist Bolshevism.[75] Although Nazi policy-makers were often ambivalent toward religion, they supported Mennonites' desire for German language worship. Himmler personally authorized the election of new elders in Chortitza and Molotschna.[76] As among other confessions, baptism became common; in 1942, the Chortitza congregation alone inducted one hundred candidates. Pacifism, however, was not promoted. "No one thought," one leader later recalled, "to emphasize or defend the Mennonite principle of nonresistance."[77] Religion more typically provided a means of currying Nazis' favor. Wehrmacht soldiers and SS officers sometimes attended Mennonite services, while ministers co-sponsored Christmas celebrations with Special Command R. One visitor to the Niederchortitza congregation reported that the entire assembly sang the German national anthem. Church buildings served as early sites for propaganda distribution. Gerhard Fast, a Mennonite ethnologist serving with Special Command Stumpp, delivered pro-Nazi speeches. "For each village we intend to prepare a report," he told one congregation; "we [want] to fill out questionnaires detailing kinship histories as far back as possible." Fast was careful to make "clear references to God," fusing Mennonite faith with racial ideology.[78]

A rebirth of church life was just one aspect of Germanization. Mennonite schools reopened with German-language instruction, while young people joined paramilitary formations. In September 1942, Himmler established a field station for the Ethnic German Office in Halbstadt. From there, SS Support Commandos radiated outward, providing aid to outlying settlements.[79] Villages received "German Shops," stocked with goods for German-only customers, as well as "German Houses," which sponsored propaganda rallies, lectures, plays, and cinema. Newsreels provided reports

Mennonite life in Nazi-occupied Ukraine became choreographed around expectations of racial purity and the production of official propaganda. During this 1942 visit to the Molotschna colony, Heinrich Himmler reviews a parade of "ethnic German" youth as photographers document the event.

of war victories, while films depicted "ethnic Germans" suffering under Judeo-Bolshevism. In 1941, the Propaganda Ministry rereleased *Frisians in Peril* under the title *Village in the Red Storm*, directly associating conquest with Mennonites in Ukraine. Pro-Nazi activists also arrived from the Reich, often as teachers, school superintendents, physicians, Red Cross nurses, or aid workers, both to build up the colonies for Germandom and to hold locals to high ideological standards. They encouraged Mennonites with "Jewish" first names like Abraham, Hannah, or Benjamin to choose new Aryan names. Teacher training institutes sprang up alongside military academies, including a major educational center near Molotschna. One lecturer reported on sessions in Chortitza and Kronau-Orloff. "There's little doubt that the German pedagogues from the Reich had never had a more grateful audience than these teachers, who swallowed with great hunger everything that was offered to them on pedagogical and political questions," he wrote. "It has never happened to me before that farm women want to rise to applaud in the midst of my presentation."[80]

Mennonite men and women joined Ukraine's new civil administration. Johann Epp, District Administrator for the entire Chortitza colony, presided over another eighteen mayors. Officials like Epp were expected to comply with the elimination of Ukraine's Jews. At the time of invasion, the villages under his jurisdiction possessed a total Jewish population of 1,066. Two years later, this number was 0.[81] Mennonites also served as mayors for towns and mid-sized cities outside the colonies. Collaborators sometimes received positions in reward for their service, as when Einsatzgruppe C promoted a volunteer named Heinrich Wiebe to the mayorship of Zaporizhia. In November 1941, Wiebe reported that all Jewish property in Zaporizhia—whose total population approached 300,000—had been seized. During the same month, Mayor Isaac Reimer of Novo-Zaporizhia reported that one hundred Jews were kept in an urban ghetto, while another four thousand were under observation. Other Mennonites staffed government offices or filled police squads. Many volunteered or were conscripted into the Wehrmacht, where they were especially used as interpreters. Most of these individuals initially remained on the Eastern Front, accompanying the army on its drive toward Stalingrad, or served on killing squads behind German lines. Jakob Reimer, a Mennonite from Halbstadt, aided the suppression of the Warsaw Ghetto Uprising in 1943 and participated in a massacre outside Lublin. He and others clubbed three hundred Jews into a pit before machine gunning them to death.[82]

Enough young Mennonites were eager for German posts that officials complained of a flight from the countryside. After forty young people left Kronau-Orloff, the Regional Commissar restricted mobility. One Chortitza administrator estimated that 2,000 "ethnic Germans" had departed for civil or military positions. Agrarian flight distressed leaders in part because of the association between Mennonites' land use and race. The confession's symbolic and economic value to the Third Reich rested on its ability to produce substantial quantities of grain. This was especially critical during the war's middle years, when Ukraine supplied food for the Eastern Front. In 1942, Hans Rempel, a Mennonite agricultural expert employed by the East Ministry, toured the colonies. Rempel took pains to dispel Soviet-era rumors that individuals of German heritage were less productive than non-Germans. "But is the labor capacity of the German farmers really lower than that of the Ukrainians?" he asked. "No!"[83] Rempel published a study in the same year to refute such assertions. Comparing land use among Black Sea settlers including Mennonites, Jews, and Protestants, he concluded that Jews were the least productive. "Unlike the other colonists," Rempel wrote, "the Jews gave no effort to cultivating the soil." When they planted winter rye, yields were dismal. Their settlements had little wheat, oats, or millet, no potatoes or legumes, and no shepherding. Neither were there spinning wheels, weaving racks, hemp, flax, or mulberries. In short, German-speaking farmers, and especially Mennonites, were in every respect "fitter and more capable" for "agricultural colonization."[84]

Rempel's findings highlight the relationship between knowledge production and the Holocaust. Since the Weimar era, "East Research" had fueled cries for an expansionist government. Now it aided colonialism and genocide. Graphs and statistics demonstrated German prowess, each data point alleging the inferiority of Russians, Ukrainians, or Jews. Studies published by the East Ministry featured Mennonites in glowing terms. In 1940, the Nazi bureaucrat Georg Leibbrandt, a longtime scholar of Mennonitism, contacted Benjamin Unruh, asking for his cooperation to "systematically identify and research the influence of Germandom in East Europe."[85] Unruh began work on a five-volume series.[86] Other Russian-born émigrés, including Gerhard Fast, Walter Quiring, and the novelist Hans Harder, undertook analogous work. East researchers became known as racial experts, whose opinions could carry the weight of life or death. Unruh served as a consultant for Nazi agencies, providing advice on the relative Jewishness of various little-known religious sects, while Leibbrandt represented the East Ministry at the 1942 Wannsee Conference, where he helped plan the Final Solution.[87]

Nazi scholars blamed the Mennonite settlements' Bolshevik-era decline on non-Germans. One researcher identified a Jewish plot to flood the colonies with foreign blood. Once they "had control of the villages in their hands," Jews supposedly ran them into the ground.[88] Chortitza's governing town provided one example. During the Soviet years, it had become a mid-sized industrial city, with only a minority of Mennonite inhabitants. The "administrative center Chortitza can today no longer be described as a German settlement," Karl Stumpp reported, "as there were 2,178 Germans before the war, as opposed to 11,507 Ukrainians and 402 Jews."[89] One alleged function of Jewish rule was a rising rate of intermarriage. In Molotschna, Special Command R found hundreds of mixed families. This "extremely high" number purportedly demonstrated "how much less the Soviet Commissars persecuted mixed marriages than pure German families."[90] The insinuation was that Jews and Bolsheviks sought to annihilate "ethnic Germans" by deporting those who married among themselves, while privileging those who diluted their bloodlines by taking non-German spouses.

Occupiers' solution was to "cleanse" the villages. Tropes of Jewish land degradation became linked to broader images of Judaism as a pestilence to be rooted out. Mennonites watched as soldiers marched Jewish men, women, and children from their homes. "They were all shot outside the village," one woman membered, "including half-Jews."[91] In the town of Felsenbach, three boys witnessed the execution of ninety-two Roma. Anyone could observe the carnage. Bloody earth coated half-dead bodies. "Three hundred people," one villager recalled at the site of a mass grave. "The covered pit moved for days."[92] Even in towns like Schönhorst, Nikolaifeld, and Tiege, which had only one or two Jewish families, each member was marked for destruction. Whether because of ideological anti-Semitism or out of fear for their own safety, townsfolk became informants, alerting authorities to the whereabouts of any remaining Jews. In Nikolaidorf, an SS commander learned that one girl had escaped. "There's a Jewess left somewhere in this area," he told villagers. She was apprehended and shot.[93] Residents recalled how their Jewish neighbors became ostracized. In Chortitza, they "lived in great fear and withdrew from public view." One day, the Mennonite Anna Sudermann passed a Jewish woman on the street—a former coworker from the town hospital. In earlier years, the women had been friendly. The Jewish nurse had even helped Sudermann find a job. But now, contact was taboo. "Our eyes met silently," Sudermann wrote; "we moved on."[94]

The fate of Stalindorf, the joint Jewish-Mennonite colony, illustrates the link between genocide and narratives of land use. In 1941, the settlement had approximately 10,000 Jews and 3,000 German speakers—the largest number in any of Ukraine's so-called Jewish districts. Contemporary Mennonite historians described their coreligionists' original position in the colony as "highly unfavorable." Because Jews had greatly outnumbered the first Mennonites, they were subjected to "arbitrary decisions regarding agriculture," while their fields suffered from nearby Jewish "waste-ground."[95] Occupiers built on such biases. Karl Stumpp claimed in his account of the settlement that "work-shy" Jews had lured Mennonites into their villages, only to use them as "slave labor." At issue, according to Einsatzgruppe C, were "unintelligent Jews who the [Russian] government considered unfit for higher purposes and 'relegated' to the countryside." There they had conducted a "terror regime," exploiting the labor of their Mennonite neighbors. Ironically, Einsatzgruppe C found the Jewish farmers too valuable to kill. In the interest of continuing agricultural work, the unit "abstained from shooting these Jews, finding it sufficient to liquidate the Jewish leadership." Only eight months later, after authorities found several thousand "ethnic German" replacements, did they murder the remainder of the colony's Jews. It was renamed "Friesendorf," or Frisian Village, in honor of Mennonites' supposedly Dutch racial heritage.[96]

Positive reports about cleansed settlements aimed to justify extermination in retrospect. The joint Protestant-Mennonite area of Kronau-Orloff received particular praise. Of all settlements in Ukraine, it was among the closest to the Nazi ideal of a closed German colony. Thirty of its forty-two villages had always been primarily German-speaking, and as Karl Stumpp happily reported, it was inherently "Jew-free." Only the Protestant administrative center of Kronau had contained "a few Jewish commissars and civil servants." Even the number of intermarriages with people believed to have Ukrainian and Russian background was "thankfully low." Of the 2,857 families Stumpp identified as German, only 65 were mixed. Most importantly, *"mixed marriages with Jews* absolutely did not occur."[97] To a greater degree than other settlements, Kronau-Orloff had also been emptied of alleged non-Germans. By November 1942, Nazi functionaries had deported four of the colony's Ukrainian-speaking villages, and the remaining eight were scheduled for removal. This facilitated a modest redistribution of land. While most of Ukraine's German speakers remained in Soviet-style collective farms—which occupiers supported in the short term to ensure wartime food production—officials in Kronau-Orloff had begun to dismantle this system. During 1942, the colony had produced 7,100 tons of wheat, a full ton more than its wartime quota; local farmers filled their egg requirement more than one and a half times; and in the month of September, they produced more milk than any of the twenty-one surrounding districts.[98]

Of course, Kronau-Orloff's success reflected preferential treatment. Nazis' racial theories predicted that Mennonites would outperform other populations. Their policies brought this to pass. While communities categorized as non-German were deliberately starved, Mennonites and other "ethnic Germans" received comparatively lavish support. In addition to luxury commodities like milk, butter, and meat, they acquired the best agricultural equipment and land available. If any Mennonites complained that their non-German neighbors were treated unfairly, this only led officials to believe that the villages "should be cleansed of other races more quickly."[99] In this way, expropriation and murder became their own solution. Germanized colonies in turn furnished propaganda for the Reich. The removal of Jews as well as Ukrainian- and Russian-speaking residents became celebrated as a triumph of racial perseverance. Nazi artists and photographers documented the process. Film footage of settlements like Chortitza and Molotschna was distributed on the home front. One reel shot in Halbstadt showed a sign reading "German Colony," followed by views of German-style buildings. Scenes of poultry and well-tended fields gave way to youth with swastika armbands. By linking agrarianism and race, propagandists demonstrated Mennonites' contribution to the war effort while promoting solidarity with other alleged Germans across Hitler's empire.[100]

If Nazi leaders imagined a Ukraine free of Jews—a dreamland where populations with German blood ruled and where Slavs lived in servile segregation—their plans came to an early end. Defeat at Stalingrad in 1943 had changed the tide of war, while repressive policies alienated much of the local population. Ukrainian nationalists had initially hoped that occupiers would support independence, but starvation and forced labor disabused them of their trust. Partisan attacks were on the rise. "The Germans have no sympathy," one Mennonite observed, "and fight—to their own detriment—hard and without forgiveness against them, forcing even the civilian population to suffer."[101] Believing that the Red Army would soon reconquer west of the Dnieper, Himmler ordered the evacuation of Ukraine's "ethnic Germans." Between September 1943 and early 1944, 200,000 German-speaking colonists, including 35,000 Mennonites, traveled by wagon, horseback, foot, and train to occupied Poland.[102] Trek leaders requisitioned supplies from Russian and Ukrainian speakers, who were generally left to fend for themselves. Mennonite men accompanied the columns in Self Defense squads or, less often, the Waffen-SS.

From Chortitza, genealogist Gerhard Fast was the last to leave. "A deathly *silence* prevailed on that Saturday morning," Fast recalled, "when I drove through the streets of Chortitza for the last time. Through the night a rain had fallen and the sunrise was beautiful when I left that apparently sleeping village." Like so many communities across Ukraine, National Socialists had emptied the colonies. As Fast put it, Nazi occupation was the "final chapter of the Mennonite settlement of the Ukraine." But, unlike thousands of Jewish shtetls, farms, and households, Mennonites had not been systematically exterminated. And unlike the purportedly substandard Russian- and Ukrainian-speaking villages depopulated to make way for "ethnic Germans," empty Mennonite settlements left a positive impression. "What a beautiful sight it was," Fast wrote, "to see the promising fields of winter wheat put out by our people." Even after the colonists had left, their land retained a sense of mystic peace. Visions of racial paradise survived here, if only for a moment. Beyond the grain lay the carnage of the retreating Wehrmacht; broken bridges and ruined cities; starving villages and mass graves. But Fast did not see these things. Instead, he dwelled on the quiet fields. Those who had sowed them were "far, far away on an endless journey."[103]

MENNONITES IN WARTHELAND

Dreams for a racial Mennonite utopia moved westward with the trek. Evacuees' journey from Ukraine brought them closer to coreligionists in Germany, enabling greater contact with the Mennonite Union. Himmler's functionaries initially dispersed the refugees across the Nazi empire, with groups settling in Upper Silesia, the Sudetenland, Saxony, and Danzig-West Prussia. Benjamin Unruh hoped to reassemble a majority in the new wartime province of Wartheland, located in occupied Poland. "I am increasingly convinced," Unruh told the Mennonite Union, "that the concentration of our co-nationals and coreligionists in Wartheland is the best plan."[104] Although some hoped for an eventual return to Ukraine, Unruh believed that Wartheland should become their new permanent home. Native Polish speakers could be displaced to make way for future Mennonite migrations. As late as 1944, Unruh was still collaborating with the Ethnic German Office to plan the "resettlement of our close co-nationals and coreligionists

Utopia displaced. Beginning in the autumn of 1943, the SS and German military evacuated most of Ukraine's "ethnic Germans," including 35,000 Mennonites. Nazi welfare officers planned to save them from Soviet advances by reconstructing their settlements in Germany and occupied Poland.

from overseas."[105] Nazi leaders supported this view. The Mennonites "form a small world power," Wartheland's official pamphlet on the confession explained. "After the war, whole groups of Mennonites overseas are prepared to settle unconditionally in the Reich. As returnees from overseas, they are especially important and welcome. Their willingness to return largely depends on how we now handle the Mennonites here."[106]

Wartheland already had a small Mennonite population. The "model province" had been created in 1939, following Poland's joint invasion by Germany and the Soviet Union. Although Nazi demographers estimated its initial German population at less than 7 percent of inhabitants, Governor Arthur Greiser vowed to Germanize the territory with unparalleled efficiency. In practice, this meant the segregation and persecution of anyone categorized as Polish or Jewish, coupled with preferential schooling, housing, and labor policies for German speakers—as well as a mass influx of "ethnic Germans" from the East. A short-lived Non-Aggression Pact with the USSR allowed hundreds of thousands to enter Wartheland, including five hundred Mennonites from war-damaged Lemberg. During the city's destruction, congregants had lost their church building and nearly all their possessions. "The homeland that our hearts had come to love," preacher Arnold Bachmann wrote to friends in Danzig-West Prussia, "has been torn away and has become foreign." Yet, just as a majority of Mennonites in Germany welcomed Hitler in 1933, those from Lemberg saw the dictator in

Christological terms. "There in the dark of our need," Bachmann continued, "like a beam of light from the heavens, came the call of our Führer: come!... And in bright streams, we rally to him."[107] Benjamin Unruh also encouraged the settlement of immigrants from Brazil and Canada who had arrived before the war. "Mennonites are all related to each other," he told the League of Germans from Russia, "and it is understandable that these families would like to settle together, and that they would like to come into an area where Germany will settle the other ethnically German Mennonites."[108] Aided by the Mennonite Union, these migrants lobbied authorities to create a series of homogeneous towns. "Everywhere one hears: '*We want to be settled together!*'" observers reported.[109] By 1941, they were living in a half dozen villages. "As hardened German pioneers," the Mennonite Union assessed, "they are ready to turn their whole energies to their current home in Wartheland."[110]

Three years later, the Union supported a greater influx. Governor Greiser, eager to recalibrate his still majority-Polish province as well as to offset Jewish labor lost to the gas chambers, agreed to admit 50,000 German speakers from the Black Sea, including transports from Chortitza and Molotschna. "These Germans are predominantly of agrarian background and possess valuable German blood," Greiser wrote in January 1944. "The acceptance of these peoples, who preserved their Germanness despite enormous Bolshevist repression, presents us with a unique opportunity to enrich the province."[111] Although lamenting the loss of their old settlements, refugees from Ukraine—like the Lemberg congregants before them—praised their new homeland. "We Germans, resettled ... in Wartheland," one Mennonite wrote, "express to our Führer Adolf Hitler our deepest gratitude for freeing us from the Jewish yoke of communism, and we are resolved to fight and to work for the German Reich, each in the place where he is put."[112] "We have nothing to lose," another settler explained, "because all that we had, we have lost. Now we only have our lives, and those we dedicate to the final victory."[113]

Arrival in the west heralded a new round of Germanization. At the border, migrants experienced routine delousing. The purification of Mennonites' bodies prefigured racial examinations awaiting them at large processing centers like Litzmannstadt—a mirror to the processes experienced by millions of Jews and Polish speakers destined for slave labor and extermination in camps like Chełmno, Bełżec, and Treblinka. By June 1944, Wartheland's Central Immigrant Office had tested tens of thousands of returnees from Ukraine, including Mennonites from both Chortitza and Molotschna. Through the creation of a "genetic catalogue," the office determined that these German speakers, despite living for more than a century "surrounded by the biologically larger power of the host population," had not developed significant "kinship with foreign races." This was attributed to their "strong religious affiliation, of which Mennonites are the outstanding example."[114] Naturalization officials echoed this evaluation when conferring German citizenship. In the Konin district, one administrator reported that "The Black Sea Germans who, including the larger children, speak and write perfect German, are the most valuable population Wartheland has yet received."[115]

Mennonite leaders assisted naturalization, weeding out members with undesirable racial traits. Johann Epp, former District Administrator of Chortitza, evaluated 7,000 Mennonites in Upper Silesia. He traveled among the camps, performing a "preliminary cleansing" to identify those unsuitable for citizenship.[116] With the help of Epp and others, authorities divided evacuees into two racial categories, labeled O and A. Mennonites in both groups received citizenship, although sometimes only on a trial basis, during which political loyalty would be monitored. Two-thirds among one group were designated "O-Cases."[117] These were the racial elite. Nazi physicians certified their suitability for settlement in Wartheland, where they, as a hearty frontier folk, were supposed to Germanize Polish land. Not all Mennonites were considered fit for this project, however. Up to a third were "A-Cases." Those of mixed race, intermarried individuals, and anyone who spoke little German received this designation. They were dispatched across the prewar borders of Germany, where they would be surrounded predominantly by German citizens. "That is good!" spokespersons assessed. "Because the majority only speak Russian, including the children; if they now return to the Russians or come near them, the Russian influence will grow."[118]

Racial processing provided a means of confessional purification. Church leaders did attempt to reduce A-Cases, especially when doing so allowed sick or elderly Mennonites to remain with relatives. But they had little sympathy for mixed families. "For our work," Benjamin Unruh noted, "there is no sense in becoming distracted with debates about *individual cases*."[119] While most migrants received O or A designations, a few were rejected altogether. Among the settlers in Upper Silesia, Johann Epp identified "pure Russians" and others "with whom the [citizenship] commission can't be bothered." Worst of all, in Epp's eyes, were the self-proclaimed "ethnic Germans" who carried Soviet papers identifying them as Russian or Ukrainian. In communist times, they had pursued social mobility by distancing themselves from Germanness. "These swine should wear the coat that they made," Epp insisted. Having spent much of the 1930s in Stalinist gulags, he disparaged all who had escaped a similar fate through Soviet collaboration. "In my need, they did not help me," Epp seethed, "and now I am supposed to support them.... they have repudiated their Germanness and trampled their forefathers into the muck, and now they ask to be considered equal to the brave and honest, to those who suffered for their Germanness?" For Epp, these turncoats were beyond redemption. He found only their children worth saving: "something can still be made of them."[120]

Wartheland's notorious religious policies also suited the interests of Mennonite leaders. Attempting to weaken alternative centers of power—especially Polish loyalty to the Catholic Church—Arthur Greiser and his functionaries savaged religious institutions. Breaking with official practice across the Reich, the governor uncoupled both Protestantism and Catholicism from his state bureaucracy, reducing the confessions to private associations. Catholic clergy in particular suffered as criminals; numerous monks and nuns were sent to concentration camps. In one Archdiocese, only 51 of 828 priests retained their posts. The rest were imprisoned, deported, or shot.[121] Yet if Protestant and Catholic leaders denounced Greiser as an enemy of religion, his dismantling of the state church system offered Mennonites—for the first time in German history—complete legal equality with fellow Christians. Spokespersons still had to ensure their own recognition. Benjamin Unruh believed that migrants' religious freedom depended on their commitment to Nazism. At the beginning of the war, when the Wehrmacht conquered French Alsace-Lorraine, the Gestapo banned local Mennonite congregations, forcing preachers to sign a statement that "we as a Free Church are dissolved."[122] Unruh aimed to avoid a similar development in Wartheland. Traveling from camp to camp, he held lectures in the day and worship services at night. The professor hoped his visits would "morally influence these true co-nationals and coreligionists and ease their integration into the Reich."[123] Speaking as often as three times a day, he regaled crowds of several hundred with praise for their "miraculous salvation from the hellish tyranny of Bolshevism."[124]

Eventually winning Governor Greiser's support, Unruh partnered with Union officials to draft a constitution for a United Mennonite Congregation in Reichsgau Wartheland. Because Greiser wanted "only *one* Mennonite Free Church in Wartheland," leaders labored to bridge historic divisions between the immigrants, bringing all members under Union auspices.[125] "The Mennonite Free Church in the East should now overcome the old schisms in a brotherly fashion," Unruh wrote.[126] He was especially eager to supply each camp with preachers who could perform weekly services as well as baptisms, marriages, communion, and burials. Inspired by Polish discrimination, he even turned an eye toward the "currently empty Catholic church buildings."[127] Spokespersons like Unruh—just as they worried about remigrants' Germanness—also harbored anxieties about their faith. "I hope the relationship with the other confessions in Wartheland will be brought to order," the professor wrote. "Some Mennonites have allowed themselves to be baptized in the Protestant Church and have converted....

We demand our confessional independence and integrity."[128] Greiser and Himmler ultimately permitted new ordinations by elders from Danzig-West Prussia and allowed ministers to move between camps. A number of baptisms occurred, as in 1944, when Bruno Ewert of Heubuden inducted fifty returnees. Such contact reminded migrants of their ancestral ties to the region. "Although our homesickness is often great," one Molotschna native wrote, "we want to become used to our new homeland, which in fact is our true homeland, from which our ancestors once emigrated and to which we have returned."[129]

But this "homeland" was not always what evacuees expected. "In most cases, the local Germans put on a friendly appearance," resettler Jacob Neufeld reported, "but they generally remain distant."[130] Another noted the incongruity of being harassed by border guards beneath a sign reading: "Welcome to the German Reich!"[131] Migrants' housing often failed to live up to promises made by Nazi leaders. As many as four hundred families crowded into each transit camp. Poor conditions contrasted with claims that Mennonites constituted a racial elite. As one administrator reported, the "living quarters were in part *so primitive* that they were not appropriate for Germans as culturally advanced as the Black Sea Germans."[132] Although Greiser ordered the camps cleared within four weeks, many operated for months. Nazi officials had already expelled hundreds of thousands of Polish speakers to make way for "ethnic Germans," yet housing shortages were chronic. "More space must be created through the evacuation of the Poles," SS leaders decided. "The numbers don't fit. There are more Black Sea Germans arriving than Poles leaving."[133] Between April and November of 1944, authorities evicted an additional 34,000 Polish speakers. Not all Mennonites approved of these measures. "We cannot understand why the Poles' houses and farms are indiscriminately taken away," Jacob Neufeld wrote. "Many of our people are supposed to receive property this way. That will be distressing for us, as years ago we ourselves were expelled from house and home."[134]

When returnees finally did receive housing, many were dissatisfied. Up to six families crammed into a single house. Some felt too restricted; others too mobile. "Do you think it will pay for us to get some chickens and hogs?" Johann Thiessen asked authorities in 1944. "It is possible that we will be settled ... some other place, and therefore we do not want to accumulate much property."[135] Thiessen's query illustrated the disparity between expectations for a new life and the often disappointing reality of Nazi resettlement programs. Wartime necessities outweighed migrants' desires. As the Red Army drew closer, Wartheland's government was unwilling to provide Mennonites with substantial farmland. Many were lucky to find even part-time employment. Some estate owners distinguished agriculture in occupied Poland from techniques in the now defunct Reich Commissariat Ukraine. Others questioned evacuees' loyalty or their racial integrity. In many cases, they simply preferred cheap Polish-speaking labor. Demographic challenges exacerbated the situation. Most adult Mennonites were women, while the majority of remaining men were drafted into the Wehrmacht or Waffen-SS.

In the war's last months, the Nazi East was on the brink of collapse. Soviet forces reached East Prussia and occupied Poland by early 1945. Along with millions of other German citizens, 45,000 Mennonites—including 10,000 from Danzig-West Prussia—began a chaotic retreat westward. Arthur Greiser had delayed evacuation until the last minute, needlessly endangering Wartheland's civilians—although his subordinates emphasized the threat, encouraging migrants to commit suicide rather than allow capture by the Red Army. "Should the Russians flood Europe, it is finished with us Russian refugees," Jacob Neufeld wrote. "The German regime has already accomplished many wonderful deeds … should they fail at the end, after so many years of the most difficult economic and military struggle? Never, no, that cannot be!"[136] But with rivers frozen in the bitter cold, Soviet tanks made rapid advances. Wartheland's Mennonites fled by train, wagon, bicycle, or foot. Many arrived in cities like Dresden and Berlin, only to experience some of the bloodiest fighting of the war. Refugees from Danzig-West Prussia attempted to escape northwest across the Baltic. Boats that evaded Soviet torpedoes and air raids landed in Holstein or Denmark. Thousands were not so lucky. Those overtaken by communist troops suffered torture, rape, and death. Others succumbed to starvation and disease. By May, Germany—its territory divided by four occupying armies—surrendered completely and unconditionally.

During the Second World War, Mennonite leaders had assisted Hitler's empire-building in Ukraine and Poland. As narratives of genetic purity and pioneering temperament became associated with racial superiority, the confession became a tool of Nazi colonialism. Whether the supposed suffering of Ukraine's settlers under "Judeo-Bolshevism" or the legendary yields of farmers in the American West, images of Mennonitism abetted National Socialists' quest for "living space" and the Holocaust of European Jews. As Nazi leaders constructed the East as a new frontier, they conceived the occupied territories as racial spaces in which some groups deserved access to land while others did not. Millions of Jews as well as Russian, Ukrainian, and Polish speakers lost their property and often their lives so that "ethnic Germans" could flourish. At the same time, this was a project of Germanization, in which Mennonites were reformed to meet certain racial and political standards. Uneven and often unsuccessful, this process drew support in varying degrees and toward different purposes from religious leaders, Nazi administrators, and individual members.

At the war's end, plans for a Mennonite utopia in Eastern Europe were destroyed as completely as the Nazi state. Churches were in ruins, congregations scattered. And yet, the conflict's conclusion did not spell the demise of the racial church. With refugees spilling out of Germany and aid workers pouring in, the postwar years would see the rise of a new brand of global Mennonite nationalism.

CHAPTER 7

MENNONITE NATIONALISM

POSTWAR AID AND THE POLITICS
OF REPATRIATION

The Mennonite refugees are undoubtedly a remnant
of a distinctly characterized people, a *"Volk,"* which
is neither Russian nor German.

—PETER DYCK, 1946[1]

On a spring evening in 1946, Robert Kreider picked his way through the
rubble of Berlin. The Mennonite Central Committee worker from Illinois
entered an abandoned building. He had heard rumors of Mennonite squat-
ters in the area and was searching for their hiding place. A noise drew his
attention. "There in the gloomy darkness," he wrote, "I saw about a dozen
people, mostly women and children. They eyed me half fearfully." At first,
the refugees refused to speak. But when Kreider told them he was a cousin
from across the seas, their shyness disappeared. He listened as they recounted the hard years under communism, their hopes on the eve of Germany's invasion, and the sobering realities of Nazi rule. In late 1943, they
had retreated with the Wehrmacht, and two years later, the Red Army's
advance forced them westward once again. Fleeing in pairs or small family
groups, they hid in farmyards and the ruins of east German cities, attempting to evade Bolshevik authorities. Hundreds, Kreider reported to MCC,
were "now slipping stealthily into Berlin in the frantic hope that this would
be an island of safety."[2]

   With the collapse of Hitler's empire in the spring of 1945, Allied leaders
announced the return of peace to the continent. But for millions of Europeans the war was far from over. In Germany alone, eight million "displaced persons," or DPs, found themselves adrift in an apocalyptic landscape. Scattered among them were some 45,000 Mennonites. Like those
Kreider met in Berlin, 35,000 had accompanied the Nazis out of Ukraine,
while 10,000 belonged to the former congregations of Poland, East Prussia,
and the Free City of Danzig. Allied officials considered the DPs an ethnic
snarl from which individuals should be untangled, separated, and returned
to their lands of origin. This was a time of national sifting, in which popu-

lation transfers begun under Soviet and Nazi auspices became reinvigorated. Mennonite refugees faced a dilemma. While most hoped to leave Europe for Canada or Paraguay, gaining travel papers required declaring their nationality. If migrants presented themselves as Ukrainian or Russian, they risked deportation to the USSR. But if they identified as "ethnic Germans"—as during the war—they confessed to Nazi collaboration and were ineligible for aid. Mennonite relief organizations advanced a third option. According to spokespersons like Kreider, the refugees were neither Russian nor German: they were Mennonite. Temporarily sanctioned by the United Nations, this claim enabled the transatlantic resettlement of thousands of Mennonite DPs.[3]

Postwar Mennonite nationalism was an accidental phenomenon. While previous leaders, especially in the USSR and the Americas, had portrayed their confession in separatist national terms, these assertions were largely discontinuous with the late 1940s. Rather than an inevitable confession-wide awakening, religious nationalism was a temporary response to historical contingencies. While its resurgence confirms the pervasiveness of collectivist thinking in war-torn Europe, it also raises questions about the nature of its appeal among minority populations. Mennonite nationalism, for all its reach, had few true converts. Refugees adopted it to access desirable services, but were often reluctant to discard Germanness; North American aid workers found it politically expedient, but—believing true Mennonitism to be bound by faith, not blood—many privately considered it theologically bankrupt. Nevertheless, through the second half of the twentieth century, it provided a baseline for debates about the confession's composition and future. Just as other nationalists sought to rebuild their communities by uniting separated families, efforts to assist Mennonite refugees reinforced notions of global cohesion, structuring responses to denazification, repatriation, and reconciliation.

ACCIDENTAL NATIONALISM

Occupied Germany at the end of the Second World War held millions of DPs—decommissioned soldiers, homeless citizens, former prisoners of war, and liberated concentration camp inmates. Hitler had imported many as forced laborers, and now they hoped to return to their countries of origin. East European governments supported repatriation as a means of rebuilding national populations, while the United Nations believed it would reduce ethnic conflict. Approximately one million DPs, however, would not or could not return to their homelands. Nearly half of these were categorized as Poles. Another 100,000 were thought to be Ukrainian; 150,000 had arrived from the Baltics; and 250,000 were Jews. Smaller numbers from Yugoslavia, Hungary, and Slovakia rounded out the total. Rather than returning

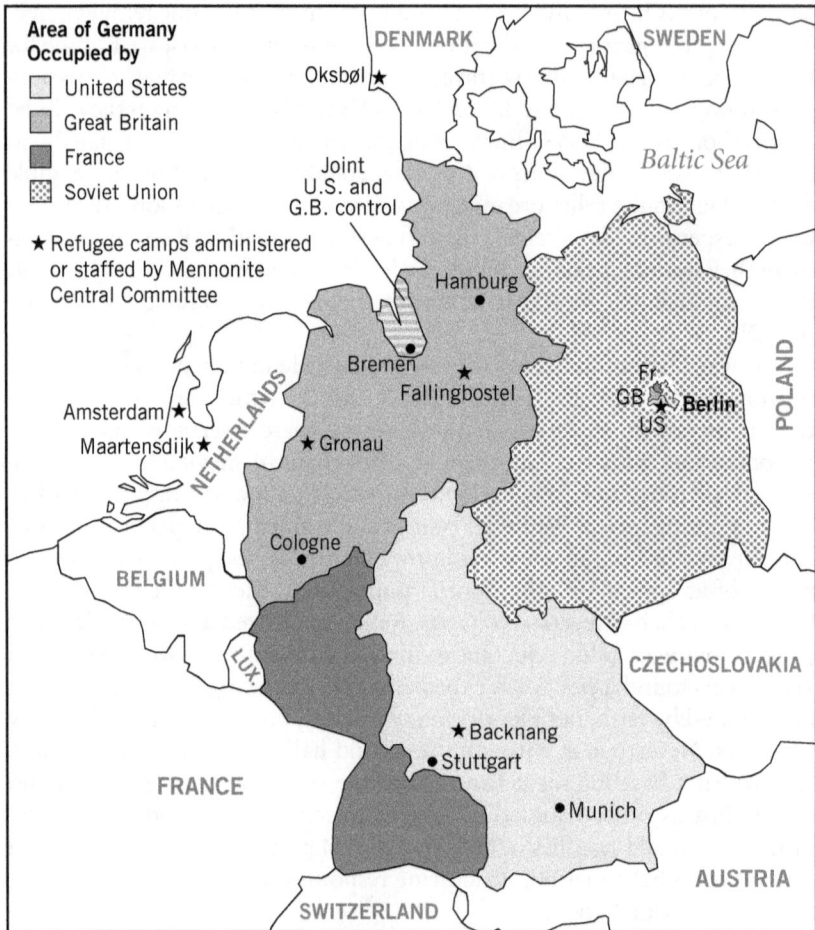

Area of Germany Occupied by

- ☐ United States
- ☐ Great Britain
- ☐ France
- ☐ Soviet Union

★ Refugee camps administered or staffed by Mennonite Central Committee

DENMARK

SWEDEN

Oksbøl ★

Baltic Sea

Joint U.S. and G.B. control

Hamburg ●

Bremen ●

★ Fallingbostel

Fr
GB ★ Berlin
US

POLAND

Amsterdam ★
Maartensdijk ★

★ Gronau

NETHERLANDS

BELGIUM

Cologne ●

LUX.

CZECHOSLOVAKIA

FRANCE

★ Backnang
● Stuttgart

● Munich

AUSTRIA

SWITZERLAND

Occupied Germany, 1947

to Eastern Europe, where refugees feared political reprisals, they sought emigration abroad, often to North or South America, Australia, or Palestine.[4] The majority of Mennonite DPs had once been Soviet citizens and were thus due for repatriation to the USSR. Stalin promoted this plan on what he claimed were humanitarian grounds. Yet Mennonites considered it hardly better than a death sentence. "We could think of nothing more terrible," one expatriate wrote, "than to be shipped back to the Soviet Union." Refugees knew that after accepting aid from National Socialists, Soviet authorities would consider them traitors. Women in particular faced retributive violence, including rape by Red Army soldiers. Repatriates anticipated hard labor in Siberian gulags. When police in Austria attempted to board one group onto a train for the USSR, they refused. "Shoot me and my children!" a woman screamed, clasping her offspring in front of her, "Do it now! Do it right here!... We are not going back to Russia."[5]

For many, time had already run out. Soviet officers rounded up thousands of Mennonites within months of capitulation. Observers feared that barely half remained. The Red Army ultimately deported 280,000 of the 350,000 "ethnic Germans" fleeing the Soviet Union, including 23,000 Mennonites.[6] On their own, there was little that church leaders in Germany could do. Occupation governments restricted mobility, downed postal systems prevented exchange, and ministers were often missing or dead. Isolated and afraid for their lives, refugees thought creatively. Denying both German and Russian identity, many claimed Mennonite nationality, a distinct culture with origins in the Dutch Reformation. In the summer of 1945, thirty-three gained entry into the Netherlands. These asylum-seekers told border guards that their ancestors had left the Netherlands four hundred years before; now they were returning to their homeland.[7] News of the group's success spread, and soon hundreds of Mennonites—all claiming Dutch heritage—were massing on the border. Migration authorities were at a loss. The refugees were certainly not Dutch in any legal sense. Most appeared to be former Soviet citizens, although many carried wartime German passports. Others had no papers at all. Their Low German language nevertheless bore similarities to certain old Dutch dialects—at least according to one philologist commissioned to study the matter. And when officials checked migrants' surnames against ancient emigration lists, they identified the majority as originating in the sixteenth-century Low Countries.[8]

Dutch authorities' interest reflected in part a desire to accommodate the North American-based Mennonite Central Committee. Since establishing modest centers in Poland, France, and England in 1939 to supply needy populations with clothes and canned goods, MCC had expanded its European presence. The organization focused primarily on domestic challenges during the war, especially supporting Mennonite conscientious objectors in the United States. But with the conflict's end, it had redirected attention across the Atlantic, establishing new offices in the Netherlands, Germany, Denmark, Austria, and Switzerland.[9] MCC was known for unrestricted generosity. "The name 'Mennonite,'" workers reported, "has a particularly good repute, just like the name 'Quaker' after the First World War."[10] In Germany alone, MCC supplied 4,500 tons of aid annually. Its soup kitchens fed 80,000 people per month, and in both 1946 and 1947, it was the single largest donor to the country's Protestant Relief Agency.[11] Yet while the organization claimed to "stand by all those in need, regardless of religion, race, or political orientation," its sponsors were especially interested in the welfare of European coreligionists.[12] As soon as workers in Amsterdam learned that a handful of refugees had arrived from Ukraine, they petitioned the Netherlands to admit any and all Mennonites knocking at its door.

Vowing to save as many as possible, MCC launched a Europe-wide rescue operation. As refugees fled westward, relief agents like Robert Kreider moved east to meet them. Often at great risk, they crept into the Russian zone, spiriting evacuees through guarded borders, into empty boxcars, and down abandoned mine shafts. MCC built on migrants' spontaneous decision to identify as Dutch, printing 5,000 official-looking "Menno Passports." These papers, displaying the phrase "Declaration of Dutch origin and permit to enter Holland," entitled bearers to joint protection under MCC and the Netherlands' General Mennonite Conference. After discovering the scheme, however, Bolshevik officials accused the country of illegally harboring Soviet citizens. When they put an end to the "hostile, secretive policy," only four hundred Mennonites had entered.[13] For MCC, the Dutch border's closing exemplified refugees' danger: if they stayed in Europe, they would either languish in German camps or disappear behind a swiftly closing Iron Curtain. As during the 1920s, migrants' preferred destination was Canada. But while this country had accepted 21,000 Russian-born Mennonites after the First World War, a reprisal appeared unlikely. It had refused immigrants perceived as ethnically German since declaring war on the Third Reich. And although MCC generally supported relocation to Canada, administrators also worried about drawbacks. Most alarming was the danger of secularization. The "subtle dangers of assimilation," according to one writer, approached the "outright animosity" of old Europe.[14]

The problem was solved in April 1946, when Paraguay agreed to accept Mennonites en masse and without restrictions. The landlocked country, which had granted autonomy to a small "Mennonite State" in 1921, was eager to attract more of "these sacrificial pioneers of peace and labor."[15] If the country desired colonists for economic development, MCC was equally interested in its "wild" Chaco. Allegedly devoid of culture, the Chaco seemed far from the perils of assimilation and the horrors of communism. "Mennonite self-government in Paraguay has been very successful," one executive assessed; "the Mennonites of the Chaco do constitute an absolutely independent state. There has never been any application of any of the laws of Paraguay to them."[16] While intervention had indeed been minimal, settlers' internal politics were plagued by divisions. Several factions had developed, due largely to Nazi propaganda; in 1944 one dispute even culminated in a rare case of Mennonite-on-Mennonite violence. While MCC downplayed the situation (one agent assured a concerned J. Edgar Hoover that "there is no indication of any pro-Nazi activity"), the organization initiated a publicity campaign of its own, attempting to divert colonists' far from non-existent Nazi sympathies into an analogous enthusiasm for Mennonite pacifism.[17] After the war, leaders continued to tout Paraguay as a destination for European migrants, believing they could preserve their religious and ethnic traditions—including exemption from military service—in homogeneous villages. Drawing on old notions of "mother" and "daughter" colonies, MCC imagined the reconstitution of tsarist Russia's once great settlements. "Just as a spider spins its web out of his body," one sociologist theorized, "so new colonies tend to spin out of their own experiences and traditions a social organization similar to that of the parent body."[18]

Migrants hoping to exit Europe underwent screening through the UN's International Refugee Organization, dedicated to addressing the continent-wide crisis. Its constitution excluded, however, all "Persons of German ethnic origin, whether German nationals or members of German minorities in other countries, who ... have fled from, or into Germany ... in order to avoid falling into the hands of Allied armies."[19] As long as they were defined as "ethnic Germans," evacuees would be ineligible for aid. Religious nationalism offered an alternative. "These Mennonite refugees are neither 'Russian' nor 'German,'" the Canada-raised MCC worker Peter Dyck told officials, drawing inspiration from contemporary efforts to form an Israeli state; "they would best be classified as 'Mennonites,' which would be doing nothing more extraordinary than that which is constantly and everywhere done in the case of the Jews." While Dyck acknowledged that few spoke about their confession in overtly nationalist terms, he argued that they nevertheless constituted a nation: the idea of Mennonitism "is not confined to religion alone, nor does it connote a church or a church membership; it means infinitely more than that, embracing all that which culture, language, tradition, and a distinct way of life implies."[20] Mennonites, like Jews, should be entitled to special treatment, privileges, and self-determination.

The International Refugee Organization was skeptical. "A doubtful origin, dating back several centuries, cannot change the character of the present generation," an analyst wrote. "These people [are] members of the German minority, in all ethnic aspects and mentality, regardless of what historical claims they may have to an obscure remote ancestry."[21] Internally, MCC was inclined to agree. One study determined that "all are distinctly of German race and wish to hold on to their German culture."[22] But spokespersons suppressed such findings. In February 1947, Europe's first postwar refugee ship sailed for Paraguay, carrying 2,303 Mennonites on board. Nearly all received funding from a forerunner of the International Refugee Organization. Although the UN never formally recognized Mennonitism as a distinct national category, it treated the confession as such, financing three additional transports to Latin America and sponsoring thousands of migrants to Canada through the early 1950s. It "is not the wish of the Organization," officials decided, to "view the Mennonites as ethnic Germans."[23] A general interest in white, Christian, anti-communist settlers aided refugees' cause. Their perceived racial and agrarian attributes rendered them desirable for governments across the Americas. Through programs that placed DPs with close relatives, many procured Canadian visas. Others gained entry as mining, forestry, or agricultural workers. Five hundred arrived in the United States through a Displaced Persons Act.

But national ambiguity cut both ways. While authorities often accepted MCC's narrative, several requested more information—a pugnacity that some leaders, invoking anti-Semitic tropes, attributed especially to Jewish emigration agents.[24] Even in the wake of the Holocaust, stories of Mennonite suffering at the hands of Jews had not subsided.[25] Scrutiny of migrants' war records led the International Refugee Organization to revoke their eligibility in July 1949. Files from Heinrich Himmler's Ethnic German Office, held at the newly established Berlin Document Center, suggested that refugees were not, as MCC insisted, a "nonpolitical group who found National Socialism under the German occupation of the Ukraine as abhorrent as the rule of communistic Russia."[26] Rather, the International Refugee Organization learned that many had acquired German citizenship as early as 1942, while virtually all adult men had performed armed service. It further determined that some had served with "reprehensible units," including the Waffen-SS, the Einsatzgruppen, and the *Sicherheitsdienst*. This knowledge rendered suspect claims of Mennonite nationality. While individuals could still receive aid upon proving that they had accepted citizenship "under stress or compulsion," new applicants had to be cross-referenced at the Berlin Document Center.[27] MCC estimated that under the altered regulations, only 5 percent would qualify.

But leaders pressed on. Rather than confirming the International Refugee Organization's interpretation, MCC retrenched its position. Spokespersons now asserted that while Ukraine's Mennonites had behaved as "ethnic Germans" during the war, they did so under coercion. A people "unmistakably other than German," they joined Nazi organizations *"exclusively and only in order that they might protect themselves from the Bolshevik agents."*[28] MCC stressed the difficulty of their position. "Remaining in the Soviet Union meant slavery or death," one administrator explained. "It is therefore understandable that the Mennonites in Russia have left the country and want to go to their relatives in Canada."[29] This logic benefited from an international climate increasingly sympathetic to ex-Nazis and Nazi collaborators. With the rise of the Cold War, anti-communism became more salient in the West than anti-fascism. Mennonite migrants took advantage of the shift, emphasizing their long-standing opposition to the USSR. "It is not only my desire to emigrate to Canada because of my relatives," one visa applicant wrote, "but it is an old and long-cherished desire born in the difficult, disastrous hours under the Bolshevik dictatorship."[30] Refugees from Ukraine downplayed their war records while simultaneously casting collaboration as a strategic partnership in the "free world's" struggle against communism.

In the end, Mennonite Central Committee prevailed. Just as during the 1920s, a dispersed network of activists, utilizing multiple strategic narratives, enlisted powerful allies to facilitate a mass population transfer. Having won influence through relief work, MCC called in its favors. US and Canadian officials contacted the International Refugee Organization at its urging, confirming that they would welcome refugees despite Nazi ties. "No change in Canadian policy re acceptance of Mennonites," Ottawa wired Geneva.[31] When refugees' eligibility was officially reinstated in October 1949, MCC's operations were nearing completion. It had already relocated most of its charges to Paraguay or Canada. Yet the resumption of support from the International Refugee Organization galvanized efforts to help those dubbed the "hard-core cases." These migrants found it difficult to leave Europe because of their medical conditions or political backgrounds. Among sixty-two applicants from the Danzig area, Canadian officials found that more than half had been Nazi Party members. Others were rejected for making false statements about their military involvement. Restrictions were nevertheless waning. In March 1950, Canada legalized the immigration of all "ethnic Germans" who had not held German citizenship before the Second World War. Six months later, the country eliminated its eleven-year ban on German citizens; in 1951, it allowed the immigration of Waffen-SS members who could prove forcible conscription; and by 1955, even volunteers could enter. MCC capitalized on these changes, concluding its refugee program by the mid-1950s. Final tallies recorded the emigration of more than 15,000 Mennonites, including nearly all non-repatriated refugees from Ukraine.[32]

UNEASY NATIONALISTS

"Can one be a Mennonite and not a Christian?" This question tugged at the consciences of MCC administrators. "In Mennonite circles," Peter Dyck observed in 1950, "one often hears the expression, 'our nation,' meaning the brotherhood, the 'Church,' the entirety of Mennonitism."[33] On one hand, Dyck endorsed the term. For him, Mennonites seemed to exhibit a cohesive set of ethnic characteristics. Dialects like Low German and Pennsylvania Dutch served as confessional languages, and while the spectrum of Mennonite dress—ranging from bonnets and suspenders to modest department store wear—was far from uniform, it supplied an endless topic of conversation. In addition to typically deep knowledge of the Bible, experiences in rural farming communities often gave members a common professional and anecdotal vocabulary. And widely held collective memories of persecution found articulation in bedtime stories, prayer, weekly sermons, and everyday discussions. Recollections of old homelands in Central and Eastern Europe were further preserved through inherited practices and material objects— hymns and worship books brought across the Atlantic, photographs, furniture, and clocks manufactured in prewar south Russia, heirloom seeds, Turkey Red Wheat, silk products, and a host of recipes and favorite baked goods: *Zwieback, Roll-Koke, Pfeffernüsse, Verenike, Bubbat, Bohne Beroge, Borscht, Portzilke, Moos*.[34] Yet Dyck regretted that for many, the confession's nationalist elements held more appeal than its theology. Speaking Low German, he noted, could make one more "Mennonite" than practicing adult baptism. The ultimate test of belonging often lay in a pool of traditional surnames: "too frequently, we consider the 'real' and 'good' Mennonites to be those named Janzen, Klassen, Dyck, Wall, and so on."[35] By focusing on ethnicity, Dyck believed that some members wrongly prioritized cultural purity over religious observance.

The irony was that MCC agents like Dyck were themselves partly responsible for creating and popularizing the notion of a Mennonite nation. What were MCC's refugee operations, after all, but an elaborate exercise in ethnic nationalism? It was no accident that newspapers and pamphlets distributed by MCC and its partner agencies aimed to "enliven the feeling of solidarity" among Mennonite migrants, as well as to reconnect missing persons to the larger confessional fold.[36] The very notion that refugees were "lost" until MCC located them served to link positive experiences of familial reunification with a feeling of global peoplehood. Efforts to construct national sensibilities were particularly evident in MCC's refugee camps. During 1946 and 1947, the organization established a series of holding areas across Germany's Allied zones. Cataloguing the names and addresses of all known evacuees, aid workers sought to assemble them into these spaces. Here, they could gain access to clothing, food, and spiritual nourishment, as well as the protection of British, French, and American military authorities. Anyone hoping to enter an MCC camp had to prove their Mennonite background—much as they would have had to pass Nazi racial tests during the war. Physical and aural characteristics became prerequisite. "They are all Low-German folk with good Mennonite names," Robert Kreider wrote of one group. "They have an unmistakable 'Mennonite appearance,' these rugged, blond, peasant folk."[37] Low German speakers and those with typical surnames were most likely to clear exams. Wearing clothing traditional to the colonies of Ukraine or the ability to sing certain songs could also help. In ambiguous cases, officers posed questions about Anabaptist history or theology.

MCC reinforced notions of Mennonite nationality through periodical literature. One biweekly, begun in 1947 and entitled *Our Paper*, provided a search service through which migrants could print the names of missing friends or family members. A year later, MCC expanded this model, introducing *The Mennonite*, a newspaper for settlers across the globe. Appearing in German—"the international language of the Mennonites"—it brought news, theological discussions, and requests for mutual aid to households throughout Europe and the Americas.[38] *The Mennonite* clarified MCC's ambition for centralized control. As Chairman P. C. Hiebert informed the "Mennonite nation" in the inaugural issue, "The Mennonites of the world have established contact and begun, more or less, to recognize the Mennonite Central Committee as the mediator and servant of all groups."[39] Nationalized interpretations spread also among non-Mennonite populations. In the Wurttemberg town of Backnang, one reporter described an MCC compound in the hills south of the train station. "A few hundred Mennonites are perched up there," the writer noted, depicting them as wayfarers who would soon "spring over to their happier coreligionists in the USA, Canada, and South America." Readers of the Backnang paper learned of their new neighbors as "Russian colonists of Flemish and northwest German descent." If their national background appeared something of a potpourri, migrants' "austere, disciplined" character went unquestioned. For Backnangers, the Mennonites' peoplehood was as timeless as their evening hymns, whose "sad wistful melodies" floated down nightly, filling the village with the sounds of the eastern steppes.[40]

In the camps, MCC instructed charges to identify as Mennonites and not as Germans. This was emphasized especially when preparing refugees for interviews with medical doctors, UN officials, or other immigration agents. "How should I answer the question about nationality?" one memo read. The correct response: "Mennonite."[41] Refugees learned that by adopting this label, they would be processed in a preferential manner. The concept was easy enough to master. Long adept at switching between claims of German, Dutch, and Russian nationality, they had little trouble grasping a Mennonite variant. Indeed for some, this narrative became a mark of pride. Proponents contrasted their confessional identity to National Socialists' "Prussian militarism," positing a comparatively healthy kind of peoplehood. One MCC executive explained that the refugees "had not been absorbed by the countries in which they lived," nor had they adopted the "militaristic spirit of the modern German state which began with Frederick the Great and continued until recent years."[42] Although some continued to see Mennonitism as a small branch on a great German tree, others disagreed. "That German 'tree,'" they responded, "does nothing to care for us; it wants at the moment nothing to do with us. And here we are aided by that controversial concept of our own 'nation,' an idea which can preserve us, keep us among our own."[43]

Mennonite nationalism was not MCC's sole property. Refugees reformulated it for their own reasons, even deploying iterations against their

Peter Dyck (front center) with baptismal candidates at MCC's Backnang camp, 1947. Refugee facilities provided space for confessional recalibration, enabling agents to identify coreligionists and to secure their theological loyalty before sponsoring migration to Paraguay or Canada.

North American benefactors. Sometimes, administrators believed they had done their job too well. Questions of everyday piety especially heightened tensions. Through MCC programs, thousands of self-identified Mennonites without congregational backgrounds came into religious orbit. Refugees who had never before shown religiosity suddenly became pious. Camp worship attendance boomed. While officials lauded the revivalist atmosphere, they also questioned migrants' sincerity. After one upswing in baptisms, suspicious leaders discovered that the rite was rumored to enhance emigration prospects.[44] The organization's services were so desirable that even non-Mennonites hoped to benefit. One Catholic imposter nearly passed the screening process at the Backnang camp. Having lived among Mennonites in Ukraine, he spoke fluent Low German and was well-versed in the confession's cultural practices. Like many imposters who sought access to refugee camps across occupied Germany, this Catholic donned certain national characteristics to gain entry. The game was up, however, when interrogators asked his place of baptism: "The River Jordan," he replied.[45] The story of the unsuccessful Catholic may have provided a good laugh for MCC executives, but it also tapped a gnawing anxiety about the premise of their program. For every devout Catholic or Protestant it turned away, MCC accepted dozens of ethnically defined Mennonites—many of whom knew or cared little about Christian faith. "It is a problem," Peter Dyck lamented, "that there are hundreds, even thousands, among us, who do not recognize

Christ as their personal savior, but who nevertheless wish to be seen as Mennonite and who are generally recognized as such."[46]

MCC's solution was to refine its requirements. Poor experiences with the first transports to Latin America had demonstrated that not all "so-called or would-be Mennonites are good Mennonites in terms of colonization in Paraguay." Upon landing, a number had refused to travel on to the Chaco. Several among those who did turned out to be war criminals from the Netherlands. Administrators learned that even migrants who used their true names often misrepresented their war records, settlement intentions, and commitment to Christianity. Officials began morality screenings in 1948. "Not all who applied to go to Paraguay," an interrogator reported, "were found eligible from our MCC office point of view. A great deal of detailed information was gathered through these interviews, some of which is encouraging; very much of which is depressing."[47] Administrators particularly condemned common law marriages. Many refugees had become separated from their spouses. Thousands were dead, imprisoned, or repatriated to the Soviet Union. Of 641 families in one Paraguayan settlement, 40 percent had no male head of household. Women's desire to remarry, even if their husbands remained alive in the USSR, threatened notions of sexual propriety and confessional purity. An international summit regulated the matter in 1949, allowing individuals to remarry as long as they had not heard from their partner for seven years.[48]

For both proponents and detractors of Mennonite nationalism, Judaism provided the most common model. "One often hears comparisons," Dyck noted, "between us Mennonites and the nation of Israel."[49] Postwar sermons were filled with references to the Book of Exodus. Preachers likened MCC leaders to Moses, spoke of Soviet territory as the Red Sea, and compared Canada and Paraguay to the land of milk and honey.[50] This language reinforced notions of Mennonitism as a chosen people, united by blood as well as faith. But while MCC explicitly termed its refugee operations a "Mennonite Exodus," officials also saw Jewish history as an admonition against religious nationalism. "Judaism," one skeptic argued, "offers us a good example of a nation that in our time is no longer primarily bound by religion. Many Jews are in fact atheists and belong to the Jewish *nation*, because they have a common history, common enemies, and common interests."[51] Both Mennonite and non-Mennonite scholars described Anabaptism in similar terms. In 1948, the sociologist E. K. Francis traced its transition "from religious group to ethnic group."[52] He concluded that through territorial isolation in Europe and the Americas, Mennonites had developed distinct national characteristics. It thus became possible for individuals to be Mennonite without holding congregational membership. Francis raised eyebrows with his claim that "the preservation of the Mennonite ethnic community took precedence over that of the faith, which had become an almost peripheral concern."[53] "Does he go beyond the diagnosis to suggest a cure?" one reviewer asked. "Few who have rubbed shoulders with the early Anabaptist martyrs can rejoice with Dr. Francis."[54]

Church leaders found the notion of Mennonite ethnicity deeply troubling. On one hand, many noted that the idea was "in part correct." Having grown up in rural Low German– or Pennsylvania Dutch–speaking households, they found it difficult to deny. Virtually all MCC affiliates perceived themselves to be genealogically descended from sixteenth-century Anabaptists as well as directly related to other members across the globe. Yet at the same time, they also feared that cultural traditions could "be seen as something godly, something religious."[55] This seemed a betrayal of the faith's most fundamental principles. As practitioners of a religion once known for piety, iconoclasm, and voluntary membership, how could they interpret ethno-nationalism as anything other than idolatrous, even blasphemous? Arguing that Mennonite nationalism was—at least theologically speaking—anti-Mennonite, spokespersons criticized the concept they had helped create. "Global Mennonitism has never been *a national* community," historian Cornelius Krahn wrote in 1952—just three years after defending Mennonite nationality to the International Refugee Organization. Such ambivalence did not only reflect religious scruples, however. Leaders also felt hampered by changing demographics. "Whether we like it or not," Krahn pointed out, "we must come to terms with the fact that only a minority of Mennonitism speaks and thinks in German."[56] By midcentury, a majority of white members spoke English. Some knew French or Russian; others were learning Spanish and Portuguese. Perhaps less apparent, but certainly on the horizon, was a growing number of converts of color. Mission stations across Asia, Africa, and the Americas were spreading the gospel to people whose histories and physiognomies differentiated them from "ethnic Mennonites."

Efforts to reframe Anabaptism as an inclusive global faith ironically ushered in new forms of religious nationalism. Even discussions of heterogeneity reinscribed the notion of a "worldwide brotherhood," separated by language and culture, but grounded in the love of Jesus Christ. With titles like *Mennonite Life*, *Mennonite Yearbook*, and *Mennonite World*, postwar literature aimed to reach and reflect global audiences. Richly illustrated, Mennonite papers, magazines, and bulletins focused on the commonplace and the everyday. Writers depicted farm work in Nebraska or pioneer construction in the Brazilian jungle. Regular topics included church architecture, food preparation, traditional clothing, and biographies of MCC heroes. Graphics of globes sometimes embellished sections of international news, grids of latitude and longitude suggesting the confession's many migration routes. Leaders typically linked their projects to a romanticized interpretation of sixteenth-century theology, known as the "Anabaptist Vision." Coined in

1943 by US historian Harold Bender, this term referred to a time when Anabaptism supposedly constituted a united movement, guided by discipleship, fellowship, and pacifism. Bender's message was that Mennonitism possessed a central essence—a set of core values whose continuity could be assessed, its purity perfected.[57]

Proponents of the "Anabaptist Vision" frequently repackaged racial interpretations for a postwar context. "Even today, every Mennonite can—with very few exceptions—say that at least the blood of some of those thousands of martyrs flows in his veins," claimed one popular history book, authored by a former Nazi. "May that be a holy obligation, to at least orient our lives according to the principles for which they *gave their lives*."[58] Invocations of Mennonite heritage served as a call to action, helping spur new, large-scale peace programs. According to Harold Bender, it was the "basic double truth" of biblical commission and cultural destiny that gave Mennonites their mandate for global peace activism. "We are the children of our past," he argued, "and that past both calls and qualifies us for the task of a world-wide Christian peace action today."[59] In 1950, MCC partnered with coreligionists in West Germany, France, the Netherlands, and Switzerland to form a Mennonite Voluntary Service program. Young adults from Europe and North America traveled the world, promoting a diversified agenda of development work, foreign missions, Latin American colonization, and anti-nuclear activism. By 1955, this organization had sponsored 1,859 camps in thirty-seven countries or territories, with nearly 70,000 participants.[60] These activities reflected an expanded understanding of peacemaking. Rather than simply opposing war, members sought to build peace. Positively connoted phrases, including "peace witness," "peace action," and "peace service," came into vogue. Although organizers entreated all Christians to join them, notions of radical discipleship retained a flavor of confessional exceptionalism. As one leader wrote, the "Mennonites are children of God, called and elected to perform a role in history."[61]

REFORMING GERMANNESS

For the 15,000 Mennonites who remained in what would become West Germany, MCC assistance carried a price. As the organization transported refugees westward across the Atlantic, it simultaneously exported ideology east. With canned goods and soap came carefully packaged notions of what it meant to be Mennonite. MCC expected coreligionists in Europe to conform to North American standards of Anabaptist propriety—especially regarding the doctrine of pacifism. Not all congregations supported aid. "There are those in our brotherhood, who have all kinds of objections against helping Germans," MCC worker C. F. Klassen admitted in 1948. "They remind us of the fact that our German brothers have not been immune to

Prussian militarism." If leaders in North America had spent the war attempting to preserve pacifism, their European counterparts had worked to stamp it out. Activists like Klassen nevertheless believed that the legacies of Nazism—if left unaddressed—would threaten efforts to construct Mennonitism as a global peace church. They claimed an obligation to reform their wayward coreligionists. By helping them build "a new church on the old Biblical and Mennonite foundation ... the bond of brotherhood tying Mennonites of the Old and the New World together will be strengthened, and international Mennonitism will see its mission responsibility stimulated."[62] Reforming Germanness was critical to reconstruction globally.

The first step was to reintroduce pacifism. MCC propagandists held lectures and distributed literature across the western zones of occupation. In September 1947, the first major gathering of Mennonites in conquered Germany brought more than one hundred youth to a retreat center in Baden. "It is clear," organizers wrote, "that these young people ... still stand under the influence of false ideologies." By setting them on the path of peace, interventionists hoped to reshape "the overall future of German Mennonitism."[63] This would not be easy. While discussions about pacifism had continued through the Third Reich, not a single member had refused conscription since the 1870s. Plaques honoring fallen soldiers from both World Wars hung in prominent locations in many sanctuaries. Yet peace activists were optimistic. "In Germany," Harold Bender reported, "a growing number is ready to take the position that they cannot participate again in war. The entire body of elders and preachers of the West Prussian Mennonite refugees in Denmark have now taken this position."[64]

Because of its symbolic importance—both as the long-alleged homeland of Mennonitism and as the perceived instigator of the Second World War—Germany received disproportionate attention from the Anabaptist welfare community. Just as Allied planners distributed billions of dollars in Marshall Plan funding to secure West European allies in the burgeoning Cold War, confessional leaders identified Germany as a new keystone in their pacifist edifice. Few Mennonite populations had exhibited uniform nonresistance during the war years. Large numbers in France, Switzerland, the Netherlands, and even the United States and Canada took up arms. But while North American spokespersons sought to strengthen pacifism among all groups, they portrayed militarism—and especially "Prussian militarism" —as a specifically German issue. Indicative was the moral pass they granted refugees from Ukraine. Due to the rule of atheistic Bolshevism, they had ostensibly been led astray through a "25-year gap in spiritual training." Despite the fact that more Mennonites from Ukraine served in Hitler's armies, it was those in Germany whom commentators chastised for ignoring "fundamental biblical teachings."[65] By readopting the "forgotten message" of nonresistance, these communities were expected to fit themselves into a larger Anabaptist collectivity from which they had fallen. Some embraced their position as Mennonitism's prodigal branch, seeing pacifism as a means of reasserting their place in the global church. Elder Bruno Enss recalled that after Hitler's rise, "our position regarding nonresistance became consciously or unconsciously ever more uncertain." Enss vowed not to rest "until many or all brothers and sisters of our Menno-folk are convinced of the correctness of nonresistance."[66]

The tentative rediscovery of pacifism among leaders like Enss came just as West Germany's new federal government debated its own position on war. Politicians were wary of repeating the Third Reich's mistakes. In 1949, constitutional framers limited the country to defensive forces, placing military operations under civilian administration and granting spending control to parliament. The most relevant section for Mennonites read, "No one may be forced to perform military service against his conscience."[67] Members in German lands could for the first time apply for noncombatant or alternative service on the basis of fundamental right. West Germany's most liberal Mennonites championed conscientious objection. Leading institutions, including the Mennonite Union, condemned war as "unchristian," while one group of young people resolved to "promote the idea of peace and its practical application in all areas of life."[68] When West Germany reinstated conscription in 1956, progressives formed a German Mennonite Peace Committee, helping youth to write anti-war statements, preparing conscripts for draft interviews, and facilitating alternative service programs.

Not all were inclined to readopt pacifism. Like many Protestants and Catholics reluctant to acknowledge complicity with Nazism, some Mennonites denied guilt. MCC administrators Harold Bender and C. F. Klassen met staunch opposition when they approached one group of churchmen. "I had five sons, three of which fell in the war," a deacon bristled, "Now are we brothers or not?" "Of course you are brothers!" Bender replied. "But it would be good," Klassen added, "if you would become nonresistant again."[69] An informal consensus developed that Mennonites who lived through the Third Reich had little for which to apologize. In part, this reflected MCC's refugee operations, which depended on a public belief in Mennonite innocence. The organization insisted from the outset that its charges were "not (a) collaborators, (b) traitors or quislings, nor (c) war criminals."[70] While such statements referred primarily to migrants from Ukraine, extending this logic to members from prewar Danzig, Poland, and Germany was a short leap. "One is often asked how it could be possible that convinced Christians—even Mennonites—were able to fall in with Hitler's views," delegate Dirk Cattepoel told the fourth Mennonite World Conference, held in the United States in 1948. "Right, but then Nazism did not approach us with concentration camps, religious persecution, extinction of the mentally ill, and gassing of the Jews; but with the motto, 'Freedom and Bread!'"

While Cattepoel considered all Germans guilty of political misjudgment, he also asserted that Mennonites and others had practiced a "resistance against Nazism ... far greater than could become known in the outside world."[71]

Spokespersons from occupied Germany claimed to have exhibited defiant heroism. In the same way that state church administrators often cast their congregations as bastions of opposition, retroactively constructing a distinction between religious integrity and Nazi depravity, selective storytelling allowed Mennonite leaders to argue that they had presented a united front against Hitler. Elder Emil Händiges, for instance, whitewashed his coworkers' activities: "even in the most critical situations they remained true to our confession of faith. When propaganda was undertaken by the 'German Christians' to promote their principles in our midst, they were warded off with [a] sharp declaration." Händiges also stated that Mennonites had taken "a very determined stand ... against the advocates of anti-Semitism."[72] By this, he meant they had defended the supposedly "Jewish" Old Testament as an integral part of the Bible. Although such examples had some basis in fact, the notion of a concerted Mennonite resistance was unabashedly ex post facto, while insinuations that leadership had done anything to help European Jews were perverse. Nevertheless, scholars of collaboration largely exonerated the confession. Conservative historian Hans Rothfels featured it in one study as an example of "constant passive resistance."[73] Had Mennonites only been more numerous, Rothfels implied, the Third Reich might have come to an earlier end. Well into the 1970s, it was not uncommon for members to proudly (and erroneously) declare: "No Mennonite was accused or convicted of war crimes."[74]

Congregants were more likely to identify as victims of Nazism than as perpetrators. Acute material deprivation allowed them to argue that Hitler had ruined their communities. Indeed, a majority of Mennonites in West Germany were expatriates from the East. Between 1944 and 1950, 12 million German citizens and "ethnic Germans" fled or were violently expelled from Eastern Europe to occupied Germany and Austria. With them came most surviving Mennonites from the Prussian east. By 1946, only two hundred remained in their old homelands. Several thousand had died in the war, remained prisoners in the Soviet Union, or immigrated to the Americas. The remaining 9,000 found new homes in the Federal Republic. Termed the "Catastrophe of the West Prussian Mennonites," their exodus became a story of terror and tears.[75] Recollections from survivors appeared in confessional periodicals, allowing readers across the globe to relive the final hours of expulsion. "Those who were fleeing westwards along the roads and were resting too often were overrun by the Red Army," one elder reported from a refugee camp in Denmark. "They experienced terrible things—plundering, raping of women of all ages, displacement, need, and suffering."[76] Reports spoke of families brutally parted, of elderly men worked to death in camps, of girls assaulted and tortured. Those lucky enough to escape saw themselves as only marginally better off. By the decade's end, two-thirds of West Germany's Mennonites remained in limbo. "They still are homeless refugees," Emil Händiges decried. "The formerly wealthy leading men of the East are now absolutely without means of support, rendering the most lowly service as farm laborers." Referencing the language of Nazi expansionism, Händiges concluded it was only now, in the wake of Hitler's defeat, that Germans had truly become a "people without space."[77]

Yet destitution was not refugees' only grievance. Händiges' bitter quip about "living space" testified that the loss of their ancestral homelands weighed heavily. As during the interwar period, when spokespersons argued that the Treaty of Versailles unfairly divided their communities, complete expulsion in 1945 seemed to shake confessional foundations. "With this catastrophe," Händiges explained, "so much was destroyed that was once the joy and glory of our hearts." Having long intertwined racial and religious identity with the land they cultivated, congregations' uprooting appeared an affront to natural order: "How much harder it was for our Mennonite farmers to separate themselves from their old homesteads! What bitter feelings arose when for the last time they tended their purebred stock and then turned them out into the cold winter, leaving them at last free and untethered until they perished!"[78] At first, some planned a return to Poland. MCC briefly operated relief centers near Danzig and Warsaw, contemplating the reestablishment of a church in areas formerly "farmed chiefly by Mennonites."[79] With the onset of the Cold War, however, the general flow of migration remained westward, not east.

Over time, the "lost" Baltic homeland became a place of mystic tragedy. Along with writers representing millions of other German-speaking expellees, Mennonite authors constructed an intricate memorial culture. They published voluminously on their old territory, stitching together every available piece of knowledge—as if amassing a complete body could reanimate the past. Popular and scholarly journals for history, genealogy, and homeland studies recounted engineering feats, tables of farm acreage, maps, migration routes, church plans, village outlays, and biographies. Behind this outpouring of minutiae—each detail obsolete and therefore fascinating—lay the gentle backdrop of landscape. For every hard-edged column and densely noted chart, there hovered the sky, the fields, and the coastline of the Baltic lowlands. In poetry and artwork, expellees depicted the Delta. Recollections of an aunt's cherry pancakes or the warm atmosphere in a church cloakroom returned key sounds, sights, and smells to "the alluring north German end moraine landscape."[80] The nostalgic paintings of Marie Bestvater, living in Buenos Aires, received particular acclaim. In 1959, a Mennonite college in Kansas received several of her pieces. "These paintings,"

A formerly Mennonite farm in northern Poland, painted by the expellee artist Marie Bestvater. If the immaculate yard invoked German order and the Dutch-style windmill recalled Anabaptist heritage, it was the expansive, melancholy landscape that spoke most to expatriates' experience of loss as well as, increasingly, to their desire for reconciliation.

the student newspaper reported, "are the result of a desire to preserve our Mennonite heritage and make it available to others. [Bestvater] found the beauty of the landscape around her Prussian home to be intimately associated with Mennonite history."[81] If Bestvater's windmills and waterways seemed out of place among Kansas prairies, the breadth of their dispersion evoked expellees' own sense of homelessness.

Yet if its Mennonite inhabitants had left, the Vistula Delta remained. Expatriates watched from afar. Many denigrated its new Polish-speaking residents, echoing Nazi-era notions of racial superiority. "The beautifully kept Werder," one elder reported, "is hardly to be recognized anymore."[82] Church buildings had become cinemas or horse stalls; farmyards were in disrepair. Nevertheless, reconciliation-oriented Mennonites began envisioning northern Poland as a space to confront their Nazi legacy. That another people tilled their precious soil provided a reminder of bad blood. Expellee Gustav Reimer reflected in 1965 from his new home in Uruguay: "'Our old homeland!' say some, when they see a picture of Danzig. 'Our homeland!' say the others, who grow up there now." For Reimer, Mennonites could not have been more dissimilar from Poland's inhabitants: they spoke different languages, practiced oppositional religions, and possessed divergent cultural backgrounds. Yet their common connection to the land "somehow binds the people together with each other!"[83] Imagining themselves both victims and aggressors in a millennia-old conflict with Poles, commentators like Reimer called for improved relations. Expellees still desired their old homes. "Do I no longer yearn for the country of my ancestors and of my youth?" one asked. "Oh yes, but for me, this is no reason to begrudge its current owners."[84]

In the early 1970s, West Germany's most progressive Mennonites proposed concrete steps for reconciliation. Following a political thaw allowing travel to Poland, Hamburg pastor Peter Foth organized a series of youth service trips. Sponsored by Operation Atonement, a West German peace organization, these journeys aimed to give young members an understanding of the Second World War and its impact on German-Polish relations. Operation Atonement had since 1967 sent small groups of volunteer laborers to Auschwitz, Majdanek, and Stutthof. As Holocaust tourism became increasingly popular, the names of these former concentration and death camps commanded heavy symbolic power. Stutthof held particular significance for Mennonites. Erected in 1939 near Danzig, it had been located in a dense area of Mennonite settlement. Among others, Mennonite contractors constructed the barracks; Mennonite guards helped staff the main facility; and Mennonite firms provided clothing, footwear, and other supplies. Mennonite farmers and industrialists throughout the Vistula Delta leased slave labor from Stutthof, exploiting dozens and even hundreds of prisoners. By liberation, 100,000 inmates had passed through the camp, which was responsible for some 60,000 deaths.[85] In the early 1970s, it served as a Holocaust memorial comprising fifty acres of facilities, including a gas chamber, crematorium, work halls, barracks, and command center. Peter Foth chose the site as his groups' primary destination.[86]

In an odd repetition of history, Mennonite youth helped rebuild the Stutthof concentration camp during the summers of 1973 and 1974. Representing congregations across West Germany, they reroofed buildings and fortified barracks originally constructed by Mennonite firms three decades earlier. These visits constituted a fluid blend of Holocaust memorialization and nostalgic sightseeing. After moving earth or mixing cement at Stutthof, work crews toured former Mennonite villages; following lectures on genocide, they worshiped in the old Danzig Mennonite church. Participants described the project as transformative. "For some of us the main reason for our trip to Poland was to visit the former Mennonite settlements," one girl reported. "But when we learned more about the history of Poland as well as about the country of today, our original purpose for taking the trip became less important to us: it was not a trip into the Mennonite past; we went there to experience the horrors of war and to show our compassion for the victims of Nazism."[87] This undertaking was not without controversy.

Especially after Chancellor Willy Brandt drew international attention for kneeling before a monument commemorating the Warsaw Ghetto Uprising, some Mennonites considered the trips untimely. One observer charged that allowing "young Germans of West Prussian heritage to perform construction work at Stutthof" was not simply insensitive; it was "distasteful and disturbing."[88] Others criticized the project on rightist grounds. Chief among these was the Mennonite historian Horst Gerlach, an expellee who sought to prove that "people of Mennonite heritage ... did not participate in the atrocities or denunciations at Stutthof."[89] While Gerlach admitted that Jews' treatment in the camp was "distressing," he insisted that the number of Jewish deaths had been overestimated, while comparable German casualties were underreported.[90]

Advocates of reconciliation decried such apologists. "In our congregations," Foth wrote, "there remains much near-sightedness and ignorance, and even naked revanchism. Still today, there is much lamenting about [Mennonites' own] suffering and at the same time much repression of the crimes that others suffered in the name of the Germans."[91] When one critic disparaged Foth's volunteer crews for refurbishing Stutthof while ignoring the dilapidation of nearby Mennonite cemeteries, the pastor retorted: "are the former concentration camps not also monstrous cemeteries?"[92] Yet even for purists like Foth, longing for the East proved inescapable. By the decade's midpoint, his Stutthof journeys had transitioned almost entirely into heritage tours. Busloads of expellees entered Poland to visit old farmyards, towns, churches, and graveyards. Visitors dwelled on their personal histories, recalling childhood stories or flight from Soviet soldiers. "It brought so many memories," one expellee reported. "For many, the tears were near."[93] If sightseers still occasionally made token stops at Stutthof, few went primarily for this purpose. More typical were the motivations of Siegfried Neufeld, who returned to his hometown of Heubuden to see the graves of his mother and sister.[94] This shift reflected in part a new consensus about confessional war guilt. "The Mennonites were steamrolled by the Third Reich," many came to believe, "just like other groups."[95] If their congregations had no resistance fighters and no conscientious objectors, they also deserved no special censure. By the mid-1970s few members in West Germany continued to see Nazi complicity as a barrier to participation in global Mennonitism. Other issues—particularly mass immigration from the Soviet Union—ensured their relevance.

THE FINAL REPATRIATION

Beginning in the 1970s, millions of migrants believed to possess German heritage relocated from the USSR to West Germany. Through "right of return" laws, the Federal Republic offered naturalization to any East European "ethnic Germans"—including nearly all Mennonites—who suffered deportation as a result of the Second World War. This program reflected both a condemnation and a continuation of Nazi race policies. Designed as a collective reparation, it constructed West Germany as a permanent homeland to which diasporic German speakers could "return."[96] Mennonite leaders across Europe and the Americas approved. Since the First World War, their own understandings of ethnic peoplehood had developed alongside campaigns to rescue coreligionists from the Soviet Union. In a report to the 1948 Mennonite World Conference, C. F. Klassen predicted the fall of Stalin's dictatorship: at that time, "it will be possible for us as the MCC to help our Mennonites and others, whose thirty years of suffering in the vast concentration camps of the USSR will call for a united relief effort greater than anything known to us heretofore."[97] As long as Mennonites stayed in communist lands, the confession would remain fractured. It was West Germany that finally offered a way out.

"Remigration" was a treasured ambition for thousands in the Soviet Union. "Our people are scattered across the country," one Mennonite wrote. *"All want to return to the German homeland, the Reich!"*[98] Those who had trekked from Ukraine to Wartheland contrasted Nazi rule with the violence, rape, and forced labor of their subsequent deportation to Siberia and Central Asia. Others recalled the kind treatment of 1918, when German forces briefly occupied south Russia. Narratives of Soviet oppression became central to Anabaptist self-understandings. "In the years of persecution, our Mennonite brotherhood has lost its best sons and daughters," one survivor mourned; "there is no confession that has as many martyrs as the Mennonite brotherhood during its four hundred years."[99] Even after Stalin's death, when the banished began emerging from work camps and labor colonies, many faced continued harassment. Their alleged Germanness drew epithets like "fascist" and "enemy of the people," while openly practicing Christians found limited opportunities in an atheist state. Prejudice ran both directions. Despite an emphasis on "friendship of the peoples," Soviet policies encouraged national distinctions. One woman later recalled: "My sorrow was that of many German mothers, particularly when surviving children reached marriageable age and lived in an area where there were few or no Germans and they married Russians."[100]

In 1956, Mennonite Central Committee established an East-West Office in Frankfurt, headed by aid worker Peter Dyck. The office prepared for extradition by cataloguing the names and locations of all known Mennonites in the USSR. "When the doors open," Dyck announced, "we want to be ready. The day of reunion and release will come."[101] Indeed, when it finally arrived more than a decade later, spokespersons in West Germany welcomed the influx. "The incorporation of the Mennonites from the USSR," the Mennonite Union declared, noting its own declining constituency, "could be very important for the further development of our confession in the Federal Republic."[102] Union leaders partnered with MCC and others in 1972 to establish a Mennonite Resettlement Program. Early estimates suggested that 20,000 hoped to immigrate. The number was in reality far higher. After the first waves became established, they brought friends and families. "If [only] everyone had been so motivated to get to heaven," one returnee later joked, "as they were to get to Germany!"[103] The final floodgates opened with the USSR's eventual demise. Of the two million "Germans from Russia" to arrive in Germany by 2004, some 280,000 were Anabaptists. While these bore various appellations, most identified as either Baptist or Mennonite. Approximately 180,000 had "Mennonite" surnames or were otherwise believed to possess Mennonite heritage. They included nearly all members from the former Soviet Union.[104]

Simply arriving in West Germany, however, was only half the battle. Upon reaching the Federal Republic, migrants faced a bevy of challenges. Local activists sought to ease their transition. Just as the Mennonite Union had always spoken for coreligionists who owed it little allegiance, the organization remained paternalistic. Although the country's extant membership was far smaller than the number of projected returnees, Chairman Hans Herzler found it "natural that we in the Union feel responsible in a special way for these coreligionists."[105] Aid workers visited individuals and families, informing them about local congregations. They further offered counseling services regarding housing, study, and career options, as well as visa assistance for those still in the USSR. Leaders across West Germany organized festivals and conferences; 2,500 attended one meeting. "There were many warm embraces and hearty handshakes, sometimes with tears," MCC News Service reported, "letters and addresses were exchanged; people strolled arm in arm around the meeting area. Some reunions ended separations of decades."[106] Others focused on church construction. "Many of the existing churches are overflowing Sunday after Sunday," observers noted. Immigrants hungered for a strong congregational life, complete with Bible study, choirs, and youth work. Invoking the atmosphere after the Second World War, the Union called for donations, asking the global Mennonite community to "sacrifice for our coreligionists from Russia."[107]

While aid poured in from Europe and North America, international sponsorship highlighted the movement's German-centrism. "One sees the need in Holland as well as in Germany," an observer in the Netherlands noted. "But because the returnees receive benefits from the German federal government and are quickly granted German citizenship, it is clear that it is more of a German matter."[108] West German policies entrenched returnees' already heightened sense of nationality. "You can see that Russian Germans here are more German in many ways," one commented, "particularly in their feelings of being German, than native Germans."[109] Upon proving ethnic identity, migrants underwent naturalization and received a sum of welcome money. West Germany granted additional resources to anyone wounded or expropriated during the war. Returnees who were older than age sixty-five obtained automatic pensions, and families received child support. "After long years of fretful waiting," read a welcome guide from the Ministry of the Interior, "you have come into this country, which shall become the new homeland for you and your children. You have given up your old homeland and with it connections that have grown over many decades, in order to live as Germans among Germans."[110] Following a short transition period, migrants were supposed to join West German society, conforming to acceptable citizenship standards.

Local Mennonites generally shared this expectation. Notions of "integration" and "assimilation" saturated discussions. When immigrants arrived, it was as if they crossed not just a physical border, but also a temporal boundary. In West German eyes, they seemed to come from a distant past. Just as earlier generations had decried the "backwardness" of rural conservatives, concerned leaders hoped to align repatriates with modernity. While many West German citizens sported liberal styles from perms to bikinis, immigrants favored modest clothing, including head coverings for women. Men and women sat on opposite sides of the sanctuary during worship. Even basic communication posed difficulties. Thick accents marked returnees' German, and in private, many preferred Low German or Russian. One North Rhine-Westphalian paper described them as "aliens from a different star."[111] Local Mennonites imagined their coreligionists to be on a journey of spiritual maturation. Informational booklets described needs generated by their "transplantation into an entirely different world" and their assumed "incorporation into the preexisting congregations."[112] Such language reinforced already condescending attitudes, casting immigrants as childlike. At the same time, it placed the onus on repatriates to adapt. "Returning" from the diaspora, they were expected to accommodate themselves to a homeland that had changed without them.

Not all were keen to assimilate. Many felt they had entered a strange and disappointing world. While returnees expected West Germany to be a Christian country, they encountered a populace largely apathetic or even hostile to religion. Between 1971 and 1982, the number of Protestants describing themselves as active church members fell from 37 percent to 14 percent; Catholics dropped from 49 to 38 percent.[113] In West German schools, evolution and sex education appeared to contradict biblical truths. "Have we come over here so that our children can be corrupted?" one mother demanded. Local congregants, who had mostly liberalized with the country around them, seemed little better. One immigrant's first disillusionment occurred in worship. "Modes of dress, hairstyles, jewelry," he recalled, "particularly the male clothing styles worn by women, shocked me. In Russia you could identify Christians by the clothes they wore on the street. In Germany, I could not see the difference even in the church sanctuary." Others commented on the laxness of Sunday attendance, critical interpretations of the Bible, and the toleration of female preachers. Most often, they questioned local Christians' commitment to their faith. How could Alexander Neufeld, a young immigrant from Estonia, feel at home in one West German youth group, when members heard "such powerful sermons and Bible teaching" on Sunday mornings, yet in the afternoon played soccer without further reflection? "In Estonia," Neufeld recalled, "we had four Sunday services."[114]

Church leaders on both sides of the Atlantic worried that immigrants remained "a foreign body in Germany," retaining "almost entirely the character of a Russian group."[115] In one sense, they praised these qualities. Affectionate descriptions of traditional customs—including "colorful babushkas" and "the long braids of young girls"—harkened to Nazi-era descriptions of Mennonites as a hearty settler folk.[116] In the wider media, onlookers expressed interest in returnees' fertility, commenting on their many children. There was also a certain idealizing of family life, in which they were alleged to possess a familial closeness "sadly missed in West German cities."[117] Yet fetishization of Mennonite bodies paled in comparison to earlier decades. The age of romantic nationalism had largely passed. And besides, nationalists had always turned on diasporic groups as soon as they stepped off the pages of story books. Most found them awkward and antiquated. Encounters produced anxieties for progressive Mennonites, not just about repatriates' well-being, but also about the confession itself. "I used to be disappointed that our and your congregations did not come together as willingly as we originally hoped," Peter Foth wrote shortly before German reunification to one immigrant elder. "We had hoped you resettlers would fill our shrinking congregations, that you would strengthen Mennonitism in Germany, and by extension, us." But a long string of uncomfortable negotiations dashed these desires. "Today I am no longer disappointed," Foth concluded. "Today I am, in the most positive sense of the word, 'ambivalent' about you."[118] Most returnees agreed. Of approximately four hundred Anabaptist congregations formed between 1972 and 2004, only one joined the Mennonite Union.[119]

Pan-confessional narratives in postwar Germany had promised an untenable future. Despite decades of fantasizing about reunification with the USSR's congregations, local leaders failed to predict the great disinterest their efforts would face. They had long mobilized around ethnic solidarity and global peoplehood. But these ideas disappointed as easily as they inspired. Even during its heyday in the 1940s, Mennonite nationalism was a fraught doctrine. Practitioners felt uneasy defending the primordialism of an idea so recently invented. Indeed, the rapidity of its spread suggests that

Mennonite Central Committee's narrative was not only, or even chiefly, the result of ideological conviction. As Peter Dyck explained in 1988, looking back through four decades, it was a temporary cloak, woven from the wool of political expediency: the refugees from Ukraine had "changed their identity when it suited them. They became chameleons.... all those in the Russian zone ... tried to pass themselves off as Germans so they would not be shipped back to Russia, but during the [International Refugee Organization] interviews they flipped and suddenly they were not Germans.... they played this game constantly." And yet, even for skeptics like Dyck, nationalism was difficult to shake. It seemed an uncomfortable truth. In "another sense, it wasn't a game," Dyck continued. The migrants "were neither German nor Russian nor even Dutch—they were Mennonite, a distinctly separate group."[120]

Mennonite nationalism was neither a unitary ideology nor a single set of practices. It constituted a diffuse set of claims and counterclaims, sometimes predicated on older practices and traditions, while also drawing from a wide repertoire of assumptions, tropes, and discourses arising at the end of the Second World War. Ethnic peoplehood held different connotations for refugees, for example, than for MCC officials. In some cases, it was merely convenient; at other moments, life or death. How individuals invoked it—whether they related it to Germanness, Russianness, communism, Nazism, or ruralism—reflected context. If constituent elements like song, dress, food, or history had long pedigrees of their own, they now assumed new legibility. Only in a land of rubble and hunger could Low German become a key to shelter and food; only in a Cold War world could knowledge of Mennonite history unlock transport to Latin America. MCC's brand of religious nationalism was one model among many. Members of color in the Global South fell outside the organization's definition. And even white populations in the USSR—typically considered emblematic of confessional ethnicity—developed alternative views. Upon arrival in Western Europe, it was precisely cultural difference that made extant congregations unacceptable to many returnees. With the ease it had once formed, postwar Mennonite nationalism could also fade away.

CONCLUSION

For no one can lay any foundation other than the one that
has been laid; that foundation is Jesus Christ.

—I CORINTHIANS 3:11[1]

"One third of the Mennonites in the world today are non-white," Executive
Secretary Cornelius Dyck reported in 1972 at the ninth Mennonite World
Conference. "They do not care much for Luther's sixteenth-century Europe,
which ethnic Mennonites consider important." Held in Curitiba, Brazil,
the assembly was meeting outside Europe and North America for the first
time since its founding nearly fifty years earlier. Organizers had chosen the
venue in response to growing concerns about the Western orientation of a
multicultural church. While white members in Germany, Paraguay, and the
United States spoke nostalgically about Swiss martyrs or lost settlements in
Ukraine, these things held little relevance for congregations of color, thousands of which had been established through missionary efforts since the
mid-nineteenth century. Voices from India and Indonesia, Ethiopia, and the
Navajo Nation were joining the confession. If all found common ground in
the gospel of Jesus Christ, narratives associated with "ethnic Mennonitism"
no longer provided a fitting foundation. Participants at the Curitiba gathering represented five continents and thirty-three countries, providing a clear
reminder of changing demographics. If the Mennonite World Conference,
Dyck charged, "is to continue as a useful instrument in the world brotherhood, it must be more than an ethnic gathering to celebrate a great past. It
must be a part of the mission Mennonites are being called to in the world,
not just white, Western Mennonites, but all Mennonites. Whether they are
in Asia, Africa, Latin America, or from minority groups in North America,
all must feel that this is their conference too."[2]

While Cornelius Dyck criticized "ethnic Mennonitism" for hindering
confessional unity, his assertion was in fact deeply ironic. The drive to form
a cohesive church was in many ways itself a product of ethnic nationalism.
Leaders like Dyck had long promoted religious globalism as a means of
uniting white communities across Europe, Central Asia, and the Americas.
Casting their faith in national terms, these leaders argued that white members' common history and collective traits rendered them part of a worldwide family. Espousing a creation myth of origins in sixteenth-century Switzerland and the Netherlands, commentators posited a culturally specific

and genetically transmissible form of peoplehood. They depicted Mennonitism, like other nationalities, as inheritable, passed from parent to child
through biological lines. Proponents celebrated this lineage, linking themselves to the confession's early martyrs. Especially during the Nazi period,
they proclaimed the confession a "racial church," describing it as an Aryan
analogue of Judaism. Notions of blood purity persisted well into the postwar era. "One of the striking developments in Germany under Hitler was
the great growth in interest in family history and genealogical research,"
US historian Harold Bender wrote. "It is encouraging to learn that a permanent interest in family history remains among the Mennonites in Germany, even after the Hitler regime has long since passed away."[3] It was the
North American Mennonite Central Committee—seeking to disassociate
the confession from National Socialism—that in the late 1940s most vocally
posited the existence of a "Mennonite nation." Supported by the United
Nations and other postwar bodies, MCC recapitulated nationalist and even
racialist interpretations, disseminating them across a global network of
white Mennonite "states," "colonies," and "settlements."

Nationalist activists have traditionally presented nations as primordial
and immutable. Formed in the mists of prehistory, they allegedly existed in
the personalities—perhaps even the blood—of their members. Historians,
sociologists, and race scientists attempted during much of the nineteenth
and twentieth centuries to pinpoint Mennonites within this framework.
Were they a Germanic people? Did they retain an original Dutch essence? Or,
alternatively, had they come to constitute their own national body? Such
formulations, however, are inadequate for describing Mennonite collectivism. Members' nationality was not an a priori trait, passively received and
uncritically lived. It was rather the subject of constant, acrimonious debate.
Whether on the Ukrainian steppes, the Canadian prairies, or in the jungles
of Brazil, congregants found nationality—like theology—an uncertain and
often divisive issue. Some chose to affiliate with Germanness; others rejected
German nationalism as un-Mennonite and un-Christian. Individuals not
infrequently adopted one stance only to reverse it a short while later. Many
were unconvinced that they should ascribe to earthly categories at all. As
Mennonites struggled to define, refine, and change their nationality, the
effects of civil war, migration prospects, regional tradition, and innumerable
other factors structured the palette of options available. Flows of events and
ideas may have enabled such debates to unfold across vast distances and
temporal spans, but particular iterations always reflected local conditions.
Depression-era Mexico necessarily produced different forms of identification
than did Cold War Kazakhstan. Contingent upon a range of rapidly changing circumstances, these processes were fluid, unpredictable, and multivalent.

The development of Mennonitism as an imagined global collectivity
would be unintelligible without the parallel rise of German nationalist

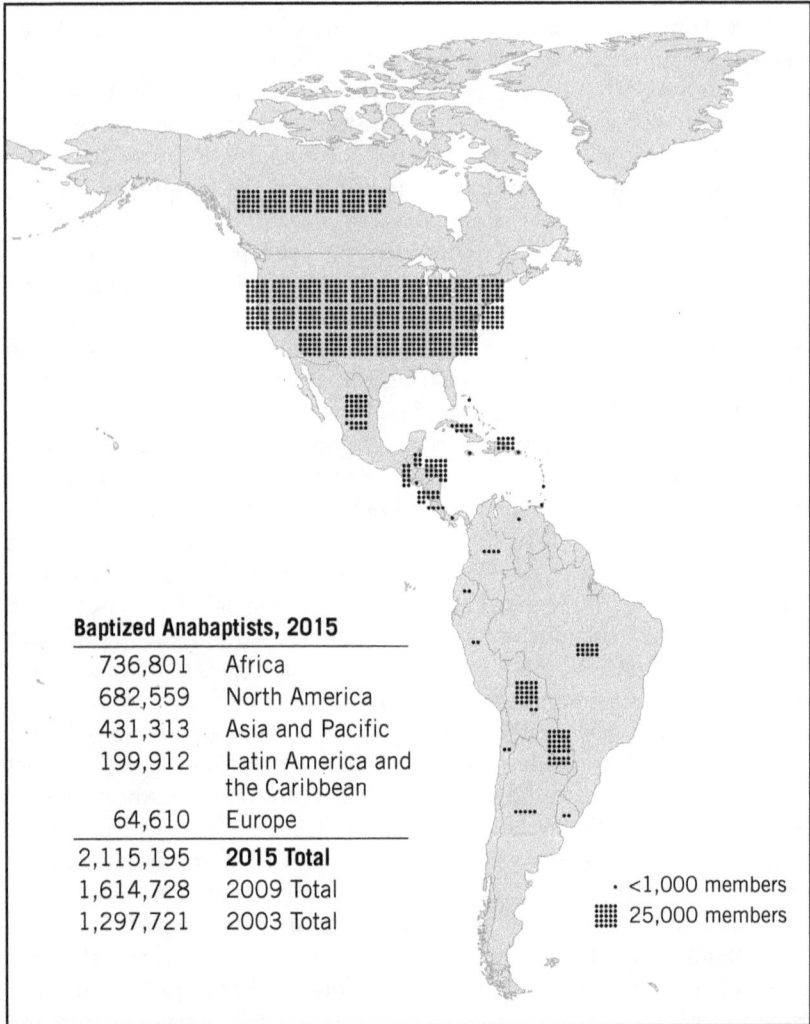

Baptized Anabaptists, 2015

736,801	Africa
682,559	North America
431,313	Asia and Pacific
199,912	Latin America and the Caribbean
64,610	Europe
2,115,195	**2015 Total**
1,614,728	2009 Total
1,297,721	2003 Total

· <1,000 members
▦ 25,000 members

In the twenty-first century, two-thirds of the world's Anabaptists are people of color. This 2015 map from Mennonite World Conference conveys the preponderance of congregations in the Global South—still a relatively recent development—while maintaining a long-standing commitment to confessional unity.

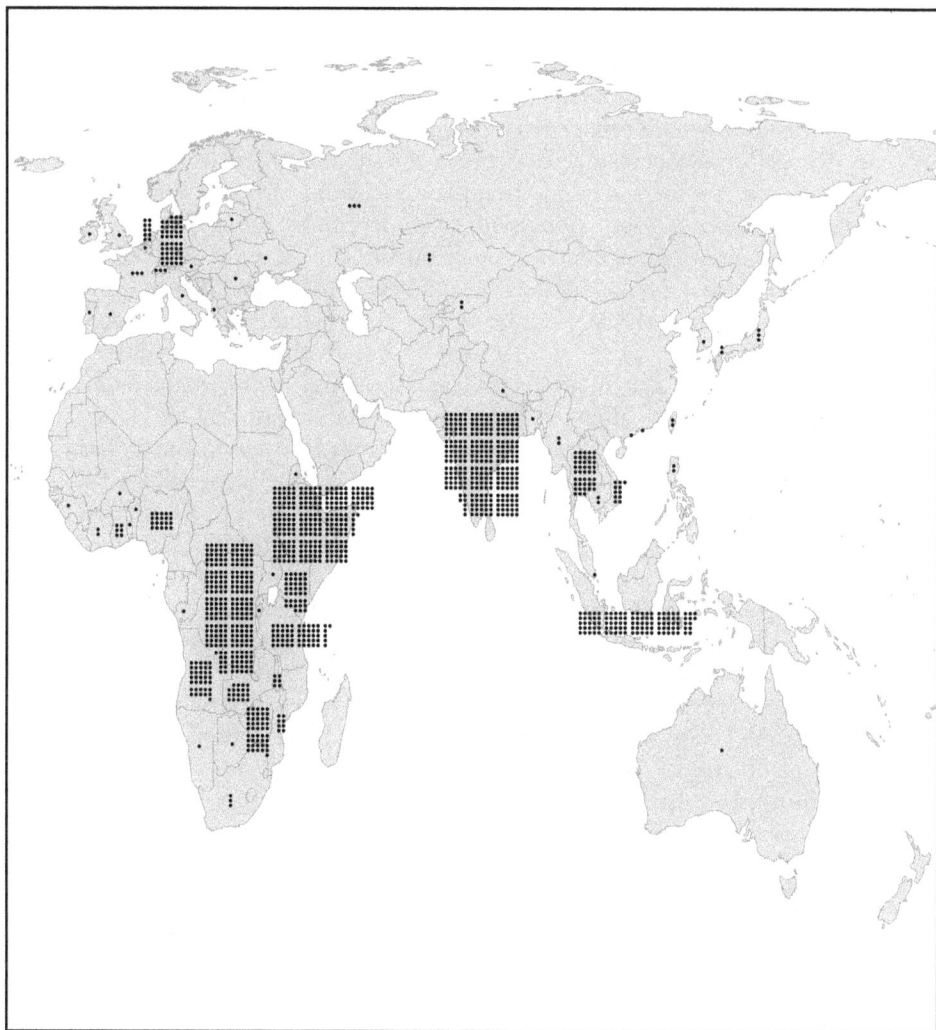

discourses. This is to say neither that Anabaptism was uniquely German nor that religious nationalisms were simply copies of older secular models. Rather, German nationalists provided a series of referents upon which confessional interpreters could draw. From the end of the eighteenth century to the opening of the twenty-first, Mennonite and German systems remained in dialogue with each other. Because allusions to Germanness nearly always influenced discussions of Mennonites' nationality, disassociating either one from the other would obscure the dialogic nature of each. It was missionary evangelism—couched in the rhetoric of nationalism—that in the 1820s first induced members across German lands to work together. While congregations in these states, along with many in the Netherlands, Imperial Russia, and elsewhere conducted "outer missions" to save the souls of distant populations in Java or Sumatra, they concurrently formulated an "inner mission" to protect the Mennonite-ness of their white, European coreligionists. Increasingly aware of their own location within a rapidly internationalizing system, a small group of visionaries sought to Germanize their confession. Especially after the founding of the German Empire in 1871, these leaders attempted to unite all members from Holstein to Baden, East Friesland to East Prussia. They appropriated the work of geographers and folklorists, claiming to identify an eternal Mennonite essence whose bearers they could systematically contact, catalogue, and cultivate. This project culminated during the 1880s in the establishment of a Union of Mennonite Congregations in the German Empire, whose scope and objectives closely followed the new nation-state's political ideology and geographic boundaries. Unionists entreated coreligionists to join on the basis of common nationality, while separatists, for their part, preferred regional working groups. Whether the Union would survive or fail depended on a collective belief in German affiliation.

Turning their attention abroad, commentators in Germany developed a sophisticated theory of worldwide diaspora. Tracing the tell-tale signs of Mennonitism across the globe, they claimed to discover places where settlers had etched their mark into local landscapes, clearing primeval forests, draining swamps, or turning arid steppes into fecund gardens of Eden. If German Mennonitism had blossomed in Central Europe, its Arcadian metaphor could also be extended to emigrant groups in Turkestan, Argentina, and the grain lands of North America. Because most diasporic members spoke German, and because they or their ancestors had once lived within the borders of what eventually became Germany, writers portrayed this territory as the common nursery of Mennonitism. Touting the achievements of diasporic communities provided a means of consolidating loyalties at home. Leaders suggested that a lively interest in their daughter settlements—especially "the consciousness that they are their mother congregations"—provided communities in Germany with a "powerful antidote to decay."[4]

Contact with their literal as well as figurative offspring abroad reminded these groups of their global ties and own innate virility. German nationalist commentators portrayed their country as the midpoint of the Anabaptist world, emphasizing its geographic centrality and historic significance. Flows of news, migration, and money were all expected to pass through this center. When the First World War threatened to snap global ties, spokespersons implored coreligionists in the Russian Empire and its successor states to "return home," initiating a process of remigration that—if modified by changing circumstances—would continue into the twenty-first century.

To be sure, there was nothing particularly novel about these events. Collectivist language had characterized Mennonite writings long before the rise of German nationalisms. Like activists of other backgrounds, confessional leaders deployed group-based narratives to induce change or stasis among their coreligionists. Whether referencing an eternal Christian church, regional conferences, or a single congregation, they invoked affiliation to motivate future action. While many scholars have associated nationalism with modernization, national discourses were neither structurally new nor did they coalesce into a coherent set of practices. Nationalist projects intertwined throughout the nineteenth and twentieth centuries with other collectivisms, many of which claimed ownership over traditions stretching back for millennia. Such alternative loyalties—whether regional, professional, religious, or otherwise—were themselves admittedly in flux. Claiming Prussian identity in 1950 meant something very different than it would have in 1850, in 1750, or at any other time. Yet if nationalist ideas differed radically from month to month, city to city, and person to person, it would be impossible to pull a common modernist thread through each iteration. Especially if the analytical net is cast wide enough to encompass conservative Anabaptists, the limitations of the modernist paradigm are clear. While those Amish and Mennonites opposed to certain forms of technology were less likely to adopt explicitly nationalist rhetoric than their more progressive coreligionists, they nevertheless existed alongside and within nationalisms. Even anti-nationalist, anti-modernist Anabaptists helped construct popular understandings of both nationalism and modernity, if only by expressing opposition. And just as conservatives rejected some technological innovations while embracing others, most adopted select nationalist precepts—community newspapers, for example, or nationally inflected terms like "peoplehood."[5]

By the same token, Mennonite collectivism cannot be examined solely through the lens of nationalism. Confessional spokespersons often encouraged coreligionists to be wary of nationalist attitudes, lest they compromise their faith. In all of Mennonite literature, I Corinthians 3:11—an appeal to base one's life on no other foundation than that of Christ—has perhaps been the most oft-cited biblical passage. This was Menno Simons' favorite quotation, and it permeated his published works. I Corinthians 3:11 emerged over subsequent centuries as an informal Mennonite motto, adorning the walls of worship houses and the mastheads of confessional periodicals. It captured for many the central tenet of Anabaptism: complete devotion to and radical discipleship of Jesus. Good Christians were to eschew actions emanating from any other principle. Indeed, Christocentrism seemed to demand the dismissal of all competing loci of authority—a belief that made many Mennonites' eventual embrace of nationalism all the more surprising. The Apostle Paul's words held a haunting power. They provided a persistent admonishment to anyone who believed that religion drew as much inspiration from earthly sources as from divine will. At the heart of any nationalism, Biblicists suspected, stood a blasphemous kernel. In this way, even the most nationalist of confessional spokespersons downplayed the profane and ostentatious elements of this-world collectivism, privileging instead the eternal Kingdom of God. When leaders like Cornelius Dyck encouraged coreligionists to foster unity in theological "content" while embracing diversity in cultural "form," they sought to re-center popular definitions of Mennonitism from ethnicity to faith.[6] Even if most white members truly were united by a common heritage, these commentators implored them to actively deemphasize this background. Such positions, ironically, reinforced a nationalized confessional structure through other means. Just as the vilification of German nationalism after the Second World War buttressed notions of a German nation from which "Nazism" and "Prussian militarism" could be expunged, calls to create a non-national Anabaptism were themselves a mode of nation-building. Popular understandings of the confession as a demographically coherent and statistically knowable body—ideas that had emerged in tandem with other European nationalist discourses—went unquestioned. As a result, observers often held heterogeneous understandings of Mennonitism that were both national and anti-nationalist at the same time.

Collectivism, for all its pervasiveness, was astonishingly frail. The ease with which populations transitioned from one narrative to another—from Germanness to Mennonitism, or from ethnic peoplehood to spiritual collectivity—undermines any theory of stable identity. Recent scholarship has sought to transcend such interpretations by treating nationalism as an ideological force, promoted by committed activists and flowing outward into broader populations. Through the dissemination of nationalist ideas, whether through newspapers, military service, elections, or other vectors, individuals supposedly come to think of themselves as part of a larger nation, most of whose members they will never meet. This view accurately demonstrates the constructed nature of collectivism, including its contingency upon ideological abstractions and material objects. In Imperial Germany, Mennonite demographers compiled address books of congregations across the country, uniting communities in Bavaria or Wurttemberg with coreligionists in Prussia and Hamburg through the proximity of printed names. Just as flags, pins, or other symbolic memorabilia could invoke larger national wholes, church directories became physical manifestations of Germanness. With the evolution of collectivist narratives, the meaning of such objects could and did shift. If nineteenth-century nationalisms were often tied to geographic boundaries, language use, cultural practices, and political affiliation, twentieth-century forms more likely emphasized racial components: blood, genealogy, and fair skin. The assembly of "racial passports" in the Third Reich allowed some Mennonites to imbue their accounts with racial characteristics. Producing knowledge about their personal and confessional heritage, family researchers symbolically infused heredity tables and ancestor lists with the blood of their forebearers. In turn, genealogists learned to re-conceptualize their own bodies, imagining their veins to pulse with the genetic legacy of the dead.

Yet collectivist narratives rarely resulted in coherent "imagined communities." This concept fails to account for the general ambivalence toward either German or Mennonite nationalisms exhibited by so many of the world's Anabaptists. Indeed, collectivist activists often possessed nearly inverse relationships with the overall mood and character of the populations they claimed to represent. The volumes leaders in Imperial Germany composed on the German nature of Mennonitism in fact signaled that their coreligionists found this idea far from compelling. Some rural conservatives expressed open hostility. Theological discrepancies, regional differences, linguistic barriers, and cultural variation all impeded the dissemination of a common vision. Similar attempts to brand the faith as nationally Dutch, Russian, or Mennonite only revealed the extent to which such claims were not self-evident. Encounters with coreligionists abroad typically served only to solidify differences. While the initial call to form a Mennonite World Conference came in 1912, the first meeting did not convene until thirteen years later. And when this and other institutions attempted to coordinate religious life among conservatives in various countries, they met with staunch opposition. Despite claiming traditionalist populations in Mexico, Pennsylvania, and elsewhere as "brethren" and "cousins," progressive spokespersons possessed little stock with many of these groups. Few knew they were supposedly part of a global Anabaptist nation. Those who did, cared little. Most were preoccupied with more immediate concerns: family, congregational life, agriculture, commerce, love. Even among those who identified in explicitly nationalist terms, Mennonitism and Germanness were just two among numerous possible categories. Individuals frequently constructed multiple national identities, developing a chameleon-like ability to blend in with their surroundings. In a single lifetime, some members—especially those from the Soviet Union—could espouse as many as six or seven different narratives: Russian, Dutch, Soviet, German, Mennonite, Paraguayan, Canadian.

Nationalist activists usually decried such side-switching. In their parlance, an inability to remain loyal to a single collectivity signaled "indifference." That this term could equally be applied in national or religious contexts demonstrates its widespread utility as a means of advocating collectivist participation. The concept's great malleability, however, suggests that it may be more accurate to see it as a motivational tool than as an adoptable stance in its own right. Indifference in one context could easily represent deep conviction in another. A conservative Mennonite might label a committed German nationalist "indifferent to religion," while simultaneously, this same nationalist might consider her Mennonite critic to be "nationally indifferent." In neither case would either individual have been truly apathetic. Suggesting otherwise would require identifying a particular mode of collectivism as normative. Only from a perspective in which nationalism or religion has already been selected as the most significant category of social analysis could indifference to one or the other become a salient diagnostic. Even within the logics of a particular collectivism, those labeled as indifferent often perceived themselves to be adopting a clear, positive stance. To take one example, Mennonite colonists in Imperial Russia faced pressure from both Russian and German nationalists to join their respective communities. Some Slavophiles encouraged them to fight in the state military, open closed colonies, and raise their children in the Russian language, while by contrast, nationalist counterparts in Germany expected these same settlers to act as Germanic farmer-soldiers, bearing the banner of Germandom deep into the heart of tsarist territory. Caught between contradictory appeals, leaders generally resisted both impulses. Instead, they claimed membership in a "little Mennonite nation," a position enabling them to appropriate desirable aspects of both German and Russian national cultures, without fully committing to either. Creating a new in-between category allowed proponents to speak Russian as well as German, while fostering relationships in each empire. These "nationally indifferent" persons were themselves nationalists.

As in this instance, observers' classifications often differed greatly from the self-understandings of those they analyzed. While commentators in Germany portrayed white Mennonite communities across the world as bastions of a single global confession, such stories presupposed a particular historical and discursive standpoint. Over the previous centuries, persons calling themselves Mennonites had indeed moved from place to place, eventually settling across much of Eurasia and the Americas. These migrants often received information about their destinations from coreligionists, or chose to relocate in order to join friends and family who had already made the transition. But it would be inaccurate to represent such complex patterns of migration and remigration as equal manifestations of one overarching process. Assertions of a single German Mennonite diaspora obscure the plurality of spatial and temporal worldviews held by migrants over the centuries. Although some members certainly did see themselves as diasporic Germans, others located their origins in Switzerland or the Netherlands. Today, hundreds of thousands across Canada, Brazil, Paraguay, the United States, and even Germany speak of their ancestors' sojourn in the Russian Empire, while conservatives in Latin America refer to their own dispersion from Canada. Nor is diaspora necessarily tied to state borders. Mennonites in North America, for example, have experienced "diaspora in the countryside."[7] And for centuries, otherworldly minded members have identified heaven as their true homeland. Like each of these narratives, the idea of a German Mennonite diaspora was culturally produced. Only in the mid-nineteenth century did some historians begin to massage a heterogeneous set of pasts into this now easily recognizable form. Such invention was itself a form of globalization, although one that was geographically unbounded. Globalist thinking could flourish within the borders of a single country, or even the confines of an individual mind.[8] Just as notions like modernity or indifference could be mapped onto formations whose character they only poorly explained, accounts of global dispersion were often predicated less on vast population movements than on the social conditions that rendered their invocation desirable.

This was without question a deeply creative process. Collectivism held the power to imbue seemingly mundane objects and practices with broad symbolic power. Depictions of Mennonite bodies offer one example. Confessional activists obsessed over the ways their coreligionists looked, dressed, and sounded. The policing of Mennonite sexuality or the fetishizing of conservative costumes thus became fused with a host of ecological, cultural, racial, and erotic fantasies; particular narratives became housed in the blondness of a braid, entangled in the knotting of a head covering. For all their ambiguity, such symbols were exceedingly rich. Mennonite bodies could serve as referents for a larger collectivity stretching across the planet, as well as back and forth along a chronological continuum. The torso of a man sawing lumber in the bush jungles of Paraguay became the temporary culmination of a greater whole, heir to centuries of blood and sweat and sex and birth. When leaders viewed charts of historic migrations—from Germany to Russia, China to Brazil, Canada to Mexico—they often saw generations of bodily processes mapped across the surface of the globe. "There is a 'family' character in colonization," one sociologist remarked. "The first inclination of daughter colonies is to reproduce, as far as possible, in the new community, the institutions, organizations, and social patterns of the parent colony." Environmental metaphors constructed the religion as an organic substance: it had "roots" that could be torn out, "tendrils" that could bud off, and "branches" that could reach across oceans and continents. This language suggested movement, change, and growth. But Mennonitism could also be immortal. Colonial advocates highlighted the "village pattern of settlement which has been transplanted from Russia to Canada, to Mexico, and to Paraguay."[9] Spreading its seed across the centuries, the confession was believed to remain biologically consistent. Such depictions erased internal space and time, collapsing Mennonitism into the tree-lined streets, the opposing houses, and the central church of its common village pattern. While members lived in an array of environments— from the Siberian steppes to the Brazilian jungle—it was their ability to resist assimilation in diverse contexts that produced Mennonites' alleged unity.

Like every aspect of activists' narratives, this unity was always understood in multiple ways. Rather than a single aspirational goal, it possessed a plurality of orientations toward varying sets of people, institutions, ideas, and practices. After all, every collectivism is also a universalism, and any invocation of Mennonitism—by conjuring a totalizing cosmology—related all known objects to its primary referent. Thus the confession could also function as an integral element of other, larger collectivities. Even in Hitler's supposedly totalitarian Third Reich, Mennonite exceptionalism found a privileged position. While scholars of fascism have long debated whether Nazi leaders drew their power from popular consent or from the coercion of their subjects, it may be more revealing to ask how notions of constituent populations developed in the first place. National Socialism was, among other things, an unusually self-aware and ethically unabashed set of collectivist claims. Absent a robust discourse of affiliation and loyalty, fascism would never have been imaginable. To take one well-documented case, the racial science undergirding so much of Hitler's domestic and foreign policy owed its authority less to some innate human difference than to preconstituted assumptions about belonging. The idea of race itself made categories like Aryan and non-Aryan conceivable. Just as collectivities such as Mennonitism could be drawn within the German national community, Nazism also relied on the production of dangerous aliens, whose exclusion helped maintain internal borders. Depending on their perceived relation to Germanness, anyone categorized as Polish, Jewish, Russian, homosexual, work-shy, or more abstractly as non-German faced fluctuating degrees of persecution. That efforts to purify the German "racial body" ranged from threats and slurs to street violence, legalized discrimination, expropriation, full-scale deportation, and genocide, while also varying between territories and populations, suggests that Nazi brutality was neither consistent in kind nor constitutive of a unitary system. Yet, as various collectivisms aligned, their boundaries could stiffen, rendering disadvantaged populations increasingly vulnerable. This occurred during the Second World War on a catastrophic scale, propelling events that would become known worldwide as the Holocaust.

Violent border-keeping was of course by no means limited to Nazism. Germany's path to fascism was historically specific and in many ways unrepeatable. But just as the potential for mass oppression resided in German nationalist thought long before Hitler's rise, so do all collectivist systems hold similar possibilities. Even pacifist Mennonite communities—typically identified as idyllic refuges from state-sponsored militarism—have always been predicated on coercion. Mennonite pioneers' seizure of native lands across Europe, Central Asia, and the Americas provides only one example. As Russian-born settlers were likely to narrate their ancestors' arrival along the Black Sea: "In culture and lifestyle they were superior to indigenous people like the Nogai. There was no possibility of amalgamating with them or of any normal integration. The indigenous people were simply displaced."[10] External difference certainly mediated internal homogeneity, but this was not because Nogai cultural practices were so dissimilar from colonists' own. Rather, the act of claiming so provided chauvinists with a means of asserting their own advancement. Likewise, racial difference per se was not responsible for the generation of conceptual, material, or legalistic distinctions between the confession's white members and those of color. It was instead an internal ambivalence toward missionary evangelism—white Mennonites' fear that spreading the gospel among people of color might erase their own privileged position—that helped produce the notion of "Mennonite ethnicity." Without a foil, this term would be toothless. Only in a context where ethnicity served as a descriptor of confessional purity could a white non-believer disparage the authenticity of a devout believer of color. Differentiated further, white congregations were themselves subject to regulation from within. Anyone considered to have violated common convictions—whether through military service, adultery, queer sexuality, or any number of other perceived faults—faced derision, humiliation, and possibly excommunication.[11]

Mennonitism was in all cases responsible for and directly produced by exclusionary force. The denunciation of a Jewish neighbor in Nazi-occupied Ukraine, the exploitation of indigenous labor in Paraguay, and the shaming of queer members in the United States were all deeply constitutive acts. Each was at least as Mennonite as bonnets, buggies, and pacifism. But if the confession was all these things, it was also none of them. As much as the weight of history informs collectivist narratives, it does not determine their evolution. Anabaptism today remains as plural and as open to new possibilities as it ever was. Just as historical circumstances are perpetually in motion, religious, national, and other collectivities constantly break and reform in new guises. Like the ability of Mennonitism to serve as a symbol for German nationalism, any number of objects, groups, places, and ideas develop fresh connotations on a regular basis. Existing in a state of perpetual contestation, these elements flow in and out of related analogues, all acting as overlapping, interlocking metaphors for each other, simultaneously producing their own difference as well as working together to construct larger wholes. Parsing the specifically national or uniquely religious elements of a given tradition would be neither desirable nor possible. Scholars attempting to explain the discrepancies between activists' claims and everyday structures will not find answers by refining their definitions. Collectivist accounts are best understood as contingent products of particular situations. Emphasizing such malleability is not meant to deny the real significance of nationalist or religious language. To the contrary, only in a state of radical interrelation does such rhetoric have meaning. Only by examining the emergence and deployment of collectivist discourses will we be able to imagine nationalism without nations, religion without religions. And only by refusing the existence of homogenous groups can we leave wide the door of change.

How present-day Mennonites will confront the legacies of their pasts has yet to be seen. Which stories they tell, who they include, and what historical events confessional leaders decide to remember will all affect how current and future members experience their faith. Since the ninth Mennonite World Conference in Curitiba, Brazil, observers like Cornelius Dyck have drawn particular attention to demographic developments. Today, two-thirds of the world's 2.1 million baptized Anabaptists live in the Global South. While white communities in Europe and the Americas have sometimes been uncomfortable ceding power to coreligionists of color, these congregations are now more numerous than their wealthier, more privileged counterparts. Emphasizing deep-seated disparities in mobility, income, and other resources, spokespersons on various continents have initiated fresh debates about the role of "Mennonite ethnicity" as an exclusionary concept. Drawing on liberation theology, queer and postcolonial theory, and radical feminism, many have advocated the reorganization of transnational institutions, while also producing new histories, maps, and sociologies as a means of ameliorating historic inequalities.[12] At the same time, progressive leaders have promoted the creation of a new "sense of Mennonite peoplehood with diverse national, racial, and ethnic origins."[13] Once again, I Corinthians 3:11 has been appropriated to fit a changing world. Theologians have most recently invoked this passage to encourage white members to discard their cultural distinctiveness. Summoning corporeal imagery, such calls have reaffirmed Mennonite bodies as sites for collectivist contestation—in turn revealing desire for a blank slate upon which to etch the ideology of the confession. And yet, as some activists strip away the ethnic trappings of their faith, they are left not with a core of values, but with a process. For Christ's foundation, as it always has, continues to shift.

ARCHIVAL SOURCES

A complete bibliography is available from the author upon request. Archives consulted for this project (with abbreviations used in the endnotes) include Archiv der Kolonie Fernheim, Filadelfia, Paraguay; Archiv der Kolonie Menno, Loma Plata, Paraguay (AKM); Archiv des Schweizerischen Vereins für Täufergeschichte, Basel, Switzerland; Archives Nationales, Pierrefitte-sur-Seine, France (AN); Archiwum Państwowe w Gdańsku, Gdańsk, Poland; Archiwum Państwowego w Poznaniu, Poznań, Poland; Bibliothek der Mennonitengemeinde zu Hamburg und Altona, Hamburg, Germany (BMHA); Bundesarchiv, Berlin, Germany (BArch); Evangelisches Zentralarchiv, Berlin, Germany; Geheimes Staatsarchive Preußischer Kulturbesitz, Berlin, Germany; Mennonite Central Committee Files, Akron, Pennsylvania, United States; Mennonite Church USA Archives, Goshen, Indiana, United States; Mennonite Heritage Centre, Winnipeg, Canada (MHC); Mennonite Library and Archives, North Newton, Kansas, United States (MLA); Mennonitische Forschungsstelle, Bolanden-Weierhof, Germany (MFS); National Archives, Kew, United Kingdom (TNA); Politisches Archiv des Auswärtiges Amts, Berlin, Germany (PA AA); Staatsarchiv der Freien und Hansestadt Hamburg, Hamburg, Germany (SFHH); Staatsbibliothek-Haus 2, Berlin, Germany (SB); Stadsarchief Amsterdam, Amsterdam, Netherlands; Steven Spielberg Film and Video Archive, United States Holocaust Memorial Museum, Washington, DC, United States (USHMM); Universität Karlsruhe, Karlsruhe, Germany (UK).

The following institutions provided illustrations (denoted by page number) used in this book: Archiv der Kolonie Fernheim (page 118); Bundesarchiv (page 161, Bild 146-1978-117-14A / Fotograf: o.Ang.); Herald Press (page 184, reprinted with permission from *Up from the Rubble*, ©1991 by Herald Press); Kunstmuseen Krefeld (page 24); Mennonite Archives of Ontario (page 167, attributed to Hermann Rossner); Mennonite Library and Archives (pages 14, 60, 109, and 192); Mennonite World Conference (pages 202–203, map used by permission of Mennonite World Conference ©2015); Mennonitische Forschungsstelle (page 54); New York Public Library (page 153); Stadsarchief Amsterdam (page 34).

NOTES

INTRODUCTION

1. *Die Bibel* (Köln: Wilh. Hassel, 1873), 14. This rendering retains the tenor of the Luther translation with which emigrating Mennonites would have been familiar.
2. Peter Dyck, "Beschreibung meiner Auswanderung nach Amerika, 1876," *Mennonitische Geschichtsblätter* 6 (1954): 43–45. On Mennonites in German lands, Mark Jantzen, *Mennonite German Soldiers: Nation, Religion, and Family in the Prussian East, 1772–1880* (Notre Dame: University of Notre Dame Press, 2010); Jakob Fehr and Diether Lichdi, "Mennonites in Germany," in *Testing Faith and Tradition: Europe*, ed. Hanspeter Jecker and Alle Hoekema (Intercourse, PA: Good Books, 2006), 97–152.
3. Wilhelm Ewert, "A Defense of the Ancient Mennonite Principle of Non-Resistance by a Leading Prussian Mennonite Elder in 1873," *Mennonite Quarterly Review* 11, no. 4 (1937): 290.
4. Carl Harder, "Die Reorganisation der Mennoniten-Gemeinden in der Provinz Preußen," *Blätter für Religion und Erziehung*, June 1869, 52. On Mennonite history and theology, Arnold Snyder, *Anabaptist History and Theology* (Kitchener: Pandora Press, 1995); Diether Lichdi, *Über Zürich und Witmarsum nach Addis Abeba: Die Mennoniten in Geschichte und Gegenwart* (Maxdorf: Agape Verlag, 2004).
5. Ewert, "A Defense," 285, 287.
6. Curatorium, "Öffentliche Erklärung," *Tägliche Rundschau*, August 23, 1888.
7. H. G. Mannhardt, *Festschrift zu Menno Simons' 400 jähriger Geburtstagsfeier* (Danzig: L. Saunier, 1892), 54.
8. Translated in Wilhelm Mannhardt, *The Military Service Exemption of the Mennonites of Provincial Prussia* (North Newton, KS: Bethel College, 2013), 340.
9. Recent scholarship has criticized this "secularization thesis," i.e., Todd Weir, *Secularism and Religion in Nineteenth-Century Germany: The Fourth Confession* (New York: Cambridge University Press, 2014).
10. On Jewish nationalism as both a response to and indicative of secularism, Mitchell Hart, *Social Science and the Politics of Modern Jewish Identity* (Stanford: Stanford University Press, 2000); Nadia Abu El-Haj, *The Genealogical Science: The Search for Jewish Origins and the Politics of Epistemology* (Chicago: University of Chicago Press, 2012).
11. Anthony Smith, *Chosen Peoples: Sacred Sources of National Identity* (Oxford: Oxford University Press, 2003), and Adrian Hastings, *The Construction of Nationhood: Ethnicity, Religion, and Nationalism* (Cambridge: Cambridge University Press, 1997) argue that religion often laid the groundwork for the formation of national communities. Linda Colley outlined the relationship between Protestantism and Britishness in *Britons: Forging the Nation, 1707–1837* (New Haven: Yale University Press, 1992), while Helmut Smith has shown how German nationalisms followed religious

lines: *German Nationalism and Religious Conflict: Culture, Ideology, Politics, 1870–1914* (Princeton: Princeton University Press, 1995).

12. Harder, "Die Reorganisation," 52.

13. Heinrich Wiehler, "Die Mennoniten und ihr Vaterland," *Mennonitische Blätter*, September 1928, 81–83.

14. Translated in John Toews and Paul Toews, eds., *Union of Citizens of Dutch Lineage in Ukraine (1922–1927): Mennonite and Soviet Documents* (Fresno, CA: Center of Mennonite Brethren Studies, 2011), 346, 348.

15. See especially recent work on transnationalism, including the forum "On Transnational History," *American Historical Review* 111, no. 5 (2006): 1441–1464; Steven Vertovec, *Transnationalism* (New York: Routledge, 2009); Gunilla Budde, Sebastian Conrad, and Oliver Janz, eds., *Transnationale Geschichte: Themen, Tendenzen und Theorien* (Göttingen: Vandenhoeck & Ruprecht, 2006); Sebastian Conrad and Jürgen Osterhammel, *Das Kaiserreich transnational: Deutschland in der Welt, 1871–1914* (Göttingen: Vandenhoeck & Ruprecht, 2004). On Mennonite transnationalism, Royden Loewen, *Village among Nations: "Canadian" Mennonites in a Transnational World, 1916–2006* (Toronto: University of Toronto Press, 2013); Troy Osborne, "The Development of a Transnational 'Mennonite' Identity Among Swiss Brethren and Dutch Doopsgezinden in the Sixteenth and Seventeenth Centuries," *Mennonite Quarterly Review* 88, no. 2 (2014): 195–218.

16. My thinking has been particularly informed by Rogers Brubaker, *Ethnicity without Groups* (Cambridge, MA: Harvard University Press, 2004), and Frederick Cooper, *Colonialism in Question: Theory, Knowledge, History* (Berkeley: University of California Press, 2005).

17. Leonhard Weydmann, *Luther: Ein Charakter und Spiegelbild für unsere Zeit* (1850), 160–161. On Weydmann and his context, Wolfgang Froese, *Sie kamen als Fremde: Die Mennoniten in Krefeld von dem Anfängen bis zur Gegenwart* (Krefeld: Mennonitengemeinde Krefeld, 1995), 105–156.

18. Martin Luther, *Luther's Works*, ed. Jaroslav Pelikan, vol. 13 (Saint Louis: Concordia Publishing House, 1956), 61.

19. Weydmann, *Luther*, 161.

20. Recent efforts to distill racial differences from human DNA, for example, have elicited searing critique: Nadia Abu el-Haj, "The Genetic Reinscription of Race," *Annual Review of Anthropology* 36 (2007): 283–300; Barbara Koenig, Sandra Lee, and Sarah Richardson, eds., *Revisiting Race in a Genomic Age* (Piscataway, NJ: Rutgers University Press, 2008). Anthony Smith has, however, shown that nationalist discourses often do draw on ancient traditions: *The Ethnic Origins of Nations* (Oxford: Blackwell Publishing, 1987). Also, Caspar Hirschi, *The Origins of Nationalism: An Alternative History from Ancient Rome to Early Modern Germany* (Cambridge: Cambridge University Press, 2011).

21. Eric Hobsbawm and Terence Ranger, eds., *The Invention of Tradition* (Cambridge: Cambridge University Press, 1992); Eric Hobsbawm, *Nations and Nationalism Since 1780: Programme, Myth, Reality* (New York: Cambridge University Press, 1992); John Breuilly, *Nationalism and the State* (Chicago: University of Chicago Press, 1994).

22. Ernest Gellner, *Nations and Nationalism* (Oxford: Blackwell, 1983), 55. See also Miroslav Hroch, *Social Preconditions of National Revival in Europe* (New York: Columbia University Press, 1985).

23. Benedict Anderson, *Imagined Communities* (London: Verso, 2006). Studies in this vein include Eugene Weber, *Peasants into Frenchmen: The Modernization of Rural*

France, 1870–1914 (Stanford: Stanford University Press, 1976); Gary Cohen, *The Politics of Ethnic Survival: Germans in Prague, 1861–1914* (Princeton: Princeton University Press, 1981); Jeremy King, *Budweisers into Czechs and Germans: A Local History of Bohemian Politics, 1848–1945* (Princeton: Princeton University Press, 2002).

24. Works emphasizing the contingency of nationalism include Pamela Ballinger, *History in Exile: Memory and Identity at the Borders of the Balkans* (Princeton: Princeton University Press, 2002); Timothy Snyder, *The Reconstruction of Nations: Poland, Ukraine, Lithuania, Belarus, 1569–1999* (New Haven: Yale University Press, 2003); Pieter Judson and Marsha Rozenblit, eds., *Constructing Nationalities in East Central Europe* (New York: Berghahn Books, 2006).

25. Celia Applegate, *A Nation of Provincials: The German Idea of* Heimat (Berkeley: University of California Press, 1990), and Alon Confino, *The Nation as a Local Metaphor: Wurttemberg, Imperial Germany, and National Memory, 1871–1918* (Chapel Hill: University of North Carolina Press, 1997) elucidate a dialectic between regionalism and nationalism.

26. H. G. Mannhardt, "Predigt über Epheser 4, 3–6," in *Zur Erinnerung an das Crefelder Maifest* (Crefeld, 1911), 4.

27. See the five-volume Global Mennonite History Series: Jecker and Hoekema, eds., *Testing Faith*; John Lapp and Arnold Snyder, eds., *Anabaptist Songs in African Hearts: Africa* (Intercourse, PA: Good Books, 2006); Jamie Prieto, *Mission and Migration: Latin America* (Intercourse, PA: Good Books, 2010); John Lapp and Arnold Snyder, eds., *Churches Engage Asian Traditions: Asia* (Intercourse, PA: Good Books, 2011); Royden Loewen and Steven Nolt, *Seeking Places of Peace: North America* (Intercourse, PA: Good Books, 2012).

28. Brubaker, *Ethnicity without Groups*. Also, Rogers Brubaker, *Nationalist Politics and Everyday Ethnicity in a Transylvanian Town* (Princeton: Princeton University Press, 2006).

29. George Williams, *The Radical Reformation* (Philadelphia: Westminster Press, 1962).

30. See James Stayer, Werner Packull, and Klaus Deppermann, "From Monogenesis to Polygenesis: The Historical Discussion of Anabaptist Origins," *Mennonite Quarterly Review* 49, no. 2 (1975): 83–121; Arnold Snyder, "Beyond Polygenesis: Recovering the Unity and Diversity of Anabaptist Theology," in *Essays in Anabaptist Theology*, ed. Wayne Pipkin (Elkhart, IN: Institute of Mennonite Studies, 1994); John Roth and James Stayer, eds., *A Companion to Anabaptism and Spiritualism, 1521–1700* (Boston: Brill, 2007).

31. On Menno, Menno Simons, *The Complete Writings of Menno Simons, c. 1496–1561* (Scottdale, PA: Herald Press, 1956); Sjouke Voolstra, *Menno Simons: His Image and Message* (North Newton, KS: Bethel College, 1997).

32. See Claus-Peter Clasen, *Anabaptism: A Social History, 1525–1618* (Ithaca: Cornell University Press, 1972); Brad Gregory, *Salvation at Stake: Christian Martyrdom in Early Modern Europe* (Cambridge: Harvard University Press, 2001), 197–249.

33. Translated in Cornelis Ris, *Mennonite Articles of Faith* (Berne, IN: Mennonite Book Concern, 1918), 53.

34. On the Amish division, John Mast, ed., *The Letters of the Amish Division of 1693–1711* (Oregon City: Chr. J. Schlabach, 1950). Today, most Amish do not consider themselves Mennonites.

35. Joh. Hirschler, "Zum 400jährigen Gedächtniss Menno Simons," *Gemeindeblatt*, December 1892, 89.

36. Ewert, "A Defense," 286.

37. Simons, *Complete Writings*, 44, 555. (Matthew 5:44).

38. See Joshua Sanborn, *Drafting the Russian Nation: Military Conscription, Total War, and Mass Politics, 1905–1925* (DeKalb: Northern Illinois University Press, 2011); Daniel Moran and Arthur Waldron, *The People in Arms: Military Myth and National Mobilization Since the French Revolution* (Cambridge: Cambridge University Press, 2002); Michael Silber, "From Tolerated Aliens to Citizen-Soldiers: Jewish Military Service in the Era of Joseph II," in *Constructing Nationalities*, ed. Judson and Rozenblit, 19–39.

39. On Anabaptists and the state, Michael Driedger, "Anabaptists and the Early Modern State," in *A Companion to Anabaptism*, ed. Roth and Stayer, 507–544; James Urry, *Mennonites, Politics, and Peoplehood: Europe—Russia—Canada, 1525 to 1980* (Winnipeg: University of Manitoba Press, 2006).

40. Paul Mendes-Flohr and Jehuda Reinharz, eds., *The Jew in the Modern World: A Documentary History* (Oxford: Oxford University Press, 1995), 49; Mannhardt, *Military Service*, 336.

41. Translated in James Urry, *None but Saints: The Transformation of Mennonite Life in Russia 1789–1889* (Winnipeg: Hyperion Press, 1989), 282–284.

42. Quoted in Theron Schlabach, *Peace, Faith, Nation: Mennonites and Amish in Nineteenth-Century America* (Scottdale, PA: Herald Press, 1988), 256–257. On Mennonites in Canada, Frank Epp, *Mennonites in Canada, 1786–1920: The History of a Separate People* (Toronto: Macmillan of Canada, 1974).

43. This figure includes emigration from Switzerland and Alsace-Lorraine. On migration to North America, Loewen and Nolt, *Seeking Places of Peace*, 19. On migration to the Russian Empire, Benjamin Unruh, *Die niederländisch-niederdeutschen Hintergründe der mennonitischen Ostwanderungen im 17., 18. und 19. Jahrhundert* (Karlsruhe: Heinrich Schneider, 1955), 231; Urry, *None but Saints*, 285–289.

44. Quoted in Curatorium, "Öffentliche Erklärung." On Mennonites and the Enlightenment, Michael Driedger, "Competing Visions of the Mennonite *Gemeinde*: Examples from Early Modern Krefeld in Their Dutch Context," in *Defining Community in Early Modern Europe*, ed. Michael Halvorson and Karen Spierling (Burlington, VT: Ashgate, 2008), 267–288.

45. Carl Harder, "Die Amischen," *Monatsschrift für die evangelischen Mennoniten*, October 1847, 16. On Amish and modernity, Donald Kraybill, Karen Johnson-Weiner, and Steven Nolt, *The Amish* (Baltimore: Johns Hopkins University Press, 2013). On anti-Enlightenment thinking and discourses of modernity, Darrin McMahon, *Enemies of the Enlightenment: The French Counter-Enlightenment and the Making of Modernity* (Oxford: Oxford University Press, 2001).

46. I.e., Isaiah Berlin, *Three Critics of the Enlightenment: Vico, Hamann, Herder* (Princeton: Princeton University Press, 2000), 208–300.

47. Cooper, *Colonialism in Question*, 147.

48. For example, Emilio Gentile, *Politics as Religion* (Princeton: Princeton University Press, 2006); Emilio Gentile, *The Sacralization of Politics in Fascist Italy* (Cambridge, MA: Harvard University Press, 1996).

49. "Herbei herbei du trauter Sängerkreis" in Fr. Semler, *Nürnberger Liederbuch* (Nürnberg: Bieling, 1872), 16.

50. "Festlied zum 4. Mai 1911," 521-5/215, vol. 2, folder 1911, SFHH.

51. Samuel Cramer, "Internationales Mennonitenthum," *Mennonitische Blätter*, May 1902, 39–40.

52. Hinrich van der Smissen, "Die Ausbildung unserer besoldeten Prediger im 19. Jahrhundert," *Mennonitische Blätter*, December 1903, 98. On globalization, Jürgen Osterhammel, *Die Verwandlung der Welt: Eine Geschichte des 19. Jahrhunderts* (Munich: C.H. Beck, 2009); Jan Scholte, *Globalization: A Critical Introduction* (New York: Palgrave, 2000); C. A. Bayly, *The Birth of the Modern World, 1780–1914* (Oxford: Wiley-Blackwell, 2003). In the context of religion, Abigail Green and Vincent Viaene, eds., *Religious Internationals in the Modern World: Globalization and Faith Communities since 1750* (New York: Palgrave Macmillan, 2012); Philip Jenkins, *The Next Christendom: The Coming of Global Christianity* (Oxford: Oxford University Press, 2004).

53. Andreas Wimmer and Nina Schiller, "Methodological Nationalism and Beyond: Nation-State Building, Migration, and the Social Sciences," *Global Networks* 2, no. 4 (2002): 301–334.

54. See James Sheehan, "What is German History? Reflections on the Role of the Nation in German History and Historiography," *Journal of Modern History* 53, no. 1 (1981): 1–23; Glenn Penny, "German Polycentrism and the Writing of History," *German History* 30, no. 2 (2012): 265–282; Dirk Hoerder, "The German-Language Diasporas: A Survey, Critique, and Interpretation," *Diaspora* 11, no. 1 (2002): 7–44.

55. On nationalist activism, Pieter Judson, *Guardians of the Nation: Activists on the Language Frontiers of Imperial Austria* (Cambridge, MA: Harvard University Press, 2006); Tara Zahra, *Kidnapped Souls: National Indifference and the Battle for Children in the Bohemian Lands, 1900–1948* (Ithaca: Cornell University Press, 2008). See also Gene Sharp, *The Politics of Nonviolent Action*, 3 vols. (Boston: Porter Sargent, 1973).

56. Translated in Suzanne Stewart-Steinberg, *The Pinocchio Effect: On Making Italians, 1860–1920* (Chicago: University of Chicago Press, 2007), 1.

57. Harder, "Die Reorganisation," 54.

58. Christian Neff, "Hinrich van der Smissen," *Christlicher Gemeinde-Kalender*, 1929, 70–90; Matthias Rauert and Annelie Kümpers-Greve, *Van der Smissen: Eine mennonitische Familie vor dem Hintergrund der Geschichte Altonas und Schleswig-Holsteins* (Hamburg: Nord Magazin, 1992), 104–106.

59. Emil Händiges, "Die heutige Verbreitung und Organisation des deutschen Mennonitentums," *Mennonitische Blätter*, September 1929, 75.

60. On the construction of diasporic communities, Stefan Manz, *Constructing a German Diaspora: The 'Greater German Empire,' 1871–1914* (New York: Routledge, 2014); Krista O'Donnell, Renate Bridenthal, and Nancy Reagin, eds., *The* Heimat *Abroad: The Boundaries of Germanness* (Ann Arbor: University of Michigan Press, 2005); Bradley Naranch, "Inventing the *Auslandsdeutsche*: Emigration, Colonial Fantasy, and German National Identity, 1848–71," in *Germany's Colonial Pasts*, ed. Eric Ames, Marcia Klotz, and Lora Wildenthal (Lincoln: University of Nebraska Press, 2005), 21–40.

61. Sebastian Conrad, *Globalisation and the Nation in Imperial Germany* (Cambridge: Cambridge University Press, 2010). See also Bradley Naranch and Geoff Eley, eds., *German Colonialism in a Global Age* (Durham: Duke University Press, 2014).

62. Translated in Max Weber, *The Protestant Ethic and the Spirit of Capitalism* (New York: Charles Scribner's Sons, 1950), 44. On Weber's racism, Andrew Zimmerman, "Decolonizing Weber," *Postcolonial Studies* 9 (2006): 53–79. On Mennonites and capitalism, Calvin Redekop, Stephen Ainlay, and Robert Siemens, *Mennonite Entrepreneurs* (Baltimore: Johns Hopkins University Press, 1995); Calvin Redekop, Victor

Krahn, and Samuel Steiner, eds., *Anabaptist/Mennonite Faith and Economics* (Waterloo, Ontario: Institute of Anabaptist and Mennonite Studies, 1994).

63. Translated in Henry Krehbiel, *The History of the General Conference of the Mennonites of North America* (St. Louis: Wiebusch & Son, 1898), 149.

64. See Urry, *None but Saints*, 242–264; Abraham Friesen, *In Defense of Privilege: Russian Mennonites and the State Before and during World War I* (Winnipeg: Kindred Publications, 2006).

65. Translated in Toews and Toews, eds., *Union of Citizens*, 348, 350. On this phenomenon, Pieter Judson, "When is a Diaspora not a Diaspora?" in *The* Heimat *Abroad*, ed. O'Donnell et al., 219–247.

66. Pieter Judson and Tara Zahra, "Introduction," *Austrian History Yearbook* 43 (2012): 27. See also Tara Zahra, "Imagined Non-Communities: National Indifference as a Category of Analysis," *Slavic Review* 69, no. 1 (2010): 93–119; James Bjork, *Neither German nor Pole: Catholicism and National Indifference in a Central European Borderland* (Ann Arbor: University of Michigan Press, 2008); Brendan Karch, "Nationalism on the Margins: Silesians between Germany and Poland, 1848–1945" (PhD diss., Harvard University, 2010).

67. Marshall Sahlins, *Islands of History* (Chicago: University of Chicago Press, 1987), 144.

68. On the agency of piety, Saba Mahmood, "Feminist Theory, Embodiment, and the Docile Agent: Some Reflections on the Egyptian Islamic Revival," *Cultural Anthropology* 16, no. 2 (2001): 202–236. In Germany, David Blackbourn, *Marpingen: Apparitions of the Virgin Mary in Nineteenth-Century Germany* (New York: Alfred A. Knopf, 1994).

69. On agency and its limits, Walter Johnson, "On Agency," *Journal of Social History* 37, no. 1 (2003): 113–124.

70. H. D. Cornies, "Konfessionell oder national?" *Der Bote*, January 28, 1925, 5.

71. Adolf Hitler, *Mein Kampf* (Munich: Zentralverlag der NSDAP, 1943), 742–743.

72. On national side-switching, Chad Bryant, "Either German or Czech: Fixing Nationality in Bohemia and Moravia, 1939–1946," *Slavic Review* 61, no. 4 (2002): 683–706. Among Mennonites, Hans Werner, *The Constructed Mennonite: History, Memory, and the Second World War* (Winnipeg: University of Manitoba, 2013); Eric Steinhart, "The Chameleon of Trawniki; Jack Reimer, Soviet *Volksdeutsche* and the Holocaust," *Holocaust and Genocide Studies* 23 (2009): 239–262.

73. Dyck, "Beschreibung meiner Auswanderung," 44–45.

CHAPTER 1: BECOMING GERMAN

1. Hinrich van der Smissen, "Der Ursprung der deutschen Mennoniten," *Mennonitische Blätter*, March 1917, 22–23.

2. Hinrich van der Smissen, "Unsere Aussichten für das Jahr 1919," *Mennonitische Blätter*, January 1919, 2–5.

3. Modernist interpretations include Anderson, *Imagined Communities*; Hobsbawm and Ranger, eds., *The Invention of Tradition*; Hobsbawm, *Nations and Nationalism*.

4. On Mennonites in the northwest German states, Michael Driedger, *Obedient Heretics: Mennonite Identities in Lutheran Hamburg and Altona during the Confessional Age* (Aldershot: Ashgate, 2002); Froese, *Sie kamen als Fremde*; J. P. Müller, *Die Mennoniten in Ostfriesland vom 16. bis zum 18. Jahrhundert* (Emden: Haynel, 1887).

5. In the Polish-Lithuanian Commonwealth and Prussian east, Peter Klassen, *Mennonites in Early Modern Poland and Prussia* (Baltimore: Johns Hopkins University Press,

2009); Jantzen, *Mennonite German Soldiers*; Peter Klassen, *A Homeland for Strangers: An Introduction to Mennonites in Poland and Prussia* (Fresno: Center for M.B. Studies, 1989).

6. In the south German states, *Documents of Brotherly Love: Dutch Mennonite Aid to Swiss Anabaptists*, vol. 1 (Millersburg: Ohio Amish Library, 2007); Ernst Correll, *Das schweizerische Täufermennonitentum: Ein soziologischer Bericht* (Tübingen: J.C.B. Mohr, 1925); Frank Konersmann, *Das Gästebuch der mennonitischen Bauernfamilie David Möllinger senior 1781–1817* (Alzey: Rheinhessischen Druckwerkstätte, 2009); Hermann Guth, *Amish Mennonites in Germany* (Metamora: Illinois Mennonite Historical and Genealogical Society, 1995).

7. Translated in "Concordat of the cities of Zürich, Bern, and St. Gall," *The Mennonite Encyclopedia*, vol. 1 (Scottdale, PA: Mennonite Publishing House, 1955), 667.

8. Quoted in Klassen, *Mennonites in Early Modern Poland*, 15.

9. On these migrations, William Schroeder and Helmut Huebert, *The Mennonite Historical Atlas* (Winnipeg: Springfield Publishers, 1996). On Anabaptists and the state, Roth and Stayer, eds., *A Companion to Anabaptism*; Urry, *Mennonites, Politics, and Peoplehood*.

10. Gerald C. Studer, "A History of the *Martyrs' Mirror*," *Mennonite Quarterly Review* 22, no. 3 (1948): 163–179.

11. Benjamin Eby, *Kurzgefaßte Kirchen Geschichte und Glaubenslehre der Taufgesinnten-Christen oder Mennoniten* (Berlin, Canada: Heinrich Eby, 1841), 136–139. Also, Mannhardt, *Military Service*, 65–100.

12. *Katalog der Kirchenbibliothek der Mennonitengemeinde zu Danzig* (Danzig: Edwin Groening, 1869).

13. On Mennonites in the Netherlands, Alastair Hamilton, Sjouke Voolstra, and Piet Visser, eds., *From Martyr to Muppy: A Historical Introduction to Cultural Assimilation Processes of a Religious Minority in the Netherlands: The Mennonites* (Amsterdam: Amsterdam University Press, 1994); S. Groenveld, J. P. Jacobszoon, and S. L. Verheus, eds., *Wederdopers, Menisten, Doopsgezinden in Nederland 1530–1980* (Zutphen: De Walburg Pers, 1980); Cor Trompetter, *Agriculture, Proto-Industry and Mennonite Entrepreneurship: A History of the Textile Industries in Twente 1600–1815* (Amsterdam: NEHA, 1997); Piet Visser, "Mennonites and Doopsgezinden in the Netherlands, 1535–1700," in *A Companion to Anabaptism*, ed. Roth and Stayer, 299–346.

14. Piet Visser, "Aspects of Social Criticism and Cultural Assimilation," in *From Martyr to Muppy*, ed. Hamilton et al., 67.

15. See the introductions to Cornelis Ris, *Die Glaubenslehre der Mennoniten oder Taufgesinnten* (Summerfield, IL, 1895).

16. Translated in "Crefeld," *Mennonite Encyclopedia*, 735. Also, Peter Kriedte, *Taufgesinnte und großes Kapital: Die niederrheinisch-bergischen Mennoniten und der Aufstieg des Krefelder Seidengewerbes* (Göttingen: Vandenhoeck & Ruprecht, 2007).

17. Driedger, *Obedient Heretics*, 24–25.

18. "Mennonitenfamilien in Zahlen," *Mennonitische Geschichtsblätter* 5 (1940): 26–45.

19. *Namensverzeichniss der Aeltesten, Lehrer und Diakonen oder Vorsteher der Taufgesinnten Mennonitischen Gemeinden* (Elbing: Agathon Wernich, 1835), 1. Volumes compiled in the Netherlands were more comprehensive.

20. Translated from Dutch in "Zur Vorgeschichte unserer taufgesinnten Missionsgesellschaft in Amsterdam," *Mennonitische Blätter*, June 1895, 46.

21. On missions, Jantzen, *Mennonite German Soldiers*, 128–130; Alle Hoekema, "Early 19th Century Baptist Influences on Dutch Mennonite Missionary Endeavors," *Mission*

Focus 14 (2006): 123–133. On Angas, F. A. Cox, ed., *Memoirs of the Rev. William Henry Angas* (London: Thomas Ward, 1834).

22. Quoted in Hans-Jürgen Bömelburg, "Konfession und Migration zwischen Brandenburg-Preußen und Polen-Litauen 1640–1772," in *Glaubensflüchtlinge*, ed. Joachim Bahlcke (Berlin: Lit Verlag, 2008), 132.

23. Klassen, *Mennonites in Early Modern Poland*, 172–173.

24. Translated in Frank Konersmann, "Middle-Class Formation in Rural Society: Mennonite Peasant Merchants in the Palatinate, Rhine Hesse, and the Northern Rhine Valley, 1740–1880," *Mennonite Quarterly Review* 86, no. 2 (2012): 247. On Mennonites and Enlightenment, Driedger, "Competing Visions"; Michael Driedger, "Gerrit Karsdorp (1729–1811): Mennonitenprediger und Förderer der Aufklärung in Hamburg," *Mennonitische Geschichtsblätter* 56 (1999): 35–53.

25. Quoted in "Der Grundsatz der Wehrlosigkeit und seine Entwickelung in unserer Gemeinschaft," *Mennonitische Blätter*, November 1910, 85.

26. On Mennonites and the Napoleonic Wars, Klassen, *Mennonites in Early Modern Poland*, 178–181; Jantzen, *Mennonite German Soldiers*, 79–110; Fehr and Lichdi, "Mennonites in Germany," 112–116; Froese, *Sie kamen als Fremde*, 105–203.

27. Translations from Mannhardt, *Military Service*, 56.

28. Jürgen Kocka and Allan Mitchell, *Bourgeois Society in Nineteenth-Century Europe* (Oxford: Berg, 1993); Bayly, *The Birth*, 325–365.

29. Quoted in "Zur Vorgeschichte unserer taufgesinnten Missionsgesellschaft in Amsterdam," *Mennonitische Blätter*, July 1895, 52.

30. Carl Harder, "Briefliche Mittheilungen," *Monatsschrift für die evangelischen Mennoniten*, October 1847, 13.

31. Quoted in "Der kleine Missionsverein 1826," *Mennonitische Blätter*, September 1907, 69–70.

32. Quoted in "Versammlung auf dem Weierhof am 9. Mai 1830," *Mennonitische Blätter*, October 1907, 77.

33. Mannhardt, *Military Service*, 345–346.

34. Ernst Crous, *Wie die Mennoniten in die deutsche Volksgemeinschaft hineinwuchsen* (Karlsruhe: Mennonitischer Geschichtsverein, 1939), 12.

35. *Namensverzeichniss der Aeltesten*, 4.

36. Some earlier examples are known, i.e., Abraham Hunzinger, *Das Religions-, Kirchen- und schulwesen der Mennoniten oder Taufgesinnten* (Speyer, 1830), i.

37. Jakob Mannhardt, "Vorwort," *Mennonitische Blätter*, January 1854, 2.

38. B. C. Roosen, "Offenes Sendschreiben an die Mennonitischen Brüder in Pennsylvanien," *Das Christliche Volks-Blatt*, June 1859.

39. Carl Harder, "Gruss," *Monatsschrift für die evangelischen Mennoniten*, October 1846, 1–4.

40. Carl Harder, "Erklärung in Betreff dieser Monatsschrift," *Monatsschrift für die evangelischen Mennoniten*, May 1848, 1.

41. Brian Vick, *Defining Germany: The 1848 Frankfurt Parliamentarians and National Identity* (Cambridge, MA: Harvard University Press, 2002). More broadly, Jonathan Sperber, *Revolutionary Europe, 1780–1850* (New York: Routledge, 2000).

42. Carl Harder, "Deutschland und Preußen," *Mittheilungen aus dem religiösen Leben*, September 1848, 1–3.

43. Quoted in Katja Beisser-Apetz, *Das weiße Blatt: Antje Brons: Ein Außergewöhnliches Frauenleben im 19. Jahrhundert* (Oldenburg: Schardt Verlag, 2011), 63–69.

44. Translated in Klassen, *Mennonites in Early Modern Poland*, 183. Also, Ulrich Hettinger, *Hermann von Beckerath: Ein preußischer Patriot und rheinischer Liberaler* (Krefeld: Mennonitengemeinde Krefeld, 2010).

45. Printed in Rudolf Muhs, "Das schöne Erbe der frommen Väter: Die Petition der badische Mennoniten an die deutschen Nationalversammlung von 1848 um Befreiung von Eid und Wehrpflicht," *Mennonitische Geschichtsblätter* 42 (1985): 97–98.

46. Translated in Jantzen, *Mennonite German Soldiers*, 149; printed in Muhs, "Das schöne Erbe," 97.

47. Carl Harder, "Briefliche Mittheilungen," *Monatsschrift für die evangelischen Mennoniten*, January 1848, 15–16.

48. Mannhardt, "Vorwort," 1.

49. *Mennonitische Blätter*, January 1854, 1–8.

50. *Namens-Verzeichniss der in Deutschland, Ost- und Westpreußen, Galizien, Polen und Rußland befindlichen Mennoniten-Gemeinden* (Danzig: Edwin Groening, 1857).

51. Mennonites in the Netherlands developed a parallel movement. The Dutch-language counterpart of Mannhardt's journal was *Doopsgezinde Bijdragen*, founded in 1861.

52. Crous, *Wie die Mennoniten*, 5.

53. Smissen, "Die Ausbildung," 98.

54. S. F. van der Ploeg, "Holländische Mennoniten-Prediger in Deutschland," *Mennonitische Blätter*, January 1904, 4.

55. Harder, "Briefliche Mittheilungen," 1847, 15.

56. Carl Justus van der Smissen, "Die Missionsgesellschaft der Taufgesinnten in Amsterdam Betreffendes," *Mennonitische Blätter*, September 1854, 47.

57. Printed in ibid. On this organization, Alle Hoekema, *Dutch Mennonite Mission in Indonesia: Historical Essays* (Elkhart, IN: Institute of Mennonite Studies, 2001).

58. B. C. Roosen, "Ein freimütiges brüderliches Schreiben an Dr. Cramer," *Mennonitische Blätter*, June 1885, 50.

59. Nicolaas Dirk Schuurmans, "Ein Brief des Missionars Schuurmans," *Mennonitische Blätter*, February 1876, 13.

60. Ploeg, "Holländische Mennoniten-Prediger," 4.

61. Heinrich Neufeld, "Anruf an sämtliche Mennoniten-Gemeinden in der alten und neuen Welt," *Mennonitische Blätter*, May 1859, 19–20.

62. On the Gustav Adolf Association, Kevin Cramer, "The Cult of Gustavus Adolphus: Protestant Identity and German Nationalism," in *Protestants, Catholics, and Jews in Germany, 1800–1914*, ed. Helmut Smith (Oxford: Berg, 2001). More broadly, Manz, *Constructing a German Diaspora*; Naranch, "Inventing the *Auslandsdeutsche*."

63. *Briefe an die Mennonisten Gemeine in Ober Canada* (Berlin, Canada: Heinrich Eby, 1840), 35.

64. Krehbiel, *History of the General Conference*, 159.

65. August von Haxthausen, *Studien über die inneren Zustände, das Volksleben und insbesondere die ländlichen Einrichtungen Rußlands* (Hannover: Hahn'schen Hofbuchhandlung, 1847), 171–196.

66. Antje Brons, *Die Ankunft der ersten Deutschen in Amerika und ihre Ansiedlung daselbst* (Altona: Heinrich Dircks, 1893).

67. Wilhelm Groos, "Die 'Täufer' (Mennoniten) als deutsche Aussenposten," *Deutsche Erde*, 1913, 172–174.

68. Mannhardt edited the world's first journal on folklore and wrote widely on Central European peasant culture. See George S. Williamson, *The Longing for Myth in*

Germany: Religion and Aesthetic Culture from Romanticism to Nietzsche (Chicago: University of Chicago Press, 2004), 259–264; Karl Scheuermann, *Wilhelm Mannhardt: Seine Bedeutung für die vergleichende Religionsforschung* (Giessen: Meyer, 1933); Richard Beitl, "Wilhelm Mannhardt und der Atlas der deutschen Volkskunde," *Zeitschrift für Volkskunde* 42 (1933): 70–84; Jantzen, *Mennonite German Soldiers*, 183–190.

69. Wilhelm Mannhardt, *Gedichte* (Danzig, 1881), vii–ix.

70. Wilhelm Mannhardt, *Die Götter der deutschen und nordischen Völker* (Berlin, 1860), Vorwort.

71. Wilhelm Mannhardt, *Germanische Mythen* (Berlin: Ferdinand Schneider, 1858), v.

72. Wilhelm Mannhardt, "Über Das Studium der Volksüberlieferung," Nachlaß Wilhelm Mannhardt, box 4, SB.

73. Mannhardt, *Germanische Mythen*, vii. On Mannhardt's methodology, Günter Wiegelmann and Joan Cotter, "The *Atlas der deutschen Volkskunde* and the Geographical Research Method," *Journal of the Folklore Institute* 5, no. 2/3 (1968): 187–197.

74. Alan Dundes, *International Folkloristics* (New York: Rowman & Littlefield, 1999), 16.

75. Translations from Mannhardt, *Military Service*, 2, 6.

76. Wilhelm Mannhardt, "Mennoniten in der Diaspora," *Mennonitische Blätter*, October 1859, 39.

77. Translated in Klassen, *Mennonites in Early Modern Poland*, 11–12.

78. Hinrich van der Smissen, "Zum Reformationsfest," *Mennonitische Blätter*, November 1903, 87. On agrarianism and civilization in German thought, David Blackbourn, *The Conquest of Nature: Water, Landscape, and the Making of Modern Germany* (New York: W.W. Norton, 2006); David Blackbourn and James Retallack, eds., *Localism, Landscape, and the Ambiguities of Place: German-Speaking Central Europe, 1860–1930* (Toronto: University of Toronto Press, 2007).

79. Mannhardt, "Mennoniten in der Diaspora," 39.

80. Mannhardt, *Die Götter*, Vorwort.

81. Wilhelm Mannhardt, "Bitte," Nachlaß Wilhelm Mannhardt, box 4, SB.

82. Antje Brons, *Ursprung, Entwickelung und Schicksale der Taufgesinnten oder Mennoniten* (Norden, 1884), 355.

83. Hinrich van der Smissen, "Vierhundert Jahre mennonitischer Geschichte," *Mennonitische Blätter*, November 1892, 165.

84. Roosen, "Offenes Sendschreiben."

85. Translated in Krehbiel, *History of the General Conference*, 36.

86. On early US missions, James Juhnke, *A People of Mission: A History of General Conference Mennonite Overseas Missions* (Newton, KS: Faith and Life Press, 1979); James Juhnke, "General Conference Mennonite Missions to the American Indians in the Late Nineteenth Century," *Mennonite Quarterly Review* 54, no. 2 (1980): 117–134. In Imperial Russia, Waldemar Janzen, "Foreign Mission Interest of the Mennonites in Russia before World War I," *Mennonite Quarterly Review* 42, no. 1 (1968): 56–67.

87. Mannhardt, *Jahrbuch*, 1.

CHAPTER 2: FORGING HISTORY

1. Brons, *Ursprung, Entwickelung und Schicksale*, v.

2. Ernst von Wildenbruch, *Der Menonit* (Berlin: Freund & Jeckel, 1892), 89. See Jantzen, *Mennonite German Soldiers*, 228–234.

3. Ewert, "A Defense," 286.

4. *Kulturkampf* here refers to Bismarck's anti-Catholic policies as well as Imperial Germany's more general religious conflict into the 1880s. Smith, *German Nationalism*; Margaret Lavinia Anderson, "The Kulturkampf and the Course of German History," *Central European History* 19, no. 1 (1986): 82–115.

5. Such logic was common in Germany and beyond: Hartmut Lehmann, "Pietism and Nationalism: The Relationship between Protestant Revivalism and National Renewal in Nineteenth-Century Germany," *Church History* 51 (1982): 39–53; William Hutchison and Hartmut Lehmann, eds., *Many Are Chosen: Divine Election and Western Nationalism* (Harrisburg, PA: Trinity Press International, 1994).

6. Harder, "Die Reorganisation," 52.

7. Translated in Mark Jantzen, "'Whoever Will Not Defend His Homeland Should Leave It!' German Conscription and Prussian Mennonite Emigration to the Great Plains, 1860–1890," *Mennonite Life* 58, no. 3 (2003): https://ml.bethelks.edu/issue/vol-58-no-3/article/whoever-will-not-defend-his-homeland-should-leave/.

8. Translated in ibid.

9. "Ein deutsches Wort an's deutsche Volk," *Gemeindeblatt* supplement, December 1870. Also, Barbara Dick and Harry Loewen, "Recollections of the Franco-German War, 1870–71," *Journal of Mennonite Studies* 7 (1989): 33–50.

10. Ulrich Hege, "Zum neuen Jahr," *Gemeindeblatt*, January 1871, 1.

11. Quoted in Christian Neff, "Hinrich van der Smissen," *Christlicher Gemeinde-Kalender*, 1929, 71–72.

12. Jakob Ellenberger, "Ein Kleines nationalfest im grossen deutschen Reich," *Mennonitische Blätter*, November 1872, 60–63. Quotation from Ernst Moritz Arndt, *Gedichte* (Berlin: Weidmannsche Buchhandlung, 1860), 233–235. On Sedan Day, Confino, *The Nation*, 27–72.

13. Translated in Mannhardt, *Military Service*, 324.

14. Wilhelm Mannhardt, "Zur Wehrfrage," *Mennonitische Blätter*, January 1870, 3.

15. Harder, "Die Reorganisation," 54. On Kant's theory, Immanuel Kant, *Political Writings* (Cambridge: Cambridge University Press, 1991), 93–130.

16. Jakob Mannhardt, "Traurede," *Mennonitische Blätter*, May 1872, 30.

17. Harder, "Die Reorganisation," 57.

18. Carl Harder, *Kurzgefaßte Geschichte der Elbinger Mennonitengemeinde* (Elbing: H. Gaartz, 1883), 22.

19. *Nachtrag zur Gemeinde-Ordnung der vereinigten Mennoniten-Gemeinde zu Danzig* (Danzig: Edwin Groening, 1870).

20. Mannhardt, *Military Service*, 324.

21. Jakob Ellenberger, *Bilder aus dem Pilgerleben* (Stuttgart: Steinkopf, 1878), 139–140.

22. Translated in Mark Jantzen, "Equal and Conscripted: Liberal Rights Confront Mennonite Conceptions of Freedom in Nineteenth-Century Germany," *Journal of Mennonite Studies* 32 (2014): 65–66.

23. Translated in Jantzen, "'Whoever Will Not Defend.'"

24. Translated in Jantzen, *Mennonite German Soldiers*, 223–225.

25. Dyck, "Beschreibung meiner Auswanderung," 43–45.

26. Ewert, "A Defense," 286, 290.

27. Translated in Harvey Dyck, "Russian Mennonitism and the Challenge of Russian Nationalism, 1889," *Mennonite Quarterly Review* 52, no. 4 (1982): 335. On this migration, Urry, *None but Saints*, 196–218.

28. Translated in Dyck, "Russian Mennonitism," 318.

29. A. Thiessen, *Die Lage der deutschen Kolonisten in Russland* (Leipzig: Robert Hoffmann, 1876), 4.

30. Translated in Dyck, "Russian Mennonitism," 318.

31. Thiessen, *Die Lage*, 16.

32. B. C. Roosen, "Die Auswanderung unserer mennonitischen Brüder aus Rußland," *Mennonitische Blätter*, January 1876, 5. On Roosen, Michael D. Driedger, "Kanonen, Schießpulver und Wehrlosigkeit: Cord, Geeritt und B. C. Roosen in Holstein und Hamburg 1532–1905," *Mennonitische Geschichtsblätter* 52 (1995): 112. On German migrations, Dirk Hoerder and Jörg Nagel, eds., *People in Transit: German Migrations in Comparative Perspective, 1820–1930* (Cambridge: Cambridge University Press, 1995).

33. Theodor Fontane, *Quitt* (Berlin: J.G. Cotta'sche Buchhandlung, 1902), 193–199. See Jantzen, *Mennonite German Soldiers*, 234–245. On Mennonites in fiction, Harry Loewen, ed., *Mennonite Images* (Winnipeg: Hyperion Press, 1980), 197–219.

34. Recounted in Antje Brons to Ludwig Keller, June 6, 1888, Ludwig Keller Collection, MLA. On "Dissidents" as a fourth confession, Weir, *Secularism and Religion*. On *Kulturkampf*-era Mennonite historiography, Abraham Friesen, *History and Renewal in the Anabaptist/Mennonite Tradition* (North Newton, KS: Bethel College, 1994).

35. Brons, *Ursprung, Entwickelung und Schicksale*, 12.

36. Müller, *Die Mennoniten in Ostfriesland*, Vorrede.

37. Brons, *Ursprung, Entwickelung und Schicksale*, 12, 354.

38. Max Schön, *Das Mennonitenthum in Westpreußen* (Berlin: Friedrich Luckhardt, 1886), Vorwort; Mannhardt, *Festschrift*, Vorwort.

39. B. C. Roosen, *Geschichte der Mennoniten-Gemeinde zu Hamburg und Altona*, vol. 1 (Hamburg: H. D. Persichl., 1886), 1–2.

40. Smith, *German Nationalism*, 51–66. Also, Rebecca Bennette, *Fighting for the Soul of Germany: The Catholic Struggle for Inclusion after Unification* (Cambridge, MA: Harvard University Press, 2012).

41. Ludwig Keller to B. C. Roosen, February 6, 1889, Ludwig Keller Collection, MLA. Karl Kautsky developed this trope in *Die Vorläufer des neueren Sozialismus* (Stuttgart: Diek, 1895), 312–436.

42. Antje Brons to Ludwig Keller, January 25, 1888, Ludwig Keller Collection, MLA.

43. Ludwig Keller to B. C. Roosen, January 3, 1888, Ludwig Keller Collection, MLA.

44. Ibid.

45. Curatorium, "Öffentliche Erklärung."

46. Hermann Wiens to Ludwig Keller, June 18, 1888, Ludwig Keller Collection, MLA.

47. Curatorium, "Öffentliche Erklärung."

48. Translated in Jantzen, *Mennonite German Soldiers*, 228.

49. Hermann Wiens to Ludwig Keller, June 3, 1888, Ludwig Keller Collection, MLA.

50. Brons to Keller, June 6, 1888.

51. Ludwig Keller, *Zur Geschichte der altevangelischen Gemeinden* (Berlin: Mittler und Sohn, 1887), 5–12.

52. Ibid., 13–53.

53. Gabriel Audisio, *The Waldensian Dissent: Persecution and Survival, c. 1170–c. 1570* (Cambridge: Cambridge University Press, 1999).

54. Carl Harder, "Ist die mennonitische Gemeinschaft eine 'Sekte' oder ist sie die 'Fortsetzung der ursprünglichen christlichen Kirche?'" *Mennonitische Blätter*, January 1888, 2–3.

55. Ludwig Keller, *Die Waldenser und die deutschen Bibelübersetzungen* (Leipzig: Hirzel, 1886), 9, 40.

56. H. G. Mannhardt, "Eine neue Ausgabe der 'Deutschen Theologie,'" *Mennonitische Blätter*, March 1887, 21–22.

57. Reported in Brons to Keller, June 6, 1888.

58. H. G. Mannhardt to Ludwig Keller, November 29, 1888, Ludwig Keller Collection, MLA.

59. Harder, "Ist die mennonitische Gemeinschaft," 11.

60. Mannhardt, "Predigt über Epheser," 2–5.

61. Brons to Keller, January 25, 1888.

62. Ludwig Keller to Hinrich van der Smissen, October 10, 1887, Ludwig Keller Collection, MLA.

63. S. Eck, "Jahrbuch der altevangelischen Taufgesinnten oder Mennoniten-Gemeinden," *Theologische Literaturzeitung*, 1888, 305–307.

64. Otto zur Linden, *Melchior Hofmann, ein Prophet der Wiedertäufer* (Haarlem: Erven Bohn, 1885), Vorwort.

65. Friedrich Nippold, *Die Theorie der Trennung von Kirche und Staat* (Bern: Wyss, 1880), 43. For context, Heinrich Bornkamm, "Die Staatsidee im Kulturkampf," *Historische Zeitschrift* 170 (1950): 41–72, 273–306.

66. Friedrich Fabri, *Wie weiter? Kirchenpolitische Betrachtungen zum Ende des Kulturkampfes* (Gotha: Freidrich Perthes, 1887), 26. On Fabri, Friesen, *History and Renewal*, 47–53; Klaus Bade, *Friedrich Fabri und der Imperialismus in der Bismarckzeit: Revolution–Depression–Expansion* (Zurich: Atlantis, 1975).

67. Ludwig Keller to Otto von Bismarck, November 1888, Ludwig Keller Collection, MLA.

68. Ludwig Keller, February 11, 1889, Ludwig Keller Collection, MLA.

69. Ludwig Keller, *Geschichte der Wiedertäufer und ihres Reiches zu Münster* (Münster: Coppernrath'schen Buch- & Kunsthandlung, 1880).

70. Ludwig Keller, *Ein Apostel der Wiedertäufer* (Leipzig: Hirzel, 1882).

71. Ludwig Keller, *Johann von Staupitz und die Anfänge der Reformation* (Leipzig: Hirzel, 1888), v.

72. Keller, *Geschichte der Wiedertäufer*, iii.

73. Georg Winter, "Ein neues Reformationsbuch," *Illustrierte Deutsche Monatshefte*, 1889, 268; J. Fischer, "Keller, Ludwig," *Das Archiv*, 1889, 88–89.

74. Franz Jostes, *Die Waldenser und die vorlutherische deutsche Bibelübersetzung* (Münster: Heinrich Schöningh, 1885), 5–6.

75. Theodor Kolde, "Keller, L.," *Göttingische gelehrte Anzeigen*, 1889, 574–585.

76. Ludwig Keller to S. J. Hingst, February 6, 1889, Ludwig Keller Collection, MLA.

77. Antje Brons to Ludwig Keller, March 14, 1883, Ludwig Keller Collection, MLA.

78. Ludwig Keller to Jacob Toeves, February 11, 1889, Ludwig Keller Collection, MLA.

79. Printed in Ernst Göbel, "Conferenz zu Ernstweiler in der Südpfalz," *Mennonitische Blätter*, June 1885, 57.

80. Keller to Toeves, February 11, 1889.

81. Printed in Göbel, "Conferenz zu Ernstweiler," 57.

82. Keller to Toeves, February 11, 1889.

83. Ludwig Keller to B. C. Roosen, August 29, 1887, Ludwig Keller Collection, MLA.

84. H. G. Mannhardt, *Bericht über die in Berlin um 2. und 3. October 1884 stattgehabte Conferenz deutscher Mennoniten* (Danzig, 1884), 13.

85. *Statut für die Vereinigung der Mennoniten-Gemeinden im deutschen Reich* (Altona: Heinrich Dircks, 1886).

86. Mannhardt, *Bericht*, 10.

87. Mannhardt, *Jahrbuch*, 112.
88. *Protokoll über die am 2. und 3. Oktober 1884 zu Berlin von einer Anzahl Mennoniten aus verschiedenen Gemeinden Deutschlands gepflogenen Verhandlungen* (Altona, 1884), 9.
89. Mannhardt, *Bericht*, 10.
90. Mannhardt, *Jahrbuch*, 107.
91. Mannhardt, *Bericht*, 10.
92. Keller to Smissen, October 10, 1887.
93. Ludwig Keller, October 16, 1888, Ludwig Keller Collection, MLA.
94. Carl Harder, "In Sachen der Keller'schen Forschungen," *Gemeindeblatt*, November 1890, 85–86.
95. H. G. Mannhardt, "Geschichte der Predigt in den deutschen Mennoniten Gemeinden," *Mennonitische Blätter*, April 1891, 37.
96. Supplement to *Reichsboten*, January 18, 1888.
97. See Pieter Judson, "Nationalism in the Era of the Nation State, 1870–1945," in *The Oxford Handbook of Modern German History*, ed. Helmut Smith (Oxford: Oxford University Press, 2011), 499–526.
98. Mannhardt, "Geschichte der Predigt," 37.

CHAPTER 3: RAISING THE FAITH

1. Göbel, "Conferenz zu Ernstweiler," 61.
2. Wiens to Keller, June 3, 1888.
3. Mannhardt, *Jahrbuch*, 108. On the religious origins of child welfare in Germany, Edward Dickinson, *The Politics of German Child Welfare* (Cambridge: Cambridge University Press, 1996), 11–34.
4. On the comparable charge of "national indifference," Zahra, "Imagined Non-Communities"; Bjork, *Neither German nor Pole*; Karch, "Nationalism on the Margins"; and the 2012 *Austrian History Yearbook*. In the context of childrearing, Judson, *Guardians of the Nation*; Zahra, *Kidnapped Souls*.
5. Richard Weikart, "The Origins of Social Darwinism in Germany, 1859–1895," *Journal of the History of Ideas* 54, no. 3 (1993): 473. Darwinism was unusually successful in Germany: Alfred Kelly, *The Descent of Darwin: The Popularization of Darwinism in Germany, 1860–1914* (Chapel Hill: University of North Carolina Press, 1981).
6. Hermann Wiens to Ludwig Keller, February 18, 1889, Ludwig Keller Collection, MLA. On children and future-oriented thinking, Lee Edelman, *No Future: Queer Theory and the Death Drive* (Durham: Duke University Press, 2004).
7. Miranda Pollard has described the social mobilization of familial discourses in *Reign of Virtue: Mobilizing Gender in Vichy France* (Chicago: University of Chicago Press, 1998). Regarding Central Europe, Tara Zahra, "Reclaiming Children for the Nation: Germanization, National Ascription, and Democracy in Bohemian Lands, 1900–1945," *Central European History* 37, no. 4 (2004): 499–540.
8. "Bericht über die zweite Badisch-Pfälzische Konferenz," November 16, 1887, Nachlaß Christian Neff, box 17, folder 130, MFS.
9. Ibid.
10. Mannhardt, "Predigt über Epheser," 5. On German nationalist rhetorical stategies, Confino, *The Nation*, 61–64.
11. H. C. Andres, "Eine kurze Antwort auf den Artikel: 'vom Leiden des Unrechts und von der Wehrlosigkeit,'" *Gemeindeblatt*, September 1888, 71.

12. Ernst Weydmann to Ludwig Keller, March 17, 1891, Ludwig Keller Collection, MLA.
13. Wiens to Keller, June 3, 1888.
14. Ludwig Keller, October 27, 1902, Ludwig Keller Collection, MLA. On Keller's later dealings with Mennonites, Friesen, *History and Renewal*, 100–112.
15. H. G. Mannhardt, "Innere Mission. II," *Mennonitische Blätter*, August 1902, 67.
16. Ibid.
17. B. C. Roosen, *Geschichte der Mennoniten-Gemeinde zu Hamburg und Altona*, vol. 2 (Hamburg: Perfiehl, 1887), 57. The overall Hamburg-Altona congregation remained robust: Mannhardt, *Jahrbuch*, 18.
18. H. G. Mannhardt, "Innere Mission. III," *Mennonitische Blätter*, September 1902, 74.
19. Christian Hege, "Wesshalb nehmen unsere Geminden beständig ab?" *Gemeindeblatt*, July 1892, 51.
20. Christian Neff, "Über Kindergottesdienst und ihre Einführung," May 15, 1889, Nachlaß Christian Neff, box 17, folder 130, MFS.
21. Translated in Mannhardt, *Military Service*, 334–335.
22. Carl Harder, "Christus will alle Menschen zu einer Familie vereinigen," *Monatschrift für die evangelischen Mennoniten*, June 1847, 9–10. On family structures, Jantzen, *Mennonite German Sold*iers, 16–22, 50–54, 161–169. Also, Benjamin Redekop and Calvin Redekop, eds., *Power, Authority, and the Anabaptist Tradition* (Baltimore: Johns Hopkins University Press, 2001).
23. Beth Kreitzer, "Menno Simons and the Bride of Christ," *Mennonite Quarterly Review* 70, no. 3 (1996): 299–318. Also, Sigrun Haude, "Gender Roles and Perspectives among Anabaptist and Spiritualist Groups," in *A Companion to Anabaptism*, ed. Roth and Stayer, 425–466.
24. Jantzen, *Mennonite German Soldiers*, 50–54, 70–77, 162–169.
25. Brons to Keller, March 14, 1883.
26. Hege, "Wesshalb nehmen unsere Geminden," 51.
27. Quoted in Driedger, "Kanonen, Schießpulver und Wehrlosigkeit," 113.
28. Brons to Keller, March 14, 1883.
29. Reprinted in *Allerhöchste Kabinetsorder vom 3. März 1868* (Marienburg: Druck von O. Halb, 1915).
30. *Nachtrag zur Gemeinde-Ordnung.*
31. Ulrich Hege, "Nachträgliches zu dem Artikel: 'Die christliche Gemeindezucht,'" *Gemeindeblatt*, July 1871, 30–31.
32. Ulrich Hege, "Die Mennofeier," *Gemeindeblatt*, July 1892, 55.
33. Christian Schmutz, "Noch einiges über die Mischehe," *Gemeindeblatt*, August 1871, 33–34.
34. Hege, "Nachträgliches zu dem Artikel," 30.
35. Carl Harder, "Gemischte Ehen," *Mittheilung aus dem religiösen Leben*, November 1848, 15.
36. Quoted in Driedger, "Kanonen, Schießpulver und Wehrlosigkeit," 113–114.
37. Mannhardt, "Innere Mission. II," 68.
38. Translated in Mannhardt, *Military Service*, 339.
39. Curatorium, "Werte Brüder!" December 1889, Uncatalogued Documents, BMHA.
40. Translated in William Klassen, "The Role of the Child in Anabaptism," in *Mennonite Images*, ed. Loewen, 23 (1 Timothy 5:8; Ephesians 6:4). More broadly, Marcia Bunge, *The Child in Christian Thought* (Grand Rapids: Eerdmans Publishing, 2001).
41. Neff, "Über Kindergottesdienst."
42. Carl Harder, "Die Familie," *Blätter für Religion und Erziehung*, March 1870, 337.
43. Neff, "Über Kindergottesdienst."

44. Philippe Ariès has demonstrated the malleability of conceptions of childhood in *Centuries of Childhood: A Social History of Family Life* (New York: Vintage Books, 1962). On later developments, Hugh Cunningham, *Children and Childhood in Western Society Since 1500* (New York: Routledge, 2014).

45. Harder, "Die Reorganisation," 59.

46. Ellenberger, *Bilder aus dem Pilgerleben* (1878), 4.

47. Ulrich Hege, "Für Kinder," *Gemeindeblatt*, January 1870, 4.

48. Christian Schowalter, "Meine lieben Kinder!" *Nachrichten aus der Heidenwelt*, January 1885, 3. Published in the United States, this paper found readership in Germany.

49. Jakob Ellenberger, *Bilder aus dem Pilgerleben*, vol. 3 (Frankfurt a.M.: Lichtenberg, 1883), 4.

50. Schowalter, "Meine lieben Kinder!"

51. "Eine Ansprache an die Baptisten Deutschlands—eine Mahnung für die Mennoniten Deutschlands," *Mennonitische Blätter*, September 1884, 69–70.

52. Neff, "Über Kindergottesdienst."

53. Ellenberger, *Bilder aus dem Pilgerleben* (1878), 3, 39.

54. Neff, "Über Kindergottesdienst."

55. Helmut Haury, *Die Lehr- und Erziehungsanstalt auf dem Weierhof* (Bolanden-Weierhof: Gymnasium Weierhof, 1992).

56. Curatorium, "Werte Brüder!"

57. Mannhardt, "Innere Mission. II," 69.

58. Hege, "Wesshalb nehmen unsere Geminden," 51.

59. "Jakob Ellenberger II," *Mennonitische Blätter*, March 1901, 21.

60. Curatorium, "Werte Brüder!"

61. Mannhardt, "Innere Mission. III," 75.

62. Kuratorium, "An den Vorstand der Mennoniten-Gemeinde," April 1894, 521–5/215, vol. 1, folder 1894, SFHH.

63. Mannhardt, "Innere Mission. II," 67.

64. H. G. Mannhardt to Ludwig Keller, April 9, 1889, Ludwig Keller Collection, MLA.

65. Smissen, "Die Ausbildung."

66. Mannhardt, "Innere Mission. III," 75.

67. "Bericht über die zweite Badisch-Pfälzische Konferenz."

68. Hinrich van der Smissen, "Die Notwendigkeit einer eigenen Anstalt zur Heranbildung von Predigern und Dienern an Gottes Wort," *Mennonitische Blätter*, April 1884, 26.

69. H. G. Mannhardt, "Aus Westpreußen," *Mennonitische Blätter*, September 1884, 68.

70. Göbel, "Conferenz zu Ernstweiler," 58–59.

71. "Bericht über die zweite Badisch-Pfälzische Konferenz."

72. Johann Töws, "Meine einfache Ansicht über des Br. Schmutz aus Baden Aufforderung," *Mennonitische Blätter*, July 1867, 46. On Mennonite skepticism, James Urry, "'The Snares of Reason': Changing Mennonite Attitudes to 'Knowledge' in Nineteenth-Century Russia," *Comparative Studies in Society and History* 25, no. 2 (1983): 306–332.

73. Paraphrased in Mannhardt, *Jahrbuch*, 121.

74. "Bericht über die zweite Badisch-Pfälzische Konferenz."

75. *Prüfungs-Ordnung für die Stipendiaten der Vereinigung der Mennoniten-Gemeinden im Deutschen Reich* (1895).

76. *Statut für die Prediger-Witwenkasse der Vereinigung des Mennoniten-Gemeinden im Deutschen Reich* (Crefeld: Lüthgen, 1897); *Satzung des Vereins* (Altona: Heinrich Dircks, 1914), 20; Christian Neff to Vorstand der Vereinigung, March 1911, 521–5/215, vol. 2, folder 1911, SFHH.

77. "Der Grundsatz der Wehrlosigkeit und seine Entwicklung in unserer Gemeinschaft," *Mennonitische Blätter*, November 1910, 82–86, and December 1910, 90–91.

78. Die Soldatenkommission, "Unsere Glaubensbrüder im deutschen Heere," *Mennonitische Blätter*, December 1901, 92.

79. Mannhardt, "Aus Westpreußen," 67. On militarism in Imperial Germany, Jost Dülffer and Karl Holl, eds., *Bereit zum Krieg: Kriegsmentalität im wilhelminischen Deutschland, 1890–1914* (Göttingen: Vandenhoeck & Ruprecht, 1986).

80. Ludwig Keller, "Vom Leiden des Unrechts und von der Wehrlosigkeit," *Gemeindeblatt*, June 1888, 46.

81. Kuratorium, "An den Vorstand."

82. Die Soldaten-Kommission, "Was können wir für unsere Soldaten thun?" *Mennonitische Blätter*, February 1900, 11.

83. *Warnungen und Winke für die Militärzeit* (Kaiserslautern: Soldaten-Kommission der Konferenz süddeutscher Mennoniten, 1908), 5–24.

84. On pacifism in Imperial Germany, Roger Chickering, *Imperial Germany and a World without War: The Peace Movement and German Society, 1892–1914* (Princeton: Princeton University Press, 1975).

85. *Satzungen der Mennoniten-Gemeinde zu Gronau i. Westf.* (Gronau: Buchdruckerei der "Gronauer Nachrichten," 1899), 3.

86. *Glaubensbekenntnis der Mennoniten in Preußen* (Marienburg: Hans Halb, 1895), 15–16.

87. *Satzung der Mennoniten Gemeinde zu Schönsee Kreis Culm* (Culm: Carl Brandt, 1902).

88. "Unsere Brüder im Felde," *Mennonitische Blätter*, September 1914, 67.

89. Smissen, "Zum Reformationsfest," 87.

90. James Regier, "Where the Two Kingdoms Merge: The Struggle for Balance Between National and Religious Identity Among Mennonites in Wilhelmine Germany" (MA thesis, Wichita State University, 2006), 89–90.

91. Mannhardt, "Predigt über Epheser," 2–3.

CHAPTER 4: WORLD WAR, WORLD CONFESSION

1. *Bericht über die 400 jährige Jubiläumsfeier der Mennoniten oder Taufgesinnten* (Karlsruhe: Heinrich Schneider, 1925), 102.

2. Quoted in Christian Neff, "Bei unseren kriegsgefangenen russischen Glaubensbrüdern," *Mennonitische Blätter*, October 1915, 85. For context, David Rempel, "Mennonite Medics in Russia during World War I," *Journal of Mennonite Studies* 11 (1993): 149–161.

3. Neff, "Bei unseren kriegsgefangenen, 86." In *The Birth of the Modern World*, C. A. Bayly has identified interconnection as a hallmark of globalization. More broadly, Jürgen Osterhammel and Niels Petersson, *Globalization: A Short History* (Princeton: Princeton University Press, 2003).

4. Marsha Rozenblit finds a similar phenomenon among Habsburg Jews: *Reconstructing a National Identity: The Jews of Habsburg Austria During World War I* (Oxford: Oxford University Press, 2001). Also, Philip Jenkins, *The Great and Holy War: How World War I Became a Religious Crusade* (New York: HarperCollins, 2014).

5. Erez Manela has described the global appeal of national self-determination: *The Wilsonian Moment: Self-Determination and the International Origins of Anticolonial Nationalism* (Oxford: Oxford University Press, 2007).

6. Hinrich van der Smissen, "Es ist Krieg," *Mennonitische Blätter*, September 1914, 66. On Mennonites in Germany during WWI, Walter Klaassen, Harry Loewen, and

James Urry, "German Nationalism and the First World War: Hermann G. Mannhardt's *Heroic Deeds and Heroes*," *Mennonite Quarterly Review* 88, no. 4 (2014): 517–536; Helmut Foth, "Mennonitischer Patriotismus im Ersten Weltkrieg und die Kriegsrede des Danziger Predigers Hermann G. Mannhardt," *Mennonitische Geschichtsblätter* 72 (2015): 47–74. On Germany at war, Roger Chickering, *Imperial Germany and the Great War, 1914–1918* (Cambridge: Cambridge University Press, 1998).

7. Matthias Pohl, "Wie der Blitz oben vom Himmel," *Mennonitische Blätter*, October 1914, 73.

8. H. G. Manhardt, "Der Krieg und wir," *Mennonitische Blätter*, October 1914, 74 (Matthew 3:12).

9. Smissen, "Es ist Krieg," 66.

10. All German states with substantial Mennonite populations exempted them from oaths. Der geschäftsführende Ausschuss der Vereinigung to Staatssekretär des Reichsjustizamts Berlin, January 8, 1910, 521–5/7, SFHH.

11. H. G. Mannhardt to Kuratorium, March 13, 1916, Vereinigung, box 1, folder Briefe 1913–1918, MFS.

12. "Es ist Erreicht," *Mennonitische Blätter*, November 1914, 84.

13. Quoted in "Ob's dismal glückt?" *Mennonitische Blätter*, October 1914, 75.

14. "Unsere Brüder im Felde," 67. Some 500 were officers.

15. Mannhardt, "Der Krieg und wir," 74.

16. "Fürsorge für unsere vom Kriege heimgesuchten Brüder," *Mennonitische Blätter*, January 1915, 4. On the 1888 flood, *Bericht über die Thätigkeit des Hülfscomites für die durch Überschwemmung heimgesuchten Mennoniten-Gemeinden 1888/89* (Altona: Heinrich Dircks, 1889). On reclamation as a national metaphor, Blackbourn, *The Conquest*. Also, Thomas Lekan, *Imagining the Nation in Nature: Landscape Preservation and German Identity, 1885–1945* (Cambridge, MA: Harvard University Press, 2004).

17. Hinrich van der Smissen, "Unser Blatt," *Mennonitische Blätter*, September 1914, 69.

18. Hinrich van der Smissen, "Unsere Brüder im Ausland," *Mennonitische Blätter*, September 1914, 70.

19. Gerlof Homan, *American Mennonites and the Great War, 1914–1918* (Scottdale, PA: Herald Press, 1994), 40.

20. "Fürsorge für unsere vom Kriege," 4.

21. Translated in Friesen, *In Defense*, 211. For context, John Friesen, ed., *Mennonites in Russia 1788–1988* (Winnipeg: CMBC Publications, 1989), 221–288.

22. Translated in Manz, *Constructing a German Diaspora*, 166. Also, David Rempel, "The Expropriation of the German Colonies in South Russia during the Great War," *Journal of Modern History* 4, no. 1 (1932): 49–67; Eric Lohr, *Nationalizing the Russian Empire: The Campaign against Enemy Aliens during World War I* (Cambridge, MA: Harvard University Press, 2003).

23. Translated in Friesen, *In Defense*, 226.

24. Cornelius Bergmann, "Die Lage der Mennoniten in Rußland," *Mennonitische Blätter*, March 1915, 19. On alternative service, Lawrence Klippenstein and Jacob Dick, *Mennonite Alternative Service in Russia: The Story of Abram Dück and His Colleagues 1911–1917* (Kitchener, ON: Pandora Press, 2002).

25. Christian Neff, "Die Zukunft unserer deutsch-russischen Brüder," *Mennonitische Blätter*, January 1916, 6.

26. W. Ludwig, "Die deutschen Kolonien in Rußland," *Mennonitische Blätter*, August 1915, 65.

27. Andrew Bell-Fialkoff, *Ethnic Cleansing* (New York: St. Martin's Press, 1996), 1–118.

28. Neff, "Die Zukunft," 6. On fears of Slavic infiltration, Kristin Kopp, *Germany's Wild East: Constructing Poland as Colonial Space* (Ann Arbor: University of Michigan Press, 2012), 96–123.

29. Vorstand der Fürsorgverein für deutsche Rückwanderer to Hinrich van der Smissen, March 1, 1912, 521–5/213, vol. 3, SFHH.

30. Benjamin Unruh, *Die Wehrlosigkeit* (Halbstadt, 1917), 5, 18.

31. Mannhardt to Kuratorium, March 13, 1916.

32. Quoted in Benjamin Unruh, "Praktische Fragen," *Der Bote*, November 4, 1936, 1.

33. Translations from Friesen, *In Defense*, 198, 449–450.

34. Quoted in Unruh, "Praktische Fragen," 1.

35. Hinrich van der Smissen, "Das Los unsere russischen Brüder in holländischer Beleuchtung," *Mennonitische Blätter*, April 1916, 27.

36. Kuratorium to Theobald von Bethmann-Hollweg, November-December 1916, Nachlaß Christian Neff, box 23, folder 178, MFS. Although printed in the *Mennonite Journal*, this letter was never sent to Bethmann-Hollweg.

37. Ibid.

38. Terry Martin, "The Russian Mennonite Encounter with the Soviet State 1917–1955," *Conrad Grebel Review* 20, no. 1 (2002): 13.

39. "Weitere Mitteilungen aus der Ukraine," *Mennonitische Blätter*, March 1918, 22–23.

40. "Die Leiden unserer Brüder in der Ukraine unter den Bolschewiken," *Mennonitische Blätter*, May 1918, 44.

41. Kornelius Unruh, "Ein Schreiben aus der Ukraine," *Mennonitische Blätter*, May 1918, 38.

42. "Die Leiden unserer Brüder," 45.

43. Lawrence Klippenstein, "The *Selbstschutz:* A Mennonite Army in Ukraine, 1918–1919," in *History and Mission in Europe: Continuing the Conversation*, ed. Mary Raber and Peter Penner (Schwarzenfeld: Neufeld Verlag, 2011), 49–82.

44. "Die Leiden unserer Brüder," 45.

45. *Proceedings of the Brest-Litovsk Peace Conference* (Washington, DC: Government Printing Office, 1918), 130.

46. Deutscher Verband in Sibirien to Georg von Hertling, June 15, 1918, Vereinigung, box 1, folder Briefe 1913–1918, MFS.

47. "Gründungs-Urkunde der Siedlungs-Gesellschaft für mennonitsche Rückwanderer," June 1918, Deutsche Mennonitenhilfe, box 27, folder DMH Protokolle 1918–1924, MFS.

48. Hinrich van der Smissen, "Zur Ansiedlungsfrage," *Mennonitische Blätter*, November 1916, 84; Kopp, *Germany's Wild East*, 67–69.

49. Abraham Jansson, "Tiege," *Mennonitische Blätter*, March 1928, 25–26.

50. Ulrich Otto, "Welche Aufgaben können die deutschrussischen Mennoniten in den afrikanischen Kolonien lösen?" *Mennonitische Blätter*, October 1918, 74.

51. "Versammlung deutsch-russischer Mennoniten auf dem Weierhof," *Mennonitische Blätter*, April 1918, 28.

52. Vejas Liulevicius, *The German Myth of the East* (Oxford: Oxford University Press, 2009), 130–170; Annemarie Sammartino, *The Impossible Border: Germany and the East, 1914–1922* (Ithaca: Cornell University Press, 2010), 18–44.

53. Hinrich van der Smissen, "Zur neuen Lage der Dinge," *Mennonitische Blätter*, December 1918, 90 91.

54. Smissen, "Unsere Aussichten," 3.

55. Smissen, "Zur neuen Lage der Dinge," 91.

56. Paul Magocsi, *A History of Ukraine: The Land and Its Peoples* (Toronto: University of Toronto Press, 1996), 498–610.

57. John Toews, "The Origins and Activities of the Mennonite *Selbstschutz* in Ukraine (1918–1919)," *Mennonite Quarterly Review* 46 (1972): 5–39; Klippenstein, "The *Selbstschutz*"; John Toews, ed., *Mennonites in Ukraine Amidst Civil War and Anarchy* (Fresno: Center for Mennonite Brethren Studies, 2013). For context, Taras Hunczak, *The Ukraine, 1917–1921: A Study in Revolution* (Cambridge, MA: Harvard University Press, 1977). More broadly, Robert Gerwarth and John Horne, *War in Peace: Paramilitary Violence in Europe after the Great War* (Oxford: Oxford University Press, 2012).

58. Translated in Nestor Makhno, *The Ukrainian Revolution* (Edmonton: Black Cat Press, 2011), xvi. On Makhno, Michael Malet, *Nestor Makhno in the Russian Civil War* (London: Macmillan, 1982). For recent interpretations, Sean Patterson, "The Eichenfeld Massacre: Recontextualizing Mennonite and Makhnovist Narratives," *Journal of Mennonite Studies* 32 (2014): 151–174; Harvey Dyck, John Staples, and John Toews eds., *Nestor Makhno and the Eichenfeld Massacre: A Civil War Tragedy in a Ukrainian Mennonite Village* (Kitchener, ON: Pandora Press, 2004).

59. Peter Letkemann, "Mennonite Victims of Revolution, Anarchy, Civil War, Disease and Famine, 1917–1923," *Mennonite Historian* 24, no. 2 (1998): 2.

60. Johann Kuhlmann, "Sehr schwere Heimsuchung der in Südrußland lebenden *deutschen* Kolonisten," *Mennonitische Blätter*, October 1919, 75–76.

61. "Aufruf," *Mennonitische Blätter*, October 1920, 80–81.

62. "Dem Blutbade entronnen," *Mennonitische Blätter*, March 1920, 22–23.

63. Quoted in David Rempel and Cornelia Carlson, *A Mennonite Family in Tsarist Russia and the Soviet Union, 1789–1923* (Toronto: University of Toronto Press, 2002), 247.

64. John Klassen, "Mennonites in Russia and their Migrations," in *Testing Faith*, ed. Jecker and Hoekema, 196–197. On Mennonites in the early USSR, Toews and Toews, eds., *Union of Citizens*; Oksana Beznosova and Aleksandr Beznosov, "The Religious Life of Mennonites in the Mid-1920s through the Eyes of the Soviet Political Police," in *History and Mission in Europe*, ed. Raber and Penner, 33–48; Lawrence Klippentein, "Mennonites and Military Service in the Soviet Union to 1939," in *Challenge to Mars: Essays on Pacificsm from 1918 to 1945*, ed. Peter Brock and Thomas Socknat (Toronto: University of Toronto Press, 1999), 3–18; Reina Neufeldt, "'We Are Aware of Our Contradictions': Russlaender Mennonite Narratives of Loss and the Reconstruction of Peoplehood, 1914–1923," *Journal of Mennonite Studies* 27 (2009): 129–154; John Toews, *Czars, Soviets and Mennonites* (Newton, KS: Faith and Life Press, 1982).

65. A. Reinmarus, *Anti-Menno: Beträge zur Geschichte der Mennoniten in Russland* (Moscow: Zentral-Volker-Verlag, 1930). Also, Harry Loewen, "Anti-Menno: Introduction to Early Soviet-Mennonite Literature," *Journal of Mennonite Studies* 11 (1993): 23–42.

66. Translated in Martin, "The Russian," 30. On resistance, Sheila Fitzpatrick, *Stalin's Peasants: Resistance and Survival in the Russian Village after Collectivization* (New York: Oxford University Press, 1994).

67. "Vor dem Hungertode!" *Mennonitische Blätter*, March 1922, 19.

68. "Aufruf," 81. On DMH (originally "Mennonitische Flüchtlingsfürsorge"), *Deutsche Mennoniten-Hilfe* (Oberursel: Deutsche Mennoniten-Hilfe, 1924).

69. P. C. Hiebert and Orie Miller, *Feeding the Hungry: Russia Famine, 1919–1925* (Scottdale, PA: Mennonite Central Committee, 1929), 447.

70. Frank Epp, *Mennonite Exodus* (Altona, MB: D.W. Friesen & Sons, 1962), 59.

71. H. G. Mannhardt, "Jahresbericht der Vereinigung der Mennonitengmeienden im Deutschen Reich," *Mennonitische Blätter*, November 1920, 84–85.

72. Emil Händiges, "Empfiehlt sich für deutsche Mennoniten die Auswanderung?" *Mennonitische Blätter*, November 1928, 101–102.

73. "Mennonitische Flüchtlingsfürsorge," *Mennonitische Blätter,* January 1921, 4.

74. John Lapp and Ed van Straten, "Mennonite World Conference, 1925–2000: From Euro-American Conference to Worldwide Communion," *Mennonite Quarterly Review* 77, no. 1 (2003): 7–46.

75. Ludwig, "Die deutschen Kolonien," 65.

76. *Deutsche Mennoniten-Hilfe,* 22–24.

77. "Mennonitische Flüchtlingsfürsorge," 4.

78. Translated in Friesen, *In Defense,* 319.

79. James Urry, "A *Mennostaat* for the *Mennovolk*? Mennonite Immigrant Fantasies in Canada in the 1930s," *Journal of Mennonite Studies* 14 (1996): 67. Also, Frank Epp, "An Analysis of Germanism and National Socialism in the Immigrant Newspaper of a Canadian Minority Group, the Mennonites, in the 1930's" (PhD diss., University of Minnesota, 1965), 133–142; 239–242, 258.

80. Translated in Friesen, *In Defense,* 276.

81. Quoted in ibid., 283.

82. J. J. Hildebrand to Pastor der Mennonitengemeinde zu Amsterdam, January 12, 1921, 521–5/222, SFHH.

83. Translated in Friesen, *In Defense,* 285.

84. Eric Weitz, "From the Vienna to the Paris System: International Politics and the Entangled Histories of Human Rights, Forced Deportations, and Civilizing Missions," *American Historical Review* 113, no. 5 (2008): 1313–1343.

85. "Evacuation of Russian Refugees of German Origin (Mennonites and Lutherans) in China to Certain Latin-American Countries," *League of Nations: Official Journal* 13, no. 7 (1932): 1207–1208.

86. Translated in Friesen, *In Defense,* 288–289.

87. Quoted in Epp, *Mennonite Exodus,* 94. On anti-Germanism globally, Panikos Panayi, ed., *Germans as Minorities during the First World War: A Global Comparative Perspective* (Aldershot: Ashgate, 2014).

88. Martin, "The Russian," 22. On Mennonite emigration, John Toews, *Lost Fatherland: The Story of the Mennonite Emigration from Soviet Russia, 1921–1927* (Scottdale, PA: Herald Press, 1967). On Soviet migration policy, Alan Dowty, *Closed Borders: The Contemporary Assault on Freedom of Movement* (New Haven: Yale University Press, 1989), 67–73.

89. Translations from Martin, "The Russian," 28–35. On Soviet disfranchisement, Golfo Alexopoulos, *Stalin's Outcasts: Aliens, Citizens, and the Soviet State, 1926–1936* (Ithaca: Cornell University Press, 2003).

90. Colin Neufeldt, "Separating the Sheep from the Goats: The Role of Mennonites and Non-Mennonites in the Dekulakization of Chortitza, Ukraine (1928–1930)," *Mennonite Quarterly Review* 83, no. 2 (2009), 221–291; Colin Neufeldt, "Reforging Mennonite *Spetspereselentsy*: The Experience of Mennonite Exiles at Siberian Special Settlements in the Omsk, Tomsk, Novosibirsk and Narym Regions, 1930–1933," *Journal of Mennonite Studies* 30 (2012): 269–314.

91. Emil Händiges, *Was ist mennonitisch?* (Sonderausdruck as der Mennonitischen Blätter, 1930), 3.

92. Auswärtiges Amt to the Reichskanzlei, November 6, 1929, Nachlaß Benjamin Unruh, box 9, folder 47, MFS. For context, James Casteel, "The Russian Germans in the Interwar German National Imaginary," *Central European History* 40, no. 3 (2007): 429–466.

93. "Brüder in Not!" *Mennonitische Blätter,* December 1929, 105. This agency was later dubbed "Hitler help" in the USSR. Terry Martin, "The Origins of Soviet Ethnic

Cleansing," *Journal of Modern History* 70, no. 4 (1998): 847; Meir Buchsweiler, *Volksdeutsche in der Ukraine am Vorabend und Beginn des Zweiten Weltkrieges: Ein Fall doppelter Loyalität?* (Suttgart: Bleicher Verlag, 1984), 64–71.

94. Translated in Andrey Savin, "The 1929 Emigration of Mennonites from the USSR: An Examination of Documents from the Archive of Foreign Policy of the Russian Federation," *Journal of Mennonite Studies* 30 (2012): 53.

95. Terry Martin, *The Affirmative Action Empire: Nations and Nationalism in the Soviet Union, 1923–1939* (Ithaca: Cornell University Press, 2001), 319–321. 1,000 German-speaking Protestants also gained exit.

96. Quotations from Epp, *Mennonite Exodus*, 242–243.

97. Printed in Otto Auhagen, *Die Schicksalswende des russlanddeutschen Bauerntum in den Jahren 1927–1930* (Leipzig: S. Hirzel, 1942), 141.

98. On Mennonites in Brazil, Peter Klassen, *Die rußlanddeutschen Mennoniten in Brazilien*, vol. 1 (Bolanden-Weierhof: Mennonitischer Geschichtsverein, 1995). On German connections to Latin America, Glenn Penny, "Latin American Connections: Recent Work on German Interactions with Latin America," *Central European History* 46, no. 2 (2013): 362–394; Stefan Rinke, *"Der letzte freie Kontinent": Deutsche Lateinamerikapolitik im Zeichen transnationaler Beziehungen, 1918–1933* (Stuttgart: Verlag Hans-Dieter Heinz, 1996).

99. Urry, "A *Mennostaat*"; John Eicher, "Diaspora Hermeneutics: Mennonite Refugee Narratives Between the World Wars," in *New Perspectives in Diasporic Experience*, ed. Connie Rapoo, Maria Coelho, and Zahira Sarwar (Oxford: Inter-Disciplinary Press, 2014).

100. Walter Laqueur, *A History of Zionism: From the French Revolution to the Establishment of the State of Israel* (New York: I.B. Tauris, 2003), 84–440.

101. Harold Bender, "Die Einwanderung nach Paraguay," in *Mennonitische Welt-Hilfs-Konferenz vom 31. August bis 3. September 1930 in Danzig* (Karlsruhe: Hinrich Schneider, 1930), 118, 121. On settler colonialism, Caroline Elkins and Susan Pedersen, eds., *Settler Colonialism in the Twentieth Century: Projects, Practices, Legacies* (New York: Routledge, 2005).

102. Juan Belaieff, "The Present-Day Indians of the Gran Chaco," in *Handbook of South American Indians*, ed. Julian Steward (Washington, DC: US Government Printing Office, 1946), 372. On Mennonite-indigenous relations, Calvin Redekop, *Strangers Become Neighbors: Mennonite and Indigenous Relations in the Paraguayan Chaco* (Scottdale, PA: Herald Press, 1980).

103. Translations from Bridget Chesterton, *The Grandchildren of Solano López: Frontier and Nation in Paraguay, 1904–1936* (Albuquerque: University of New Mexico Press, 2013), 97–101. On Mennonites in Paraguay, Peter Klassen, *The Mennonites in Paraguay*, vol. 1 (Hillsboro, KS: Print Source Direct, 2004); Edgar Stoesz, *Like a Mustard Seed: Mennonites in Paraguay* (Scottdale, PA: Herald Press, 2008).

104. El Senado y Camara de Diputados de la Nacion Paraguay, "No. 514," July 26, 1921, Gesetz Nr. 514 und Gesetz Nr. 914, AKM.

105. Bender, "Die Einwanderung," 121–122.

106. John Toews, "Die Flucht rußlanddeutscher Mennoniten nach China (1929–1934)," *Mennonitische Geschichtsblätter* 36 (1979): 27–48.

107. Harold Bender, "Church and State in Mennonite History," *Mennonite Quarterly Review* 13, no. 2 (1939): 100–101.

108. Translations from Klassen, *Mennonites in Paraguay*, 74–84.

109. *Die Mennoniten-Gemeinden in Rußland während der Kriegs- und Revolutionsjahre 1914 bis 1920* (Heilbronn a. Neckar: Kommissions-Verlag der Mennon. Flüchtlingsfürsorge, 1921), 111. Shulamit Volkov has identified a similar phenomenon in the Jewish context: "Jewish History: The Nationalism of Transnationalism," in *Transnationale Geschichte*, ed. Budde et al., 190–201.

110. Emil Händiges, *Die Lehre der Mennoniten in Geschichte und Gegenwart* (Kaiserslautern: Julius Lösch, 1921), 79.

CHAPTER 5: THE RACIAL CHURCH

1. Michael Horsch, "Die bevorstehende Einigung der deutschen Mennonitengemeinden," *Sonder-Beilage zum Gemeindeblatt Nr. 8*, April 15, 1934.

2. Friedrich Keiter, *Rußlanddeutsche Bauern und ihre Stammesgenossen in Deutschland* (Jena: Gustav Fischer, 1934), the twelfth volume in *Deutsche Rassenkunde*, synthesized racial studies conducted among Mennonites since 1930. Photographs of Mennonite women from the USSR appear in Tafeln V, VI, and IX.

3. Geoff Eley, "Hitler's Silent Majority? Conformity and Resistance Under the Third Reich," *Michigan Quarterly Review* 42, no. 2 (2003): 389–425 and 42, no. 3 (2003): 550–583.

4. See Detlev Peukert's classic *Inside Nazi Germany: Conformity, Opposition and Racism in Everyday Life* (New Haven: Yale University Press, 1987), and more recently Eric Johnson, *Nazi Terror: The Gestapo, Jews, and Ordinary Germans* (New York: Basic Books, 2000); Robert Gellately, *Backing Hitler: Consent and Coercion in Nazi Germany* (Oxford: Oxford University Press, 2002); Geoff Eley, *Nazism as Fascism: Violence, Ideology, and the Ground of Consent in Germany 1930–1945* (New York: Routledge, 2013); Richard Evans, *The Third Reich in Power* (New York: Penguin, 2004). My analysis draws on Ian Kershaw's notion of "working towards the *Führer*," especially *The Nazi Dictatorship: Problems and Perspectives of Interpretation* (New York: Bloomsbury, 2015), 81–108.

5. On racial science and Nazism, Michael Burleigh and Wolfgang Wippermann, *The Racial State* (Cambridge: Cambridge University Press, 1991); Robert Proctor, *Racial Hygiene: Medicine Under the Nazis* (Cambridge, MA: Harvard University Press, 1990); Paul Weindling, *Health, Race, and German Politics between National Unification and Nazism, 1870–1945* (Cambridge: Cambridge University Press, 1989).

6. On Mennonites in the Third Reich, Diether Lichdi, *Mennoniten im Dritten Reich* (Weierhof im Bolanden: Mennonitischer Geschichtsverein, 1977); James Irvin Lichti, *Houses on the Sand? Pacifist Denominations in Nazi Germany* (New York: Peter Lang, 2008); Hans-Jürgen Goertz, "Mennoniten und der Nationalsozialismus," in *Christen im Dritten Reich*, ed. Philipp Thull (Darmstadt: Wissenschaftliche Buchgesellschaft, 2014), 68–84; Astrid von Schlachta, "'in unbedingter Treue' … 'keine Verfechter der Wehrlosigkeit': Volksgemeinschaft, Staatstreue und das Bild, das von den Mennoniten herrschen sollte," *Mennonitische Geschichtsblätter* 72 (2015): 117–132.

7. On Mennonites and Jews in Nazi Germany, Helmut Foth, "Juden, Täufer, Mennoniten: Ein Überblick über ihre 500 Jahre während Beziehungsgeschichte," *Mennonitischer Geschichtsblätter* 70 (2013): 23–54; Diether Lichdi, "Minderheiten, die sich lange fremd blieben: Mennoniten und Juden in der Zeit des Nationalsozialismus,"

in *Freikirchen und Juden im 'Dritten Reich,'* ed. Daniel Heinz (Göttingen: Vanden-hoeck & Ruprecht, 2011), 65–76; Gerhard Rempel, "Mennonites and the Holocaust: From Collaboration to Perpetration," *Mennonite Quarterly Review* 84, no. 4 (2010): 507–549.

8. Diether Lichdi, "Römer 13 und das Staatsverständnis der Mennoniten um 1933," *Mennonitische Geschichtsblätter* 32 (1980): 74–95. On the rise of Nazi Germany, Rich-ard Evans, *The Coming of the Third Reich* (New York: Penguin, 2004); Detlev Peu-kert, *The Weimar Republic* (New York: Hill and Wang, 1993).

9. Quoted in Emil Händiges, *Grundsätzliches über die deutschen Mennoniten, über ihre Stellung zu Wehrpflicht und Eid und ihr Verhältnis zum Dritten Reich* (Elbing: Rein-hold Kühn, 1937), 2. For context, Horst Penner, *Die ost- und westpreußischen Menno-niten*, vol. 2 (Karlsruhe: Heinrich Schneider, 1987), 122–145.

10. Benjamin Unruh, "Zur Frage der Rücksiedlung rußlanddeutscher Mennonitenfam-ilien aus Übersee," September 13, 1940, R 127518, PA AA. On Mennonites and the Party, John Thiesen, "Menno in the KZ or Münster Resurrected? Mennonites and National Socialism: Historiography and Open Questions," paper presented at Mar-ginal or Mainstream? Anabaptists, Mennonites and Modernity in European Soci-ety, Bethel College, North Newton, KS, June 25–26, 2010; Gerhard Rempel, "Hein-rich Hajo Schroeder: The Allure of Race and Space in Hitler's Empire," *Journal of Mennonite Studies* 29 (2011): 227–254; Christiana Duschinsky, "Mennonite Responses to Nazi Human Rights Abuses: A Family in Prussia/Danzig," *Journal of Mennonite Studies* 32 (2014): 81–96.

11. Bender, "Church and State," 91.

12. "Trauerfeier für Ernst Penner," *Mitteilungen des Sippenverbandes der danziger Mennoniten-Familien*, February 1941, 1–7.

13. Translated in Horst Gerlach, "The Final Years of Mennonites in East and West Prus-sia, 1943–45," *Mennonite Quarterly Review* 66, no. 2 (1992): 240.

14. Benjamin Unruh to D. Hege, July 28, 1933, Nachlaß Benjamin Unruh, box 2, folder 8, MFS.

15. Richard Steigmann-Gall, "Apostasy or Religiosity? The Cultural Meaning of the Protestant Vote for Hitler," *Social History* 25 (2000): 267–284.

16. Richard Steigmann-Gall, *The Holy Reich: Nazi Conceptions of Christianity, 1919–1945* (Cambridge: Cambridge University Press, 2003), 114–189.

17. Benjamin Unruh, "Aufätze," October 1933, Nachlaß Benjamin Unruh, box 2, folder 8, MFS.

18. Kuprich, "Vom Dritten Reich zur Dritten Kirche," *Elbinger Zeitung*, August 11, 1933.

19. "Zur Kirchenfrage der Mennoniten," *Mennonitische Blätter*, September 1933, 86.

20. *Vereinigung der Deutschen Mennonitengemeinden: Verfassung vom 11. Juni 1934* (Elbing: Reinhold Kühn, 1936), 3. The conservative *Verband* declined to join the reorganized Union. Ältesten- und Predigerversammlung des Bad. Württ. Bayr. Gemeindeverbandes to Vereinigung, June 22, 1934, Nachlaß Benjamin Unruh, box 2, folder 8, MFS.

21. Quoted in Lichdi, *Mennoniten im Dritten Reich*, 84. On the German Christians, Doris Bergen, *Twisted Cross: The German Christian Movement in the Third Reich* (Chapel Hill: University of North Carolina Press, 1996). Also, Susannah Heschel, *The Aryan Jesus: Christian Theologians and the Bible in Nazi Germany* (Princeton: Princeton University Press, 2008).

22. Quoted in Lichdi, *Mennoniten im Dritten Reich*, 217.

23. Quoted in Benjamin Unruh, "Auszüge aus 'Zur Kirchenfrage der Menn.' Nr. 1," October 1933, Nachlaß Benjamin Unruh, box 2, folder 8, MFS.

24. Benjamin Unruh to Simon Gorter, July 19, 1937, Nachlaß Christian Neff, box 22, folder 163, MFS.

25. Steffen Wagner, "'Aus weltanschaulichen Gründen besonders bekämpft und gehaßt?' Die Weierhöfer Schule und ihre Umwandlung in eine NS-Eliteanstalt im Jahr 1936," *Mennonitische Geschichtsblätter* 68 (2011): 110–113.

26. Unruh to Gorter, July 19, 1937.

27. Quoted in Lichdi, *Mennoniten im Dritten Reich*, 233–234.

28. Quoted in Vereinigung der Deutschen Mennonitengemeinden to Reichswehrministerium, March 15, 1935, Vereinigung, box 2, folder March–September 1935, MFS.

29. Vereinigung der deutschen mennonitengemeinden to Reichsregierung and Reichsparteileitung der NSDAP, May 1935, Vereinigung, box 2, folder March–September 1935, MFS.

30. Quoted in Friedrich Zipfel, *Kirchenkampf in Deutschland 1933–1945: Religionsverfolgung und Selbstbehauptung der Kirche in der nationalsozialistischen Zeit* (Berlin: Walter de Gruyter, 1965), 207.

31. Lichdi, *Mennoniten im Dritten Reich*, 87–91.

32. "Heimtückische Angriffe gegen das deutsche Volkstum," *Katholische Kirchenzeitung*, December 22, 1935.

33. Händiges, *Grundsätzliches*, 4.

34. Tim Grady, *The German-Jewish Soldiers of the First World War in History and Memory* (Liverpool: Liverpool University Press, 2011), 122–157. Also, Derek Penslar, *Jews and the Military: A History* (Princeton: Princeton University Press, 2013).

35. Emil Händiges, Christian Neff, and Abraham Braun, "Vereinigung der Deutschen Mennonitengemeinden," *Mennonitische Blätter*, June 1937, 47.

36. Quoted in Lichdi, *Mennoniten im Dritten Reich*, 224.

37. Emil Händiges to Christian Neff, October 1, 1937, Nachlaß Christian Neff, box 22, folder 163, MFS.

38. Quotations from Lichdi, *Mennoniten im Dritten Reich*, 224–225.

39. *Bericht über die 400 jährige Jubiläumsfeier*, 63; "Die Mennonitischen Gemeinden in den Niederlanden," *Mennonitische Blätter*, March 1923, 18–19.

40. "Bekenntnisentwurf," ca. 1933, Vereinigung, box 1, folder Briefw. 1933–1934, MFS.

41. Ernst Crous to Daniel Pohl, September 18, 1935, Vereinigung, box 2, folder March–September 1935, MFS.

42. Willi Kraus, *Friesennot* (Ufa, Delta-Filmproduktion, 1935), based on the novel Werner Kortwich, *Friesennot* (Leipzig: Insel, 1933). On the film, David Welch, *Propaganda and the German Cinema: 1933–1945* (London: I.B. Tauris, 2006), 207–213; David Hull, *Film in the Third Reich* (Berkeley: University of California Press, 1969), 86–87.

43. Benjamin Goossen, "Mennoniten als Volksdeutsche: Die Rolle des Mennonitentums in der nationalsozialistischen Propaganda," trans. Helmut Foth, *Mennonitische Geschichtsblätter* 71 (2014): 54–70. For literature about Mennonites, Otto Schowalter, "Die Mennoniten in der allgemeinen deutschen Literatur," in *Beiträge zur Geschichte der Mennoniten* (Weierhof: Mennonitischer Geschichtsverein, 1938), 83–88; Karl Klein, *Literaturgeschichte des Deutschtums im Ausland* (Leipzig: Bibliographisches Institut, 1939).

44. Walter Quiring, *Rußlanddeutsche suchen eine Heimat* (Karlsruhe: Heinrich Schneider, 1938), 7. On Mennonite anti-Bolshevism, Jonas Driedger, "'Wohin wir blicken, sehen wir Feinde': Wie sich preußische Mennoniten von 1913 bis 1933 als Teil einer christlich-antibolschewistischen Volksgemeinschaft neu erfanden," *Mennonitische Geschichtsblätter* 71 (2014): 71–102.

45. Franz Nieskens, "Hie Bibel—hie Revolver?" *Katholische Kirchenzeitung*, December 15, 1935, 14. Charges of pacifism did sometimes disadvantage Mennonites. I.e., Chef des Sicherheitshauptamts to Chef des Rasse- und Siedlungshauptamts, April 9, 1938, NS 2/220, BArch.

46. Benjamin Unruh, "Die ev. Mennoniten: Eine kurze konfessionskundliche Auskunft," ca. 1939, Nachlaß Christian Neff, box 23: folder 21, MFS.

47. Emil Händiges to Noske, January 17, 1936, Nachlaß Christian Neff, box 20, folder Friesennot, MFS.

48. "Die Antwort auf den Artikel von Melchior Crosack in dem Katholischen Kirchenblatt," 1936, Nachlaß Christian Neff, box 20, folder Friesennot, MFS.

49. C. Henry Smith, *The Story of the Mennonites* (Berne, IN: Mennonite Book Concern, 1941), 345. On Smith, Perry Bush, *Peace, Progress, and the Professor: The Mennonite History of C. Henry Smith* (Harrisonburg, VA: Herald Press, 2015). On Nazism among US Mennonites, John Thiesen, "The American Mennonite Encounter with National Socialism," *Yearbook of German-American Studies* 27 (1992): 127–158. In the Netherlands, Gerlof Homan, "'We Must and Can Stand Firmly': Dutch Mennonites in World War II," *Mennonite Quarterly Review* 69, no. 1 (1995): 7–36; Elisabeth Brussee-van der Zee, "Broederschap en national-socialisme," *Doopsgezinde Bijdragen* 11 (1985): 118–129; and the 2015 issue of *Doopsgezinde Bijdragen*.

50. D. Löwen and N. Weige, "Paraguay," *Der Auslanddeutsche* 16, no. 21 (1933): 542. On Nazism among Mennonites in Latin America, John Thiesen, *Mennonite and Nazi? Attitudes Among Mennonite Colonists in Latin America, 1933–1945* (Kitchener, ON: Pandora Press, 1999).

51. Heinrich Schröder, *Rußlanddeutsche Friesen* (Julius Beltz: Langenfalza, 1936), 31.

52. Unruh, "Die ev. Mennoniten."

53. On "East Research," Michael Burleigh, *Germany Turns Eastwards: A Study of Ostforschung in the Third Reich* (London: Macmillan, 1988).

54. Uwe Hoßfeld, *Geschichte der biologischen Anthropologie in Deutschland: Von den Anfängen bis in die Nachkriegszeit* (Steiner: Stuttgart, 2005), 188. On Mennonites and racial science, Benjamin Goossen, "Measuring Mennonitism: Racial Categorization in Nazi Germany and Beyond," *Journal of Mennonite Studies* 34 (2016): 225–246.

55. Keiter, *Rußlanddeutsche Bauern*, 1.

56. Adolf Ehrt, *Das Mennonitentum in Rußland: von seiner Einwanderung bis zur Gegenwart* (Berlin: Julius Beltz, 1932), 6.

57. Keiter, *Rußlanddeutsche Bauern*, 31.

58. Schröder, *Rußlanddeutsche Friesen*, 25.

59. Ehrt, *Das Mennonitentum*, 18.

60. Ibid., 4.

61. Heinrich Schröder, "Was heisst Völkisch," *Mennonitische Volkswarte*, April 1936, 252–256.

62. Wiehler, "Die Mennoniten und ihr Vaterland," 81.

63. Horst Penner, *Ansiedlung mennonitischer Niederländer im Weichselniederungsgebiet von der Mitte des 16. Jahrhunderts bis zum Beginn der preußischen Zeit* (Weierhof: Mennonitischer Geschichtsverein, 1940), v–vi, 66.

64. Händiges, *Was ist mennonitisch?* 16.

65. Wiehler, "Die Mennoniten und ihr Vaterland," 82.

66. For example, "Mennonitenfamilien in Zahlen"; Gustav Reimer, *Die Familiennamen der westpreussichen Mennoniten* (Weierhof: Mennonitischer Geschichtsverein, 1940).

67. Jacob Quiring, *Die Mundart von Chortitza in Süd-Rußland* (Munich, 1928); Walther Mizka, *Die Sprache der deutschen Mennoniten* (Danzig: A.W. Kasemann, 1931).

68. Karl Götz, "Sippenkundliche Randbemerkungen zu einer Amerikareise," *Jahrbuch für auslandsdeutsche Sippenkunde* 3 (1938): 127–128.

69. Keiter, *Rußlanddeutsche Bauern*, 2.

70. My analysis follows Peter Fritzsche, *Life and Death in the Third Reich* (Cambridge, MA: Harvard University Press, 2008), 76–142; Eric Ehrenreich, *The Nazi Ancestral Proof: Genealogy, Racial Science, and the Final Solution* (Bloomington: Indiana University Press, 2007). Also, Nadia Abu El-Haj, *The Genealogical Science: The Search for Jewish Origins and the Politics of Epistemology* (Chicago: University of Chicago Press, 2012).

71. Christian Hege, *Chronik der Familie Hege* (Frankfurt a.M., 1937), 2. On Mennonite genealogical practice, Benjamin Goossen, "From Aryanism to Anabaptism: Nazi Race Science and the Language of Mennonite Ethnicity," *Mennonite Quarterly Review* 90 (April 2016): 140–148.

72. Ernst Correll, "The Value of Family History for Mennonite History," *Mennonite Quarterly Review* 2, no. 1 (1928): 66–67.

73. Kurt Kauenhowen and Walter Kauenhowen, "Zum Geleit," *Die Kauenhowen*, January 1926, 2–4.

74. Horst Quiring, *Grundworte des Glaubens: Achtzig wichtige biblische Begriffe für den Menschen der Gegenwart* (Berlin: Furche-Verlag, 1938), 36–38.

75. "Satzungen des Mennonitischen Geschichtsvereins," *Mennonitische Geschichtsblätter* 1 (1936): 5–6. On this organization, Helmut Foth, "'Wie die Mennoniten in die deutsche Volksgemeinschaft hineinwuchsen': Die Mennonitischen Geschichtsblätter im Dritten Reich," *Mennonitische Geschichtsblätter* 68 (2011): 59–88.

76. "Arbeitsgemeinschaft für mennonitische Sippenkunde," *Mennonitische Geschichtsblätter* 2 (1937): 63–64.

77. Traute Leitholf, "Familienforschung im Kleinen," *Der Berg*, 1939, 4.

78. Fritz van Bergen, "Embryo," *Der Berg*, 1936, 119.

79. Joseph Goebbels to Fritz van Bergen, April 29, 1935, printed in *Der Berg*, 1935, 85.

80. "Trauerfeier für Ernst Penner," 2.

81. Nathan Stoltzfus, *Resistance of the Heart: Intermarriage and the Rosenstrasse Protest in Nazi Germany* (New Brunswick: Rutgers University Press, 2001), 311.

82. Gustav Reimer, "Die Kirchenbücher der Menno. Gemeinden in West- und Ostpreußen," *Der Berg*, 1940, 83.

83. Benjamin Unruh, "Eidesstattliche Erklärung," September 3, 1936, R 127518, PA AA.

84. Alfred Rosenberg, *Der Mythus des 20. Jahrhunderts* (Munich: Hoheneichen-Verlag, 1934), 265. On Rosenberg, Robert Cecil, *The Myth of the Master Race: Alfred Rosenberg and Nazi Ideology* (New York: Dodd, Mead & Co., 1972). On Nazi anti-Semitism, Alon Confino, *A World without Jews: The Nazi Imagination from Persecution to Genocide* (New Haven: Yale University Press, 2014).

85. Ehrt, *Das Mennonitentum*, 15.

86. Walter Quiring, *Deutsche erschliessen den Chaco* (Karlsruhe: Heinrich Schneider, 1936), 9, 204.

87. Ehrt, *Das Mennonitentum*, 16.

88. Hermann Rüdiger, "Zahl und Verbreitung des deutschen Volkes," in *Das Buch vom deutschen Volkstum*, ed. Paul Gauß (Leipzig: F.A. Brockhaus, 1935), 4.

89. Quiring, *Rußlanddeutsche*, 194.

90. Quoted in Alwin Müller, "'So lange die Juden nicht frei sind, sind wir selbst nicht frei': Die Diskussion um die Judenemanzipation auf den preußischen Provinzialtagen nach dem ersten Vereinigten preußischen Landtag," *Geschichte in Köln* 17 (1985): 39.

91. Translated in Alf Lüdtke, *Police and State in Prussia, 1815–1850* (Cambridge: Cambridge University Press, 1989), 206.

92. Johannes Foth, "Die geistliche Not unserer Gemeinden," *Mennonitische Blätter*, June 1929, 56.

93. Quoted in Foth, "Juden, Täufer, Mennoniten," 42.

94. Erich Göttner, "Christentum und Volkstum," *Mennonitische Blätter*, August 1927, 72.

95. Quoted in Lichdi, *Mennoniten im Dritten Reich*, 206.

96. Heinrich Schröder, *Die systematische Vernichtung der Rußland-Deutschen* (Berlin: Julius Beltz, 1934), 23–24.

97. Schröder, *Rußlanddeutsche Friesen*, 30–31.

98. Emil Händiges to Ehrenvorsteher und den Arbeitsausschuß der Vereinigung, May 29, 1937, Nachlaß Christian Neff, box 22, folder 163, MFS.

99. Gustav Kraemer, *Wir und unsere Volksgemeinschaft* (Krefeld: Consistorium der Krefelder Mennonitengemeinde, 1938), 15.

100. Benjamin Unruh to S.H.N. Gorter and G. S. Altmann, December 4, 1938, Nachlaß Benjamin Unruh, box 2, folder 7, MFS. On this trope, Casteel, "The Russian Germans," 429–466.

101. Lorna Waddington, "The Anti-Komintern and Nazi Anti-Bolshevik Propaganda in the 1930s," *Journal of Contemporary History* 42, no. 4 (2007): 573–594.

102. Harry Loewen, ed., *Shepherds, Servants and Prophets: Leadership among the Russian Mennonites, ca. 1880–1960* (Kitchener, ON: Pandora Press, 2003), 247–264, 265–278, 313–336, 401–426. For context, James Casteel, "The Politics of Diaspora: Russian German Émigré Activists in Interwar Germany," in *German Diasporic Experiences*, ed. Schulze et al., 117–129.

103. Quoted in Abraham Kroeker, *Unsere Brüder in Not! Bilder vom Leidensweg der deutschen Kolonisten in Rußland* (Striegau: Theodor Urban, 1930), 135–137.

104. Quiring, *Rußlanddeutsche*, 4.

105. Ehrt, *Das Mennonitentum*, 16.

106. Keiter, *Rußlanddeutsche Bauern*, 8–9.

107. Tara Zahra, *The Great Departure: Mass Migration from Eastern Europe and the Making of the Free World* (New York: W.W. Norton, 2016), 143–180.

108. Penner, *Ansiedlung mennonitischer Niederländer*, 65.

109. Schröder, *Rußlanddeutsche Friesen*, 3.

110. Quoted in Kurt Kauenhowen, "Bücher, die uns angehen," *Mitteilungen des Sippenverbandes Danziger Mennoniten-Familien*, August 1937, 144.

111. Quoted in Epp, *Mennonite Exodus*, 324.

112. Oskar Schmieder and Herbert Wilhelmy, *Deutsche Ackerbausiedlungen im südamerikansichen Grasland, Pampa und Gran Chaco* (Leipzig: Deutschen Museums für Länderkunde, 1938), 127. On this work, Ulrike Bock, "Deutsche Lateinamerikaforschung im Nationalsozialismus," in *Der Nationalsozialismus und Lateinamerika*, ed. Sandra Carreras (Berlin: Ibero-Amerikanisches Institut Preußischer Kulturbesitz, 2005), 7–22.

113. Translated in Klassen, *Mennonites in Paraguay*, 92.

114. Quoted in Manfred Kossok, "Die Mennoniten-Siedlungen Paraguays in den Jahren 1935–1939," *Zeitschrift für Geschichtswissenschaft* 8 (1960): 369.

115. Quotations from Kossok, "Die Mennoniten-Siedlungen," 370–371. On Kliewer, Jakob Warkentin, *Die deutschsprachigen Siedlerschulen in Paraguay: im Spannungsfeld staatlicher Kultur- und Entwicklungspolitik* (Münster: Waxmann, 1998), 182–280.
116. Translated in Epp, "An Analysis of Germanism," 258. Also, Alan Davies and Marilyn Nefsky, *How Silent Were the Churches? Canadian Protestantism and the Jewish Plight during the Nazi Era* (Waterloo: Wilfrid Laurier University Press, 1997), 106–116.
117. Quotations from Urry, "A *Mennostaat*," 65.
118. Ibid., 73; Klassen, *Mennonites in Paraguay*, 83–99.
119. A. B. Dyck, "Ein Geleitwort vom Herausgeber," *Mennonitische Volkswarte*, January 1935, 1–2. On this paper, Al Reimer, "The Role of Arnold Dyck in Canadian Mennonite Writing," *Journal of Mennonite Studies* 9 (1991): 83–91. Other papers in the Americas with significant Mennonite audiences that printed pro-fascist articles included *Das Mennoblatt* (Paraguay), *Die Brücke* (Brazil), *The Defender* (United States), and in Canada: *Der Bote*, *Mennonitische Rundschau*, and *Deutsche Zeitung für Canada*. Mennonite fascism never exceeded the first or second stage of Robert Paxton's taxonomy: *The Anatomy of Fascism* (New York: Random House, 2007).
120. Walter Quiring to Ernst Kundt, October 7, 1935, R 127518, PA AA.
121. Walter Quiring to Ernst Kundt, November 10, 1936, R 127518, PA AA.
122. Heinrich Unruh, *Fügungen und Führungen: Benjamin Heinrich Unruh, 1881–1959* (Detmold: Verein zur Erforschung und Pflege des Russlanddeutschen Mennonitentums, 2009), 460–464. Many of these were duplicates or published piecemeal.
123. Epp, "An Analysis of Germanism," 68–69.
124. Quiring to Kundt, October 7, 1935.
125. Unruh, "Praktische Fragen," 1.
126. Fritz Kliewer, "Mennonite Young People's Work in the Paraguayan Chaco," *Mennonite Quarterly Review* 11, no. 2 (1937): 126. On national indifference among conservative Mennonites in Latin America, Loewen, *Village among Nations*.
127. Götz, "Sippenkundliche Randbemerkungen," 127–128.
128. Karl Götz, *Deutsche Leistung in Amerika* (Berlin: Franz Eher, 1940), 69–70.
129. Erich Göttner, "Warum wachsen unsere mennonitischen Gemeinden nicht?" *Mennonitische Blätter*, March 1927, 19.
130. Margarete Boie, *Hugo Conwentz und seine Heimat* (Stuttgart, 1940), 22.
131. Nieskens, "Hie Bibel—hie Revolver?" 14.
132. "Heimtückische Angriffe."
133. Werner Zimmermann, "Über die sogenannte 'Inzucht' in den Danziger Mennonitenfamilien," *Mitteilungen des Sippenverbandes Danziger Mennoniten-Familien*, December 1941, 162–167.
134. Fritz van Bergen, *Der Berg*, 1940, 62.

CHAPTER 6: FATHERLAND

1. Unruh to Gorter and Altmann, December 4, 1938.
2. Ibid. On Unruh, see Unruh, *Fügungen und Führungen*; Jakob Warkentin, "Benjamin Heinrich Unruh: Lehrer, Forscher, Staatsmann," *Jahrbuch für Geschichte und Kultur der Mennoniten in Paraguay* 6 (2005): 9–32.
3. Translated in Adolf Hitler, *Hitler's Table Talk: His Private Conversations* (New York: Enigma Books, 2008), 55. On Nazi empire-building, Mark Mazower, *Hitler's Empire: Nazi Rule in Occupied Europe* (New York: Penguin Books Limited, 2009), 78–470.

In Ukraine, Wendy Lower, *Nazi Empire-Building and the Holocaust in Ukraine* (Chapel Hill: University of North Carolina Press, 2005); Karel Berkhoff, *Harvest of Despair: Life and Death in Ukraine under Nazi Rule* (Cambridge, MA: Harvard University Press, 2004); Alexander Dallin, *German Rule in Russia, 1941–1945: A Study of Occupation Policies* (New York: Macmillan, 1957).

4. Karl Götz, *Das Schwarzmeerdeutschtum: Die Mennoniten* (Posen: NS-Druck Wartheland, 1944), 4.

5. Emil Meynen, *Die deutschen Siedlungen in der Sowjetunion: Ukraine mit Krim* (Berlin: Sammlung Georg Leibbrandt, 1941), 3.

6. Hitler, *Hitler's Table Talk*, 55. On Manifest Destiny as a (limited) model for German expansionism, Kopp, *Germany's Wild East*; Jens-Uwe Guettel, *German Expansionism, Imperial Liberalism and the United States, 1776–1945* (Cambridge: Cambridge University Press, 2012).

7. Wendy Lower, "From Berlin to Babi Yar: The Nazi War Against the Jews, 1941–1944," *Journal of Religion & Society* 9 (2007): 2; Ray Brandon and Wendy Lower, eds., *The Shoah in Ukraine: History, Testimony, Memorialization* (Bloomington: Indiana University Press, 2008). More broadly, Peter Longerich, *Holocaust: The Nazi Persecution and Murder of the Jews* (Oxford: Oxford University Press, 2010).

8. Lower, *Nazi Empire-Building*, 40–41; Eric Steinhart, "Creating Killers: The Nazification of the Black Sea Germans and the Holocaust in Southern Ukraine, 1941–1942" (PhD diss., University of North Carolina, 2010), 323. On Himmler, Richard Breitman, *Himmler and the Final Solution: The Architect of Genocide* (London: Pimlico, 2004).

9. "'Notizen,' über die Unterredung des Reichsführers SS Heinrich Himmler mit dem Vertreter der Rußlanddeutschen in der Ukraine," Nachlaß Benjamin Unruh, box 2, folder 7, MFS. On this meeting, Benjamin Unruh to Emil Händiges, January 27, 1943, Vereinigung, box 3, folder 1943, MFS; Götz, *Das Schwarzmeerdeutschtum*, 11; Heinrich Himmler, *Der Dienstkalender Heinrich Himmlers 1941/42* (Göttingen: Wallstein Verlag: 1999), 660.

10. Karl Stumpp, *Bericht über das Gebiet Chortitza im Generalbezirk Dnjepropetrowsk* (Berlin: Publikationsstelle Ost, 1943), 6–8. For context, Neufeldt, "Separating the Sheep"; Neufeldt, "The Fate of Mennonites"; Peter Letkemann, "Mennonite Victims of the 'Great Terror,' 1936–1938," *Journal of Mennonite Studies* 16 (1998): 33–58; Marlene Epp, *Women Without Men: Mennonite Refugees of the Second World War* (Toronto: University of Toronto Press, 2000), 17–41.

11. SD, "Ereignismeldung UdSSR Nr. 134," November 17, 1941, R 58/219, BArch.

12. Unruh, "Die ev. Mennoniten."

13. Quoted in Benjamin Unruh to Ernst Kundt, April 26, 1940, R 127518, PA AA.

14. Translated in Thiesen, *Mennonite and Nazi?* 67.

15. Ibid., 135–138. Also, Peter Klassen, *Die deutsch-völkische Zeit in der Kolonie Fernheim, Chaco-Paraguay (1933–1945)* (Bolanden-Weierhof: Mennonitischer Geschichtsverein, 1990).

16. Urry, *Mennonites, Politics, and Peoplehood*, 195–203; Benjamin Redekop, "Germanism Among Mennonite Brethren Immigrants in Canada, 1930–1960: A Struggle for Ethno-Religious Integrity," *Canadian Ethnic Studies* 24 (1992): 20–42; Epp, "An Analysis of Germanism"; Jonathan Wagner, *Brothers Beyond the Sea: National Socialism in Canada* (Waterloo: Wilfrid Laurier University Press, 1981).

17. Benjamin Unruh to Orie Miller, July 4, 1939, Nachlaß Benjamin Unruh, box 9, folder 48, MFS.

18. Quoted in Lichdi, *Mennoniten im Dritten Reich*, 213.
19. Quoted in Kossok, "Die Mennoniten-Siedlungen," 372.
20. Heinrich Bergen, "Ein Gruß aus Übersee," *Der Berg*, 1938, 264.
21. Quoted in Urry, "A *Mennostaat*," 72; Hitler, *Mein Kampf*, 449.
22. Unruh to Miller, July 4, 1939.
23. Stieve, February 25, 1939, R 127502, PA AA.
24. See Thiesen, *Mennonite and Nazi?* 67; Rempel, "Heinrich Hajo Schroeder," 235.
25. Unruh to Miller, July 4, 1939.
26. "Chortitza," R 6/621, BArch.
27. Jakob Stach, "Zur Einführung der Sammlung," in Christian Kugler, *Großliebental* (Leipzig: S. Hirzel, 1939), viii. Also, J. Geiger, "Ansiedlung von Deutschen in der Krim," March 18, 1942, R 6/19, BArch.
28. Meynen, *Die deutschen Siedlungen*, 3.
29. G. Franz, "Kugler, Christian, Großliebental," *Jahrbücher für Nationalökonomie und Statistik* (1941): 120. On "ethnic Germans" in the Soviet Union, Ingeborg Fleischhauer, *Das Dritte Reich und die Deutschen in der Sowjetunion* (Stuttgart: Deutsche Verlags-Anstalt, 1983); Ingeborg Fleischhauer and Benjamin Pinkus, *Soviet Germans Past and Present* (London: Hurst, 1986); Irina Mukhina, *The Germans of the Soviet Union* (New York: Routledge, 2007); O'Donnell et al., eds., *The Heimat Abroad*, 187–218, 267–286.
30. Sundicani, "Schicksal und Leistung der Schwarzmeerdeutschen," January 20, 1944, R 69/215, BArch. Also, Nicolai Rupert, "Friesisches Kolonistentum in Rußland," *Odal: Monatsschrift für Blut und Boden* 7, no. 2 (1938): 112–121; Walter Kuhn, *Die mennonitische Altkolonie Chortitza in der Ukraine* (Sonderabdruck aus den "Deutschen Monatsheften," 1942).
31. Walter Kuhn, *Deutsche Sprachinsel-Forschung* (Plauen, i.V.: Günther Wolff, 1934), 328.
32. Sundicani, "Schicksal und Leistung."
33. *Die Mennoniten-Gemeinden in Rußland während der Kriegs- und Revolutionsjahre, 1914 bis 1920* (Heilbronn a. Neckar: Kommissions-Verlag der Mennon. Flüchtlingsfürsorge, 1921), 28–30.
34. Helmut Anger, *Die Deutschen in Sibirien: Reise durch die deutschen Dörfer Westsibiriens* (Berlin: Ost-Europa-Verlag, 1930), 33–34.
35. Sonderkommando Rußland, "Das Deutschtum im Raum von Kriwoi-Rog-Saporoshje-Dnepropetrowsk," November 1, 1941, translated in Gerhard Rempel, "Himmler's Pacifists: German Ethnic Policy and the Russian Mennonites," ch. 2, Gerhard Rempel Collection, MLA.
36. Alfred Rosenberg, "Besichtigungsreise durch die Ukraine vom 18.6 bis 26.6.42," translated in Rempel, "Himmler's Pacifists," ch. 3.
37. Himmler planned to resettle both colonies to Crimea. Himmler, *Der Dienstkalender*, 566–567. On General Plan East, Mechtild Rössler and Sabine Schleiermacher, eds., *Der "Generalplan Ost": Hauptlinien der nationalsozialistischen Planungs- und Vernichtungspolitik* (Berlin: Akademie Verlag, 1993); Czeslaw Madajczyk, *Vom Generalplan Ost zum Generalsiedlungsplan* (Munich: Saur, 1994).
38. Fleischhauer, *Das Dritte Reich*, 170–173.
39. Translations from Lower, *Nazi Empire-Building*, 19–26.
40. Hitler, *Hitler's Table Talk*, 54.
41. Lower, *Nazi Empire-Building*, 162–179.
42. "Bericht des SS-Sonderkommandos der Volksdeutschen Mittelstelle über den Stand der Erfassungsarbeiten bis zum 15. März 1942," NS 19/2385, BArch.

43. Fleischhauer, *Das Dritte Reich*, 170–171.
44. Hans Rempel, "Die Bodenfrage in den deutschen Siedlungen in der Ukraine," R 6/109, BArch; R. Sch., "Ein Besuch in Franzfeld und Chortitza im Mai 1942," *Mitteilungen des Sippenverbandes Danziger Mennoniten-Familien*, February 1943, 15–20.
45. Quoted by Benjamin Unruh in Lichdi, *Mennoniten im dritten Reich*, 141.
46. Unruh, "Zur Frage der Rücksiedlung."
47. M. C. Lehman, "Report on German-Poland Project of Mennonite Central Committee," ca. October 1941, R 127518, PA AA.
48. Sundicani, "Schicksal und Leistung."
49. Unruh, "Die ev. Mennoniten."
50. "'Notizen,' über die Unterredung."
51. Ibid.
52. See Unruh's testimony at the Nuremberg Trials: "Case #8 Tribunal 1 US vs Ulrich Greifett, et al. Volume 7 Transcripts," December 17, 1947, SA.I.184, MLA. Unruh heard firsthand about genocide in the Mennonite colonies during the war. Rempel, "Himmler's Pacifists," ch. 8. On public awareness of genocide, Fritzsche, *Life and Death*, 225–308.
53. Heinrich Hamm, "Schilderung vom Volksdeutschen," November 12, 1941, translated in Rempel, "Himmler's Pacifists," ch. 2.
54. J. Janzen, "Eine Schilderung aus dem Leben der Schwarzmeerdeutschen im Gebiet Molotschna (Ukraine)," March 16, 1944, R 69/215, BArch.
55. My thinking follows Doris Bergen, "The Nazi Concept of 'Volksdeutsche' and the Exacerbation of Anti-Semitism in Eastern Europe, 1939–45," *Journal of Contemporary History* 29 (1994): 569–82; Wendy Lower, "Anticipatory Obedience and the Nazi Implementation of the Holocaust in the Ukraine: A Case Study of Central and Peripheral Forces in the Generalbezirk Zhytomyr, 1941–1944," *Holocaust and Genocide Studies* 16, no. 1 (2002): 1–22; Götz Aly, *Hitler's Beneficiaries: Plunder, Racial War, and the Nazi Welfare State* (New York: Metropolitan Books, 2007).
56. Translated in Rempel, "Mennonites and the Holocaust," 528–529.
57. Anne Konrad, *Red Quarter Moon: A Search for Family in the Shadow of Stalin* (Toronto: University of Toronto Press, 2012), 152–153.
58. Stumpp, *Bericht über das Gebiet Chortitza*, Tafel A.
59. Harvey Dyck, ed., *A Mennonite in Russia: The Diaries of Jacob D. Epp, 1851–1880* (Toronto: University of Toronto Press, 1991), 39.
60. I.e., David Epp, *Die Chortitzer Mennoniten* (Odessa, 1889), 144–145.
61. Friesen, *In Defense of Privilege*, 319; Urry, "A Mennostaat," 67.
62. Quoted in Buchsweiler, *Volksdeutsche in der Ukraine*, 367.
63. "Fragebogen zur sippenkundlichen Aufnahmen des Rußlanddeutschtums," R 6/621, BArch. On the village reports, Richard Walth, *Flotsam of World History: The Germans from Russia between Stalin and Hitler* (Essen: Klartext Verlag, 2000).
64. Lower, *Nazi Empire-Building*, 35.
65. "Dorfbericht," R 6/621, BArch.
66. Hamm, "Schilderung vom Volksdeutschen."
67. Translated in Jacob Neufeld, *Path of Thorns: Soviet Mennonite Life under Communist and Nazi Rule* (Toronto: University of Toronto Press, 2014), 44–45. See also Colin P. Neufeldt, "The Public and Private Lives of Mennonite Kolkhoz Chairmen in the Khortytsia and Molochansk German National Raïony in Ukraine (1928–1934)," *Carl Beck Papers in Russian and East European Studies*, no. 2305 (2015): 58–63.
68. Janzen, "Eine Schilderung."

69. Rempel, "Mennonites and the Holocaust," 540–547. On killing squads, Christopher Browning, *Ordinary Men: Reserve Police Battalion 101 and the Final Solution in Poland* (New York: Harper Collins, 1992).

70. Alexander Rempel, "Ein Protest gegen die Judenvernichtung," Alexander Rempel Fonds, file 3440, MHC. See reports from Einsatzgruppe C in SD, "Ereignismeldung UdSSR Nr. 135," November 19, 1941, and SD, "Ereignismeldung UdSSR Nr. 143," December 8, 1941, R 58/219, BArch; as well as Helmut Krausnick, *Hitlers Einsatzgruppen: die Truppe des Weltanschauungskrieges, 1938–1942* (Frankfurt a.M.: Fischer Taschenbuch Verlag, 1985), 166–175.

71. SD, "Ereignismeldung UdSSR Nr. 134."

72. Heinrich Himmler to Werner Lorenz, April 10, 1942, NS 19/2385, BArch. On the squadrons, Horst Gerlach, "Mennonites, the Molotschna, and the *Volksdeutsche Mittelstelle* in the Second World War," *Mennonite Life* 41, no. 3 (1986): 4–9; Gerhard Lohrenz, ed., *The Lost Generation and Other Stories* (Steinbach, MB: Derksen Printers, 1982). Also, Werner, *Constructed Mennonite*.

73. Quoted in Gerhard Fast, *Das Ende von Chortitza* (Winnipeg: Regehr's Printing, 1973), 48.

74. Translated in Alyssa Schrag, "Peace or Persecution: Mennonite Involvement in the Holocaust," *Mennonite Life* 66, no. 2 (2012): https://ml.bethelks.edu/issue/vol-66/article /peace-or-persecution-mennonite-involvement-in-the/.

75. Karel Berkhoff, "Was There a Religious Revival in Soviet Ukraine under the Nazi Regime?" *Slavonic and East European Review* 78, no. 3 (2000): 536–567.

76. Benjamin Unruh to Vereinigung and Verband, September 23, 1943, Vereinigung, box 3, folder 1943, MFS.

77. Jacob Neufeld, "Die Flucht 1943–1946," *Der Mennonit*, March 1951, 42. On religious life, Gerhard Fast, "Mennonites of the Ukraine under Stalin and Hitler," *Mennonite Life*, vol. 2 (1947): 21.

78. Fast, *Das Ende von Chortitza*, 14–15.

79. Stabsbefehl SS und Pol. Führer Dnjepropetrowsk, September 4, 1942, R 59/66, BArch. On the occupation, Neufeld, *Path of Thorns*, 218–234; Horst Gerlach, *Die Rußlandmennoniten*, vol. 1 (Kirchheimbolanden: Selbstverlag, 1992), 81–104, and vol. 2 (2007), 328–353.

80. Translated in Eric Schmaltz and Samuel Sinner, "The Nazi Ethnographic Research of Georg Leibbrandt and Karl Stumpp in Ukraine, and Its North American Legacy," *Holocaust & Genocide Studies* 14, no. 1 (2000): 46. On Nazi activists in the East, Elizabeth Harvey, *Women and the Nazi East* (New Haven: Yale University Press, 2003).

81. Stumpp, *Bericht über das Gebiet Chortitza*, Tafel A.

82. Steinhart, "Chameleon of Trawniki," 246–247.

83. Rempel, "Die Bodenfrage."

84. Hans Rempel, *Deutsche Bauernleistung am Schwarzen Meer: Bevölkerung und Wirtschaft 1825* (Leipzig: S. Hirzel, 1942), xvii–xviii.

85. Georg Leibbrandt to Benjamin Unruh, December 17, 1940, Bestand 10001, Signatur 2392, UK.

86. Benjamin Unruh to Vereinigung, November 21, 1944, Nachlaß Benjamin Unruh, box 4, folder 21, MFS.

87. I.e., Benjamin Unruh, "Subotniki," September 24, 1936, R 127518, PA AA. On knowledge production and the Holocaust, Ingo Haar and Michael Fahlbusch, eds., *German Scholars and Ethnic Cleansing, 1920–1945* (New York: Berghahn Books, 2005); Isabel Heinemann and Patrick Wagner, eds., *Wissenschaft, Planung, Vertreibung:*

Neuordnungskonzepte und Umsiedlungspolitik im 20. Jahrhundert (Stuttgart: Franz Steiner Verlag, 2006), 45–118.

88. Karl Götz, "Kurzbericht über die Schwarmeerdeutschen," January 26, 1944, R 69/215, BArch.

89. Karl Stumpp, *Bericht über das Gebiet Chortitza*, 6–7.

90. "Bericht des SS-Sonderkommandos."

91. Translated in Rempel, "Mennonites and the Holocaust," 529.

92. Konrad, *Red Quarter Moon*, 149–159.

93. Quoted in Susanna Toews, *Trek to Freedom: The Escape of Two Sisters from South Russia during World War II* (Winkler, MB: Heritage Valley Publications, 1976), 20. Also Lohrenz, ed., *The Lost Generation*, 135–136.

94. Translated in Rempel, "Mennonites and the Holocaust," 529.

95. "Judenplan," in *Mennonitisches Lexikon*, vol. 2, ed. Christian Hege and Christian Neff (Frankfurt am Main, 1937), 439–440.

96. Quotations from Buchsweiler, *Volksdeutsche in der Ukraine*, 349, 379–383. See also Special Command Stumpp's village reports for Friesendorf in R 6/623, BArch.

97. Karl Stumpp, *Bericht über das Gebiet Kronau-Orloff* (Berlin: Publikationsstelle Ost, 1943), 4.

98. Rempel, "Die Bodenfrage."

99. Ibid.

100. "Germans in Occupied Ukraine," 1943, RG-60.0648, USHMM.

101. Printed in Jacob Neufeld, *Tiefenwege: Erfahrungen und Erlebnisse von Russland-Mennoniten in zwei Jahrzehnten bis 1949* (Virgil, ON: Niagara Press, 1958), 167–168.

102. "Übersicht über die Herkunft und den jetztigen Aufenthalt der Volksdeutschen nach dem Stand v. 15.12.43," R69/222, BArch. On the trek, Horst Gerlach, "Rußlanddeutsche Umsiedlung 1943/44 nach Westpreußen und dem Wartheland," *Westpreußen-Jahrbuch* 29 (1979): 145–154; Peter Dyck and Elfrieda Dyck, *Up from the Rubble* (Scottdale, PA: Herald Press, 1991), 87–99; Epp, *Mennonite Exodus*, 351–365; Epp, *Women Without Men*, 42–51.

103. Fast, "Mennonites of the Ukraine," 44.

104. Benjamin Unruh to Vereinigung, May 17, 1944, Nachlaß Benjamin Unruh, box 4, folder 21, MFS.

105. Benjamin Unruh to Wolfrum, January 19, 1944, Nachlaß Benjamin Unruh, box 4, folder 21, MFS.

106. Götz, *Das Schwarzmeerdeutschtum*, 3. On "ethnic German" resettlement, Valdis Lumans, *Himmler's Auxiliaries: The Volksdeutsche Mittelstelle and the German National Minorities of Europe, 1933–1945* (Chapel Hill: University of North Carolina Press, 1993); Robert Koehl, *RKFDV: German Resettlement and Population Policy 1939–1945: A History of the Reich Commission for the Strengthening of Germandom* (Cambridge, MA: Harvard University Press, 1957).

107. "Rundschreiben," January 21, 1940, Vereinigung, box 3, folder 1940 Januar–Juni, MFS. On the Lemberg Mennonites, Peter Bachmann, *Mennoniten in Kleinpolen: 1784–1934* (Lemberg, 1934). On Wartheland, Catherine Epstein, *Model Nazi: Arthur Greiser and the Occupation of Western Poland* (Oxford: Oxford University Press, 2010), 124–304.

108. Benjamin Unruh to Verband der Rußlanddeutschen, October 20, 1939, R 127518, PA AA.

109. Emil Händiges to Ernst Crous and Abraham Braun, March 27, 1940, Vereinigung, box 3, folder 1940 Januar–Juni, MFS.

110. Emil Händiges, "Kurzbericht über unsere Reise," November 14, 1941, Vereinigung, box 3, folder 1940 Juli–Dezember, MFS.

111. Arthur Greiser, "Anordnung für alle Kreisleiter," January 14, 1944, R69/222, BArch.

112. Janzen, "Eine Schilderung."

113. Quoted in Benjamin Unruh to Vereinigung, January 7, 1944, Nachlaß Benjamin Unruh, box 4, folder 21, MFS.

114. EWZ-Kommission XXVII-Sonderzug Gesundheitsstelle, "Bericht über die Durchschleusung der Rußlanddeutschen im Warthegau," June 29, 1944, R69/418, BArch.

115. Hangel to Ortsgruppenleiter et al., February 8, 1944, R69/222, BArch.

116. Quoted in Unruh to Vereinigung, January 7, 1944. On Epp, "Johann Epp, der Rayonchef von Chortitza, 1898–1998," in *Diese Steine: Die Russlandmennoniten*, ed. Adina Reger and Delbert Plett (Steinbach, MB: Crossway Publications, 2001), 124–127.

117. "Erfahrungsbericht über die Erfassung der Rußlanddeutschen im Gau Danzig-Westpreußen," February 26, 1944, R69/418, BArch.

118. Quoted in Unruh to Vereinigung, January 7, 1944.

119. Unruh to Vereinigung, January 7, 1944.

120. Quoted in ibid.

121. Epstein, *Model Nazi*, 225–226. See also Bernhard Strasiewski, "Die Kirchenpolitik der Nationalsozialisten im Warthegau 1939–1945," *Vierteljahrshefte für Zeitgeschichte* 7 (1959): 46–74.

122. Emil Kempf to Emil Händiges, August 10, 1941, Vereinigung, box 3, folder 1940 Juli–Dezember, MFS.

123. Benjamin Unruh to Gauleitung in Posen, May 16, 1944, Nachlaß Benjamin Unruh, box 4, folder 21, MFS.

124. Benjamin Unruh to Wolfram, January 1944, Nachlaß Benjamin Unruh, box 4, folder 21, MFS.

125. Benjamin Unruh, "Bericht über Verhandlungen im Warthegau im März 1944," March 30, 1944, Nachlaß Benjamin Unruh, box 4, folder 21, MFS.

126. Quoted in Unruh, *Fügungen und Führungen*, 417.

127. Benjamin Unruh to Peter Bergmann, June 6, 1944, Nachlaß Benjamin Unruh, box 4, folder 21, MFS.

128. Benjamin Unruh to Vereingung, November 21, 1944, Nachlaß Benjamin Unruh, box 4, folder 21, MFS.

129. Janzen, "Eine Schilderung."

130. Printed in Neufeld, *Tiefenwege*, 179–180.

131. Translated in Rempel, "Himmler's Pacifists," ch. 11.

132. Hangel to Orstsgruppenleiter, February 8, 1944.

133. Quoted in Isabel Heinemann, *"Rasse, Siedlung, deutsches Blut": Das Rasse- & Siedlungshauptamt der SS und die rassenpolitische Neuordnung Europas* (Göttingen: Wallstein Verlag, 2003), 471–472.

134. Printed in Neufeld, *Tiefenwege*, 179–180. Heinrich Hamm, by contrast, welcomed resettlement to a formerly Jewish residence. Heinrich Hamm, "Die Umsiedlung der Volksdeutschen aus Dnjepropetrowsk im September 1943," *Nachrichtenblatt des Sippenverbands Danziger Mennoniten-Familien*, December 1943, 3–4.

135. Johann Thiessen to Hermann Roßner, April 2, 1944, translated in Rempel, "Himmler's Pacifists," ch. 11.

136. Printed in Neufeld, *Tiefenwege*, 212–213. On war's end, Epp, *Women Without Men*, 51–69.

CHAPTER 7: MENNONITE NATIONALISM

1. Peter Dyck, "Mennonite Refugees in Germany," July 1946, FO 1050/1565, TNA.
2. Quoted in Epp, *Mennonite Exodus*, 367. Also, Robert Kreider, *My Early Years: An Autobiography* (Kitchener, ON: Pandora Press, 2002), 415–416.
3. On postwar aid as national reconstruction, Tara Zahra, *The Lost Children: Reconstructing Europe's Families after World War II* (Cambridge, MA: Harvard University Press, 2011); Rogers Brubaker, "Migrations of Ethnic Unmixing in the New Europe," *International Migration Review* 32 (1998): 1047–1065.
4. Gerard Cohen, *In War's Wake: Europe's Displaced Persons in the Postwar Order* (Oxford: Oxford University Press, 2011); Peter Gatrell, *The Making of the Modern Refugee* (New York: Oxford University Press, 2013), 89–117.
5. Translations from Dyck and Dyck, *Up from the Rubble*, 94. On sexual violence, Marlene Epp, "The Memory of Violence: Soviet and East European Mennonite Refugees and Rape in the Second World War," *Journal of Women's History* 9, no. 1 (1997): 58–87. On Soviet occupation, Norman Naimark, *The Russians in Germany: A History of the Soviet Zone of Occupation, 1945–1949* (Cambridge, MA: Harvard University Press, 1995).
6. Benjamin Unruh to Abraham Braun, November 16, 1945, Nachlaß Benjamin Unruh, box 4, folder 21, MFS; Fleischhauer and Pinkus, *Soviet Germans*, 101.
7. Dyck and Dyck, *Up from the Rubble*, 81–131; Friesen, *In Defense*, 328–335; Gerlof Homan, "'We Have Come to Love Them': Russian Mennonite Refugees in the Netherlands, 1945–1947," *Journal of Mennonite Studies* 25 (2007): 39–59.
8. H.M.L.H. Sark et al., "Dutch origins of the Russian Mennonites who have lately emigrated to Paraguay," February 24, 1947, AJ/43/462, folder Mennonites, AN. See Goossen, "From Aryanism to Anabaptism," 148–157.
9. On MCC, John Unruh, *In the Name of Christ: A History of the Mennonite Central Committee and Its Service, 1920–1951* (Scottdale, PA: Herald Press, 1952). Also, Herbert Klassen and Maureen Klassen, *Ambassador to his People: C. F. Klassen and the Russian Mennonite Refugees* (Winnipeg: Kindred Press, 1990).
10. Dirk Cattepoel, "The Mennonites of Germany, 1936–1948, and the Present Outlook," in *Fourth Mennonite World Conference Proceedings* (Scottdale, PA: Herald Press, 1950), 20.
11. Pascal Maeder, *Forging a New Heimat: Expellees in Post-War West Germany and Canada* (Göttingen: V&R Unipress, 2011), 116.
12. *Mennonite Central Committee: Im Namen Christi* (Akron, PA: MCC, April 1947).
13. Translations from Dyck and Dyck, *Up from the Rubble*, 112, 124.
14. Harold Bender, "Introduction," in Sanford Calvin Yoder, *For Conscience Sake: A Study of Mennonite Migrations Resulting from the World War* (Scottdale, PA: Herald Press, 1945), ix–x.
15. Ministerio de Economia, *Las Colonias Mennonitas en el Chaco Paraguayo* (Asunción: Imprenta Nacional, 1934), Foreword.
16. Bender, "Church and State," 100–101.
17. Quoted in Thiesen, *Mennonite and Nazi?* 167. On US anti-Nazi efforts, Max Paul Friedman, *Nazis and Good Neighbors: The United States Campaign Against the Germans of Latin America in World War II* (Cambridge: Cambridge University Press, 2003).
18. Winfield Fretz, "Factors Contributing to Success and Failure in Mennonite Colonization," in *Fourth Mennonite World Conference*, 175. On Fretz, Ben Nobbs-Thiessen,

"Mennonites in Unexpected Places: Sociologist and Settler in Latin America," *Journal of Mennonite Studies* 28 (2010): 203–224.

19. "Constitution of the International Refugee Organization," in *Treaties and Other International Agreements of the United States of America, 1776–1949*, vol. 4 (Washington, DC: US Government Printing Office, 1970), 300.

20. Dyck, "Mennonite Refugees in Germany."

21. M. W. Royse, "Volksdeutsche in Austria," January 27, 1948, AJ/43/462, folder 149, AN.

22. Quoted in Steven Schroeder, "Mennonite-Nazi Collaboration and Coming to Terms with the Past: European Mennonites and the MCC, 1945–1950," *Conrad Grebel Review* 21, no. 2 (2003): 10.

23. Quoted in Horst Klaassen, "Nationalität: Mennonit? Mennonitische Auswanderungslager in Backnang 1947 bis 1953," *Mennonitischer Geschichtsblätter* 54 (1997): 108–109.

24. Ted Regehr, "Of Dutch or German Ancestry? Mennonite Refugees, MCC, and the International Refugee Organization," *Journal of Mennonite Studies* (1995): 13, 17.

25. Anti-Semitic references occur in some Mennonite memoir literature, i.e., Neufeld, *Path of Thorns*, 61–65, 117, 162–163. References to a "Mennonite holocaust" in the USSR emphasize Mennonite suffering. For example, Donovan Smucker, *The Sociology of Canadian Mennonites, Hutterites, and Amish* (Waterloo: Wilfrid Laurier University Press, 1977), 118.

26. Mennonite Central Committee, "Memorandum on the Mennonite Refugees from South Russia," April 6, 1948, AJ/43/572, folder Political Dissidents – Mennonites, AN.

27. Quoted in Epp, *Mennonite Exodus*, 406.

28. C. F. Klassen, "Statement Concerning Mennonite Refugees," July 16, 1948, AJ/43/572, folder Political Dissidents – Mennonites, AN.

29. Quoted in Klaassen, "Nationalität: Mennonit?" 108.

30. Quoted in Epp, *Mennonite Exodus*, 420.

31. Quoted in ibid., 407.

32. In total, 8,158 European Mennonites relocated to Canada, 4,914 to Paraguay, 1,184 to Uruguay, and 1,108 to the United States. Ibid., 391–498.

33. Peter Dyck, "Unser Volk," *Der Mennonit*, September 1950, 81.

34. Spellings from Edna Kaufman, *Melting Pot of Mennonite Cookery, 1874–1974* (North Newton, KS: Bethel College Women's Association, 1974); *Off the Mountain Lake Range* (Mountain Lake, MN: Mountain Lake Junior Historians, 1949).

35. Dyck, "Unser Volk," 82. My analysis draws on Dominique Reill's study of "fearful nationalists": *Nationalists Who Feared the Nation: Adriatic Multi-Nationalism in Habsburg Dalmatia, Trieste, and Venice* (Stanford: Stanford University Press, 2012).

36. Siegfried Janzen, "Liebe Flüchtlingsgeschwister!" *Unser Blatt*, October 8, 1947.

37. Quoted in Epp, *Mennonite Exodus*, 367.

38. C. F. Klassen, "Zum Geleit," *Der Mennonit*, January/February 1948, 1–2.

39. P. C. Hiebert, "An die zerstreuten Mennoniten der Welt," *Der Mennonit*, January/February 1948, 3.

40. Quoted in Klaassen, "Nationalität: Mennonit?" 103.

41. Translated in Schroeder, "Mennonite-Nazi Collaboration," 9.

42. Quoted in Epp, *Mennonite Exodus*, 376. On "Prussian militarism," Christopher Clark, *Iron Kingdom: The Rise and Downfall of Prussia, 1600–1947* (Cambridge, MA: Harvard University Press, 2008), xii–xviii, 670–688.

43. "Mennonitischer Nationalismus?" *Mennonitische Welt*, September 1950, 8–9.

44. Epp, *Mennonite Exodus*, 385.

45. Quoted in Klaassen, "Nationalität: Mennonit?" 110.
46. Dyck, "Unser Volk," 82.
47. Quoted in Epp, *Mennonite Exodus*, 387–388.
48. Ibid., 453–454.
49. Dyck, "Unser Volk," 81. Also, Daphne Naomi Winland, "The Quest for Mennonite Peoplehood: Ethno-Religious Identity and the Dilemma of Definitions," *Canadian Review of Sociology & Anthropology* 30, no. 1 (1993): 121.
50. Schroeder, "Mennonite-Nazi Collaboration," 11–13.
51. Dyck, "Unser Volk," 82.
52. E. K. Francis, "The Russian Mennonites: From Religious to Ethnic Group," *American Journal of Sociology* 54 (September 1948): 101–107. On Francis, James Urry, "The Mennonite Commonwealth in Imperial Russia Revisited," *Mennonite Quarterly Review* 84, no. 2 (2010): 229–247. On Mennonite "ethnicity," Hans Werner, "Peoplehoods of the Past: Mennonites and the Ethnic Boundary," *Journal of Mennonite Studies* 23 (2005): 23–35; Rodney Sawatsky, "Mennonite Ethnicity: Medium, Message and Mission," *Journal of Mennonite Studies* 9 (1991): 113–121; Urry, *Mennonites, Politics, and Peoplehood*, especially 205–228.
53. E. K. Francis, "Anabaptism and Colonization," in *The Recovery of the Anabaptist Vision*, ed. Guy Hershberger (Scottdale, PA: Herald Press, 1957), 250.
54. William Klassen, "Review: *In Search of Utopia*," *Mennonite Quarterly Review* 30, no. 4 (1956): 299–300.
55. Dyck, "Unser Volk," 81.
56. Cornelius Krahn, "Form und Inhalt," *Mennonitische Welt*, July 1952, 4.
57. Harold Bender, "The Anabaptist Vision," *Church History* 13, no. 1 (1944): 3–24. On Bender, Albert Keim, *Harold S. Bender, 1897–1962* (Scottdale, PA: Herald Press, 1998).
58. Horst Penner, *Weltweite Bruderschaft: Ein mennonitisches Geschichtsbuch* (Karlsruhe: Heinrich Schneider, 1955), 209.
59. Harold Bender, "Mennonite Peace Action Throughout the World," in *Fourth Mennonite World Conference*, 263.
60. Calvin Redekop, *European Mennonite Voluntary Service: Youth Idealism in Post-World War II Europe* (Telford, PA: Cascadia Publishing, 2010), 106–109. Also, Calvin Redekop, *The PAX Story: Service in the Name of Christ, 1951–1976* (Kitchener, ON: Pandora Press, 2001).
61. Klassen, "Review," 299–300.
62. C. F. Klassen, "Mennonite Refugees—Our Challenge," in *Fourth Mennonite World Conference*, 185–186. On denazification, Alexander Biddiscombe, *The Denazification of Germany: A History 1945–1950* (Stroud: Tempus, 2007). On Mennonites in North America, Paul Toews, *Mennonites in American Society, 1930–1970: Modernity and the Persistence of Religious Community* (Scottdale, PA: Herald Press, 1996); Ted Regehr, *Mennonites in Canada, 1939–1970: A People Transformed* (Toronto: University of Toronto Press, 1996).
63. Theo Glück, *Botschaft und Nachfolge: Berichte und Vorträge der mennonitischen Studientagung auf dem Thomashof 1947* (Karlsruhe: Mennonitische Schriftenreihe, 1948), 5.
64. Harold Bender, "Die Friedenstätigkeit der Mennoniten," *Der Mennonit*, September/October 1948, 87.
65. Epp, *Mennonite Exodus*, 447.
66. Bruno Enss, "Erfahrungen unserer Brüder in Westeuropa nach dem zweiten Weltkrieg," *Der Mennonit*, September/October 1949, 69.

67. *Das Grundgesetz für die Bundesrepublik Deutschland*, May 23, 1949, I. Die Grundrechte, Article 4, Paragraph 3. On rearmament, David Large, *Germans to the Front: West German Rearmament in the Adenauer Era* (Chapel Hill: University of North Carolina Press, 1996).

68. Quotations from Stefanie Kuntz, "'Christus ist unser Friede': Die Erneurerung des Friedenszeugnisses im deutschen Mennonitentum nach 1945" (Thesis, Ruprecht-Karls-Universität Heidelberg, 2000), 19, 24.

69. Penner, *Die ost- und westpreußischen Mennoniten*, 156–157. On Protestants, Matthew Hockenos, *A Church Divided: German Protestants Confront the Nazi Past* (Bloomington: Indiana University Press, 2004); Clemens Vollnhals, *Evangelische Kirche und Entnazifierung 1945–1949: Die Last der nationalsozialistischen Vergangenheit* (Munich: Oldenbourg, 1989).

70. Dyck, "Mennonite Refugees in Germany."

71. Cattepoel, "The Mennonites of Germany," 15–22. See Cattopoel's anti-euthanasia sermon: "Predigt über Gal. 6 Vers 2," September 21, 1941, Nachlaß Ernst Crous, folder D. Cattepoel Predigten 1941/42, MFS.

72. Emil Händiges, "The Catastrophe of the West Prussian Mennonites," *Mennonite Quarterly Review* 24, no. 2 (1950): 126–127.

73. Hans Rothfels, *The German Opposition to Hitler: An Appraisal* (Hinsdale, IL: Regnery, 1948), 40.

74. Translated in Gerlach, "The Final Years," 397. On Mennonite war criminals, Epp, *Mennonite Exodus*, 412–421; Thiesen, *Mennonite and Nazi?* 206–207; Steinhart, "The Chameleon"; Rempel, "Mennonites and the Holocaust."

75. Händiges, "The Catastrophe," 124. On expulsion, R. M. Douglas, *Orderly and Humane: The Expulsion of the Germans After the Second World War* (New Haven: Yale University Press, 2012). Among Mennonites, Ted Regehr, "Polish and Prussian Mennonite Displaced Persons, 1944–50, *Mennonite Quarterly Review* 66, no. 2 (1992): 247–266.

76. Quoted in Horst Gerlach, "The Final Years of Mennonites in East and West Prussia 1943–45," *Mennonite Quarterly Review* 66, no. 3 (1992): 417.

77. Händiges, "The Catastrophe," 128–129.

78. Ibid. 124. On "lost" landscapes, Blackbourn, *The Conquest of Nature*, 311–321.

79. Quoted in Schroeder, "Mennonite-Nazi Collaboration," 10.

80. Siegfried Neufeld, "Eine Reise nach Danzig im August 1976," 521–5/336, HSFHH.

81. "College Receives Oil Paintings," *Bethel Collegian*, August 24, 1959, 4.

82. Translated in Gerlach, "The Final Years," no. 3, 418.

83. Quoted in Helmut Reimer, "Die Mennoniten im Kreis Marienburg," in *Neues Marienburger Heimatbuch*, ed. Rainer Zacharias (Herford: Wendt Groll, 1967), 399.

84. Ibid.

85. On Mennonites and Stutthof, Rempel, "Mennonites and the Holocaust," 507–525. For context, Hermann Kaienburg, *Die Wirtschaft der SS* (Berlin: Metropol Verlag, 2003); Christopher Browning, *Remembering Survival: Inside a Nazi Slave-Labor Camp* (New York: W. W. Norton, 2010).

86. Peter Foth, "Abschlusserklärung der Polengruppe 1973," August 1973, 521–5/335, vol. 1, SFHH.

87. Translated in Kazimierz Mezynski, "The German Mennonites on Their Way to Reconciliation with Poland," *Mennonite Quarterly Review* 50, no. 4 (1976): 289.

88. Rolf Fieguth to Peter Foth, October 2, 1972, 521–5/335, vol. 1, SFHH.

89. Horst Gerlach, "Stutthof und die Mennoniten," in Lichdi, *Mennoniten im Dritten Reich*, 248.

90. Horst Gerlach to Ott-Heinrich Stobbe, October 4, 1973, 521–5/335, vol. 1, SFHH.
91. Peter Foth, "Was wir vorhaben – was uns erwartet," ca. 1974, 521–5/335, vol. 2, SFHH.
92. Peter Foth to Gerhard Wiebe, November 12, 1973, 521–5/335, vol. 1, SFHH.
93. Käthe Grenda, "Fahrt nach Danzig, 24. August bis 1. September 1976," 521–5/336, HSFHH.
94. Neufeld, "Eine Reise."
95. Lichdi, *Mennoniten im Dritten Reich*, 12. Also, Diether Lichdi, "Vergangenheitsbewältigung und Schuldbekenntnisse der Mennoniten nach 1945," *Mennonitische Geschichtsblätter* 64 (2007): 39–54.
96. Stefan Wolff, "The Politics of Homeland," in *The* Heimat *Abroad*, ed. O'Donnell, et al., 287–312; Klaus Bade and Jochen Oltmer, eds., *Aussiedler: deutsche Einwanderer aus Osteuropa* (Osnabrück: Universitätsverlag Rasch, 1999).
97. Klassen, "Mennonite Refugees—Our Challenge," 185–186.
98. Quoted in Benjamin Unruh, "Verkürzte Abschrift eines schreibens aus dem Ural," December 31, 1956, Nachlaß Benjamin Unruh, box 2, folder 7, MFS. On Mennonites in the postwar USSR, Walter Sawatsky, *Soviet Evangelicals since World War II* (Kitchener, ON: Herald Press, 1981); Heinrich Löwen, *Deutsche Christen in Russland und in der Sowjetunion* (Hamburg: Disserta Verlag, 2014); and the 2012 *Journal of Mennonite Studies*.
99. Letter to Hans Niessen, ca. 1978, 521–5/333, SFHH.
100. Translated in Werner, "'Feeling at Home': Soviet Mennonites in Bielefeld, Germany, 1950–1990," *Journal of Mennonite Studies* 20 (2002): 165. On Soviet nationalities, Martin, *Affirmative Action Empire*.
101. Quoted in Epp, *Mennonite Exodus*, 462.
102. Hans Herzler to Peter Dyck, 1973, 521–5/333, SFHH.
103. Translated in Werner, "Feeling at Home,'" 155.
104. Klassen, "Mennonites in Russia," 217–232. Also, Hans Werner, *Imagined Homes: Soviet German Immigrants in Two Cities* (Winnipeg: University of Manitoba Press, 2007).
105. Hans Herzler to Peter Dyck, November 9, 1973, 521–5/333, SFHH.
106. Lydia Penner, "Sängerfest Highlights Treffen," August 14, 1978, 521–5/333, SFHH.
107. "Eine Aufgabe, die uns alle angeht," July 1976, 521–5/333, SFHH.
108. Jo de Vries to Hans Hertzler et al., October 30, 1973, 521–5/333, SFHH.
109. Translated in Werner, "Feeling at Home,'" 172.
110. *Wegweiser für Aussiedler*, Bundesminister des Innern (n.p., n.d.).
111. Quoted in Werner, "'Feeling at Home,'" 177. On integration, Ilan Troen and Klaus Bade, eds., *Returning Home: Immigration and Absorption into their Homelands of Germans and Jews from the Former Soviet Union* (Beer Sheva: Ben-Gurion University of the Negev Press, 1994); Sabine Ipsen-Peitzmeier and Markus Kaiser, *Zuhause fremd: Russlanddeutsche zwischen Russland und Deutschland* (Bielefeld: Transcript, 2006).
112. "Zur Situation der Umsiedler," 1977, 521–5/333, SFHH.
113. Werner, "Feeling at Home,'" 170.
114. Translations from ibid., 170–171, 177.
115. H. J. Hildebrant to Peter Foth, June 21, 1978, 521–5/333, SFHH.
116. Penner, "Sängerfest."
117. Translated in Werner, "Feeling at Home,'" 167.
118. Printed in Peter Foth, *Was bleibt? Texte 1987 bis 1992* (Hamburg, 1993), 56–58.
119. Klassen, "Mennonites in Russia," 218; Gerlach, *Die Rußlandmennoniten*, vol. 1, 173.
120. Quoted in Schroeder, "Nazi Mennonite Collaboration," 10.

CONCLUSION

1. *The New Oxford Annotated Bible* (Oxford: Oxford University Press, 2007), New Testament 272.
2. Cornelius Dyck, *Jesus Christ Reconciles: Proceedings of the Ninth Mennonite World Conference* (Elkhart, IN: Mennonite World Conference, 1972), xxii–xxiii. For context, Lapp and van Straten, "Mennonite World Conference"; and the Global Mennonite History Series.
3. Harold Bender, "Mitteilungen des Sippenverbandes der danziger Mennoniten-Familien Epp-Kauenhowen-Zimmermann," *Mennonite Quarterly Review* 24, no. 2 (1950): 173–174.
4. Brons, *Ursprung, Entwickelung und Schicksale*, 355.
5. I.e., Donald Kraybill and Marc Olshan, *The Amish Struggle with Modernity* (Hanover, NH: University Press of New England, 1994).
6. Krahn, "Form und Inhalt," 3.
7. Royden Loewen, *Diaspora in the Countryside: Two Mennonite Communities and Mid-Twentieth-Century Rural Disjuncture* (Toronto: University of Toronto Press, 2006).
8. On the global as "charismatic," Anna Tsing, "The Global Situation," *Cultural Anthropology* 15, no. 3 (2000): 327–360.
9. Winfield Fretz, "Factors Contributing to Success and Failure in Mennonite Colonization," in *Fourth Mennonite World Conference*, 175–176.
10. Translated in Toews and Toews, eds., *Union of Citizens*, 346.
11. On difference and exclusion, Tobin Shearer, *Daily Demonstrators: The Civil Rights Movement in Mennonite Homes and Sanctuaries* (Baltimore: Johns Hopkins University Press, 2010); Felipe Hinojosa, *Latino Mennonites* (Baltimore: Johns Hopkins University Press, 2014); Stephanie Krehbiel, "Pacifist Battlegrounds: Violence, Community, and the Struggle for LGBTQ Justice in the Mennonite Church USA" (PhD diss., University of Kansas, 2015).
12. Examples include John Lapp, "The Global Mennonite/Brethren in Christ History Project: The Task, the Problem, the Imperative," *Conrad Grebel Review* 15, no. 3 (1997): 283–290; Alain Weaver, ed., *A Table of Sharing: Mennonite Central Committee and the Expanding Networks of Mennonite Identity* (Telford, PA: Cascadia, 2011).
13. Werner, "Peoplehoods of the Past," 32. Also, Stuart Murray, *The Naked Anabaptist: The Bare Essentials of a Radical Faith* (Scottdale, PA: Herald Press, 2010); John Roth, "'Blest Be the Ties That Bind': In Search of the Global Anabaptist Church," *Conrad Grebel Review* 31, no. 1 (2013): 5–43.

INDEX

Page numbers followed by *f* indicate a figure; those followed by *t* indicate a table.

GPSR Authorized Representative: Easy Access System Europe - Mustamäe tee 50, 10621 Tallinn, Estonia, gpsr.requests@easproject.com

www.ingramcontent.com/pod-product-compliance
Lightning Source LLC
Chambersburg PA
CBHW031414270326
41929CB00010BA/1455